Russia's Foreign Policy

Russia's Foreign Policy

Change and Continuity
in National Identity

Fourth Edition

Andrei P. Tsygankov

ROWMAN & LITTLEFIELD
Lanham • Boulder • New York • London

Published by Rowman & Littlefield
A wholly owned subsidiary of The Rowman & Littlefield Publishing Group, Inc.
4501 Forbes Boulevard, Suite 200, Lanham, Maryland 20706
www.rowman.com

Unit A, Whitacre Mews, 26-34 Stannary Street,
London SE11 4AB, United Kingdom

British Library Cataloguing in Publication Information Available

Library of Congress Cataloging-in-Publication Data
Names: Tsygankov, Andrei P., 1964- author.
Title: Russia's foreign policy : change and continuity in national identity /
  Andrei P. Tsygankov.
Description: Fourth edition. | Rowman & Littlefield : Lanham, 2016. |
  Includes bibliographical references and index.
Identifiers: LCCN 2015043662 (print) | LCCN 2015044211 (ebook) |
  ISBN 9781442254015 (cloth : alk. paper) | ISBN 9781442254022 (pbk. : alk.
  paper) | ISBN 9781442254039 (electronic)
Subjects: LCSH: Russia (Federation)—Foreign relations. | Soviet Union—
  Foreign relations. | Great powers. | Russia (Federation)—Foreign
  relations—Western countries. | Western countries—Foreign relations—
  Russia (Federation) | Nationalism—Russia (Federation) | Social change—
  Russia (Federation)
Classification: LCC DK510.764 .T785 2016 (print) | LCC DK510.764 (ebook) |
  DDC 327.47—dc23
LC record available at http://lccn.loc.gov/2015043662

Printed in the United States of America

Contents

List of Tables   vii

Note on the Transliteration   xi

Chronology of Key Foreign Policy Events, 1985–2015   xiii

Preface   xxvii

1 Understanding Change and Continuity in Russia's
   Foreign Policy   1

2 The Cold War Crisis and Soviet New Thinking   33

3 The Post–Cold War Euphoria and Russia's Liberal
   Westernism   59

4 New Security Challenges and Great Power Balancing   97

5 The World after September 11 and Pragmatic Cooperation   135

6 U.S. Regime Change Strategy and Great Power
   Assertiveness   177

7 Global Instability and Russia's Vision of Modernization   209

8 The West, the Non-West, and Russia's "Civilizational" Turn   233

9 Conclusions and Lessons   261

Further Reading	281
Topics for Discussion or Simulation	285
Index	289
About the Author	305

Tables

1.1	Russia's Foreign Policy: Change and Continuity	9
1.2	International Relations Theories and Their Perspectives on Foreign Policy	16
1.3	Constructivist Explanation of Foreign Policy: A Causal Process	18
1.4	Explaining Russia's Foreign Policy after Communism	23
2.1	Gross National Product for the USSR and the United States, 1960–1985	37
2.2	New Thinking (NT): View of National Interest	39
2.3	New Thinking (NT): Contending Views	42
2.4	Gorbachev's Legacy in Security Policy	44
2.5	Growth Rates for the Soviet Economy, 1985–1991	46
2.6	The Rise of Ethnonationalism in the Union Republics, 1989–1991	49
2.7	Limits on Arms Accepted or Proposed by Gorbachev, 1983–1991	52
2.8	The Record of New Thinking	54
3.1	Westernist Course: View of National Interest	62

Tables

3.2 The Spectrum of Russia's Post-Soviet Foreign Policy
Thinking 65

3.3 Westernism: Contending Views 69

3.4 External Aid and Investment: Russia and Other
Recipients, 1990–1995 75

3.5 Post-Soviet Economic Decline: Russia Relative to Other
Ex-Republics 86

3.6 Russia and the Ex-Republics: Economic, Military,
and Cultural Dependencies 88

3.7 The Record of the Westernist Course 91

4.1 Great Power Balancing (GPB): View of National Interest 101

4.2 Great Power Balancing (GPB): Contending Views 105

4.3 Russia's Power Resources Relative to Other
Powerful States (%) 106

4.4 Russia's Government Revenue and Expenditure,
1992–1998 (% of GDP) 109

4.5 Russia and China: Demographic and Economic
Disparities in the Far East, 1997 115

4.6 Russia's Power Capabilities Relative to Former Soviet States 117

4.7 The Record of Great Power Balancing 127

5.1 Russia's Economic Recovery, 1998–2001 (% of 1998) 136

5.2 Russia's Increased Military Budget, 1999–2002 139

5.3 Pragmatic Cooperation (PC): View of National Interest 140

5.4 Pragmatic Cooperation (PC): Contending Views 144

5.5 Russia's Foreign Policy Discourse after September 11 145

5.6 Favorable View of the United States (%) 151

5.7 The Record of Pragmatic Cooperation 169

6.1 Russia's Basic Economic Indicators, 1999–2007
(% annual change) 181

6.2 Great Power Assertiveness (GPA): View of National Interest 185

6.3 Great Power Assertiveness (GPA): Contending Views 188

6.4	Russia's Foreign Policy Discourse	190
6.5	The Record of Great Power Assertiveness	203
7.1	Alliances for Modernization (AM): View of National Interest	213
7.2	Alliances for Modernization (AM): Contending Views	214
7.3	The Record of Alliances for Modernization	227
8.1	State-Civilization (SC): View of National Interest	239
8.2	State-Civilization (SC): Contending Views	241
8.3	The Record of State-Civilization	255
9.1	Russia's Seven Visions of the World and National Interest	265

Note on the Transliteration

In transliterating names from the Russian, I have used "y" to denote "й," " ' " to denote "ь" and "ъ," "yu" to denote "ю," "ya" to denote "я," "ï" to denote "й" and "ий," "iyi" to denote double "и," "e" to denote "э," "kh" to denote "х," "zh" to denote "ж," "ts" to denote "ц," "ch" to denote "ч," "sh" to denote "ш," and "sch" to denote "щ." I have also used "Ye" to distinguish the sound of "E" (such as "Yevropa") at the beginning of a word from that in the middle of a word (such as "vneshnei"). Everywhere, I did not distinguish between "e" and "ё." Original spelling is retained in quotations.

Chronology of Key Foreign Policy Events, 1985–2015

1985

March	U.S.-Soviet arms negotiations in Geneva
April	Gorbachev announces a unilateral moratorium on deployment of intermediate-range nuclear missiles and proposes a moratorium on all nuclear weapons tests
	Eduard Shevardnadze succeeds Andrei Gromyko as Soviet foreign minister
July	Soviet Union imposes five-month moratorium on nuclear weapons tests, making its extension contingent upon a similar U.S. response
September	Moscow proposes at Geneva negotiations that the United States and the USSR reduce long- and medium-range nuclear weapons by 50 percent

1986

January	Gorbachev proposes a ban on all nuclear weapons by the year 2000
June	Warsaw Pact meeting in Budapest proposes mutual Warsaw Pact–NATO troops reduction of 100,000 to 150,000 men and the reduction of military capabilities to those "necessary for defense"
July	Gorbachev announces in Vladivostok a five-point plan for cooperation in the Asia-Pacific region and advocates closer ties with China
October	Reagan and Gorbachev meet in Reykjavik, Iceland

1987

May   General Dmitri Yazov is named the new Soviet defense minister

December   Gorbachev and Reagan sign in Washington the INF treaty eliminating all 2,611 Soviet and U.S. intermediate-range nuclear forces

1988

January   Gorbachev announces the need for "innovative policies" in Eastern Europe

May   U.S.-Soviet summit in Moscow

December   Gorbachev announces before the United Nations General Assembly a unilateral reduction of Soviet forces by some 500,000 men, 10,000 tanks, 8,500 artillery pieces, and 800 combat aircraft

1989

April   Soviet crackdown on Georgian nationalists in Tbilisi; twenty demonstrators killed and two hundred wounded
             Unilateral withdrawal of Soviet forces begins from Hungary

May   Gorbachev before Council of Europe promises not to interfere militarily in political events in Eastern Europe

October   Shevardnadze proclaims before the Supreme Soviet that the Soviet invasion in Afghanistan in 1979 "violated the norms of proper behavior" and that the Krasnoyarsk radar installation is illegal under the 1972 antiballistic missile treaty

December   "Big Four" (United States, France, Great Britain, and USSR) meet to discuss the status of Berlin

1990

January   Soviet troops are deployed to Azerbaijan in the wake of massive anti-Armenian demonstrations

February   "Two Plus Four" talks on German reunification announced

March   In response to Lithuania's declaration of independence, Soviet paratroopers seize the headquarters of the Lithuanian Communist Party

May   U.S.-Soviet summit in Washington

July   Gorbachev and Kohl announce agreement to allow reunified Germany to belong to NATO

November   NATO and Warsaw Pact states sign the CFE treaty and the Charter of Paris at the CSCE Summit
             Gorbachev proposes a new Union treaty

December   Shevardnadze resigns as Soviet foreign minister

1991

January   Soviet troops crack down on pro-independence forces in Lithuania and Latvia; 19 protesters are killed

March   In the Soviet referendum, voters choose to preserve the union; Baltics, Armenia, Georgia, and Moldova boycott the vote

July   Warsaw Pact is disbanded in Prague

                 Bush and Gorbachev reach an agreement in Moscow on the Strategic Arms Reduction Treaty (START)

                 Ten Soviet republics reach an agreement on a new Union treaty to be signed on August 20

August   Coup against Gorbachev

December   Russia, Ukraine, and Belarus establish the CIS in Minsk

                 Gorbachev resigns as president of the USSR

1992

February   Foreign Ministry conference "The Transformed Russia in the New World"

March   Kozyrev briefly travels to China

April   Bush, supported by Kohl, announces $24 billion package for Russia

                 Yeltsin orders withdrawal of troops from Nagorno-Karabakh and asks for the deployment of NATO troops

                 Russia places the Fourteenth Army in Moldova under its control

May   Russia supports the United Nations' sanctions against Yugoslavia

                 Russia signs the CIS Collective Security treaty

                 Russia joins the IMF and World Bank

June   Russia and the United States agree on terms of START II

July   Yeltsin at G-7 summit

                 Yeltsin and Moldova's president Snegur sign peace agreement over Transdniestr conflict

December   Yeltsin visits China

                 Kozyrev acknowledges the need to be more active on the eastern front

1993

January   Yeltsin attends the Civic Union's congress

                 Bush and Yeltsin sign START II

April   New Foreign Policy Concept signed into law

May   Russia initiates the CIS Economic Union agreement at Moscow summit

July	The Tokyo G-7 summit declares a $43.4 billion package of assistance for Russia
October	Russia withdraws from the ruble zone
	U.S. secretary of state Warren Christopher promises Yeltsin not to push for NATO expansion immediately and to focus on Partnership for Peace instead
November	Russia adopts new military doctrine
December	Westernizers lose party elections to nationalist Zhirinovski

1994

January	Clinton announces that the question of enlarging NATO is not whether it will happen, but when
July	Kozyrev announces change in his foreign policy course
September	Washington summit; Clinton pledges NATO enlargement will be guided by "three nos"—no surprises, no rush, and no exclusion of Russia
December	Kozyrev refuses to sign up for Partnership for Peace
	Yeltsin warns of "cold peace"
	Russian military launches offensive in Chechnya
	Russia joins G-7

1995

May	Russia begins dialogue with NATO and signs Partnership for Peace
December	In Russian parliamentary elections, Westernizers lose to Communists
	Kozyrev is removed from office
	Primakov replaces Kozyrev as foreign minister

1996

April	Treaty on the Formation of the Russia-Belarus Union State is signed
May	IMF announces $10.2 billion to be disbursed to Russia monthly from March 1996 to March 1999
June	Yeltsin approves the concept of the state nationalities policy of the Russian Federation and states the goal of a multi-ethnic Russia; he also initiates the search for a new "national idea"
July	Yeltsin is reelected as president
November	Yeltsin and the Japanese prime minister meet and commit themselves to signing a peace treaty in 2000
December	Primakov visits Tehran and declares that Russia-Iran relations are "developing along an ascending curve"

Russia is admitted to the Asian and Pacific Economic Council (APEC)

1997

March — Yeltsin meets Clinton in Helsinki and insists that NATO not include former Soviet states

CIS adopts Concept of Economic Integrational Development

April — Russia and China sign the "Joint Declaration on a Multipolar World and the Formation of a New International Order"

May — Yeltsin signs NATO-Russia Founding Act at summit with NATO leaders in Paris

Russia and Ukraine sign the "Big Treaty," which legalizes the borders

June — Peace treaty to end the Tajik civil war is signed in Moscow

October — Georgia, Ukraine, Azerbaijan, and Moldova establish a security group to balance Russia

December — Russia adopts new National Security Concept

Primakov responds to the U.S. threat to attack Iraq by entering an alliance with France and negotiating an agreement for the return of the UN inspections to Iraq

1998

February — Russia and Ukraine sign the ambitious Program of Economic Cooperation

May — Yeltsin and Clinton meet in Birmingham; Russia officially joins the G-8

September — Primakov assumes the post of prime minister

Igor' Ivanov becomes foreign minister

December — Russia withdraws ambassadors from London and Washington to protest U.S. and British air strikes against Iraq

Primakov speaks of desirability of Russia-China-India alliance as a "new pole in world politics"

1999

February — Russian Duma narrowly ratifies the Russia-Ukraine "Big Treaty"

March — Russia begins negotiating restructuring of its approaching $17.5 billion foreign debt payment

NATO's air strikes against Serbia begin; Primakov cancels the upcoming negotiations with the United States and the IMF in Washington

April	Yeltsin appoints Viktor Chernomyrdin as Russia's special envoy on Yugoslavia Russian Duma refuses to ratify the START II
May	Sergei Stepashin replaces Primakov as prime minister
June	Chernomyrdin and Finnish president Martti Ahtisaari secure Milošević agreement to NATO terms for ending war
	Russian troops begin participation in the multilateral peace-keeping force in Kosovo "Common Strategy of the EU on Russia" is adopted
July	First meeting of Russia-NATO Permanent Council since it was boycotted by Russia in March
August	Russia sends troops to counter Chechen incursions into Dagestan
	Putin replaces Stepashin as prime minister
	Chechen rebels occupy parts of Dagestan; Kremlin resumes military operation
	Bombs explode in Moscow, killing hundreds of residents
October	Russia adopts new military doctrine
December	Yeltsin resigns; Putin becomes acting president of Russia

2000

March	Putin is officially elected president
June	Putin holds summit with Clinton in Moscow
September	Russia, India, and Iran sign an agreement, according to which all signatories will get relief from import tax and customs duties

2001

February	The secretary of the Security Council, Sergei Ivanov, announces the new "pragmatic" course of bilateral relations in the former Soviet region
June	Putin meets George W. Bush in Ljubljana, Slovenia
September	Terrorist attacks on the United States
	Putin announces support for the United States and pledges intelligence assistance
November	Putin and Bush meet in Crawford, Texas

2002

February	Putin emphasizes Russia as a reliable energy alternative to the Middle East; he also proposes creating a "gas OPEC" group
April	Putin proclaims Russia's European foreign policy a priority in a Duma address

May	Russia and the United States sign a joint declaration on energy cooperation in Moscow
October	Russia-U.S. "energy summit" in Houston
November	At the EU summit, Russia proposes to have a visa-free arrangement in Kaliningrad
December	Russia shuts down the OSCE mission in Chechnya

2003

January	Russia joins the antiwar coalition and argues for the United Nations as the only legitimate body to sanction the use of force in Iraq
April	Russia and Turkmenistan sign a strategic gas agreement
May	Russia and five other ex-Soviet states form the Collective Security Treaty Organization for fighting terrorism
June	Putin proposes that visas between EU countries and Russia be abandoned altogether by the year 2006
August	Putin seals a joint venture with British Petroleum worth over $6 billion
	Moscow withdraws its peacekeeping mission from Bosnia and Kosovo
September	Russia signs an $800 million deal with Iran and pledges to build two more nuclear reactors in Iran
	Russia signs a partnership agreement with Azerbaijan
	Russia signs an agreement with Saudi Arabia pledging cooperation in the energy sector and in setting the international price of oil
October	The head of Russia's state electric company, Anatoli Chubais, announces that Russia's main goal is to build a "liberal empire" in the former USSR

2004

March	Putin is reelected president
May	EU incorporates ten new members
	Russia and the EU agree on conditions to extend the Partnership and Cooperation Agreement with the EU to the ten new members
September	Terrorist attack in Beslan, northern Ossetia
	Putin announces reform in the political system
November	Orange Revolution in Ukraine; Russia supports Viktor Yanukovich in Ukraine's presidential election

2005

January	Putin-Bush summit in Bratislava

March   Change of power in Kyrgyzstan through a mass protest;
             Russia takes no side
April   Putin visits Middle East
             Russia and Germany agree to build a gas pipeline under the
             Baltic Sea
May   Celebration of victory in World War II in Moscow
             Riots and their brutal suppression in Uzbekistan; Russia
             supports the government
June   Russia-China-India meeting in Vladivostok to discuss pros-
             pects of strategic partnership
             Russia and Georgia reach agreement on withdrawal of Rus-
             sia's military bases
December   Russia-Ukraine dispute over natural gas

2006
June   Russia declares opposition to Ukraine or Georgia joining
             NATO
September   Russian economic and political sanctions against Georgia
December   Russia-Belarus dispute over natural gas

2007
February   Putin's speech at the Munich Conference on Security Policy
March   The Foreign Ministry report "A Review of the Russian
             Federation's Foreign Policy" is released
April   The United States announces plans to deploy elements of a
             missile defense system in Eastern Europe
May   Kazakhstan, Turkmenistan, and Uzbekistan agree to
             increase exports of energy via Russia's pipelines
             Putin announces a moratorium on implementing the Con-
             ventional Forces in Europe treaty
             Russia-EU summit in Samara
December   Russia announces plans to reequip its new missiles, SS-27,
             with multiple warheads

2008
March   Medvedev is elected president
April   Russia blocks Georgia and Ukraine from receiving the
             Membership Action Plan for NATO
June   President Medvedev proposes a new pan-European treaty
             beyond NATO
             Russia-EU summit in Khanty-Mansiysk
July   Russia and China complete border demarcation
August   Russia-Georgia war

	Russia recognizes the independence of Abkhazia and South Ossetia
December	Russia's new National Security Strategy through 2020 is released

2009

April	Russia expresses concern over the EU's Eastern Partnership project
May	NATO conducts a military exercise in Georgia
	Russia-EU summit in Khabarovsk
June	SCO summit in Ekaterinburg
July	U.S.-Russia summit in Moscow
	Russia agrees to U.S. military overflights to and from Afghanistan
	Russia conducts a large military exercise in the Caucasus
September	Medvedev critically assesses Russia's prospects in the article "Go, Russia!"
October	Russia proposes that Iran send spent nuclear fuel outside for reprocessing
	Russia agrees to supply natural gas to China beginning in 2014–2015
November	Medvedev proposes to judge the effectiveness of foreign policy "by a simple criterion: Does it improve living standards in our country?"

2010

February	The Foreign Ministry report focuses on strengthening Russia's economic position
April	The United States and Russia sign the new START treaty
	Ukraine agrees to extend the lease on Russia's Black Sea Fleet for twenty-five more years in exchange for the reduction of gas prices by 30 percent
May	Russia-Turkey agreement to carry oil from the Black Sea to the Mediterranean
June	Violent change of power occurs in Kyrgyzstan; Russia does not interfere
	Russia supports UNSC sanctions against Iran and refuses to supply Iran with an S-300 air defense system
July	In a meeting with Russia's ambassadors, Medvedev highlights the need to establish "modernization alliances" with foreign powers
	Customs Union of Russia, Belarus, and Kazakhstan comes into force

September	Russia completes an oil pipeline to China, and two gas pipelines are planned
November	Russia and China agree to use national currencies in bilateral trade
December	Medvedev expresses disappointment with the lack of progress on the proposed pan-European treaty

2011

January	Karzai visits Moscow to meet Medvedev
March	Russia abstains in the UNSC resolution that authorized airstrikes against Libya
April	Russia invites Ukraine to join Customs Union
	Russia creates a new antiterrorism center in Kyrgyzstan
	The Russia-controlled CSTO amends its mission by pledging to defend its members from internal "unconstitutional disturbances"
August	Russia hosts a trip by North Korea's leader Kim Jong Il; the idea of a trans-Korean pipeline is explored
September	Russia's state oil company, Rosneft, concludes an agreement with ExxonMobil to develop Russia's Arctic Basin
	Putin announces his decision to run for the presidency
October	Putin proposes to build a new Eurasian Union among the CIS states
December	Russia completes negotiations over WTO membership

2012

February	Russia and China veto UNSC Syria resolution
March	Putin is elected president in the first round
	The Kremlin approves NATO use of an airport in Ulyanovsk as a transit point for moving soldiers and cargo to and from Afghanistan
May	Russia warns the U.S. Congress against adopting the bill imposing visa bans and asset freezes on human rights violators in Russia
June	Putin's first foreign trips include Belarus, Germany, France, Uzbekistan, China, and Kazakhstan
	Putin meets President Obama in Mexico
July	Putin addresses Russian ambassadors and permanent representatives in international organizations
August	Russian court sentences members of the punk band Pussy Riot to two years in jail for hooliganism; Western governments express their strong disagreement with the decision

October	Russia refuses renewal of the Nunn-Lugar Cooperative Threat Reduction Program and additional cuts in strategic nuclear warheads; Putin stresses the need to address the U.S. MDS plans in Europe
December	Putin addresses the Federation Council and speaks of new demographic and moral threats
	The U.S. Congress, while normalizing trade relations with Russia, passes the Magnitsky bill that imposed sanctions against human rights violators in Russia
	The Russian Duma passes the "Anti-Magnitsky Act" that bans the adoption of Russian children by U.S. citizens

2013

February	Russia releases a new Foreign Policy Concept that discusses competition of different "values and development models"
June	The former CIA employee Edward Snowden defects to Russia; the Kremlin refuses to turn him over to the U.S.
	The Russian Duma passes Law against "propaganda of non-traditional sexual relations among minors"; Western governments express their disappointment
August	Russia grants Snowden asylum; Obama expresses his disappointment and cancels a bilateral summit with Putin
	The U.S. accuses Syria of using chemical weapons against opposition and threatens force; Russia disagrees and proposes a process of eliminating Syrian chemical weapons
September	The U.S. and Russia reach an agreement on phased elimination of Syria's chemical weapons
	The G-20 summit in St. Petersburg
	Putin visits Japan and signs investment and trade agreements
October	Putin's speech at Valdai Club on "the desire for independence and sovereignty in spiritual, ideological and foreign policy spheres"
November	Ukraine refuses to sign an Association Agreement with the EU; mass protests take place in Kiev pressuring the government to reverse the decision
December	In his address to the Federation Council Putin positions Russia as a "conservative" power and the worldwide defender of traditional values

2014

February	Russia and the West disagree on Syria in Geneva negotiations
	Russia holds successful Olympics in Sochi

	Revolutionary change of power in Ukraine
	Russia sends additional troops to Crimea
	The West condemns Russia's actions and threatens to apply sanctions
March	Russia annexes Crimea after its referendum and desire to join Russia
	The U.S. introduces sanctions against the Russian economy
April	The downing of Malaysian airplane with 286 passengers on board
	The EU joins the U.S. sanctions against Russia
May	Putin travels to China to sign massive natural gas deals
	Moscow writes off North Korean debt and agrees to build a gas and rail link into the south
July	The sixth BRICS summit in Fortaleza, Brazil
September	The Minsk-I agreement on cease-fire in Ukraine
	At the Valdai forum Putin is critical of the U.S. "destabilizing" role in world affairs
October	The ruble loses about 40 percent of its value
November	Russia participates in APEC summit
	Another massive natural gas deal between Russia and China
December	In his address to the Federation Council Putin justifies incorporation of Crimea in terms of consolidating Russia's centuries-old "civilizational and sacred significance"

2015

January	Putin travels to Istanbul and proposes a gas pipeline through Turkish territory to Europe's borders
February	The Minsk-II agreement on cease-fire in Ukraine
May	The 70th anniversary Victory Day parade in Moscow is not attended by Western leaders
	China's president attends the Victory Day parade and signs important economic agreements in Moscow
	Leaders of Russia and China sign an agreement on cooperation between the Eurasian Union and the Silk Road
	Russia and the Eurasian Union sign a free trade treaty with Vietnam
	Kerry arrives in Moscow to discuss the Middle East
	Putin signs Law on "Undesirable" Organizations giving prosecutors the power to shut down international organizations
July	Russia hosts summits of SCO and BRICS in Ufa

The U.S., UK, France, Russia, China, and Iran sign a nuclear agreement on limiting Iranian nuclear program in exchange for the lifting of international sanctions

Sources: Partly adapted from: Coit D. Blacker, *Hostage to Revolution: Gorbachev and Soviet Security Policy, 1985–1991* (New York: Council on Foreign Relations, 1993), ix–xviii; Strobe Talbott, *The Russia Hand* (New York: Random House, 2002), 423–29; Karen Dawisha and Bruce Parrott, *Russia and the New States of Eurasia* (Cambridge, UK: Cambridge University Press, 1994), 298–310; Ted Hopf, *Social Construction of International Politics: Identities and Foreign Policies, Moscow, 1955 and 1999* (Ithaca, NY: Cornell University Press, 2002), 212–13.

Preface

Winston Churchill once famously observed that the key to understanding Russia's "enigma" is its national interest. However, he failed to explain what that interest was. It is therefore our scholarly task to uncover what Russians themselves understand to be their foreign policy interests and objectives. In contrast to the direction of Churchill's thought, there has been a great deal of change in Russia's perceptions of its national interest. Thus, President Boris Yeltsin and his first foreign minister, Andrei Kozyrev, defined national interest as that of integration with Western economic and security institutions. The second foreign minister, Yevgeni Primakov, saw the need to restore Russia's great power status and balance hegemonic aspirations of the United States. Finally, Vladimir Putin and Dmitri Medvedev adopted their own distinct vision of national interest, which balanced Russia's great power status with the need to have special relationships with the West in general and the United States in particular. In the wake of the global economic crisis and rise of non-Western powers, Russia is yet again reassessing its interests and relations with the West.

This book seeks to contribute to our understanding of the national interest formation in Russia's foreign policy. Instead of assuming that national interest is about power or modernization, as mainstream international relations theories tend to do, I maintain that we ought to study the complex forces behind its formation. Upon closer inspection, we discover that much of Russia's foreign policy and national interest can be understood in the context of the country's relations with the West. Russia's attempts to embrace Western liberalism, as well as its insistence on great power status, make sense when we consider the significance of Western recognition in affirming Russia's actions. Western actions serve to reinforce or undermine dominant political forces inside Russia. Extending recognition emboldens Russian liberals insisting on their country's belongingness with the West. Withholding such recognition strengthens Russia's traditionally strong supporters of greater independence from the West. It is therefore domestic identity coalitions competing for influence in the context of Western actions that help to make sense of Russia's foreign policy formation. Chapter 1 explains my approach in greater detail.

The book does not claim to break new ground in empirical research. My objectives are more modest: to assist fellow academics in their teaching needs and to suggest a plausible interpretation of Russia's foreign policy. In my own teaching, I continue to feel a deficit of broadly targeted textbooks appropriate for senior undergraduate and graduate courses in the field of post-Soviet studies. With the second decade of the post-Soviet changes underway, there is still surprisingly little written that would meet this criterion. Fortunately, there are exceptions. There is also a good deal written by specialists on various specific aspects, issues, and periods in the development of Russia's foreign policy after communism. In my book, I relied heavily on this literature in attempting to synthesize it into a relatively broad overview of the subject. In addition to highlighting in endnotes the impact of some specific sources on my thinking, I list in a "further reading" section some of the readings that influenced this book.

While writing with teaching needs in mind, I have advanced an argument and taken an explicit analytical perspective. My choice of explaining Russia's foreign policy turns by changes in the nation's identity, rather than by material capabilities or leadership's perspectives alone, was a conscientious one. I fully realize that for the purpose of advancing scholarship, many of the book's assertions would require much greater documentation. I hope, however, that my framework is helpful for presenting material, asking interesting questions, and organizing in-class discussion. After all, no textbook is neutral, and instructors usually try to balance the dominant text(s) by assigning additional materials with conflicting viewpoints and perspectives. In my own teaching, I also commonly employ articles and materials by authors holding diverse views. Provoking thinking and sparking debates in class is essential for learning, as it is through arguing and sometimes only through arguing that we deepen our understanding. Although this may seem like a challenging way of teaching, our students deserve nothing less. I therefore intentionally present material in a somewhat polemical way, as a debate among different social and political groups in Russia.

I also make an effort to differentiate myself from more common treatment of Russian foreign policy in the West. My own perspective on the development of Russia's foreign policy is neither pro-Western liberalism nor anti-Western nationalism. Both of these perspectives have influenced Russian foreign policy formation, but, in my judgment, each has defended views of relatively narrow elite circles and ultimately failed to respond to broader needs of Russian society. I hope that Russia is now closer to having developed an appropriate formula of national interest, which appreciates the value of international cooperation in a globalizing world, but is also sensitive to Russia's local conditions and the country's special position in the international system. I also hope that scholars across the world pay close attention to future developments in Russia's foreign policy. Russia is no longer a threat to the West, and that alone has directed some of the sharpest pens away from studying that country's attitudes and behavior. Yet we have not come to understand this nation better just because the iron curtain is no longer in place. Russia also retains its political significance, and engaging it as a legitimate member of world society remains a key to peace and security in the new era. Such engagement requires that we improve our knowledge of Russia's perceived national interests.

The book is divided into nine chapters. The first chapter provides a brief historical overview of Russia's foreign policy and spells out the book's approach to understanding Russia's post-Soviet international behavior. I situate my approach relative to more mainstream international relations theories, realism and liberalism, and I argue the insufficiency of these traditional theoretical perspectives for understanding Russia. The rest of the book is a detailed analysis of several distinct concepts of national interest that guided Russia's international policies in the late Soviet and post-Soviet years. The latter parts are broken down further in order to cover such stories as the International Monetary Fund (IMF), the North Atlantic Treaty Organization (NATO), China, Yugoslavia, Iran, Commonwealth of Independent States (CIS) ties, the United States, the Iraq war, bilateral relations with newly independent states, and others. These are cases that instructors can choose from in order to stimulate a more focused discussion in class. Instructors may elect to assign longer articles or those materials that interpret Russia's actions differently than I do. Chapter 2 analyzes Gorbachev's New Thinking philosophy and what it meant for the country's foreign policy. Chapters 3–8 each explore the formation and consequences of other distinct visions of national interest— integration with the West (early Yeltsin and Kozyrev), great power balancing (late Yeltsin and Primakov), pragmatic cooperation (early Putin), great power assertiveness (Putin since 2007), renewed pragmatic cooperation under Medvedev, and return to Putin's assertiveness since spring 2012 in a new international context. In each of the substantive chapters, I specify the international and domestic context of foreign policy formation. I provide a brief overview of domestic debates on national interest, and then review

Russian policies toward the West, the East, and the former Soviet region. Furthermore, in each chapter, I offer an assessment of each period's foreign policy record. Criteria for my assessment are spelled out in the first chapter. The final chapter summarizes my explanation of change and continuity in Russia's foreign policy and its implications for Russian and Western policymakers.

Writing this book would have been impossible without the support of my friends, colleagues, students, and family. Naturally, full responsibility for the book's content is my own. For financial assistance, I wish to thank the Office of the President at San Francisco State University, which granted me an Award for Professional Development of Probationary Faculty and therefore made it possible for me to complete this book. I owe special thanks to Susan McEachern and Andrzej Korbonski. In the spring of 2002, they each, independently, suggested to me the idea of a textbook on Russian foreign policy. Since then they have been supportive of the project and confident in my ability to finish it. Comments and criticisms by Ronald Linden and an anonymous reviewer have been instrumental in improving the book, and I hope the final version will satisfy some of their expectations. I am also grateful to the University of Chicago's Program on International Politics, Economics, and Security (PIPES) for inviting me to deliver a paper and for providing a stimulating theoretical critique of this book's central argument. I thank especially Charles Lipson, Michelle Murrey, Alexander Wendt, as well as all other Program participants for their helpful reactions and suggestions. Sanjoy Banerjee and David Holloway shared their time to discuss central ideas of this book. Julia Godzikovskaya and Anna Radivilova were good enough to provide feedback on individual chapters. Furthermore, I thank many of my students in classes on Russia, post-Soviet states, and United States–Russia relations in Eurasia. The writing process would have been much less rewarding without their reactions to various portions of the book. It has been a pleasure to teach the subject of my own fascination, and to a group of interested and motivated individuals.

Many thanks to Rowman & Littlefield Publishers for smoothing out my prose and for all their assistance. While revising the book for the second, third, and fourth editions, I have greatly benefited from comments and suggestions made by Susan McEachern and anonymous reviewers who have used the text in their teaching. In addition, six years have passed since the book was first published. During these years, I have received many helpful comments from teachers, scholars, journalists, and members of the policy community in reaction to the published book and my other writings on Russia's international policy. Finally, I have a special debt to my family for their love and support. I dedicate this book to the youngest members of my family, my daughter Dasha, my son Pasha, and my grandson Slava.

1

Understanding Change and Continuity in Russia's Foreign Policy

When political formulas, such as "national interest" or "national security" gain popularity they need to be scrutinized with particular care. They may not mean the same thing to different people. They may not have any precise meaning at all.

—Arnold Wolfers[1]

This chapter provides analytical tools for understanding the subject of this book. It reviews Russia's international behavior across history and identifies several patterns of change and continuity in the country's foreign policy. Russia's traditional foreign policy debates survived the fall of the Soviet system, and Russia's postcommunist behavior should therefore be understood in the historical context. The chapter offers a framework for understanding Russian foreign policy, comparing and contrasting it with some prominent analytical perspectives. My approach focuses on Russia's relations with the outside world, and it views Russia's behavior as particularly influenced by the development and behavior of Western nations. What often determines Moscow's foreign policy choices is whether or not the West's international actions are perceived by Russian officials as accepting Russia as an equal and legitimate member of the world. The chapter also develops standards for evaluating Russia's foreign policy record. Finally, it orients the reader regarding the book's methodology and organizational structure.

RUSSIA'S FOREIGN POLICY:
CHANGE AND CONTINUITY

Russia's foreign policy was formed in different external contexts, while responding to some similar sets of security challenges. This combination provides Russia's historical foreign policy with elements of change and continuity.

Changing Contexts

At least since Peter the Great, Europe and—after World War II—the West in general played an especially prominent role in creating for Russia the system of meanings in which to defend international choices. To many Russians, the West represented a superior civilization whose influences were to be emulated or contained, but never ignored. Yet Western contexts were changing over time, presenting Russia with different policy dilemmas. More specifically, different Wests have been associated respectively with sovereign monarchy, the rise of a liberal political system, and finally the consolidation of a liberal political system.

Sovereign monarchy emerged as a dominant political form in seventeenth-century Europe after the era of religious wars. It was the era of increasingly secular sovereign statehood, and it was in this context that Peter the Great assumed power in 1694. In the context of European secularism, Peter introduced a new ideology of state patriotism, or loyalty to the state—a sharp break with the religious autocratic Russia that had emerged after the two-centuries-long rule by the Mongols. Despite opposition from the Eastern Orthodox Church, the czar decisively turned Russia in the secular nationalist direction. Although religion was still playing an important role, it was increasingly subjected to considerations of the state. European international politics, and with it Russia's international politics, was becoming the politics of accumulating national power rather than affirming religious values.

The liberal and egalitarian ideas of the French Revolution of 1789 further changed Europe by splitting it into progressive and antirevolutionary camps. The era of the rising Europe of Enlightenment, constitutionalism, and capitalism presented Russia with new international dilemmas. Russian rulers had to decide between the old monarch-centered vision of sovereignty and the new popular sovereignty, and this choice was then to shape the nation's international behavior. Some rulers—most prominently Alexander II—attempted to yet again redefine the country's identity in line with the new European ideas of freedom and equality. Their moderate foreign policies reflected the need for Russia to undergo considerable domestic changes. Other rulers were fearful of the new Europe and sought to defend the basic features of the old monarchic regime. Thus, Alexander I insisted on the need to defend the status quo in the post-Napoleonic Europe and embraced antirevolutionary Germany and Austria, rather than progressive France, as his role models. Alexander III also continued policies of siding with European autocracies and repression at home.

As Europe was fighting its way through the crisis of rising liberal ideas, some Russians began to advocate a break with both old and new Europe. Alexander Herzen, for instance, grew disappointed with European conservative restorations of the 1840s and argued for Russia's own, non-European way of "catching up" economically and socially. The Bolsheviks pushed this line of thinking to its extreme and adopted a fundamentally different political system and foreign policy. The Bolshevik revolution of October 1917 reflected the crisis of European identity and the Russian leadership's inability to choose between the two Europes. The czar failed to prevent the country from the nearing destruction, revolution, and civil war. The rule of Nicholas II was symbolic in this respect. In 1904, he dismissed his finance minister, Count Sergei Witte, a proponent of the new Europe and an economic reformer, and chose to sacrifice domestic reforms to the goals of foreign policy expansionism by going to war against Japan. By then entering World War I, Nicholas further brought the European crisis closer to home and made it impossible to prevent the spread of extremist Marxist ideas in Russia, a move which brought his downfall in the Bolshevik revolution of 1917. In recognition of the West's world role, however, even the Bolsheviks sought to engage Western nations and related to their technological and material power. The Bolsheviks' concept of Soviet power and proletarian democracy was also a response to egalitarian ideas of the French Revolution. Furthermore, Bolsheviks' foreign policy, after the early efforts to overthrow the "bourgeois" governments in Europe, was that of rapprochement and pragmatic cooperation with the West.

As Europe reemerged as a consolidated liberal-democratic continent after World War II, the Soviet rulers sought to preserve a connection with the new West. The intercourse with the West grew stronger under Nikita Khrushchev and then Mikhail Gorbachev. Soviet leader Nikita Khrushchev's famous de-Stalinization speech at the XXth Communist Party congress broke many taboos of the old thinking and was meant, among other things, to bring Soviet Russia closer to Europe.[2] Despite Khrushchev's removal, the impact of de-Stalinization proved to be irreversible—a considerable part of a new intellectual generation now referred to themselves as the "children of the XXth party congress" and worked within and outside the establishment to bring Soviet Russia closer to the West. The post-Stalin period saw, in particular, growth of specialized institutions in which researchers carefully analyzed Western viewpoints, such as those generated by American international relations (IR) scholars.

Ultimately, the new Western influences contributed greatly to the discourse of human rights and democracy in the Soviet Union, creating the environment for reformers and helping Gorbachev come to power. Although he never meant for the socialist system to be replaced by that of Western liberalism, Gorbachev proclaimed a new era in relationships with the West and therefore greatly contributed to the new fundamental change. In addition to Khrushchev's policies of de-Stalinization and peaceful coexistence, Gorbachev drew from ideas of Russian liberal-minded scientists, such as Vladimir Vernadski, Pyotr Kapitsa, and Andrei Sakharov—all long-term advocates of developing relationships with the West. The leader of perestroika was also building on European social-democratic ideas, as well as American theories of transnationalism and interdependence. The Soviet collapse of 1991 completed the process of the country's difficult adjustment to the new international context and laid the groundwork for the establishment of Russia's liberal foreign policy orientation. The new liberal context continues to be highly contested in Russia and will be shaped further by the country's interaction with Western nations. If the West remains a relatively consolidated liberal entity with a clear and unambiguous message to the world, the new liberal identity has a good chance of taking stronger root in post-Soviet Russia.

Three Schools of Foreign Policy Thinking

Although Russia's foreign policy was a response to various international contexts, it also displayed a remarkable degree of historical continuity. Across the eras of monarchy and liberalism, Russia's engagement with the world followed several persistent patterns of thinking and behavior. As a borderland nation in an uncertain, often volatile external environment, Russia had to continuously respond to similar challenges to its security. These challenges included unrest in neighboring territories, threats of external invasion, and difficulties in preserving internal state integrity. Over time, the country has developed three distinct traditions, or schools, of foreign policy thinking—Westernist, Statist, and Civilizationist. Throughout centuries, Westernizers, Statists, and Civilizationists sought to present Russia's international choices in ways consistent with the schools' historically established images of the country and the outside world.

Westernizers placed the emphasis on Russia's similarity with the West and viewed the West as the most viable and progressive civilization in the world. The early Westernizers sought to present Russia as a loyal member in the family of European monarchies. Historically the emergence of this school of thinking can be traced back to Peter the Great's military Westernization. Peter was the first to admire the West for its technological superiority and to raise the possibility of borrowing Western technology to overcome Russia's backwardness. Alexander I was more consistent in defending the values of the old Europe and vigorously opposing the spread of French egalitarian ideas. After the defeat of Napoleon, Alexander championed the so-called legitimist policies and established the Holy Alliance with Germany and Austria in order to suppress revolutionary activities on the Continent.

Liberal Westernizers identified with the Western values of constitutional freedoms and political equality. After the era of great reforms and Russia shifting its relations from Germany to France and Britain under Alexander II, the czarist government seemed more willing to embrace the new European values of constitutionalism. Pavel Milyukov, once a foreign minister and a leader of Russian liberals, took the most active pro-European position by insisting that Russia must stay in World War I as an active member of the anti-German coalition. To Milyukov, support for the European allies—despite all the devastation that the war had brought to Russia—was a matter of principle and the country's identity orientation.

Westernizers within the Soviet system saw Russia as standing not too far apart from European social democratic ideas. For instance, one of Gorbachev's favorite lines of thinking was that the Soviet Union had to "purify" itself of Stalinist "distortions" and become a democratic, or "human," version of socialism (*gumannyi sotsializm*). In his foreign policy, Gorbachev pursued the notion of mutual security with the West and presided over a series of revolutionary arms-control agreements with the United States, as well as over the Soviet military withdrawals from Europe and the third world. By introducing the idea of a "common European home," Gorbachev meant to achieve Russian-European integration based on the principles of European social democracy.

Finally, the liberal Westernizers in post-Soviet Russia argued for the "natural" affinity of their country with the West based on such shared values as democracy, human rights, and a free market. Liberal Westernizers warned against relations with former Soviet allies and insisted that only by building Western liberal institutions and joining the coalition of what was frequently referred to as the community of "Western civilized nations" would Russia be able to respond to its threats and overcome its economic and political backwardness. Andrei Kozyrev and Boris Yeltsin's vision of "integration" and "strategic partnership with the West" assumed that Russia would develop liberal democratic institutions and build a market economy after the manner of the West. Throughout 2009–2012, President Dmitri Medvedev advocated a new era of improving relations with the Western nations based on a common assessment of security threats and greater openness in economic and political systems. He initiated a new pan-European security treaty and argued for liberalizing the economic and political system in order to overcome Russia's backwardness, corruption, and rigidity.

Statists have emphasized the state's ability to govern and preserve the social and political order. This is, arguably, the most influential school of Russia's foreign policy thinking. It is explicit in choosing values of power, stability, and sovereignty over those of freedom and democracy. Critical to Statism is the notion of external threats to Russia's security. Ever since the two-centuries-long conquest by the Mongols, Russians have developed a psychological complex of insecurity and a readiness to sacrifice everything for independence and sovereignty. Multiple wars in Europe and Asia further reinforced this mentality and provided Statism's supporters with extra justifications for their reasoning. For instance, when justifying the need for rapid industrialization, the leader of the Soviet state, Josef Stalin, famously framed his argument in terms of responding to powerful external threats.

> The history of the old Russia was the continual beating she suffered because of her backwardness. She was beaten by the Mongol khans. She was beaten by the Turkish beys. She was beaten by the Swedish feudal lords. She was beaten by the Polish and Lithuanian gentry. She was beaten by the English and French capitalists. She was beaten by the Japanese barons. All beat her—for her backwardness. . . . We are fifty or a hundred years behind the advanced countries. We must make good this distance in ten years. Either we do it, or we shall be crushed.[3]

The Statists, however, are not inherently anti-Western; they merely seek the West's recognition by putting emphasis on economic and military capabilities. The Statists of the monarchical era valued Russia's autocratic structure of power, partly because such were the structures of European monarchies as well. In foreign policy, Statists often trace their intellectual and policy origins to Prince Alexander Gorchakov. Gorchakov labored as Alexander II's foreign minister to recover Russia's lost international positions after the defeat in the Crimean War. He pursued the policy of "concentration" by developing a system of flexible alliances and limiting Russia's involvement in European affairs.[4] Other Statists trace their roots to Peter the Great. Unlike Westernizers emphasizing Peter's Europeanness, Statists relate to Peter's military competitiveness. It was state security and military competitiveness, they argue, that brought about the czar's notion of getting closer to Europe.

The socialist Statists insisted on the importance of the Communist Party's firm control over the society for the purpose of maintaining political order and averting external "capitalist" threats. Within the Soviet leadership, this school was always suspicious of efforts to activate political institutions outside the party and opposed Gorbachev's democratization reform. In foreign policy, some Statists advocated relative accommodation with the West, while others favored balancing strategies. Maksim Litvinov, for instance, supported a "collective security" system in Europe in order to prevent the rise of fascism. Nikita Khrushchev, too, wanted to break taboos of isolationism and bring Soviet Russia closer to Europe. He also called for a return to Lenin's principles of "coexistence" with the capitalist world, although he later slipped into several incidents of confrontation with the West. Both Litvinov and Khrushchev saw themselves as supporters of the late Lenin's course toward giving up the idea of the world revolution and learning to live and trade with the potentially dangerous capitalist world.

On the other hand, Stalin's pact with Hitler, as well as Leonid Brezhnev's "correlation of forces" strategy, reflected the will to balance perceived dangerous influences from the outside world. By signing the treaty of friendship with Nazi Germany, Stalin hoped to isolate Russia from World War II or at least to buy enough time to prepare for it. His successors operated on a world scale and, with the "correlation of forces" doctrine, they meant to respond to the perceived growing global influence of the West. Both strategies meant to preserve Russia's independence in world affairs and had some elements of Gorchakov's described strategy of concentration.

The liberal Statists of the post-Soviet era no longer supported a single-party state, and they agreed with the importance of building a market economy and political democracy. However, they were not ready to sacrifice to these new values the historically tested notion of a strong state, and they argued that liberal values should be established to strengthen, not weaken, the state. The liberal Statists believed that Russia continued to be exposed to external threats and must remain a great power capable of responding to those threats anywhere in the world. Yet they proposed different strategies to achieve the great power status. The distinction between Primakov's and Putin's policies is a case in point. Both camps have at one point or another referred to Gorchakov as their inspiration, and both viewed Russia's greatness and strength as key goals of their foreign policies. In their domestic policies, both wanted to bring more order and control to social and political life. Primakov sought to control big business. Putin continued in the same vein, but also tightened his grip over the legislature, party building, regions, and electronic media, while at the same time declaring his commitment to the newly established political institutions and economic liberalization. The critical foreign policy difference between the two, however, is that Primakov was trying to rebuild the former Soviet Union and contain the United States through a strategic alliance with China and India, whereas Putin emphasized bilateral relations in Russia's periphery and was ambitious to develop a partnership with the United States to deter terrorism.

Finally, Civilizationists have always seen Russian values as different from those of the West, and they have always attempted to spread Russian values abroad, outside the West. Their response to Russia's security dilemmas has been more aggressive than that of the more status quo–oriented Statists. As a foreign policy philosophy, Civilizationism dates back to Ivan IV's ("Ivan the Terrible's") "gathering of Russian lands" after the Mongol Yoke and to the dictum "Moscow is the third Rome," which was adopted under Ivan. Unlike Westernizers and Statists, Civilizationists have sought to challenge the Western system of values, insisting on the cultural distinctiveness of Russia and Russia-centered civilization. Some representatives of this school advocated a firm commitment to values of Orthodox Christianity, while others viewed Russia as a synthesis of various religions.

The early Civilizationists advocated the identity of the "Russian empire." They recognized the constraints set by the West-centered external context and recommended that Russia expand beyond its eastern and southern borders. Yet they were eager to defend what they saw as a cultural unity in their outer area. For instance, in the nineteenth century, Civilizationists defended the notion of Slavic unity, and their ideology of Pan-Slavism affected some of the czar's foreign policy decisions.

The socialist Civilizationists went further and challenged the West in a most direct fashion. The Lenin-Trotski doctrine of the world revolution was the Soviet version of Civilizationist thinking. Although it had died as an official philosophy in 1921 with Lenin's commitment to coexistence with capitalism, many in the official and social circles remained convinced of the virtues of the thinking. For example, in the late Soviet and the post-Soviet context, some hard-line political and intellectual movements often defend a widespread external expansion as the best means of ensuring Russia's security. The so-called Eurasianists view Russia as a constantly expanding land-based empire in a struggle for power against sea-based Atlanticism, associated especially with the United States.[5] Born out of the agony of two Europes, Soviet Russia saw itself as superior to the "decadent" and "rotten" Western capitalist civilization. Yet even the Soviet Civilizationists sought to justify their foreign policy expansionism by the need to respond to the "global imperial expansion" of the West. The expansionism therefore was seen by Russian rulers as legitimate and permissible in the international context. It remains to be seen which forms Russia's post-Soviet liberal Civilizationism might take.[6]

The continuity of Russian schools of foreign policy thinking in different external contexts is summarized in table 1.1.

Table 1.1.   Russia's Foreign Policy: Change and Continuity

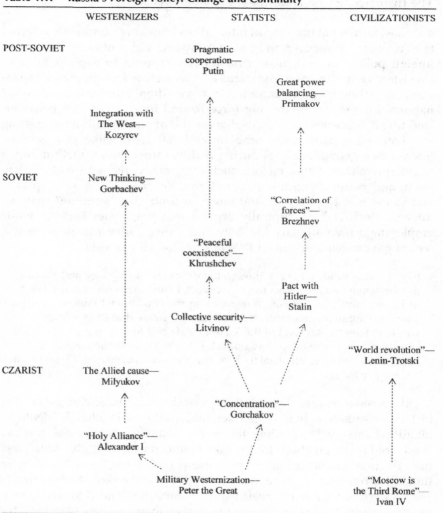

	WESTERNIZERS	STATISTS	CIVILIZATIONISTS
POST-SOVIET		Pragmatic cooperation— Putin	
			Great power balancing— Primakov
	Integration with The West— Kozyrev		
SOVIET	New Thinking— Gorbachev		
			"Correlation of forces"— Brezhnev
		"Peaceful coexistence"— Khrushchev	
			Pact with Hitler— Stalin
		Collective security— Litvinov	
			"World revolution"— Lenin-Trotski
CZARIST	The Allied cause— Milyukov		
		"Concentration"— Gorchakov	
	"Holy Alliance"— Alexander I		
		Military Westernization— Peter the Great	"Moscow is the Third Rome"— Ivan IV

EXPLAINING CHANGE AND CONTINUITY
IN RUSSIAN FOREIGN POLICY

This section introduces various explanations of Russian foreign policy and argues for the insufficiency of traditional approaches. In attempting to address the shortcomings of these approaches, I offer a framework for understanding Russian behavior as shaped by the nation's interaction with the West.

The Insufficiency of Traditional Explanations

The most influential tradition of international thinking, commonly referred to as realism, has focused on historical patterns and continuity in Russia's foreign policy. In particular, scholars have sought to explain Russia's consistent commitment to the status quo, as well as foreign policy expansionism. Scholars in this tradition have often emphasized Russia's national interest as the driving force behind its international behavior. Defining it as preservation and enhancement of power within the existing international system, many scholars and statesmen alike saw national interest as a geopolitically enduring reality, rather than something open to interpretations. Other factors, such as ideology, the nature of government, and political culture, mattered, too. Yet their role was to specify, and sometimes to cover for, but never to contradict "genuine" national interest. Realists have typically argued that the Soviet leaders, while employing a revolutionary ideology and acting under a totalitarian system of government, defended Russia's traditional interests.

> Soviet leaders did not act as though the demands of ideology and those of the Russian national interest were in conflict. Lenin, in negotiating the Treaty in Brest-Litovsk, and Stalin, in negotiating the Nazi-Soviet Pact and in the wartime summit conferences, were constantly aware that their first priority was to ensure the survival of the Russian state and to seek ways to enhance its security. . . . When they had opportunities to expand, the territories that interested them were identical to those that the tsars had sought, for identical strategic reasons.[7]

Others have pointed to underlying consistencies in Soviet policy. For instance, Nathan Leites, in his seminal study of Bolshevik ideology, identified three rules guiding the Soviet behavior: "never risk already conquered major positions for the sake of uncertain gains," "anything less than the exertion of maximum pressure is ineffective," and "mastery in the skill of retreating is as necessary as mastery in the skill of advancing."[8] For Western policymakers, realist studies implied the need to stay firm in resisting Russia's power aspirations, rather than to keep searching for common solutions, and to apply what during the Cold War would be called "containment." As Winston Churchill put it in his famous "iron curtain" speech, "There is nothing they [Russians] admire so much as strength, and there is nothing for which they have less respect than for . . . military weakness."[9]

More recent developments in realist thinking point to the structure of the international system—namely, the absence of a legitimate authority (anarchy)—as the central force that affects Russia's international behavior. For example, some realists have explained Russia's liberal momentum of the late 1980s–early 1990s and the searches for active accommodation with the West by the Soviet defeat in the Cold War and the need to respond to the emergence of an America-centered global unipolar system. In this perspective, Russia's hegemonic policy in the former Soviet area and a nonconfrontational engagement with the West is the only rational strategy, given the fundamental weakness of Russia's post–Cold War capabilities.[10] The new or structural realists continue to view power and national interest as the underlying force of Russia's international behavior. Even when they employ factors other than power, such as perceptions and domestic politics,[11] they assign to these factors secondary roles relative to the role attributed to the structure of the international system. Introducing perceptions and domestic politics therefore does not change the overall thrust of the realist analysis, according to which the international environment is anarchic in nature and states have a constant drive for security and power (national interest).

By focusing on foreign policy continuity, realists employ a very narrow perspective on "change," limiting it to fluctuations of available power capabilities. In the realist tradition, there is little room for foreign policy patterns shaped by considerations other than power, such as indigenous ideas or cultural beliefs. As a result, realists typically overlook and wrongfully interpret some far-reaching changes in Russia's foreign policy that are potent for cooperation with Western nations. Realism seems to work when the actual policies at play are of a zero-sum nature, but it errs when the zero-sum reality is not in place. For example, in his engagement with two leading realists, Robert English pointed to the inaccuracy of presenting Gorbachev as the overseer of the Soviet strategic retreat. He argued that the origins of Gorbachev's New Thinking dated back to the late 1950s and 1960s and had to do with domestic changes and the revival of cultural links to the West, not defense calculations and economic needs.[12] If this criticism is correct, realism is unable to account fully for Russia's liberal changes. It has a built-in tendency to misrepresent the scope and the origins of Russia's foreign policy changes. It follows that it is simply unfit for fully understanding Russian liberal-minded statesmen, such as Pavel Milyukov, Mikhail Gorbachev, or Andrei Kozyrev. Even when realists are able to correctly identify the direction of Russia's "realist" policymakers, such as Primakov and Putin, their excessive emphasis on the international structure of power makes them neglectful of important domestic/local sources that often shape Russia's foreign policy.[13]

A less prominent, but still influential, tradition in international relations concentrates on understanding foreign policy changes. Western scholars working in this tradition have challenged the realist notion of foreign policy continuity by pointing to such episodes as Khrushchev's early arms control efforts, the Soviet policies of détente, and Gorbachev's sweeping international initiatives. Frequently referred to as liberals, these scholars have also sought to undermine the concept of national interest as something objective and geographically defined. In particular, they have pointed to considerable disagreements among state elites regarding Russia's international priorities and interests. They have also identified multiple coalitions and interest groups with different foreign policy agendas and ways to influence the policymaking process. Furthermore, they identified some learning curves in Russian/Soviet foreign policymaking.[14]

The end of the Cold War produced new expectations of increasing policy convergence across nations and pushed liberals toward developing theories of foreign policy that would be more sensitive to the structure of the international system. The liberal view of the international system is principally different from that of the realists. Unlike realists, who emphasize international anarchy and cyclical development, liberals have argued the global and progressive ascendancy of Western political and economic values. Francis Fukuyama pioneered the claim and insisted on the arrival of "the universalization of Western Liberal democracy as the final form of human government."[15] In this spirit, many scholars and policymakers took the end of the Cold War as an opportunity to assert that economic and political modernization, rather than geopolitically defined national interest, should serve as the primary foreign policy goal. Theories on the transition to a free-market economy and pluralistic democracy became dominant in academic and political discourse. Behind those theories lay a deep conviction in the progressive nature of international relations and the ability of market democratic institutions to turn the world into a more peaceful and prosperous place.

Three different schools emerged in the liberal community to challenge the realist outlook. One school promoted economic globalization and the growing "common marketization" of international relations as a guarantee of the diminution of the likelihood of large-scale conflict between states. Its supporters questioned the realist belief in the primacy of states by insisting that in an increasingly "borderless world," the state role will be reduced to providing the necessary infrastructure for competitive behavior in the global market.[16] Another school concentrated on democracy building as a guarantee for peace in international relations. In line with the old ideas of the German philosopher Immanuel Kant and U.S. president Woodrow Wilson, this school embraced the proposition that democracies are essentially peaceful in relations with one another, and therefore democracy promotion will keep the peace in the world.[17] Yet another group argued the significance of various transnational ties—transnational expert communities, political ideas, and social movements—

in challenging the realist notion of international anarchy.[18] It was the transnational ties, the scholars insisted, that had become especially important in foreign policy formulation. The case of Mikhail Gorbachev's leadership has become especially important to liberals.[19]

The power of the liberal outlook was reflected in policy actions. Policymakers, such as U.S. president Bill Clinton, committed themselves to transforming the world in line with the liberal internationalist ideas of Kant and Wilson. The democratic peace theory became the official justification of the United States' foreign policy actions in the 1990s. Clinton's 1994 national security strategy stated, "Our national security strategy is based on enlarging the community of market democracies while deterring and containing a range of threats to our nation, our allies and our interests. The more that democracy and political and economic liberalization take hold in the world, particularly in countries of geo-strategic importance to us, the safer our nation is likely to be and the more our people are likely to prosper."[20] In their speeches, Clinton and his advisers were arguing, just as Clinton's senior adviser and top Russia expert Strobe Talbott did, that "democracy . . . is the one big thing that we must defend, sustain, and promote wherever possible, even as we deal with the many other tasks that face us."[21]

Despite the increased sophistication of its foreign policy analysis, liberalism is a limited guide in understanding Russia's foreign policy. It cannot offer a comprehensive theory of foreign policy because of its unrealistic assumptions and selective focus. While rejecting the anarchy-based perspective as inaccurate, liberals produced a vision of an international system that is restrictive in its own way. Unlike that of realists, the liberal vision of foreign policy change is progressive and cumulative. However, this vision does not account fully for conservative turns in Russia's foreign policy. Such turns are normally viewed as "setbacks" that imply Russia's future "return" to the track of progressive liberal changes. For instance, in acknowledgment of scholars of Clinton's Russia policies, "for the Clinton team, Yeltsin the man *was* reform, while his enemies represented regression and the possible return of communism."[22] It is not surprising that the Clinton White House miscalculated many of Russia's developments and often did not want to admit some obvious facts. For instance, as late as the second half of 1993, American officials believed that Russia's transition was on track and, as a result, they were completely unprepared for the nationalist victory in Russia's December 1993 parliamentary election. When the extreme nationalist Vladimir Zhirinovski did win the election, Clinton's officials attributed the win to economic hardship under reform, never questioning the principal applicability of pro-Western democratization and marketization to Russia's inherent conditions. Even after Russia's financial default to the International Monetary Fund (IMF) in August 1998, Washington did not believe in the failure of Russia's liberal experiment and pointed instead to the "imperatives of the global marketplace." Rather than try to understand Russia's specific conditions, the Clinton team explained the nation's shift "away from the unabashedly pro-Western reformers and toward nationalistic bureaucrats who had been waiting in the shadow" in terms of insufficient financial aid for the Russian reform.[23] Just as realists view Russia's liberal shifts as an anomaly, liberals consider the country's conservative shifts as tenuous and short term. Some larger assumptions seem to be in play here: while realists study zero-sum interactions, liberals are interested primarily in positive-sum changes. It seems symptomatic and hardly accidental that liberals, who devoted so much energy to explaining the New Thinking and Russia's liberal "revolution," have produced no systematic accounts of Russia's return to great power thinking in the post-Soviet era. As a result, liberals have failed to fully understand the changes that Yevgeni Primakov and Vladimir Putin brought to Russia's foreign policy.

Social Constructivism and Its Promise

Overall, there are two problems with realist and liberal accounts of foreign policy. First, both theories tend to emphasize one aspect of the international system at the expense of others. Rather than acknowledging the validity of both power and modernization/democratization imperatives in foreign policy formation, they choose to highlight one or the other. In so doing, the two approaches refrain from developing a comprehensive and complex explanatory framework. In such a framework, realism would need to be modified to account for liberal changes in Russia's foreign policy, whereas liberalism should be revised to explain Russia's periodic retreats to great power thinking. The second problem is that both realism and liberalism are ethnocentric in the sense that they view Russia's foreign policy through similar Western cultural lenses and do not pay sufficient attention to Russia's indigenous history and system of perceptions. While realists are committed to the notion of Western power and dominance in the world, liberals advocate economic and political modernization by making little effort to apply any but the Western definition of the notion. Developed in the West, by the West, and for the West, these two approaches are increasingly problematic in a world that is multicultural and multimeaningful. In order to address their limitations, they both need to be sensitized to social conditions in which the various changes in Russia's foreign policy take place. If we are to understand the diversity of national foreign policies, we ought to first understand what "national" is.

In the field of international relations, the perspective that begins the analysis by asking what "national" is and that exposes the "nation" to various meanings and interpretations is called social constructivism. Constructivists are different from realists and liberals in viewing the international system as a social or cultural phenomenon. In addition to military and institutional constraints or facilitators of state actions, as emphasized by the other two theories, constructivists concentrate on the cultural contexts and meanings in which these actions take place. From this perspective, the international system is not merely a terrain for applying available military, economic, and diplomatic instruments; rather, the role of the international system is in assisting states in their socialization and understanding of interests in world politics. The international environment constructs state actions and interests. Such actions and interests are not rationally uniform, and they differ depending on individual states' experiences with the international system and its parts. Constructivists argue that because particular social contexts define national interests, the formation of such interests should be carefully studied, rather than merely assumed to be rational or irrational. In the words of a leading constructivist, "It is striking how little empirical research has been done investigating what kind of interests state actors actually have."[24]

The central category of the constructivist theory of international politics is identity. Before nations figure out how to best defend their interests with available material and diplomatic means, they first seek to understand what these interests in the international society are. By interacting with other members of international society, nations develop affiliations, attachments, and—ultimately—their own identities. Historically, some nations or cultural communities emerge as more important than others, and it is through these significant Others that national Selves define their appropriate character and types of actions. The very existence of the Self becomes difficult without recognition from the Other. National identity therefore is a system of meanings that expresses the Self's emotional, cognitive, and evaluative orientations toward its significant Other. The significant Other establishes the meaningful context for the Self's existence and development and therefore exerts decisive influence on the Self. Through its actions, the Other may reinforce or erode the earlier established sense of national identity. Depending on whether these influences are read by the Self as extending or denying it recognition, they may either encourage or discourage the Self to act cooperatively. (Table 1.2 summarizes the constructivist perspective on foreign policy, relative to those of realism and liberalism.)

Table 1.2.   International Relations Theories and Their Perspectives on Foreign Policy

	International Influences	Foreign Policy Actor	Foreign Policy Objective
Realism	Anarchy	State	State power
Liberalism	Western economic and political progress	Individuals, groups	Modernization and democratization
Constructivism	Significant Other	National Self	Self's acceptance by the Other

At the same time, one must not privilege international social practices at the expense of those of local origins. Local conditions, such as the state of the economy, relations among different social groups, or the type of political regime, are just as important in shaping national perceptions. These and other conditions have long been part of foreign policy analysis, and the initially international system–oriented constructivism is now moving toward incorporating domestic-level variables.[25] Foreign policy begins when a state manages to transcend the dichotomy of internal/ external pressures and develops multiple strategies for responding to world challenges.[26] With distinct social conditions in place, nations have distinct concerns and therefore view the world in their own ways. For instance, perceptions of reality by rich nations will differ from perceptions of reality by those that are considered poor. Some local concerns are more historically stable and are formed across a relatively long time, while others are more immediate and emerge in response to short-term developments. But in both cases, they serve as cultural lenses through which a nation views the outside world.

A nation, however, is not a homogenous entity. Different traditions or schools of thinking about the world develop in response to international and local conditions, and these schools compete for political influence. They hold different images regarding a nation's identity, the nature of the external world, and appropriate policy response. In a relatively open society, they compete openly for the dominant position and are supported by various social groups or coalitions. Constructivists do not view foreign policy as a product of a unitary state's advancing power, as in realism, or as a particular group pursuing modernization interests, as in liberalism. Rather, the role of a coalition is to put forward a particular image of national identity that will speak to the existing local conditions and be recognized by the significant Other. Identity coalitions are broader and more fundamental than interest coalitions, and they seek to achieve social recognition, rather than to maximize wealth or power.

To summarize, both international influences and local conditions are critical in understanding the processes of foreign policy formation and change. International influences by the Other create the meaningful context in which the national Self evolves and then shapes foreign policy. Past interactions with the external environment, as well as local conditions, establish identity as a relatively stable system of meanings with a well-consolidated context in which to act. Therefore, a nation has relative autonomy in influencing foreign policy, and that autonomy is historically established. On a more contemporary level, however, identity is a product of discursive competition among different groups and coalitions, drawing on different actions of the Other and interpreting contemporary international and local influences in a way that suits the groups' interests. The process that links international and local conditions, national identity and foreign policy, is a complex one, and it includes vigorous debates over the nature of national identity and national interests. Because international society contains multiple norms and influences, some of them may conflict in influencing the Self. For instance, realists emphasize the need to be strong, while liberals insist that the world revolves around values of free economy and society. Both strength and liberty can serve as powerful normative messages the modern West sends to the outside world. However, just as realists and liberals disagree, the norms of strength and liberty can conflict in shaping the identity of the Self.

At this point, identity becomes highly contested. Different identity coalitions form to promote their visions. Promoted by various identity groups in both public and private spaces, identity contestation is especially intense until one of the available visions becomes predominant. Activities of political entrepreneurs, appropriate material and ideational resources, conducive institutional arrangements, and historical practices can considerably facilitate this process of persuading the general public and elites. When this persuasion part of the process is complete, the state appropriates the dominant national identity vision as a guide in policy-making (national interest). Foreign policy, then, is a highly political phenomenon. It evolves with the rise and fall of various identity visions, as advocated by different social and political groups. Individual leaders' views and ideologies, as creative and autonomous they may be, too frequently reflect group visions of national identity. Other factors and influences may interfere with a decision-making process, yet if all the other factors are equal, one can expect a reasonable degree of foreign policy consistency based on an adopted image of national identity. (Table 1.3 spells out the causal influences on foreign policy as viewed from the constructivist perspective.)

Table 1.3. Constructivist Explanation of Foreign Policy: A Causal Process

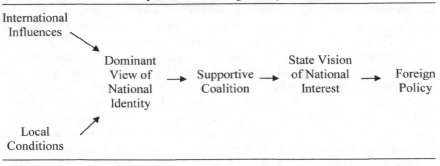

The Social Construction of Russia's Foreign Policy

In Russia's case, Europe and the West in general played the role of the significant Other and prominently figured in debates about national identity. It was Europe and the West that created the meaningful environment in which Russia's rulers defended their visions of national identity and national interest. Russia has historically sought to be recognized by the Western Other and to modernize after the manner of the West. In 1917—partly because of the West's own agonizing split between autocracy and liberalism and partly because of the special local conditions and the leadership's errors—Russia went through the experience of a social revolution and ceased experimenting with liberal reforms. The liberal West therefore rejected Russia as its own, and Bolshevik leaders sought to be recognized for their strength, rather than for the nature of their domestic institutions. Statist thinking prevailed in the Soviet discourse, reflecting the desire to maintain the balance of power with the West. As the West consolidated its liberal institutions after World War II, liberal thinking returned to the Soviet Union, paving the way for possible future changes. Gorbachev's arrival signaled that Soviet liberalism had grown strong enough to challenge the tenets of the old Statist and Civilizationist thinking.

However, Gorbachev was unable to stay his course. Under the conditions of extreme polarization between the old Statists and Civilizationists and the new liberal Westernizers, Gorbachev lost his initial support among elites and the general populace and subsequently had to resign. Although he never meant for Russia's socialist identity to be replaced by that of pro-Western liberalism, Gorbachev undoubtedly greatly contributed to the rise of domestic Westernizers. The 1991 collapse of the Soviet Union presented Russia's new liberals with an opportunity to fashion a pro-Western course of foreign policy. President Boris Yeltsin and his foreign minister Andrei Kozyrev pursued policies of strategic partnership and Integration with the West and its institutions. Externally, they were inspired by the Western promises of support, and they expected to "join" the West within a few years. They saw the West's victory in the Cold War as the promise and the opportunity of the new liberal era. Domestically, the Westernizing coalition included—in addition to liberal-minded leadership—intellectuals, human rights activists, and new procapitalist elites, particularly those with export interests in the West. The new identity coalition pursued a revolutionary agenda of transforming the old Soviet institutions into those of a pro-Western nation-state. It seemed as if the new liberal identity was finally to be established in Russia.

But Soviet disintegration did not end the old identity debates. In fact— partly because of the Soviet breakup—the new post-Soviet identity became deeply contested, and the liberal momentum did not last. Soon the pro-Western policies were met with a formidable opposition, in which the new Statists played the key role. The new Statists were different from their Soviet counterparts in acknowledging the necessity of building a market economy and democratic institutions. At the same time, they shared the old line of Statist reasoning, according to which all reforms had to be subjected to the main objective of strengthening the state. The new Statist coalition included military industrialists, the army, and the security services—those who saw only marginal benefits in adopting the Western model. Led by presidential adviser Sergei Stankevich and then the chief of foreign intelligence Yevgeni Primakov, the new Statists insisted that the national interest had not changed significantly and still had to do with defending Russia's great power status. Over time, this reasoning proved to win the support of the elites and masses, and the state had to adopt the Statist concept of national interest. Primakov—now Russia's newly appointed foreign minister—argued for more restrained relations with the West and for a more "balanced" and "diverse" foreign policy. Primakov believed that Russia's new liberal values did not erase the need to maintain the status of a distinct Eurasianist great power and to balance Western influences. One of his prominent proposals was that Russia develop a strategic alliance with China and India.

Statists were able to defeat Westernizers because of the power of the old Statist identity, the establishment of which could be traced as far back as the 1920s. The Statists were also successful in using the weakness of the new liberal state and mobilizing various informal channels for influencing policymaking. In particular, they benefited politically from the failure of Westernist radical economic reform. Externally, the identity struggle between Statists and Westernizers took place in the changed context. Looking to protect Russia's security, Statists were soon able to identify several threatening developments. Newly emerged instabilities and conflicts in the former Soviet republics and inside the country (Chechnya) in the early to mid-1990s made it extremely difficult for Westernizers to sustain their policies of disengagement from the periphery. Importantly, the West—Russia's significant Other—greatly strengthened the Statist discourse by making a decision to expand the North Atlantic Treaty Organization (NATO) eastward and exclude Russia from the process. This strengthened the sense that the West was not accepting Russia as one of its own. All these developments provided the context for constructing the sought image of external threat and solidified the influence of the new identity coalition. On the other hand, Westernism did not have sufficient public support to be able to reduce the power of the Statists.

The arrival of Vladimir Putin as the new president signaled yet another change in policies and a renewed interest in engaging the West. In a stunning strategic reversal, the state adopted another distinct view of national interest—different from those of Westernizers and Primakovites. Although Putin insisted on Russia's priority of preserving great power status, his strategy for achieving this objective differed considerably from Primakov's. Instead of continuing the policy of balancing against the West, Putin explicitly sided with Europe and the United States and insisted that Russia was a country of European and Western, rather than Asian, identity.

Why such a modification in the previous Statist thinking? The unresolved identity question, the shifting balance in the Statists-Westernizers debate, and the new international context help to explain Putin's strategic innovation. Domestically, Putin's course of "pragmatic cooperation" with the West was the project of a mixed-identity coalition that included both Westernist and Statist interests. Sometimes referred to as the alliance of oligarchs and chekists,[27] the new domestic coalition brought Putin to power and gained strength in the new world context, which held both threats and opportunities for Russia. Opportunities came from domestic economic stabilization and cooperation with the United States after the September 11, 2001, terrorist attacks, and threats were defined by the new leadership as being of a terrorist nature and emanating from both inside and outside of Russia. The public strongly supported Putin's approach. His vision of the national interests, which included the preservation of Russia's security and identity, socioeconomic development, and the strengthening of political institutions,[28] resonated with the domestic public better than the security-underplayed Westernism of Kozyrev or the security-overplayed Eurasianism of Primakov. In response to the colored revolutions and perceived Western pressures, Russia's policy obtained a more assertive dimension. The Kremlin sought to consolidate Russia's position by challenging the Western nations to open their markets to Russian business and not expand their military infrastructure closer to Russia's borders.

Once the international context began to change, Russia's identity competition resumed. With the global financial crisis severely undermining the country's economy, the liberal Westernizers reemerged to promote Russia's modernization according to Western standards of free market competition, political pluralism, and transparency. They embraced Medvedev's vision of a cautious modernization and sought to push it toward a radical revision of Putin's Statist model and assertive relations with the West. Medvedev's foreign policy was based on the notion of international alliances for modernization and served to bring Russia closer to Europe and the United States. Although a number of serious issues remained unresolved, Russia and the West signed a new START (Strategic Arms Reduction Treaty) treaty, cooperated on securing Afghanistan, and occasionally coordinated their policies toward the Middle Eastern region. In 2012, Russia also joined the WTO (World Trade Organization).

However, the international context continued to encourage Statist thinking inside Russia. The Western expansion of military infrastructure such as the Missile Defense System in Europe, attempts to limit Moscow's influence in the former Soviet region, and promotion of Western values contributed to Putin's perception of the West as seeking to internally weaken Russia. The Ukraine crisis further exacerbated Russia's sense of strategic vulnerability by pushing it further away from the West toward non-Western nations, especially China.

Neither realism nor liberalism is fully satisfactory in explaining the identified changes and continuity in Russia's foreign policy. For example, realist arguments that post-Soviet Russia was merely looking to consolidate its great power capabilities fail to acknowledge the socialist Westernist nature of Gorbachev's policies and the liberal Westernist vision of Russia's first post-Soviet foreign minister. Both Gorbachev and Kozyrev were thinking in terms of the priority of cooperation and engagement with the world, rather than preserving or reviving Russia's material power. They had roots in domestic international thinking, but were also motivated and encouraged by the West's liberal developments. Because of the failure to acknowledge the true origins of the identified liberal foreign policy developments, realists also misrepresented the scope of changes resulting from these developments. Both changes implied fundamental breaks with the Statist past and went far beyond strategic adaptation to the growing military power of the West. Liberals, on the other hand, have difficulty with making sense of Russia's retreat to great power thinking. To them, this retreat does not seem rational, since in the world of globalization, preoccupation with great power status may be an impediment to development and, ultimately, the survival of the country. Indeed, it is all too common to see Western politicians' references to Putin as a paranoid and irrational thinker.[29]

Ultimately, both realism and liberalism are inadequate in identifying the genuine nature and origins of various concepts of national interest guiding Russia's international behavior. In particular, they miss the fact that national interest is not about power or modernization. Instead, it is about social adaptation to the constantly changing international and local conditions, and it is about recognition by the identified significant Other. For both Westernizers and Statists, the West is a key point of reference, although each school understands its nature differently. Even Civilizationists, who rarely held a prominent position in domestic discourse, aspired to be respected by the West. What matters in national-interest formation is how debate about national identity is shaped by (1) a population's most pressing local concerns and (2) contemporary behavior of Western nations toward Russia that vindicates or erodes the earlier established images of the West. In addition, as I try to show in the following chapters, each school must work hard to make use of available material and institutional resources in the society. Ultimately, it is the described local conditions combined with considerations of international recognition and respect, rather than a position in the international economy or the balance of power, that determine the concept of national interest adopted by the state as a foreign policy guide. Russia's post-Soviet concepts of national interest and their formation are summarized in table 1.4 (see facing page). The remaining chapters of the book further develop the above-suggested explanation of Russia's foreign policy.

EVALUATING RUSSIA'S FOREIGN POLICY

In addition to describing and explaining Russia's foreign policy, one should also attempt to evaluate the record of its efficiency. This section introduces the evaluative standards adopted in this book and briefly illustrates their application with examples from the post-Soviet era. The remaining chapters offer a more detailed assessment of the accomplishments and losses of each of the described foreign policy courses.

Evaluative Standards

Four criteria deserve to be carefully considered in evaluating foreign policy record—security, welfare, autonomy, and identity. Security typically refers to the absence of military threats to the nation, particularly (but not limited to) from outside. The welfare criterion implies that foreign policy assists the nation in creating external conditions for the improvement of standards of living that may have to do with economic growth, new jobs, and social services. Autonomy has to do with the state's ability to make decisions by withstanding possible pressures of special interests from inside and outside the country. Finally, a successful foreign policy is

Table 1.4. Explaining Russia's Foreign Policy after Communism

	Local Conditions				
	National-Democratic Revolution	*Economic Depression; Political Instability*	*Economic Recovery; New Security Threats*	*Economic Decline; Remaining Security Threats*	*Ongoing Domestic Crisis*
Support	INTEGRATION WITH THE WEST				
Behavior of Europe/West NATO expansion Renewed support		BALANCING	PRAGMATIC COOPERATION		
Regime change Engagement			ASSERTIVENESS		
Expansion				ALLIANCES FOR MODERNIZATION	CIVILIZATION

not fundamentally disruptive to the existing system of cultural values. Rather, such a policy relies on these values by reshaping and mobilizing them in a manner that would further the nation's interests and assist the nation in accomplishing its principal goals.

In general, a foreign policy is about protection of a nation's external security, economy, and social lifestyle. Each of these criteria or objectives can be measured by a variety of indicators. A more secure nation, for example, is one that has relatively few military threats from outside and therefore can afford to reduce its military expenditures. A more prosperous nation has stable growth and improving living standards for the general population. A more autonomous nation has a state that is capable of defending the interests of the people as a whole and is not hostage to some powerful influences at home, such as big business or military, or from abroad. Determining the state's foreign policy autonomy requires comparing how the proclaimed goals of defending the interests of the national majority stand against specific international actions of the state, as well as to what extent these actions represent interest groups at the expense of the rest of the society. Finally, a culturally sensitive foreign policy reflects the already-established historical patterns and usually has the population's support with regard to the asserted relationships with the nation's significant Other. Approval of the society in each of these categories expressed through public opinion polls (should such polls be available) may serve as additional evidence for evaluating a foreign policy record.

The foreign policy of each time period can be evaluated using these criteria as they apply during a specified period. Foreign policy is successful if at a given time it has provided a balanced defense of all the listed objectives using the available resources.

From New Thinking to Pragmatic Cooperation

Russia's foreign policy record is complex. Overall, the country's leadership has tried to defend its security by relying on limited resources available and without resorting to an imperialist course. After the collapse of the economy in the early 1990s, it began a difficult process of recovery, and the society on the whole has begun to feel the difference of the post-Yeltsin era. Under Putin, during the 2000s the state has restored a good measure of policy autonomy, and key international decisions have become more reflective of the social consensus than those of the early to mid-1990s. Polls of the general public on some pressing international issues during the past two years or so consistently demonstrate that people on the whole are satisfied with the country's foreign policy. Finally, as a result of a more moderate foreign policy course, Russia has been able to strike a better cultural balance between the necessity to rethink the old Soviet legacy and the need to respect some traditional values, such as the defense of Russian-language speakers abroad. Geopolitically, Russia's foreign policy reflects the nation's desire to have strong ties with European, or Western, civilization, while preserving special relations with Muslim and Asian neighbors.

In none of the specified areas, however, has Russia's foreign policy been perfectly efficient. For instance, terrorism continues to pose a serious challenge to the nation's internal and external security. The economic improvement is still more of a product of the 1998 currency devaluation and favorable world oil prices than of competitive domestic restructuring. In a number of areas, interest groups have preserved their influence on state policy. And the crisis of Russia's post-Soviet identity has not yet been fully resolved. The transition to a relatively balanced foreign policy course has also not been easy or straightforward. Rather, it has emerged as a result of zigs and zags of different strategies different leaders pursue in concert with their views of Russia's national interest. Nevertheless, the overall improvement in foreign policy efficiency has been evident if one examines the record over the past twenty years. Polls of the general public on some pressing international issues during the past two years or so consistently demonstrate that people on the whole are satisfied with the country's foreign policy. What follows is a brief assessment of four distinct periods in Russia's international activities.

Gorbachev's foreign policy course was based on an innovative under-standing of national interest that called for rethinking the Soviet system and its international environment (New Thinking). Its most important accomplishment was a radical improvement of Russia's national security, which resulted mainly from fundamentally changed relationships with the West. Thanks largely to Gorbachev's personal leadership and commit-ment, several key arms-control agreements were concluded, and the whole era of highly adventurous arms races was gone forever. The disap-pearance of the threat from the West liberated a great deal of resources that had been previously spent to feed one of the most powerful military machines in the world.

The New Thinking record is not as impressive in areas outside security. Gorbachev's preoccupation with matters of arms control did not assist him in reforming the Soviet economy or improving people's standards of living. From 1988 to 1989, polls began to register growing disappointment with reforms and a lack of trust in the central leadership. While Moscow was busy negotiating with Western nations over security matters, such as thresholds of nuclear sufficiency and withdrawals of troops from the third world and Eastern Europe, the economy was increasingly losing

control, eventually collapsing in 1990. This development severely handi-
capped Gorbachev in his ability to pursue the originally designed international course. Already in 1990, this course was on its way to changing
from the Soviet one in terms of initiative and design into a largely West-
controlled one. The leader of New Thinking was weakened and had to
make many more concessions to Western leaders than he had envisioned.
He no longer had the initiative or policy autonomy required for sustaining his course, and U.S. president George H. W. Bush was therefore correct to proclaim the West's "victory" in the Cold War in his 1992 State of
the Union address. In addition, Gorbachev's foreign policy failed to
mobilize Russian cultural identity. Introduced to reinvigorate the country's social energy and initiative, New Thinking left the nation's citizens
deeply divided and unsure about their future. Already in 1989, 34 percent
of the public felt that the Soviet Union could not serve as an example to
the outside world, compared with only 5 percent in 1988.[30]

The course of Integration with the West, pursued by President Yeltsin
and his foreign minister Kozyrev, was meant to capitalize on the already-
achieved security and improved relations with Western nations. The
post-Soviet leaders went much further than Gorbachev in their proclaimed
convergence of the interests of new Russia with those of the West. Whereas
Gorbachev saw the Soviet Union and the West as culturally distinct enti-
ties, the new leadership proposed that Russia become a full-fledged
member of Western civilization by borrowing key Western values, such as
individualism, the market economy, and political democracy. Partly, the
new concept of national interest, which emphasized rapid economic and
political modernization, was designed to attract Western economic assistance and therefore address the welfare criterion of foreign policy. Yeltsin
and Kozyrev hoped that after proclaiming their commitment to Western
values and adopting principles of rapid marketization, or the so-called
shock therapy, private investments and financial assistance would quickly
revive the half-alive and continuously deteriorating economy.

The reality was different. Western investments remained scarce. Through
the use of IMF and World Bank loans, the economy was stabilized, but at
the heavy price of stagnation, collapsed social services, and skyrocketing
poverty. The failure of shock therapy to bring Russia into the family of
rich Western nations alienated a considerable portion of the elites and
general public, making it difficult to defend the foreign policy record of
the pro-Western leadership. Increasingly, the populace felt that strategic
partnership with the West was not working, and many developed resentment toward Western nations, particularly the United States. For instance,
during 1993–1995, the number of those viewing the United States as a threat
increased from 26 to 44 percent among the general public and from 27 to

53 percent among the elites.[31] In addition, many judged that Russia was effectively ceding its policy autonomy to the West in economic and other affairs. In 1995, 75 percent of the population believed that the economy was essentially in foreign hands.[32] The number of those perceiving the West as seeking to weaken Russia also increased. The increased dependency on the West in economic affairs went hand in hand with loss of autonomy in security affairs, as Washington was often dictating Moscow's foreign policy in such critical areas as the Balkans and Iraq.

Perhaps worst of all, security issues returned to the agenda. Partly the result of Kozyrev's overconcentration on the Western direction, the security threats reemerged in the form of ethnic and military conflicts in the former Soviet Union and even inside Russia (Chechnya). All these developments further exacerbated the sense of Russian hurt pride and identity. The pro-Western foreign policy course did little to address those feelings. Accompanied by failures to protect the nation's security, economy, and policy autonomy, this course in fact deepened the sense of cultural loneliness among Russians. Shrunken in size after the Soviet Union's disintegration and confronted with NATO's decision to expand eastward, Russia was bound to seriously rethink the assumptions of its pro-Western foreign policy.

When the leading critic of the West-oriented course, Yevgeni Primakov, replaced Kozyrev as foreign minister, Russia's foreign policy changed greatly. As much as was possible under Yeltsin's leadership, the new foreign minister pursued policies of restoring great power status. He addressed the new security threats through intense diplomatic involvement in the former Soviet region, particularly in the areas of military confrontations and civil wars (Tajikistan, Moldova), and through the initiation of economic and security projects aimed at tightening the ties among the former Soviet republics under the leadership of Russia. Primakov was also successful in restoring some measure of foreign policy autonomy. While Russia's dependence on Western lending agencies continued, the new course was pursued with greater respect for public perception of the national interest, and it was considerably less tolerant of Washington's attempts to shape Russia's policies toward the Balkans, Iraq, and the former Soviet region. Both elites and the general public expressed their strong support for the new course, welcoming its greater independence and concentration on solving security issues in the former Soviet Union. In line with the new course, the public was supportive of strengthening the army and relations with the former republics.[33]

The strategy of Great Power Balancing was not as successful in improving the welfare of Russians. The project of integrating the former Soviet region proved to be excessively geopolitically driven and not as founded on economic grounds. The economy continued to stagnate, not bringing any foreign investments and increasing the burden of foreign debt. The new foreign policy strategy was also dubious with respect to the criterion of identity. Primakov addressed the new cultural fear of the West by attempting to pragmatically defuse the crisis in relations with NATO and by proposing to build a strategic triangle of Russia, China, and India to balance American hegemonic growth in world politics. NATO's military intervention in Yugoslavia in 1999 further pushed Russia away from the West. Yet the Westernist component of Russia's cultural identity is a well-established reality, and the strategy of Eurasia-oriented Great Power Balancing failed to address this part of the Russian national psyche.

Vladimir Putin's course of Pragmatic Cooperation has been more successful in terms of meeting the criteria of security, welfare, autonomy, and identity. Creatively borrowing from both Westernist and Statist thinking of the post-Soviet era, the president forcefully responded to the new security challenge of terrorism in Chechnya, the Caucasus, and central Asia, simultaneously improving somewhat damaged relations with the West. Dmitri Medvedev's policy of modernization continued the effort to pragmatically engage the West in order to strengthen ties with most advanced economies, while preserving a good measure of state autonomy. As a result, the economy and social welfare have improved. Russia finally gained membership in the World Trade Organization (WTO)—in part to continue with the country's efforts of economic modernization. Finally, Pragmatic Cooperation helped to preserve both Westernist and Statist components of Russia's identity by orienting Russians to adjust to the West while preserving their own cultural legacy and long-standing relations with non-Western nations in Asia and the Muslim world.

However, since the early 2010s, the course of Pragmatic Cooperation has demonstrated limitations, as Western nations declined to recognize Russia's distinct security interests and values. Following the Orange Revolution in Ukraine, Russia sought to consolidate its political system in order to prevent the Ukraine-like destabilization and the West's potential interference in Russia's internal affairs. Putin's new vision of Russia as a state-civilization with distinct interests and values since 2012 sought to compensate for weaknesses of Medvedev's cooperative and West-centric approach. The new course has aimed to stand the ground on security issues by not allowing Ukraine to be absorbed by the West's political and military institutions. Russia also wanted to take advantage of new opportunities presented by rise of non-Western powers. It remains to be seen how successful the overall record of the new course will be.

METHODOLOGY AND ORGANIZATION OF THE BOOK

This study combines two methods. In order to explore the indigenous system of Russian perceptions, I explore the content and intensity of Russian foreign policy debates by comparing arguments made by the identified schools of thinking. For understanding the process of contestation of national interests, I employ the method of "schools of thought" analysis. Following Martin Wight's conceptualization,[34] I identify three distinct schools of thinking about national interest that existed in Russia before and after Gorbachev's perestroika (Westernism, Statism, and Civilizationism). Careful exploration of the arguments made by various schools and participants in Russian discourse allows me to identify existing foreign policy alternatives and to present a comprehensive picture of the country's international thinking.

For understanding changes in Russia's post-Soviet foreign policy, I employ a method of "over time comparison." Beginning with the next chapter, I offer a detailed analysis of the rise and fall of several distinct concepts of national interests—New Thinking, Integration with the West, Great Power Balancing, Pragmatic Cooperation, Assertiveness, Alliances for Modernization, and Civilization—as well as policies that stemmed from each of these concepts. I trace how each of these visions first emerged outside the state and the process through which it then came to define leadership's perceptions and adopted international policies. The book's central argument is that it is these visions of national interest, rather than Russia's position in the international economy or balance of power that have determined the country's foreign policy after communism. During the 1990s through the early 2000s, neither structural power conditions nor the international economic position of Russia has changed sufficiently to fully account for its foreign policy choices.

The book's organization is straightforward. The chapters that follow study national interests and foreign policy formation through four distinct periods from the late 1980s until mid-2012. In each chapter, I describe the international and local contexts in which Russian debates about national interest took place. I analyze the process through which one of the foreign policy visions prevailed and obtained the status of state vision. I then review specific international policies pursued by leaders toward the former Soviet Union and the outside world in attempting to satisfy their visions of national interest. Finally, I attempt to evaluate the accomplishments and losses of each of the pursued foreign policy courses. The concluding chapters reflect on the future choices of Russia's foreign policy and summarize the analysis by comparing the diverse concepts of national interest and evaluating their relative performance. The final chapter also draws lessons for Russian and Western policymakers.

NOTES

1. Arnold Wolfers, "'National Security' as an Ambiguous Symbol," in *Classics of International Relations*, 2nd ed., ed. John A. Vasques (Englewood Cliffs, NJ: Prentice Hall, 1990), 135.

2. Khrushchev's Europeanism was limited, and it pursued the objective of greater European independence in the context of a power struggle with the Americans. Yet his position that the European Economic Community become a reality emboldened those in domestic politics who wanted to improve relationships with Bonn and other European nations. See Iver B. Neumann, *Russia and the Idea of Europe: A Study in Identity and International Relations* (London: Routledge, 1996), 140–41.

3. As cited in Richard Sakwa, *The Rise and Fall of the Soviet Union, 1917–1991* (London: Routledge, 1999), 187–88.

4. See Yevgeni Primakov, "Rossiya v mirovoi politike," *Mezhdunarodnaya zhizn'* 5 (1998); I. Ivanov, *Vneshnyaya politika Rossiyi* (Moscow: Mezhdunarodnyye otnosheniya, 2001) 313–30; *Strategiya dlya Rossiyi: Povestka dlya prezidenta—2000*. Russian Westernists, on the other hand, are often critical of Gorchakov's diplomacy (see, for example, Yuri Fedorov, "Krizis vneshnei politiki Rossiyi," *Pro et Contra* 6, nos. 1–2 [2001]).

5. Aleksandr Dugin, *Osnovy geopolitiki* (Moscow: Arktogeya, 1997); Aleksandr Mitrofanov, *Shagi novoi geopolitiki* (Moscow, 1998).

6. Interestingly enough, Yeltsin's former privatization czar and current head of Russia's state electric company, Anatoli Chubais, recently wrote that Russia's main goal in the twenty-first century should be to build up a "liberal empire" through the strengthening of its position in the former Soviet Union. "EES Head Calls for Russia to Become a 'Liberal Empire,'" RFE/RL Newsline, September 26, 2003; Anatoli Chubais, "Missiya Rossiyi v XXI veke," *Nezavisimaya gazeta*, October 1, 2003.

7. Robert H. Donaldson and Joseph L. Nogee, *The Foreign Policy of Russia* (Armonk, NY: M. E. Sharpe, 1998), 59.

8. Nathan Leites, *The Operational Code of the Politburo* (New York: McGraw-Hill, 1951), as cited in Celeste A. Wallander, "The Sources of Russian Conduct," in *The Sources of Russian Foreign Policy after the Cold War*, ed. C. A. Wallander (Boulder, CO: Westview Press, 1996), 5.

9. Sakwa, *The Rise and Fall of the Soviet Union*, 295.

10. Neil MacFarlane, "Realism and Russian Strategy after the Collapse of the USSR," in *Unipolar Politics*, ed. Ethan B. Kapstein and Michael Mastanduno (New York: Columbia University Press, 1999); Allen Lynch, "Realism of Russian Foreign Policy," *Europe-Asia Studies* 53, no. 1 (2001).

11. Gideon Rose, "Neoclassical Realism and Theories of Foreign Policy," *World Politics* 51, no. 1 (1998).

12. Robert English, "Power, Ideas, and New Evidence on the Cold War's End," *International Security* 26, no. 4 (Spring 2002): 78–82.

13. In fact, both Primakov's and Putin's foreign policies can be understood in terms of Russia's responses to new domestic challenges, such as economic poverty and insecure borders. As some scholars have argued, outside the Western Hemi-

sphere, states' international responses often explain the need to stabilize political regimes internally. See, for example, Mohammed Ayoob, *Third World Security Predicament: State Making, Regional Conflict, and the International System* (Boulder, CO: Lynne Rienner, 1995).

14. For a more detailed overview of Russia's foreign policy studies, see Wallander, "The Sources of Russian Conduct."

15. Francis Fukuyama, "The End of History?" *National Interest* (1989): 4.

16. See, especially, Kenichi Ohmae, *The Borderless World: Power and Strategy in the Interlinked Economy* (New York: Harper Perennial, 1991) and Thomas L. Friedman, *The Lexus and the Olive Tree* (New York: Farrar, Straus & Giroux, 1999).

17. For overviews, see Michael E. Brown, Sean M. Lynn-Jones, and Steven E. Miller, eds., *Debating the Democratic Peace* (Cambridge, MA: MIT Press, 1996); Fred Chernoff, "The Study of Democratic Peace and Progress in International Relations," *International Studies Review* 6 (2004).

18. George W. Breslauer and Philip E. Tetlock, eds., *Learning in U.S. and Soviet Foreign Policy* (Boulder, CO: Westview Press, 1991); Peter Haas, "Introduction: Epistemic Communities," *International Organization* 46, no. 2 (1992); Thomas Risse-Kappen, ed., *Bringing Transnational Relations Back In* (Cambridge: Cambridge University Press, 1995); M. E. Keck and Katherine Sikkink, *Activists beyond Borders: Advocacy Networks in International Politics* (Ithaca, NY: Cornell University Press, 1998).

19. Liberal scholars have linked Gorbachev's policies to principal economic and political changes in the West, as well as to activities of transnational expert communities, ideas, and social movements. See, for example, Celeste A. Wallander, "Opportunity, Incrementalism, and Learning in the Extension and Retraction of Soviet Global Commitments," *Security Studies* 1 (Spring 1992); Matthew Evangelista, *Unarmed Forces: The Transnational Movements to End the Cold War* (Ithaca, NY: Cornell University Press, 1999); Robert D. English, *Russia and the Idea of the West: Gorbachev, Intellectuals and the End of the Cold War* (New York: Columbia University Press, 2000).

20. As cited in James N. Goldgeier and Michael McFaul, *Power and Purpose: U.S. Policy toward Russia after the Cold War* (Washington, DC: Brookings, 2003), 11.

21. Goldgeier and McFaul, *Power and Purpose*, 90.

22. Goldgeier and McFaul, *Power and Purpose*, 11.

23. Strobe Talbott, *The Russia Hand: A Memoir of Presidential Diplomacy* (New York: Random House, 2002), 367, 407–8; Goldgeier and McFaul, *Power and Purpose*, 133–34.

24. Alexander Wendt, *Social Theory of International Politics* (Cambridge: Cambridge University Press, 1999), 133.

25. As one scholar suggests, "Identity explanations are likely to become 'foreign policy-ized' by connecting identity to other factors and theories that have long been part of the FPA agenda." Juliet Kaarbo, "Foreign Policy Analysis in the Twenty-First Century: Back to Comparison, Forward to Identity and Ideas," *International Studies Review* 5 (2003): 160. International relations scholars have recognized the internal/external bind by referring to it as a "two-level game." Robert D. Putnam, "Diplomacy and Domestic Politics: The Logic of Two-Level Games," *International Organization* 42, no. 2 (1988).

26. For additional hypotheses about international influences and their interaction with local conditions, see Jack Snyder, "International Leverage on Soviet Domestic Change," *World Politics* 42, no. 1 (1989); James Richter, *Khrushchev's Double Bind: International Pressures and Domestic Coalition Politics* (Baltimore, MD: Johns Hopkins University Press, 1994).

27. *Chekist* originates from the Russian *CheKa*, the original name of the Bolsheviks' security service. It was led by People's Commissar Feliks Dzerzhinski. Oligarchs are, of course, superrich captains of Russia's newly privatized economy.

28. See Vladimir Putin, "Rossiya na rubezhe tysyacheleti," *Nezavisimaya gazeta*, December 2, 1999.

29. Suffice it to recall German Chancellor Angela Merkel's remarks to President Barack Obama following Russia's intervention in Crimea that Putin is living "in another world" (Peter Baker, "Pressure Rising as Obama Works to Rein in Russia," *The New York Times*, March 2, 2015 http://www.nytimes.com/2014/03/03/world/europe/pressure-rising-as-obama-works-to-rein-in-russia.html?hp)

30. Yuri Levada, ed., *Est' mneniye! Itogi sotsiologicheskogo oprosa* (Moscow: Progress, 1990), 284.

31. William Zimmerman, *The Russian People and Foreign Policy* (Princeton, NJ: Princeton University Press, 2002), 91.

32. Zimmerman, *The Russian People*, 92.

33. Zimmerman, *The Russian People*, 91; Fond Obschestvennoye Mneniye, at www.fom.ru.

34. Martin Wight, *International Theory: The Three Traditions* (Leicester, UK: Leicester University Press, 1991).

2

The Cold War Crisis and Soviet New Thinking

Taking into account the new situation in the world, the problem of interests must be addressed in a new way.

—Mikhail Gorbachev[1]

With Gorbachev, Russia's story of engagement with the West took a sharp turn. While being a convinced socialist, Gorbachev pursued a radically different interpretation of Russia's socialist identity, which he viewed as distinct yet compatible with Western ideas of democracy and which eventually collapsed under the heavy weight of Western modernity. Before we analyze the leader of perestroika's worldview and perceptions, we must, however, review the context in which Gorbachev formulated his foreign policy vision. For it was this context that shaped Soviet Russia's new understanding of national interest.

THE COLD WAR AND SOVIET FOREIGN POLICY

During the Cold War, the Western Other changed in some fundamental ways. These changes, as well as their influences on the Soviet Union, can be viewed in at least two different lights. On the one hand, the West emerged as a more unified civilization committed to values of democracy, liberal capitalist reconstruction, and human rights. The success of the Marshall Plan in post–World War II Europe, as well as a considerable improvement in living standards, made a positive impression on some officials in Soviet Russia and encouraged reformers inside the country.

On the other hand, the Cold War warriors in the West pushed for increased military expenditures and a tougher stance toward Russia, which made it more difficult for the Soviet reformers to advocate change and rapprochement with Western nations. As the logic of confrontation was gaining the upper hand in Russia-West relations, the two sides were increasingly losing sight of many other important international issues, such as poverty and environmental degradation. In this context, everything was progressively viewed through the lens of who gains more power and who manages to more successfully weaken the opponent.

In this contradictory context, the Soviet schools of foreign policy thinking drew their inspiration from different developments in the West. The Soviet Westernizers emphasized the West's democratic consolidation and policies of détente. They sought to acquire Western recognition by conducting domestic reforms and advocating a more robust international cooperation. In Europe, it was social democratic ideas that most closely resembled this group's views. Through support of détente, European social democrats made it easier for the Soviet reformists to press on with their international and domestic agenda.[2] Gorbachev, as well as his reformist predecessors, such as Nikita Khrushchev, did not see the West as inherently evil. They identified with the West of reform and moderation, rather than with that of containment or defeat of the Soviet "evil empire" in an arms race competition. Outside the political class, this nonconfrontational vision appealed to the Soviet middle class—the highly educated social strata that were eager to break the taboos of Soviet isolationism and develop mutually beneficial relationships with the West.

A more nationalist group within the Soviet establishment, the Statists, made a note of détente, but also saw the West's militarism and policies aimed at preventing the Soviet Union from influencing world affairs. Many in the Soviet bureaucratic and military establishment, therefore, did not believe in any far-reaching changes and instead advocated limited reforms and coexistence with the "world of capitalism." This group was not closed to changes in world politics, but was prepared to cooperate with the West in a reciprocal manner only. Continuation of détente was viewed to be possible, but only to the extent that the West itself was committed to it. Similarly to Western realists insisting on reaching a balance of power between the Soviet and Western poles, this group advocated the notion of "correlation of forces" between socialism and capitalism. Members of the group saw the goal of achieving international status and acceptance in terms of preservation of strength, both military and economic.

Finally, there were also some die-hard Bolsheviks committed to the ideology of winning the competition between socialism and capitalism.

Unlike Westernizers and pragmatically oriented nationalists, this group stood for the authentic "socialist values" that were deemed to be superior to those of capitalism. The supporters of such views, or Civilizationists, had zero trust in détente and rapprochement with the West and associated all the Western activities with aggressive "imperialist" intentions. There could be no middle ground in the struggle with imperialism, and the Cold War was ultimately a competition between the two systems' cultural values, rather than merely economic or military systems. It was through the spreading of values that the group planned to achieve the appropriate recognition of the Soviet Union by the outside world. This group included some leading Communist Party ideologists and eventually emerged as the main opposition to the future New Thinking.

It was Statists who were primarily in control of the actual foreign policymaking during the Cold War era. Immediately after the 1917 revolution, the Bolsheviks were conducting two foreign policies—one was aimed at stabilizing relations with the Western leaders and conducted by the Commissariat on Foreign Affairs, whereas the other sought to undermine the West through the activities of Comintern. That duality receded into the past as Stalin took charge and shifted the effort away from the highly ideological communist rhetoric and toward winning recognition of Soviet Russia as a "Great Power" and, later, a "Superpower."[3] Stalin's Statism therefore won over the Comintern-like Civilizationism in foreign affairs. Only during the so-called second Cold War of the late 1970s through the early 1980s did the Soviet Civilizationists regain some of their former prominence, partly in response to the rise of hard-line thinking toward Soviet Russia in the West. The arguments about the need to expand into Afghanistan and other third world countries were partly provoked by the West's own military buildup, opposition to the ratification of the Strategic Arms Limitations Talks (SALT II), and the decision by NATO to deploy American missiles in Europe. In addition to aiding Afghanistan, the Soviets supplied communists in Vietnam and Angola. When in 1983 U.S. president Ronald Reagan announced the Strategic Defense Initiative, also known as the Star Wars program, the Soviet leaders were divided between the more status quo–oriented Statists and the more expansionist Civilizationists. Westernizers were hardly in the picture; they occupied much less prominent positions and could not be taken very seriously given the extent of tensions with the West. After the death of Konstantin Chernenko, Gorbachev was elected general secretary of the Communist Party for his vigor and youth rather than his policy beliefs. At the time, his worldview and policy beliefs were hardly known to his comrades in the Politburo.

GORBACHEV AND THE CONCEPT OF NEW THINKING

In the mid-1980s, Gorbachev was not known for his radical international ideas. After being elected general secretary, he moved cautiously and first proposed the strategy of accelerating scientific and technological progress as a way to improve the state of the Soviet economy. The idea, although well received by the ruling establishment, brought little practical results, and the new leader used the momentum to advance his more radical vision of economic, political, and international changes known as perestroika. Gorbachev also insisted that perestroika could take place only if accompanied by New Thinking, or radical transformation of the traditional outlook on world affairs.

The New Vision of World Politics

By introducing New Thinking, Gorbachev did not mean to replace the Soviet system with one similar to that of the West. He was a product of the system and a firm believer in the Soviet Union's principal viability. At the same time, Gorbachev was highly critical of how the system had performed in the past and he wanted to renew it in some fundamental way. In particular, he dreamed of releasing human potential and social creativity that, in his opinion, were suppressed under the Stalinist regime. Eventually Gorbachev meant to bring the system closer to the model of Scandinavian societies, in which democracy was combined with strong egalitarian principles in the economy.

Yet Gorbachev proved to be especially innovative in the area of world politics. Seeking to break the Cold War hostilities and be accepted by the Western nations as an equal member of the world, Gorbachev proposed a vision that required the Cold War enemies to cooperate.[4] The new vision sought to present the old enemies with a notion of a common threat, leaving them little choice but to abandon their old hostilities. At the heart of the vision lay the notion of a global and principally nondivisive world, which was argued to be in danger of annihilation. The Cold War, with its arms races and power struggle, put humankind on the verge of nuclear, ecological, and moral catastrophe. New Thinking diagnosed the catastrophe as one that was global in nature and could be resolved only through global efforts. To quote from the author of New Thinking, "For all the contradictions of the present-day world, for all the diversity of social and political systems in it, and for all the different choices made by the nations in different times, this world is nevertheless one whole. We are all passengers aboard one ship, the Earth, and we must not allow it to be wrecked. There will be no second Noah's Ark."[5]

It was therefore critical to acknowledge the primacy of values "common to all humankind" and to understand that security could only be mutual. The reasons for this were the threat of mutual destruction in a nuclear war, as well as an increased level of economic and ecological interdependence in the world.

The origins of New Thinking therefore had little to do with the necessity of a strategic retreat in the face of the growing economic and military strength of the West—the argument often advanced by realists.[6] To argue this is to neglect Gorbachev's domestic intellectual roots. It is true that the Soviet economy was in decline by the time of Gorbachev's arrival (see table 2.1). Yet the new leader did not make sense of the world in terms of economic or military capabilities. He was not a member of the Statist school, and his entire thinking about international politics was shaped by a desire to reach out to a liberal and social democratic West. This thinking also had a distinct domestic tradition stretching back at least to Nikolai Bukharin's and Nikita Khrushchev's foreign policy liberalizations.

Table 2.1.   Gross National Product for the USSR and the United States, 1960–1985

	1965	1970	1975	1980	1985
USSR	4.8	4.9	3.0	1.9	1.8
U.S.	4.6	3.0	2.2	3.4	2.5

Source: David Kotz and Fred Weir, *Revolution from Above: The Demise of the Soviet System* (London: Routledge, 1997), 42.

Achieving recognition by Western nations was extremely difficult given the legacy of the Cold War. For at least a decade, conservatives were in power, and they originally received the arrival of Gorbachev and his ideas of perestroika and New Thinking with suspicion. Such recognition was all the more difficult because Gorbachev was not a believer in the primacy of the Western values of political democracy and the market economy. Instead, he envisioned some global unity from contributions of both capitalist and socialist systems. He was prepared to learn from other systems and other nations,[7] while remaining a socialist and a believer that the whole world would continue to be influenced by the socialist experience and "socialist values."[8]

The Domestic Appeal

The new vision of world politics was designed to appeal to all the main groups of the Soviet political class. Westernizers were to be attracted to ideas of democratization, reform, and rapprochement with the West. Gorbachev himself was influenced by the ideas of European social democrats, as well as liberal-minded scientists, such as Vladimir Vernadski, Pyotr Kapitsa, and Andrei Sakharov. His concept of a "common European home" also had its roots in Nikita Khrushchev's efforts to bring Soviet Russia closer to Europe. Khrushchev saw Russia as culturally close to Europe, and at one point he even proposed the concurrent disbandment of NATO and the Warsaw Pact. New Thinking also sought to appeal to at least some of the Statists, who understood the necessity of responding to Western military pressures by reducing diplomatic tensions and moving in the direction of a new détente. Finally, Gorbachev's vision meant to engage some of the most forward-thinking members of the Civilizationist school, because it offered a new, admittedly very unorthodox, way of capitalizing on "socialist values." The leader of perestroika traced his origins to the late Lenin's notion of coexistence with capitalism, and he kept emphasizing that his project was a development, not an abandonment, of socialism. As utopian as it was, the vision had global ambitions and even elements of a moral messianism. It was therefore a creative synthesis that attempted to engage representatives of the entire political class.

But Gorbachev's vision was never a purely elite product. Socially, it reflected the worldview of the Soviet middle class that grew stronger during the 1960–1986 period. The proportion of highly educated and qualified urban specialists had increased during the indicated period fourfold. The overall number of urban dwellers in the total population had grown by over two-thirds, by some calculations.[9] The Soviet middle class was dissatisfied with Brezhnev's unwillingness to initiate change, and increasingly expected reforms in the rigid economic and political system. Many representatives of this class were also in touch with the outside world's technological developments, and their perceptions of the world began to conflict with those of Brezhnev's *nomenklatura* and hardline military. Increasingly, Soviet society supported accommodation, not confrontation, with the outside world. Although the Soviet system's resources were far from exhausted, the anticipation of and the eagerness for change were already in the air.

Redefining National Interest

The above-described vision left little room for national interest as pursued independently of the interests of other members of the global society. Gorbachev did not expect the Soviet Union or any other nations to give up what they perceived to be in their interests. Yet he called for acknowledging the futility of class and narrowly viewed national gains and for developing a globally integrated approach based on the notion of mutual responsibility and "balance of interests." Practically speaking, he proposed compromises and multilateral negotiations as a way to implement the new vision.

For the Soviet Union, New Thinking implied the necessity of formulating its national interest and foreign policy objectives in a way that would be respectful of world opinion and nonthreatening toward others. In particular, Gorbachev proposed rethinking the nature of capitalism. The old ideological vision assumed that the Soviet Union had to contain the influence of world capitalism, because at its highest stage of development, imperialism, capitalism was intrinsically related to expansion and war. Without containing imperialism, the Soviet Union would be destroyed. As Josef Stalin said in a slightly different context, "Either we do it, or we shall be crushed."[10] The Gorbachev vision posited something very different. In February 1988, he criticized the very notion of imperialism as being no longer accurate. He argued that capitalism had developed domestic democratic mechanisms for resisting expansion and war and was therefore self-containing. Such criticism had its roots in the Soviet postwar debates. Already in the late 1940s, Yevgeni Varga, director of the Moscow Institute of World Economy and World Politics, began arguing that postwar capitalism could regulate its contradictions and had relatively stabilized. After Stalin's death, those emphasizing the depth of imperialist contradictions and the inevitability of the capitalist decline gathered around Richard Kosolapov, the editor in chief of *Kommunist* and a member of the Central Committee of the Communist Party, while those opposing this hard-line view assembled at the Institute of World Economy and World Politics.[11] Siding with supporters of the anti-imperialism view of capitalism allowed Gorbachev to present the notion of military sufficiency in an entirely different light and to call for a reevaluation of Soviet defense expenditures. It provided the basis for terminating the arms race in which the Soviet Union had been previously heavily involved. Clarifying the new approach, the foreign minister Eduard Shevardnadze argued that attempts to reach military parity with all the potential enemies were in fact against Soviet national interests.[12] (Table 2.2 summarizes the New Thinking view of national interest.)

Table 2.2.   New Thinking (NT): View of National Interest

What?	Global responsibility and "balance of interests"
How?	Military sufficiency Multilateral negotiations Diplomatic compromises

The introduction of the notion of "national interest" was partly strategic and was designed to preempt possible criticism that New Thinking was nothing but a series of concessions to capitalism. Multiple withdrawals from Eastern Europe and the third world, as well as proposals to eliminate entire classes of nuclear missiles, could now be presented as something that was part of a long-term strategy. For example, the "loss" of Eastern Europe after the 1989 fall of the Berlin Wall could now be presented as a net "gain" in a general calculus of creating a favorable international environment. In February 1990, Shevardnadze insisted along these lines, "Our national, as well as historic and everyday, interest is that our neighbors are stable and prosperous. We will only benefit from this."[13]

DOMESTIC CRITICS OF NEW THINKING

Despite Gorbachev's efforts to be a consensus builder, his New Thinking was soon attacked from two different directions. Conservative forces charged that Gorbachev was "selling out" the Soviet interests to the West, whereas liberals saw him as indecisive in abandoning the "outdated" Soviet outlook. Revolutionary changes in the country further polarized the process of foreign policy formation, making it impossible to sustain the originally devised plan with appeal to all main social groups. The original coalition of New Thinkers was fairly broad, representing the industrial, military, party, and academic establishment. Over time, however, that coalition began to fall apart, and the struggle of ideas around New Thinking suggested in which directions some future social and politicoeconomic groups were to emerge.

Conservative Opposition

Conservative opposition to Gorbachev consisted of some representatives of Statist and Civilizationist schools. Intellectually heterogeneous, conservatives were united in their hatred of New Thinking, perceiving it as leading to the Soviet Union's social and political disintegration. Conservative Statists remained highly skeptical of the ideas of détente and domestic reform and were prepared to discuss only military modernization. Conservative Civilizationists put their emphasis on what they saw as key socialist values, such as economic and political centralization of the system. Both groups had much to agree on and enjoyed sufficient support in the military and party establishments, as well as in the wider society.

Conservatives rejected the idea that the West had made a considerable contribution to world development and insisted that Soviet Russia had little to learn from Western modernity. To them, the moral authority in the world lay unquestionably outside the West, whereas the West was viewed as an inferior community united by the aspiration to become rich at the expense of the world. The global crisis diagnosed by Gorbachev could therefore not be solved by appeals to the West itself. Nor could there be dialogue with those who exploit the world economically and corrupt it morally. To Statists, New Thinking was to result in destroying the Soviet military capabilities, and to Civilizationists, it was to erode the very spirit of Soviet society. Religious nationalists, who followed the philosophy of the nineteenth-century Slavophiles and viewed Russia as a holder of Orthodox religious beliefs not to be corrupted by Western Christianity, reinforced the position of the latter.[14]

Not tempted by New Thinking's emphasis on common human values, conservatives recommended that the Soviet Union stay firm and preserve its own historical and cultural tradition. They insisted on the need to continue to resist the influences from the West. Some proposed to accumulate power through economic and technological development, and to abstain from global military conflicts, while others suggested an offensive strategy of expansion to fill the geopolitical vacuum between the Soviet Union and the West.[15]

Liberal Opposition

Conservative perspectives initially remained marginalized in Soviet society. As Gorbachev's reforms were failing to live up to rising expectations, there was still little in Western behavior that could have justified the conservative fears of the West attempting to destroy Russia. On the contrary, a number of successful negotiations with Western leaders made Russians trust the West more and attracted them even more to its values.

This situation improved the position of liberal-minded Westernizers in the national discourse and provided conditions for the consolidation of a Westernist coalition. Originally sympathetic to Gorbachev's agenda, members of the new coalition now felt that he was too slow and inconsistent in his policies. The coalition included representatives of the Soviet middle class, liberal intellectuals, and some party *nomenklatura*, all of whom were growing impatient with the pace of Gorbachev's domestic and external changes. Eventually Boris Yeltsin, a former provincial party secretary, emerged as the leader of the Westernist coalition. Supported by some ethnic republics, liberals were attracted to the "Western" model of development and were disappointed in Gorbachev's "socialist" character of reform.

Liberal critique of New Thinking was just the opposite of that of conservatives. It insisted that Gorbachev's philosophy failed to attribute most common human values to Western civilization. In the view of one scholar, common human values are those "that are based on the criteria of the Western civilization, with its liberal-democratic values and the level of scientific-technological development."[16] Whereas Gorbachev was proposing a globally integrated approach based on the notion of mutual responsibility, liberals viewed the West as the ultimate moral authority and the model to follow. With the nineteenth-century thinker Petr Chaadayev, who believed that "we [Russians] are placed somewhat outside of the times,"[17] the Soviet liberals had little faith in the national tradition of development. In their view, the dilemma before Soviet Russia was either modernization-Westernization or autarchy and backwardness. Any alternative ways of development were no longer available, and Gorbachev's renewed socialist project was nothing but a harmful utopia.

Table 2.3 summarizes contending views on the New Thinking.

Table 2.3.   New Thinking (NT): Contending Views

Conservatives:		Liberals:
NT weakens the Soviet state	vs.	NT fails to change the Soviet system

NEW THINKING ABROAD:
BANKING ON THE WEST'S RECOGNITION

It follows that both conservative and liberal critics of New Thinking had a tendency to view national interest in zero-sum terms. While conservatives saw the Soviet national interests as anti-Western, liberals tended to equate them with those of the West. Gorbachev's complex and dialectical perspective on the Soviet Union in world politics was hardly acceptable to either one of his opponents. To stay his course at home, he needed major support from the West. Obtaining such support in response to New Thinking initiatives could have improved Gorbachev's domestic credibility and assisted him in keeping together his fragile coalition of support. Banking on recognition from the West became a crucial part of the new Soviet strategy. The inadequacy of Western reciprocity, along with Gorbachev's own errors in reforming the economic and political system, ultimately contributed to his failure.

Promises and Disappointments

Gorbachev's ambitious foreign policy agenda included far-reaching disarmament measures, particularly in the area of Soviet-American relations, withdrawal of military assistance and troops from the external imperial territories in Eastern Europe and the third world, and strengthening global institutions (see the chronology earlier in this book for a summary of key events during Gorbachev's tenure). The latter was crucial for fighting militarization, poverty, and environmental degradation across the world, and Gorbachev placed a high premium on the United Nations in accomplishing these goals. The New Thinking vision assumed the emergence of a new global community, in which diverse socioeconomic systems would cooperate in the spirit of mutual trust and reciprocity.

Initially, Gorbachev planned to engage the West through multiple disarmament and demilitarization initiatives. Already in 1985 he argued that military doctrine should become more defensive, announced a unilateral moratorium on nuclear tests, insisted on the need to dissolve military blocs, and made known the Soviet readiness to make disproportionately large cuts in conventional forces.[18] He followed up by proposing more far-reaching changes during several summits with Western leaders. In January 1986, Gorbachev proposed to eliminate all nuclear weapons by 2000, and he offered some major cuts in strategic weapons. He then made several significant concessions on the issue of intermediate nuclear forces, and at the end of 1987, he traveled to Washington to sign the agreement that dismantled the whole class of medium-range and short-range missiles (see table 2.4 for a summary of Gorbachev's security record). No less crucial were decisions to withdraw military assistance and troops from Eastern Europe and the third world. In 1987, the Eastern European leaders were informed that the Soviets were considering troop withdrawal, which was fully consistent with New Thinkers' beliefs in freedom of choice and noninterference in Eastern European domestic affairs. In early 1988, Gorbachev announced the decision to withdraw from Afghanistan, as well as from other third world countries. Gorbachev himself had made these decisions much earlier; indeed, he came to office convinced of their necessity.[19] Finally, in the spirit of strengthening global institutions, the leader of New Thinking took to heart the idea of reforming the United Nations. He supported more extensive resources for peacekeeping forces, proposed to renounce the use of force by the permanent members of the Security Council, and argued for a number of new agencies and agreements. Consistent with these proposals, the new Soviet leadership paid the United Nations $200 million for peacekeeping operations that the old leaders had refused to support since 1973. It also contributed to mediating political resolutions of conflicts in Africa and Latin America.[20]

Table 2.4. Gorbachev's Legacy in Security Policy

The INF Treaty (December 1987). The United States and the USSR agreed to eliminate 1,600 intermediate-range missiles. Also eliminated were approximately 1,100 shorter-range missile systems (500–1,000 km) deployed in Europe.

The CFE Treaty (November 1990). Signed by sixteen NATO states and six members of the Warsaw Pact, the Treaty on Conventional Armed Forces in Europe placed restrictions on the number of conventional weapons within the agreed zone. The treaty deprived the USSR of the ability to mount a credible attack against NATO in Europe.

START (July 1991). The Strategic Arms Reduction Treaty limited each side to a total of 1,600 long-range ballistic missiles and heavy bombers.

Withdrawals of troops from Eastern Europe. Gorbachev decided not to interfere in Eastern Europe before or after anticommunist revolutions there and began to withdraw the Soviet troops in April 1989.

The unification of Germany. Gorbachev endorsed the "Two Plus Four" formula to produce the final settlement on Germany, to acquiesce in West Germany's virtual absorption of its eastern neighbor (largely on Western terms), and to accept a united Germany becoming a full member of NATO.

The radical upturn in U.S.-Soviet relations. By the time of the Bush-Gorbachev summit in December 1989, the two sides converged on many international issues, such as the desirability of a negotiated peace in Nicaragua and El Salvador and a reduction of the Soviet assistance to Cuba. Bush was even at first reluctant to accept the reality of the December 1991 Soviet breakup, when the leaders of Ukraine, Russia, and Belarus announced the creation of the Commonwealth of Independent States.

Adapted from: Coit D. Blacker, *Hostage to Revolution: Gorbachev and Soviet Security Policy, 1985–1991* (New York: Council on Foreign Relations, 1993), 184–89.

Despite all these efforts, the Western leaders were not as cooperative as Gorbachev had hoped. Although Ronald Reagan and British prime minister Margaret Thatcher liked Gorbachev personally, they did not feel convinced by his arguments against nuclear deterrence and nuclear weapons as an "absolute evil." During 1985–1987, they were also not persuaded that the Soviet Union was sincere about renouncing the "Brezhnev doctrine" in Eastern Europe or withdrawing its troops from the third world. The core of the mistrust had to do with the uncertain nature of Soviet reform and a fear of a conservative comeback to power. As a result, many of Gorbachev's initiatives were met with skepticism. For instance, the Geneva Summit in November 1985 produced nothing but a declaration of the inadmissibility of nuclear war. Reykjavik, too, failed, as the Soviet proposals were left unreciprocated. Gorbachev also found no support on the issue of nonuse of force and nonintervention in the internal affairs of other states,[21] which was crucial for him to reciprocate his "freedom of choice" principle with regard to the former outer empire of the Soviet Union. Increasingly, he was left in a difficult position to respond to conservative critics at home.

Conservatives in the party and military establishment opposed New Thinking with a growing vigor. Initially, Gorbachev's coalition was a fairly broad one and even included the chief of the general staff Sergei Akhromeyev and the Politburo member Yegor Ligachev, who agreed with a number of military cuts and withdrawals. In particular, both supported Gorbachev's decision to withdraw from Afghanistan. Yet the more radical the New Thinkers were in their proposals, the more vigorous was the opposition. The military was critical of Reykjavik and of the notion of defense "sufficiency," which was meant to make military doctrine more defense oriented and to prepare the ground for future military cuts. Party officials objected to the principle of "freedom of choice" with regard to Eastern Europe. For instance, Oleg Rakhmanin, head of the Central Committee department for relations with socialist countries, publicly defended the Brezhnev doctrine of limited sovereignty and denounced any changes in bloc relations.[22] Gorbachev fought back by pushing for more military cuts and concessions to the West. He took advantage of the system's failures, such as Chernobyl's nuclear accident and a foreign private aircraft's landing in Red Square, using them as a pretext for replacing hard-liners with those more loyal to his course. In addition, although there was initially no direct connection between his foreign policy initiatives and the state of the Soviet economy, the leader of perestroika was constantly making this connection to maintain conservative support for his course.

Decline and Capitulation

After 1988, the domestic situation took a sharp turn. An economic slowdown, a dramatic worsening of people's living standards, and political separatism of some of the Soviet republics severely affected Gorbachev's ability to stay the course that had already been undermined by the West's reluctant cooperation. The economy was especially important. Although it was growing at the rate of 2.2 percent after the cyclical decline of the early 1980s, it began to decline again during the 1987–1989 period and then collapsed after 1989[23] (see table 2.5). The collapse of the economy was a likely reaction to the vacuum of power resulting from the abolition of state orders. The "law of state enterprise" that came into effect in 1988 replaced state orders with nonbinding control figures. The economy that for decades had been state regulated had not yet developed market-based incentives and was now in a free fall.

Table 2.5.   Growth Rates for the Soviet Economy, 1985–1991

	Western Estimates (gross national product)	Official Soviet Data (net material product)
1985	1.8	3.2
1986	4.1	2.3
1987	1.3	1.6
1988	2.1	4.4
1989	1.5	2.5
1990	−2.4	−3.9
1991	−12.8*	−15*

*Estimate excludes Georgia and the Baltic republics.
Source: David Kotz and Fred Weir, Revolution from Above: The Demise of the Soviet System (London: Routledge, 1997), 75.

As a result, domestic politics was growing increasingly polarized, with conservatives and liberals pulling in opposite directions. Conservatives feverishly tried to restore control over the system and argued for preservation of the class perspective in international relations. But with the Eastern European revolutions underway, the reality was slipping away. The spring 1989 elections in Poland and Hungary brought to power anticommunist forces, and November 1989 saw a key symbol of the Cold War, the Berlin Wall, falling. As the old system was largely discredited, political attention was turning to liberals, who attacked Gorbachev for his indecisiveness and unwillingness to follow the West's model of development. As the leader of New Thinking was losing control, liberal forces were consolidating around Boris Yeltsin, who was soon elected president of the Russian Federation. Even Gorbachev's closest supporters, such as Aleksandr Yakovlev and Eduard Shevardnadze, were now leaving him disappointed. Finally, the general public, too, grew dissatisfied with the results of reform. For instance, in 1989, 39 percent associated the difficulties of reforms with the government's indecisiveness, while only 22 percent of the public attributed such difficulties to the activities of conservative forces.[24]

These domestic changes affected the course of New Thinking negatively. Initially designed as a middle ground between Western capitalism and Stalinist socialism, New Thinking was now seriously endangered and increasingly looked like a failure. After 1988, as Gorbachev was losing ground at home, his foreign policies toward the West were losing their momentum and originality. Symptomatically, in November 1989, the foreign minister Eduard Shevardnadze publicly admitted a lack of "conceptual ideas" and "deficit of counterarguments" in responding to conclusions about the coming triumph of Western liberal ideology.[25] In the meantime, the general public was losing its faith in the country. While in

1988 only 5.3 percent of respondents had felt that the Soviet Union could not serve as an example to the outside world, in 1989 the share of those expressing that feeling reached the level of 34 percent.[26] Western leaders understood Gorbachev's inability to sustain his originally globalist course and pressed for more concessions, without offering much in return. Yegor Ligachev, Gorbachev's powerful conservative opponent, had reason to charge that certain forces in the United States were "linking perestroika with the dismantling of socialism."[27] Gorbachev still tried to save what was left of his course by resisting unified Germany's membership in NATO and insisting on diplomatic solutions to the Persian Gulf crisis. But the Cold War was over, and after having initiated the change, the Soviet Union had little say in negotiating its outcomes. Banking on the West's recognition proved to be a flawed strategy.

On balance, Gorbachev contributed greatly to improving his country's security by relieving an extremely heavy burden of military expenditures that by the time of his arrival had reached the share of some 16.5 percent of the gross national product (GNP).[28] Yet, even if judged by Gorbachev's own standards and expectations, New Thinking was a failure and a capitulation before the West. As an identity project, it did not serve the formulated purposes. Few of Gorbachev's hopes matched the reality. One of them was that far-reaching disarmament initiatives would break down the old Western mistrust and produce some global commitments to demilitarization. Convinced of the viability of socialism, Gorbachev also declared the "freedom of choice" principle with regard to Eastern Europe and the third world. He hoped that these areas would remain neutral and might eventually turn social democratic. He expected the old bipolar security system to be gradually replaced by that of nonconfrontation and cooperation. The old military blocs, such as the Warsaw Pact and NATO, were to recede into the past, and European security would have been organized around the inclusive Organization for Security and Co-operation in Europe (OSCE), the origins of which were in the 1975 Helsinki Accord signed by the Soviet Union. Finally, the United Nations was expected to develop enough muscle to successfully deal with the possible vacuum of power and rising instabilities in the third world after the Soviet withdrawals.

Such were the hopes. The reality, however, was different. Western leaders expressed a willingness to negotiate arms-control agreements, but showed no desire to go as far as Gorbachev expected them to. Neither Margaret Thatcher nor Ronald Reagan shared Gorbachev's vision of complete demilitarization and denuclearization. Eastern European states had their own memory of being a part of the Soviet outer empire and, once the opportunity presented itself, rushed to join Western economic and security institutions, first and foremost NATO. Germany reunited.

The Warsaw Pact disappeared, but NATO persisted and even decided to expand all the way to the Russian borders. The United Nations remained relatively weak and unable to adequately deal with growing violence in the third world. Afghanistan in particular is a case in point. The Soviet withdrawal from there ultimately resulted in that state's collapse. Afghanistan's leader Najibulla was executed, while the new regime of the Taliban became a safe haven for terrorists and their training camps.

THE CRISIS FOR NATIONALITIES AND THE REVENGE
OF NEW THINKING AT HOME

The Soviet Union was an empire, in which the center effectively controlled the sovereignty of the peripheral republics. The Kremlin, rather than Russia and the Russians, played the role of the center—in many ways, Russia was just as heavily exploited by the authorities for the sake of maintaining the empire's economic and political cohesion. Although the Soviet authorities maintained the principle of representation of indigenous nationalities in the power structures, they also relied on political coercion, economic redistribution, and forceful migration—all the traditional tools of empire building. Yet the principle of nationalities' representation developed and reinforced the sense of peripheral distinctiveness from the empire. Historically, it paved the way for nationalist mobilization during imperial decline, particularly among those republics that had developed a sense of national Self before incorporation into the Soviet empire.

Given this nature of relationships between Moscow and the Soviet republics, changing the Soviet territorial power structure should have been high on Gorbachev's list of priorities. If, externally, the Soviet national interests were to be pursued in balance with the interests of other nations, that principle should have applied internally as well. Yet until the early 1990s, Gorbachev failed to address the problem, and his way of dealing with the imperial decline and nationalities crisis presents us with another illustration of how naïve and divorced from power considerations New Thinking ideas were. Gorbachev failed to recognize the Soviet Union as an empire and simply did not see the need for major power changes. By not reacting to national uprisings in a timely and systematic manner, he lost some valuable time (table 2.6 summarizes the rise of ethnonationalism in the Soviet Union). Only in March 1990 did he raise the question of a new union treaty as a way to avoid political disintegration. By that time, nationalists in the Baltic republics and elsewhere had been active for more than three years. Six republics—the Baltic ones, Georgia, Moldova, and Armenia—announced their intent of nonpartici-

Table 2.6. The Rise of Ethnonationalism in the Union Republics, 1989–1991

Union Republic	Main Ethnonationalist Movement (date of foundation)	Sovereignty Declaration (rank)
Armenia	Karabakh Committee (Feb. 1988)	July 1990 (8)
Azerbaijan	Azeri Popular Front (July 1988)	Sept. 1989 (4)
Belarus	Renewal (Andradzhen'ne) (June 1989)	June 1990 (7)
Estonia	Estonian Popular Front (July 1988)	Nov. 1988 (1)
Georgia	Committee for National Salvation (Oct. 1989)	Nov. 1989 (5)
Kazakhstan	Nevada Semipalatinsk Movement (Feb. 1989)	Sept. 1990 (9)
Kyrgyzstan	Openness (Ashar) (July 1989)	Nov. 1990 (10)
Latvia	Latvian Popular Front (July 1988)	May 1989 (2)
Lithuania	Sajudis (June 1988)	July 1989 (3)
Moldova	Moldovan Popular Front (Jan. 1989)	May 1990 (6)
Russia	Democratic Russia (1990)	May 1990 (6)
Tajikistan	Openness (Ashkara) (June 1989)	July 1990 (8)
Turkmenistan	Unity (Agzybirlik) (Jan. 1990)	July 1990 (8)
Ukraine	Popular Front (Rukh) (Nov. 1988)	June 1990 (7)
Uzbekistan	Unity (Birlik) (Nov. 1988)	May 1990 (6)

Adapted from: Graham Smith, *The Post-Soviet States: Mapping the Politics of Transition* (London: Arnold, 1999), 39; Ann Sheehy, "Factsheet on Declarations of Sovereignty," *Report on the USSR*, November 9, 1990.

pation in the new union treaty, and Russian liberal critics of Gorbachev were already debating the idea of confederation. Later, the leader of perestroika himself admitted that he had "underestimated the strength of national feelings and aspirations."[29]

By the time Gorbachev had formulated his concept of a revived union, he had to defend it against the well-elaborated positions of conservatives and Westernizers. Conservatives advocated the idea of empire. Some popularized the essentialist notion of Soviet Eurasia as a new continental empire and a distinct civilization, and recommended the use of force in preserving territorial integrity. Liberal Westernizers around Yeltsin and his supporters criticized the Soviet Union as a hypercentralized state, attacking it from a colonial nationalist perspective. Increasingly, they saw the solution in separating Russia from the center and building Russia's own state institutions. Gorbachev's perspective was not an essentialist one. Rather than advocating an empire or a nation-state, he argued for the Soviet Union as a reformed federation and a community of various peoples. Culturally, he saw this community in transnational terms. A European in his social and political outlook, Gorbachev saw the need to maintain a cultural balance. After 1987 he upgraded his "common European home" formula by adding the Asian dimension and more frequently referring to the Soviet Union as an Asian, as well as a European, country. His foreign minister Eduard Shevardnadze also touted this vision. For example, in October 1988 in his welcoming message to foreign guests attending the Asia-Pacific region conference in Vladivostok, he stressed the Soviet Union as a "great Eurasian space" and a "world of worlds" (*mir mirov*), and argued that Russia had to live in a complex world of both European and Asian nations.

That vision had broad popular support. For example, even as late as during the March 1991 referendum on the future of the new union—a referendum that was conducted in all of the Soviet republics except the Baltics, Armenia, Georgia, and Moldova—147 million people voted and 76.4 percent approved the preservation of the union. The wording of the question was: "Do you support the preservation of the union as a renewed federation of sovereign republics in which the rights of a person of any nationality are fully guaranteed?"[30]

Yet it was a struggle of elites, rather than involvement of the general public, that was about to determine the future of the Soviet Union. The referendum for a renewed union took place in the context of Gorbachev's struggle against liberal elites on the one hand and conservatives on the other. Yeltsin's umbrella organization, Democratic Russia, openly called for the dissolution of the Soviet Union and even tried (unsuccessfully) to convince Yeltsin to campaign for a "no" vote in the referendum. Liberals turned nationalists presented the Soviet Union as an "empire" that was to be dismantled for the sake of Russian prosperity. Throughout the political campaigns of 1990 and 1991, Yeltsin had advanced the "Russia-victim" argument, and it was his advisers who eventually wrote a scenario for dissolving the union. Conservatives, too, did what was in their power to sabotage Gorbachev's efforts. In early 1991, Soviet troops cracked down on the rebellious Lithuania and Latvia. Gorbachev denied responsibility by putting the blame on his defense minister, Dmitri Yazov. Yet liberals in Russia widely associated the crackdown with Gorbachev, and this association worsened the problem. The conservative coup in August was meant to prevent the scheduled signing of the new union treaty between the center and nine republics, but it only made the Soviet disintegration inevitable. The nationalism of the republics' political leadership then reached its highest degree, with Russia and Ukraine playing a particularly important role. On December 25, 1991, after Russia-Ukraine-Belarus had concluded a separate treaty creating the Commonwealth of Independent States (CIS) without consulting the center, Gorbachev resigned.

Paradoxically, New Thinking contributed to the breakup of the Soviet Union. By aiming for the West's support and recognition, it inserted itself into the arena of Western, modern nation-states, making it increasingly difficult to discourage the Soviet ethnic republics from embarking on nationalist projects. Soon after the beginning of perestroika, nationalists were openly referring to the Soviet Union as the last empire in the "age of decolonization." By announcing glasnost and democratization, New Thinking also provided nationalists in Russia and other republics with the required channels for political mobilization. The organization of mass demonstrations in the Baltic republics and then election to national parliaments of those who saw the future only in terms of complete independence greatly facilitated the undermining of the Soviet Union. Finally, Gorbachev's own vision made little room for timely changes in nationalities policy. Despite mounting evidence of strong secessionist sentiments displayed by several republics, he kept insisting that the republics formed a natural historical unity and that they should be "grateful" to the Soviet Union for their social and economic development. Such "New Thinking" undoubtedly stimulated peripheral nationalism. Although public support for the preservation of the union was sound, the extreme polarization of the political space by elites deprived Russia of a chance to reformulate its transnational identity.

UTOPIA AND REALITY: ASSESSMENT OF GORBACHEV'S FOREIGN POLICY

Gorbachev's New Thinking project was introduced to renew the Soviet national identity and to save it as the idea of a reformed socialism open to an outside world yet loyal to some of the already developed social values. Over time, however, the project of saving the national idea regressed into a national defeat. Most of New Thinking's expectations regarding the outside world failed to materialize. The Cold War ended on terms that Gorbachev himself found difficult to accept. The Soviet Union unilaterally withdrew from most areas of the world where it had been present, and it did so without receiving the satisfaction of strengthening global institutions, such as the United Nations, or being given credit for changing the world's thinking. Instead, it was widely accepted that the Soviets lost the Cold War to the West, and it was the West that emerged as the triumphant civilization and the guarantor of peace and security in the world. As if this were not enough, the forces of nationalism in Russia and several other republics added to Gorbachev's domestic defeat. He acknowledged the defeat and resigned as president of a country that was no more. His overall project of external openness and domestic liberalization had been initially widely supported in Soviet society and among elites, who felt ready to move away from the stiffening bureaucratic and militaristic system. But in the process of being implemented, New Thinking lost appeal both externally and domestically, and it contributed to the loss of governance in the country. This section offers a more detailed assessment of Gorbachev's foreign policy record. It reflects on the causes of what happened and draws lessons from the failure of New Thinking.

The Record: Accomplishments and Losses

Gorbachev and his team should be given great credit for initiating a new progressive thinking about the future of the country and the world. Liberals worldwide have been appreciative of the intellectual effort to reactivate social initiative and put a human being in the center of state policy. It is highly misleading to view New Thinking as driven by some power necessities or as an ideology meant to cover the Soviet system's prime desire to rebuild its economic and military capabilities. Gorbachev may have been naïve in his expectations and strategic design, but he certainly was not a cynical power calculator whose main concern was to save the Soviet economic and military machine from defeat in the Cold War. In fact, he did not need to be a New Thinker for power purposes, as the old system could have survived for another generation or so.[31] Nor did he believe, when he came to power, that the Soviet economy was in serious trouble. Gorbachev could have continued to enjoy power without introducing any changes, or he could have introduced limited measures to reform the economy and fight corruption, as favored by his predecessor Yuri Andropov and the majority of the leadership. Instead he initiated what he himself liked to refer to as a "social revolution."

One undisputed accomplishment of New Thinking has been a break with the old Soviet-style isolationism and a radical improvement in military security (see tables 2.4 and 2.7 for summaries). It is only thanks to major theoretical innovations and subsequent arms-control agreements that the Soviet leadership was able to avert the threat of war and move to a realistic military budget. After the 1987 agreement with Washington about the elimination of an entire class of nuclear forces, the very idea of a war with Western countries seemed anachronistic. The state could now concentrate on what it declared as its major tasks—improving people's lives and making the system more accountable to society.

Table 2.7.   Limits on Arms Accepted or Proposed by Gorbachev, 1983–1991

Delivery Systems (warheads)	START, 1983	START, 1991*
Strategic nuclear delivery vehicles	12,580	6,000
Ballistic missiles	10,180	4,900
Heavy ICBMs	3,080	1,540
Sea-launched ballistic missiles	3,080	Limits
Bombers	2,400	1,100

*As proposed in 1987
Adapted from: Michael McGwire, *Perestroika and Soviet National Security* (Washington, DC: Brookings, 1991), 79.

Yet it was in the areas outside military security that the state failed to deliver. Gorbachev's foreign policy failed when judged by the three key criteria of social welfare, policy autonomy, and cultural identity. First, New Thinking did little to improve living standards at home, and it did not result in the expected active participation of the West in reforming the domestic economy. In some ways, Gorbachev's active foreign policy even harmed the domestic reforms, as it precluded the leader of New Thinking from concentrating on what required his full attention at home. Although Gorbachev visualized partial privatization of the economy, he never seriously tried it. Partly, he was too busy with his revolutionary foreign policy. But he was also fearful that private property would lead to a capitalist system at home, subverting what he saw as accomplishments of socialism. For instance, in September 1990, several Soviet and Western economists developed the "500 days" plan, which included economic restructuring, privatization, and active involvement of foreign capital. Gorbachev backed away from the plan, viewing it as leading to a restoration of capitalism. But even before then he missed many opportunities to introduce a more decentralized system and economic incentives. Unlike his more pragmatic teacher Vladimir Lenin, who was not afraid of large foreign concessions and a "dual economy" with a relatively large private sector during the post–civil war reconstruction, Gorbachev proved to be a much less flexible reformer. As a result of his hesitancy, even a mixed economy, in which only small and medium-sized businesses are in private hands, never appeared. The economy remained heavily centralized, and it was unrealistic to expect considerable Western participation in the process of economic reform. It was even less realistic to expect such participation after the Soviet economy had collapsed.

As a result of the collapsing economy, Gorbachev was increasingly perceived abroad as weak and unable to sustain his foreign policy course. Western leaders pressed for more concessions, as in negotiations over Germany's reunification and its role in European security, and the leader of New Thinking was surrendering one position after another. Increasingly, the West, in its own policy calculations, successfully used him. Although this did not yet amount to a loss of Soviet foreign policy autonomy or the ability to make independent decisions, it may have created preconditions for future diminished autonomy. Finally, Gorbachev's foreign policy failed to deliver what New Thinking saw as perhaps the most important of its promises—reformulation of the Soviet cultural identity. Isolation from the world and the West was to be replaced by an image of a more open, democratic, and yet socialist nation confidently looking forward and even providing the world with an example to follow. Instead, Russia found itself a deeply divided nation, with an identity crisis extending well into the post-Soviet era.

Table 2.8 summarizes the record of the New Thinking.

Table 2.8.	The Record of New Thinking
Security	New arms-control agreements
	End of Soviet isolationism
Welfare	State disintegration
	Collapsed economy
Autonomy	Voluntary concessions
	Growing dependence on the West
Identity	A culturally divided nation

Lessons of New Thinking's Failure

New Thinking failed to achieve its objectives abroad and at home not because it had developed a wrong vision for the world's future, but because it had chosen a wrong course to implement that vision by largely divorcing itself from domestic and international power considerations. No grand idea can materialize if it is promoted without due consideration for the existing political context. Although Gorbachev had started his reforms supported by a relatively broad coalition, which included intellectuals and members of the middle class, the military, and party bureaucracy, he was ultimately left alone with his vision. The larger society also began to withdraw its support as early as 1988–1989, and this registered in polls as well as in growing support for Gorbachev's liberal opposition. Sadly, this did not lead to a major rethinking of the initial strategy, or to attempts to rebuild the coalition of support.

Externally, giving due attention to the political and power context would have meant an effort to achieve genuine reciprocity from the West in response to the breathtaking Soviet initiatives. One after another, countries in the West politely declined or ignored Gorbachev's initiatives—on nuclear disarmament, abandonment of the principle of deterrence, nonuse of force and nonintervention in the internal affairs of other states, and strengthening the United Nations. Yet the leader of New Thinking kept going with his own agenda of unilateral withdrawals and military concessions. Believing that his efforts would somehow be rewarded and appreciated externally and at home was naïve, all the more so because he was rapidly losing important bargaining chips in promoting his own revolutionary agenda, just as he was losing domestic support for his course. Gorbachev and his team simply did not think in the categories of preserving power and the capabilities of the state. This was enormously costly to them because the West was not as naïve in negotiating with New Thinkers in the Kremlin, and the Western leaders did give power factors their due consideration.

It was also very costly to the New Thinkers because over time they lost the ability to sell the course at home. And, if the first lesson to learn from their failure is that a successful foreign policy requires reciprocity, then the second lesson should be that a foreign policy must match domestic needs and have strong roots at home. Trying to revolutionize foreign policy simultaneous with fundamental reforms in the economy, the political system, and the area of center-periphery relations is an admirable, but ultimately impossible, task. Priorities should have been chosen, and such priorities should have been domestic, rather than external. Ironically, the harder Gorbachev seemed to push for foreign policy changes, the less control he had left at home. First, in 1988 he lost control over the economy after replacing state orders with nonbinding control figures. Then, he lost control over the political situation after his leading opponent, Boris Yeltsin, was elected president of Russia—first by the parliament and then by popular vote—while Gorbachev remained an essentially nonelected politician. Before 1989, Gorbachev still had a chance to acquire more domestic legitimacy and to strengthen the status of the Soviet president through nationwide elections; after that, such an opportunity was no longer available. By not dealing with the nationalities crisis in a timely manner, he further worsened his domestic standing, and the public had difficulties with trusting his course. Symptomatically, during 1988–1989 the percentage of those viewing nationalities relations as worsening increased from 38 to 72 percent, and in 1989, 30 percent of the respondents thought that a future civil war was likely.[32]

In sum, liberal ideas cannot succeed when they are not backed by power, and they can succeed only to the degree they successfully shape power and use it to achieve their own agenda. Such power can include the support of influential elites, the general public, or developed states abroad, but it must remain a part of the course's support. Liberal ideas should guide a course strategically, but their promoters should also take care to retain sufficient domestic and foreign support of their efforts.

NOTES

1. Mikhail Gorbachev, *On My Country and the World* (New York: Columbia University Press, 2000), 190.

2. For instance, the human rights provisions of the Helsinki Accords, signed by the Soviet Union during détente, emboldened domestic reform-oriented forces and, albeit indirectly, gave rise to a network of committed activists in the Soviet Union and Eastern Europe. For details, see Robert G. Herman, "Identity, Norms, and National Security: The Soviet Foreign Policy Revolution and the End of the Cold War," in *The Culture of National Security*, ed. Peter J. Katzenstein (New York: Columbia University Press, 1996), 292; Robert D. English, *Russia and the Idea of the*

West: Gorbachev, Intellectuals and the End of the Cold War (New York: Columbia University Press, 2000), 154–55.

3. Eric Ringman, "The Recognition Game: Soviet Russia against the West," *Cooperation and Conflict* 37, no. 2 (2002).

4. On Gorbachev as a thinker who sought to improve the Soviet Union's world status through an innovative strategy of engaging the West, see Deborah Welch Larson and Alexei Shevchenko, "Shortcut to Greatness: The New Thinking and the Revolution in Soviet Foreign Policy," *International Organization* 57 (Winter 2003).

5. Mikhail Gorbachev, *Perestroika: New Thinking for Our Country and the World* (New York: Harper & Row, 1987), 12.

6. See, for example, Stephen M. Walt, "The Gorbachev Interlude and International Relations Theory," *Diplomatic History* 21, no. 3 (1997); Stephen G. Brooks and William C. Wohlforth, "Power, Globalization, and the End of the Cold War: Reevaluating a Landmark Case for Ideas," *International Security* 25, no. 3 (Winter 2000/2001).

7. Gorbachev, *Perestroika*, 152.

8. For example, in his book *On My Country and the World*, Gorbachev discusses at length the October Revolution's global significance.

9. Graham Smith, *The Post-Soviet States: Mapping the Politics of Transition* (London: Arnold, 1999), 23. See also Moshe Lewin, *The Gorbachev Phenomenon: A Historical Interpretation* (Berkeley: University of California Press, 1991).

10. As cited in Richard Sakwa, *The Rise and Fall of the Soviet Union, 1917–1991* (London: Routledge, 1999), 188.

11. For a detailed analysis of debates between Old and New Thinkers, see English, *Russia and the Idea of the West*.

12. Stephen Sestanovich, "Invention of Soviet National Interest," *National Interest* 20 (1990).

13. Sestanovich, "Invention of Soviet National Interest," 10.

14. See, for example, Igor' Shafarevich, "Russofobiya," *Nash sovremennik* 6, no. 11 (1989); Yuri Borodai, "Treti put," *Nash sovremennik* 9 (1991).

15. Sergei Kurginyan et al., *Postperestroika* (Moscow: Politizdat, 1990); Aleksandr Prokhanov and Shamil' Sultanov, "Izmenit'sya, chtoby vyzhit," *Den'* 6 (1991); Aleksandr Dugin, "Anatomiya mondializma," *Den'* 16 (1991).

16. El'giz A. Pozdnyakov, "Formatsionnyi i tsivilizatsionnyi podkhody i mezhdunarodniye otnosheniya," in *SSSR v mirovom soobschestve*, ed. Nodar A. Simoniya (Moscow: Progress, 1990), 143. For a broader context, review the articles published in Russia's academic and literary journals during 1987–1991.

17. Petr Chaadayev, "Apology of a Madman," in *Readings in Russian Civilization*, 2nd ed., ed. Thomas Riha (Chicago: University of Chicago Press, 1969), 304.

18. English, *Russia and the Idea of the West*, 201–2.

19. English, *Russia and the Idea of the West*, 203–4.

20. Larson and Shevchenko, "Shortcut to Greatness," 98.

21. Larson and Shevchenko, "Shortcut to Greatness," 99.

22. English, *Russia and the Idea of the West*, 204.

23. David Kotz and Fred Weir, *Revolution from Above: The Demise of the Soviet System* (London: Routledge, 1997), 76.

24. Yuri Levada, ed., *Est' mneniye! Itogi sotsiologicheskogo oprosa* (Moscow: Progress, 1990), 290.

25. Eduard Shevardnadze, "Vneshnyaya politika i nauka," *Mezhdunarodnaya zhizn'* 2 (February 1990): 17, 18.

26. Levada, *Est' mneniye*, 284.

27. *Sovetskaya Rossiya*, February 6, 1991.

28. Some estimate the defense budget at 20 percent of the GNP and even higher (English, *Russia and the Idea of the West*, 200, 323n31). The official Soviet figures were 8.1 percent for 1975 and 4.6 percent for 1984. See *Finansy i statistika* (Moscow, 1985) as quoted in Janos Kornai, *The Socialist System: The Political Economy of Communism* (Princeton, NJ: Princeton University Press, 1992), 137.

29. Mikhail Gorbachev, *Dekabr' 1991: Moya pozitsiya* (Moscow: Novosti, 1992), 175–76.

30. Kotz and Weir, *Revolution from Above*, 147.

31. Michael Ellman and Vladimir Kontorovich, eds., *The Disintegration of the Soviet Economic System* (London: Routledge, 1992); see also Michael Ellman and Vladimir Kontorovich, "The Collapse of the Soviet System and the Memoir Literature," *Europe-Asia Studies* 49, no. 2 (1997); and Vladimir Kontorovich, "Economists, Soviet Growth Slowdown and the Collapse," *Europe-Asia Studies* 53, no. 5 (2001).

32. Levada, *Est' mneniye*, 280, 288.

3

The Post–Cold War Euphoria and Russia's Liberal Westernism

Our country . . . was turned into a hostage of messianic ideas, on behalf of which it sacrificed its national interests.

The United States and other Western democracies are as natural friends and eventual allies of the democratic Russia as they are foes of the totalitarian USSR.

—Andrei Kozyrev[1]

THE WORLDVIEW OF RUSSIA'S WESTERNIZERS AFTER THE COLD WAR

Soviet disintegration ended the previously established sense of national identity in Russia and opened up a space for identity reformulation by the new state. The leaders of post-Soviet Russia developed a pro-Western vision of national identity and foreign policy, which was consistent with their vision of the world. Before we describe this vision in greater detail, let us review the context in which the new foreign policy thinking was to take shape.

The Brave New Liberal World

The most powerful force that shaped the worldview of new Russia's leadership was the economic and political rise of the West. In contrast to steadily growing Western economies, Russia's gross domestic product (GDP) showed about a 60 percent cumulative decline from 1985 to 1992.[2]

59

In addition, the West reemerged as a powerful and cohesive civilization whose political unity contrasted with disarray in the former Soviet Union. Finally, in the late 1980s, many Western commentators were in a self-congratulatory mood, which also contributed to the perception of the worldwide ascendancy of Western values and institutions. By the time conservatives had been in power for a good decade and with the decline of Soviet power, they became convinced of the West's victory in the Cold War struggle.

For example, Francis Fukuyama's argument about the "end of history" defended the worldwide ascendancy of Western-style liberal capitalism and captured the vision dominant in American policy circles.[3] In Europe, such admirers of civil society and "participatory democracy" as Andrew Arato, Ralf Darendorf, and Timothy Garton Ash expressed similar Western democratic triumphalism and saw the Soviet decline as a catalyst for a revival of civic norms of plurality and publicity in Eastern Europe. British journalist Timothy Garton Ash forcefully stated the mood by maintaining that the European revolutions "can offer no fundamentally new ideas on the big questions of politics, economics, law or international relations. The ideas whose time has come are old, familiar, well-tested ones"—liberal ideas about the rule of law, parliamentary government, and an independent judiciary.[4]

Although politically the Western leaders were supportive of Gorbachev's gradual efforts to dismantle the Soviet system, most of them were critical of his socialist intentions and hoped for the emergence of a Western-like system in place of the Soviet Union. Many increasingly perceived the Soviet system as "the grand failure,"[5] and as early as 1989 such a perception had won the support of the mainstream intellectual and political discourse in the West. The leading policy establishment journal *Foreign Affairs* soon issued the verdict that "the Soviet system collapsed because of what it was, or more exactly, because of what it was not. The West 'won' because of what the democracies were—because they were free, prosperous and successful, because they did justice, or convincingly tried to do so."[6] The vision was finally legitimized on the highest policy level when U.S. president George H. W. Bush announced the Cold War "victory" of the United States in his 1992 State of the Union message.

It was this fundamental belief in the superiority of the Western system that also shaped the minds of the liberal coalition that emerged in Russia. Boris Yeltsin and his liberal foreign minister Andrei Kozyrev believed that history in a sense had ended and presented no alternatives to pro-Western development. Before Soviet disintegration, they used these ideas to discredit Gorbachev's socialist and therefore "utopian" worldview. Consistent with the Western critics of socialism, they insisted that the Soviet Union could not be reformed and that Russia needed to adopt a Western capitalist model of development. After the peaceful end of the

Cold War, the arguments of Russia's Westernizers about the "nonconfrontational" nature of the international system and the absence of security threats made their insistence on rapid modernization and Westernization all the more compelling to the public. Geopolitics seemed irrelevant, while Westernization seemed inevitable and imminent.

The Westernist Vision of Russia's Identity

Loyal to the intellectual tradition of Westernism, the new Russia's leaders saw their country as an organic part of Western civilization whose "genuine" Western identity had been hijacked by Bolsheviks and the Soviet system. In the Westernist perspective, during the Cold War Russia had acted against its own national identity and interests, and now it finally had an opportunity to become a "normal" Western country. Thus, Kozyrev argued that the Soviet Union was not merely a "normal" or "underdeveloped" country, but a "wrongfully developed" one.[7] This vision was a clear product of a long tradition of Russia's Westernist thinking. Such eminent nineteenth-century historians as Vasili Klyuchevski and Pavel Milyukov saw Russia's national characteristics, but insisted that their country would nevertheless develop in the same direction as the West and go through the same stages of development.

Why such a linear worldview? Because the West was perceived as the only viable and progressive civilization. In this perspective, world society was increasingly based on democratic values and respect for human rights as articulated by Western civilization.[8] Main threats to Russia were to come from its economic backwardness and its association with non-democratic countries, especially with some of the former Soviet allies. Accordingly, the key division in the world, overriding all other divisions, was the one between democratic countries and those in the process of democratic transition, on the one hand, and those that were still practicing authoritarian forms of government, on the other. The West and its supporters had the right to push for their human rights agenda and even intervene anywhere in the world when gross violations of human rights were taking place. With respect to the agencies that were to enforce a human rights–centered world order, it was best if human rights interventions were sanctioned through the United Nations Security Council.

The new Westernist coalition consisted of idealistic reformers and pragmatic representatives of the former Communist *nomenklatura*. The reformers, such as Gennadi Burbulis, Yegor Gaidar, and Andrei Kozyrev, advocated radical policies that they hoped would bring Russia in line with the politicoeconomic standards of Western countries within a limited period of time. Typically, these reformers talked about one or two years of necessary reforms, after which Russians were to considerably improve their living standards. Members of the former party *nomenklatura* realized that the return to the Soviet past was no longer possible. Some of them, especially those originating from the Komsomol (the youth branch of the Communist Party) apparatus and directors of large state enterprises, had entered private business during 1989–1991 and now wanted to obtain control over the state property that had previously been managed under the leadership of the Central Committee. The goals of reformers and the former *nomenklatura* were compatible: reformers wanted pro-Western capitalist reforms, while the party *nomenklatura* was eager to become a class of new capitalists.

United by the popular president Boris Yeltsin, the Westernist coalition found itself in a position to act on its foreign policy beliefs. Gorbachev's reforms had been effectively discredited, and the failed coup of August 1991 eliminated the appeal of the old communist ideas.

The Westernist Concept of National Interest

The defeat of Gorbachev by liberal Westernizers led to the assertion of a different concept of national interest. While accepting the general premises of New Thinking, the new Russia's leaders developed these premises in a more sweeping philosophy of Integration with the West and its economic, political, and security institutions. In Kozyrev's words, the country's very system of values was to be changed, as Russia was to accept the priority of the individual and the free market over society and state. As the result, a "natural partnership" with Western countries was to develop, and Russia was to be brought to the front-rank status of such countries as France, Germany, and the United States within ten to twelve years. In the spirit of liberalism, Kozyrev formulated the national interest, saying "in transforming Russia into a free, independent state, formalizing democratic institutions, setting up an effective economy, guaranteeing the rights and freedoms of all Russians, making our people's life rich both materially and spiritually."[9] (Table 3.1 summarizes the Westernist view of national interest.)

Table 3.1.   Westernist Course: View of National Interest

What?	"Natural partnership" with the West
How?	Rapid membership in Western organizations
	Isolationism in the former Soviet region
	Radical economic reform

It is worth emphasizing three key components of the asserted vision of national interest—radical economic reform, rapid membership in the Western international institutions, and isolationism from the former Soviet states. First, Yeltsin and Kozyrev advocated a strategy of radical economic reform, the so-called shock therapy, so that Russia's transition to a Western-style system would be both fast and irreversible. The argument was made that in the contemporary post–Cold War world, Russia should stop worrying about military power and geopolitics and, instead, invest its resources in the creation of a modern economy and political system. The new leadership linked the idea of radical reform to that of strategic partnership with the West, and the calculation was that the latter would be instrumental in implementing the former. Russian Westernizers hoped that the West had finally recognized Russia as one of its own and would therefore invest the required resources in Russia's transition. For instance, in addressing a joint session of the U.S. Congress in June 1992, Yeltsin saw no reason to hide his expectations for massive external assistance in reforming the country's economy. He even chose to be dramatic in linking the success of Russia's reform to U.S. aid and told the joint session that his country had only one chance to survive: "There will be no second try . . . the reforms must succeed. . . . If we [that is, you Americans] do not take measures now to support Russia, this will not be a collapse of Russia only, it will be a collapse of the United States, because it will mean new trillions of dollars for the arms race."[10]

Joining international organizations was the second critical element in the strategy of Integration with the West. Since the United States and other Western countries were now "natural allies," Russia should gain a full-scale status in such transatlantic economic and security institutions as the European Union, North Atlantic Treaty Organization (NATO), International Monetary Fund (IMF), G-7, and so on. In this brave new world of economic interdependence and Western institutional predominance, Russia would no longer need to pursue its "greatness"; it should instead prepare for a relative decrease of status in a postconfrontational world and try to solve its problems by way of joining the Western "community of civilized nations."[11]

Finally, the new concept of national interest assumed that Russia's Integration with the West would take priority over the relationships with the ex-Soviet republics. The new leadership believed that, just as Russia had suffered from isolation from the West, it had also taken on the excessively heavy Soviet imperial burden. The argument was made that the Soviet Union had been a constant drain on Russian resources, as Russia had had to subsidize other republics. Russia was therefore turned into an "internal colony" of the Soviet Union. The solution was found in the eventual separation of the country from the former republics economically, politically, and culturally. The concept of "little Russia" was introduced to assist the leadership in justifying little, if any, responsibility for the former Soviet region. In the economic realm, Russia's leaders planned to stop subsidies for the ex-republics. In the security area, they wanted to gradually withdraw Russia's military and to rely on the assistance of international organizations, such as the Organization for Security and Co-operation in Europe (OSCE), in solving possible conflicts in the region. Politically, they viewed the organization newly established in place of the Soviet Union—the Commonwealth of Independent States (CIS)—as a mechanism for completing the republics' separation from Russia, rather than for promoting or preserving their integration.

The liberal Westernist concept of national interest shaped the new foreign policy concept prepared in late 1992 and signed into law in April 1993. The concept heavily influenced by the documents and charter of the OSCE favored the promotion of Russia's interests in the first place through participation in different international organizations. The foreign minister's emphasis on Western international institutions in part reflected his own professional experience; for sixteen years (1974–1990), Kozyrev had worked in the Directorate of International Organizations at the Soviet Foreign Ministry. He saw international institutions as the main avenue for resolving conflicts outside the essentially peaceful and prosperous Western Hemisphere, including between the former Soviet republics.

This concept of national interest was in many ways unprecedented— never before had Russia's officials been as supportive of dismantling their imperial institutions, as critical of their own history, and as trusting of Western intentions. In Yeltsin and Kozyrev's design, Russia was not only supposed to cooperate with the West on a broad range of international issues, as Gorbachev had planned, it was to become the West at the expense of its own historically developed identity. Gorbachev wanted the Soviet Union to be more respectful of other nations, but he did not propose to abandon what he saw as his country's socialist values and interests. He argued that security must be mutual, especially in the context of U.S.-Soviet relations, and that it should be broadened to incorporate various aspects of economic and environmental interdependence. But Gorbachev never went as far as to suggest that the West would become the teacher of the rest of the world, whereas Yeltsin and Kozyrev developed their outlook almost exclusively from their infatuation with Western civilization and its accomplishments. This outlook implied that countries outside the West could no longer make a creative contribution to the world's development; at this posthistorical point, all that was left to the non-Western world was to patiently and passively wait to be absorbed by West-defined modernization. This kind of Westernism would have not been possible without New Thinking, but it became far more extreme and far more critical of the Soviet developments than that of Gorbachev.

Contrary to what realists might assert, the new Russia's leaders did not pursue the strategy of Integration with the West because of a weakness of Soviet material capabilities. The reformers' idealistic worldview could hardly be likened to pragmatic calculations of a weakened superpower. On the contrary, many reformers saw the Soviet collapse as an opportunity to establish a new identity for Russia. Liberal theorists of international relations are closer to the truth when they point to the impact of Western ideas of modernization on Russia's liberals. Yet these theorists could hardly have predicted the intensity of growing opposition to Russia's new Westernist course.

THE DEBATE ON FOREIGN POLICY WESTERNISM

The Westernist vision of Russia's identity and foreign policy turned out to be deeply contested and soon was challenged by various political classes as well as the larger society (table 3.2 summarizes the spectrum of Russia's

Table 3.2. The Spectrum of Russia's Post-Soviet Foreign Policy Thinking

Principal School of Thought	Vision of Russia and Its External Threats	Proponent
WESTERNIZERS		
Liberals	Russia is a part of the West and should integrate with Western economic and political institutions; the main threats to Russia come from nondemocratic states	Andrei Kozyrev
Social Democrats	Russia is an independent part of international society; it has its own specific interests, but also shares some common interests with others; the main threats to Russia come from violation of basic human rights and disrespect for cultural pluralism	Mikhail Gorbachev
STATISTS	Russia is a sovereign state and a great power with its own specific interests in maintaining the stability of the international system; the main threats to Russia come from state-revisionists seeking to change the existing balance of power	Yevgeni Primakov
CIVILIZATIONISTS		
National Communists	Russia is an independent socialist civilization and a great power/superpower; its interests are incompatible with those of the West and include the restoration of a balance of power between socialism and capitalism and the spread of the influence of Russian civilization; the main threats come from the West and its imperialist intentions	Gennadi Zyuganov
Hard-line Eurasianists	Russia is a land-based geopolitical empire; its interests are mutually exclusive of those of sea-based powers and include the preservation and expansion of Russia's geopolitical sphere of influence; the main threats come from sea-based powers	Vladimir Zhirinovski

post-Soviet foreign policy thinking). The old Civilizationists argued that the West was interested only in global hegemony and weakening Russia. Gorbachev's supporters embraced the government's attempts to engage the world, but condemned the sectarian nature of foreign policy formation and its narrowly procapitalist orientation. But the most formidable challenge to Westernism came from the revived tradition of Statist thinking. The new Statists agreed with the need to cooperate with the West in the interests of rebuilding the economy, but insisted that the guiding principle behind all reforms and foreign policy actions remained the preservation of great power status. As the West began to lose interest in Russia, Statists received an important advantage in asserting their influence. The local conditions that helped them to consolidate their support were the failure of shock therapy, growing instability in the former Soviet region, and the institutional channels of a low centralized political system.

Civilizationists

The end of the Soviet Union did not change Civilizationists, who still refused to part with the core principles of the Soviet society. One group—National Communists—was merging some old communist ideas with those of nationalism and was particularly influenced by Josef Stalin's doctrine of "socialism in one country," which acknowledged the need for Russia to focus on developing military and economic capabilities within Soviet boundaries. The most active promoter of this group's ideas was Gennadi Zyuganov, the leader of the Communist Party of the Russian Federation.[12] Another hard-line group referred to itself as Eurasianists, and viewed the world in terms of the geopolitical struggle between land-based and sea-based powers. Unlike National Communists, who portrayed themselves as adherents to conservative beliefs such as religion and social stability, Eurasianists argued that conservatism was not enough and advocated the notion of a "conservative revolution" and geopolitical expansion.[13] While National Communists had no ambitions beyond restoring the Soviet Union, Eurasianists wanted to build a larger geopolitical axis of allies—such as Germany, Iran, and Japan—in order to resist the American influences. They attracted some support from hard-line military and nationalist political movements, such as Vladimir Zhirinovski's Liberal Democratic Party.

Both groups attacked Kozyrev's course as serving the interests of the West at the expense of Russia. To them, Russia's national interest was, almost by definition, anti-Western. They had no regard for the market economy and political democracy and viewed Russia's institutions as diametrically opposed to those of the West. The West's liberalism, they argued, was nothing more than United States–based unipolarity in the making. Russia's adequate response should include rebuilding military capabilities, reforming the economy on the model of China's gradual state-oriented style, and preserving control over Eurasia or the post-Soviet world. In the words of the conservative periodical *Molodaya gvardiya*, "The historical task before Russia and other nations of the world is not to allow for the 21st century to become the American century."[14]

Civilizationist ideas were not principally different from those advanced during the Gorbachev era, and at the time they were not particularly attractive to the elites or the broader society. The mainstream political class typically viewed these ideas as dangerous and too extravagant to be implemented. The general public, too, had little faith in the imperialist policies. National Communists and Eurasianists therefore remained relatively marginalized in Russian discourse.

Social Democrats

Social Democrats were the former supporters of Gorbachev; they occupied the Westernist part of the foreign policy spectrum during the Soviet era. This group supported the elements of international openness and cooperation present in Kozyrev's thinking, but criticized his excessively pro-Western orientation and isolationism in relations with the ex-Soviet republics. This isolationism and radical Westernism, Social Democrats argued, was a product of sectarian thinking that had underlaid the breakup of the Soviet Union and that had no regard for popular opinion or aspirations to preserve the union.[15]

Following the earlier line of Gorbachev's arguments, Social Democrats advanced a vision of the emerging international system that was liberal, and yet very different from Kozyrev's liberalism. They insisted that in constructing Russia's national interest, it was important to identify and creatively follow some preestablished historical values, rather than to passively absorb values and institutions of the West. Social Democrats recommended that Russia actively participate in building a new international order, but they condemned any attempts to shape the world in accordance with a particular culture's standards. In addition, they argued that it was the relations with the whole world, not the West alone, that were of key significance.[16]

Despite the significance of the Social Democrats' critique, their public visibility in debates on Russia's foreign policy was low. Closely associated with Gorbachev, this group was yet to recover from the devastating blow of the Soviet breakup. As Kozyrev's foreign policy began to unravel, the vacuum of ideas emerged and was soon filled by revived Statist thinking.

The Revival of Statist Thinking

As the proposed vision of radical reform and strategic partnership with the West was failing to bring any visible improvements in people's living standards, the population was becoming disillusioned and skeptical. At home, Russians experienced a drastic decline in living standards. Externally, the prospects of NATO expansion toward Russia's borders and military conflicts in the Russian periphery created a sense of insecurity, undermining the Westernist foreign policy course. The disintegration of the Soviet Union added to the change in attitude; socialized in the tradition of the Soviet Statist thinking, many Russians felt that economic failures were now exacerbated by the significant loss of territory and world status. The grand strategy of Integration with the West was increasingly perceived as a flawed one. According to one poll, public support for the U.S. model of society fell from 32 percent in 1990 to 13 percent in 1992, or by more than two-thirds. A similar trend was observed with regard to Russian popular opinion about Japanese and German models of society.[17] The biggest demonstration of declining support for Yeltsin and Kozyrev's policies came during the December 1993 parliamentary elections, when liberal parties lost to those of nationalist orientation.

The official Westernist course faced growing resistance, yet Westernizers came across as defensive and unable to offer any new ideas. Many continued to insist on economic and political modernization as the country's only national interest without attempting to address the new fears of insecurity, instability, and poverty. Some lost their faith in liberalism and began to gravitate to nationalist political camps. For example, the executive secretary of the parliamentary constitutional commission, Oleg Rumyantsev, and the prominent writer and athlete Yuri Vlasov—both formerly supportive of the liberal agenda—switched to the ranks of the National Communists. Very few liberals were willing to argue the need for the state to be taking on a stronger role in dealing with instabilities at home and abroad.

Under the new geopolitical and economic situation, a number of members of the political class began to advocate a principally different vision of national interest that included a stronger role for the state and revival of Russia's great power status. Influenced by both Westernizers and Civilizationists, Statists positioned themselves to unite supporters of the old and the new Russia. Under the leadership of Yevgeni Primakov, at the time heading the Foreign Intelligence Service, the new coalition united many former Soviet industrialists, state bureaucrats, and members of the military and security services. The members of the new coalition had no faith in the West's willingness or ability to integrate Russia. Instead, they believed in the state's role in preserving security and conducting a less painful economic reform. Statists also had in mind a different model of

Russia's relationships with the outside world, and the Westernist vision of the country's identity was soon to be defeated. In late 1995, Kozyrev was removed from office and replaced by Primakov, his prominent critic and the father of Russia's new Statism. The next chapter elaborates on the Statist philosophy and foreign policy record.

Table 3.3 summarizes contending views on the Westernist view of national interest.

Table 3.3. Westernism: Contending Views

Social Democrats:		Statists:
Westernism undermines Russia's social democratic potential		Westernism undermines Russia's statehood
	vs.	
National Communists:		**Eurasianists:**
Westernism destroys Russia's socialist system		Westernism eliminates Russia's geopolitical independence

Statism's Institutional Advantages

In addition to the West's disengagement and Russia's domestic instabilities, the rise of Statism became possible because of various institutional channels available to the school's advocates. The combination of a historically dominant nationalist political culture and low centralized democratic system provided the new Statists with some institutional advantages. Effective use of institutions, such as parliament, media, and influential nongovernmental organizations, helped Statists to promote their vision and undermine that of Kozyrev.

Parliament, or the Supreme Soviet, played a particularly important role in challenging the Westernist course. One of the earliest critics of Kozyrev's foreign policy was the chairman of the Foreign Affairs Committee of the Supreme Soviet, Yevgeni Ambartsumov. A former supporter of Gorbachev and Yeltsin's team, Ambartsumov had been responsible for formulating the concept of enlightened imperialism in the former Soviet region that was later publicized by his associate Andranik Migranyan. The concept defined the entire territory of the former Soviet Union as the sphere of Russia's vital interests by drawing parallels with the early-nineteenth-century policy of American special rights in the Western Hemisphere (the Monroe Doctrine).[18] Another prominent critic of Kozyrev was parliamentarian and future ambassador to the United States Vladimir Lukin, who cautioned against the one-sided pro-Western orientation and expressed his support for a more diversified foreign policy.

An influential agency with direct access to Yeltsin was the Primakov-led Foreign Intelligence Service. Throughout 1992–1994, the agency was arguing the need to reconsider Russia's foreign policy priorities and concentrate on the former Soviet area. In contrast to Kozyrev's emphasis on Russia's "natural partnership" with the West, even at the expense of relationships in the former Soviet Union, Primakov saw his role as pointing to economic and security disintegrations in the post-Soviet area and proposing remedies. One of these reports, "Russia-CIS: Is the West's Position in Need of Adjustment?" had been a direct response to NATO's expansion initiative, and it eventually influenced Yeltsin's own thinking. In late 1995, Primakov replaced Kozyrev as foreign minister and announced that the former Soviet area would become his first priority.

Other important government channels included the Presidential Administration and Security Council. Presidential adviser Sergei Stankevich had taken issue with Kozyrev since the latter's first attempt to systematically formulate Russia's national interests at the Foreign Ministry conference "The Transformed Russia in the New World" in February 1992. Stankevich promoted the vision of Russia as a cultural bridge between Europe and Asia and insisted that Russia needed to defend the rights of ethnic Russians in the former Soviet republics.[19] The Russian Security Council was yet another governmental body through which Statists were able to challenge the Westernist course. Already in the summer of 1992, representatives of the foreign, defense, and security ministries united under the Security Council—at that time headed by Yuri Skokov—to challenge Kozyrev's foreign policy vision and to draw up "Guidelines for the Foreign Policy of the Russian Federation." The eventual document prescribed that Russia take its place as a world power, as a bridge between East and West, with specific interests in the "Near Abroad."

Outside the state, several organizations became prominent in advancing the Statist vision. The Council for Foreign and Defense Policy served as the nongovernmental umbrella think tank expressing views of industrialists, businessmen, intellectuals, and mass opinion leaders. The council has consistently advocated Russia's more "Near Abroad"–oriented policies and pragmatism in relationships with the West.[20] The political movement Civic Union consolidated various voices critical of the Westernist policies. Influential individuals associated with the Civic Union's philosophy included Vice President Aleksandr Rutskoi, the chief of the Security Council Yuri Skokov, and the speaker of the Supreme Soviet Ruslan Khasbulatov. In January 1993, the Civic Union adopted its own Concept of Russian Foreign Policy, which advocated Russia's national interests defined in terms of achieving a great power status in Eurasia. Civic Union acted from inside the mainstream, gradually changing the balance of power within the political class. The organization sought to reestablish economic ties with the ex-Soviet republics, and operated throughout the entire post-Soviet space. Intellectually, the Civic Union worked closely with the Council for Foreign and Defense Policy, and the two advocated similar philosophies.

The End of Russia's Westernist Momentum

The Westernist course began to lose its momentum toward the end of 1992. The absence of practical outcomes was all too visible, and the opposition's criticisms were beginning to bite. Kozyrev had to acknowledge the end of the "honeymoon period" in relations with the West.[21] Yeltsin expressed similar feelings by criticizing the United States for its tendency to "dictate its own terms." Echoing Statist sentiments, he declared that Russia's relations with the West "had to be balanced. After all, we are a Eurasian state."[22] The radical Westernist coalition was falling apart, with some of its members joining the ranks of moderate or even radical opposition. The rhetoric and the agenda of the Statists were gaining currency. Geopolitics was quickly becoming the name of the national discourse, and Westernizers could no longer be taken seriously without framing what they had to say in geopolitical terms.

The calculations of Yeltsin and Kozyrev that the West would recognize Russia as its own and provide all the necessary assistance to integrate it into its midst proved to be flawed. Although the Western governments provided some substantial financial aid to Russia and were willing to cooperate on matters of security and arms control (the next section returns to this point), these measures could not meet the existing highly inflated expectations for Western assistance. Trying to rally domestic support around such expectations was unrealistic. Credit and investment were too negligible to buttress the credibility of the liberal Westernist vision, let alone transform Russia's institutions. In the realm of security, the importance of the Russia-favored OSCE declined visibly, and Russia made no progress in getting closer to NATO. Although Russia gained a nominal standing within an expanded G-8, its formal inclusion did not come about until July 1994. In addition, some influential foreign policy experts in the West spoke of "the premature partnership" with Russia,[23] a statement that came as a cold shower to the Yeltsin-Kozyrev team.

Yeltsin and Kozyrev found themselves in a very difficult position. On the one hand, they had already committed their policies to first-priority relations with Western countries and understood the importance of not alienating the West for both tactical and strategic reasons. On the other hand, the Westernist foreign policy course clearly lost its domestic appeal and had to be modified. Some serious concessions to the Statist opposition had to be made.

In response to this new predicament, Russia's leaders attempted to preserve the strategy of integration, while tempering their expectations and casting the course more in terms of shared interests than shared cultural

values with the West. Abroad, they continued to insist that strategic partnership with Russia remained the best choice for the West because of "a
historic opportunity to facilitate the formation of a democratic, open Russian state and the transformation of an unstable, post-confrontational world
into a stable and democratic one."[24] At home, the leadership sought to
consolidate support among influential elites. It allowed some of the former
economic and party *nomenklatura* to privatize the lucrative energy industry, thereby turning them into the wealthiest businessmen with Western
trading preferences. It continued to reward loyal members of the media
and banking community with government credits, often interest-free. In
early 1993, Yeltsin also attended a Civic Union congress, thereby acknowledging the organization's significance. And in late 1994—partly in his bid
for the support of the army elite—Yeltsin made a decision about military
intervention in Chechnya. Kozyrev supported the decision and demon-
stratively resigned from the parliament's most pro-Western faction, Russia's
Choice.

In addition, both Yeltsin and Kozyrev added the geopolitical dimension to their publicly displayed views of national interest. Yeltsin spoke
about moving away from a Western emphasis in Russian diplomacy.
Kozyrev acknowledged the importance of preserving economic and cultural relationships with the former Soviet states and became more critical
of Western policies toward Russia. In early 1994, writing in the *New York
Times*, he warned of "the chauvinistic new banners that flap in the Washington wind." "I must say, sadly, that in these confused days sometimes
we are neither understood nor adequately supported by our natural
friends and allies in the West. Even at this critical moment in Moscow,
when democracy needs all the help it can get, we hear Western threats to
reduce economic cooperation with Russia . . . it appears that some Western politicians, in Washington and elsewhere, envision Russia not as an
equal partner but as a junior partner. In this view a 'good Russian' is
always a follower, never a leader."[25]

All these measures, however, were primarily of a tactical and rhetorical
nature. The larger society and much of the political class remained dissatisfied and unaffected by the modification of the course. No less importantly,
the general public and elites remained mistrustful of the leaders in charge.

TOWARD INTEGRATION WITH THE WEST

As brief as Russia's Westernist momentum was, Yeltsin and Kozyrev did
try to act on their beliefs. This section reviews their policies toward the
outside world, which demonstrate the depth of their convictions about

Western civilization's primacy in the world. Russia's leaders turned their full attention to the West, while remaining neglectful of relationships with the Asian and Middle Eastern regions.

The West as the Savior

Much like Mikhail Gorbachev, Westernizers predicated their entire course on recognition by the West. The new Russia's leaders hoped that the West would provide all the required material and moral support for reform when it saw how committed Russia was to a liberal transformation. At times the Russians sounded dramatic and even desperate for massive Western material and moral support because they believed that, short of such support, their reforms were doomed to failure. In the absence of the West's quickly throwing its entire weight behind helping Russia, argued the Kremlin officials, a fascist coup was likely to happen. Much like Gorbachev, Yeltsin and Kozyrev fully acknowledged the groundbreaking nature of their relationships with the West, referring to them as a revolution in cooperation among the states of the civilized world. Unlike Gorbachev, however, they wanted to be fully integrated within Western civilization. Whereas Gorbachev wanted to be recognized as a country with distinct values (socialism), the new Russia's leaders equated recognition with integration and loss of their country's distinct identity. Whereas Gorbachev saw diversity and multiple contributions to world development, the new Westernizers recognized only the triumph of one civilization (the West) over the rest of the world. At the time, Russia's leaders made little distinction between North America and Europe, viewing them as firmly united by common values of the market economy and political pluralism.[26] It therefore seemed inevitable to sacrifice Russia's historical identity to that of the West, and the leadership saw no tragedy in it. Indeed, losing such an identity seemed necessary only if Russia were to be transformed into a Western nation.

There is no reason to doubt the sincerity of Russia's leaders, and any attempts to present them as cynical calculators of material rewards in exchange for rhetorical loyalty to the West would be highly misleading. Their utopian ideological considerations were the primer in shaping Russia's perception of the world. Rational interests came in a distant second and reemerged as a key foreign policy motivation only at a later stage. It is consistent with Westernist ideological beliefs that Russia's leaders were ready to do everything in their power to gain membership in Western international organizations and support the West's agenda in international security affairs.

Striving to Join Western International Organizations

The leaders of the new Russia had very high expectations about joining Western international organizations. In economic affairs, they did not merely expect loans or assistance in debt restructuring and currency stabilization; they wanted a flow of massive Western investments, and they were correct to measure the success of Russia's integration into the world economy by such investments, rather than high-interest loans. For instance, in July 1992 Yeltsin declared at a G-7 summit that a $24 billion package would not save Russia and that foreign direct investment in the amount of several hundred billion dollars was necessary to do the job. Kozyrev, speaking at a Western forum in September 1992, formulated the idea of a new SDI—Strategic Democratic Initiative (a contrast with the old SDI, the Strategic Defense Initiative)—which was to include attracting Western investments to Russia's economy, supporting small and medium-sized businesses, conducting military conversion, and creating favorable conditions for Russia's exports abroad.[27] Most Russian politicians expected a grand bargain with Russia, something comparable to the Marshall Plan or the "500 Days" plan that had been articulated but never implemented during the Gorbachev era. The latter included $100 billion of support over four years for reforming the Soviet Union, alongside an orthodox IMF program.[28]

Such expectations, of course, assumed an unprecedented level of trust in the new Russia by Western leaders and the world business community—a condition that was hardly in place. The West was neither willing nor able to launch something similar to the massive Marshall Plan for postcommunist Russia. All Western nations could offer was to work through the IMF in trying to reform Russia. Germany embarked on the reunification project, which soon proved to be extremely costly. The United States—at the time the key supporter of the new Russia—also was going through an economic downturn and was hardly in a position to put all its eggs in the highly uncertain basket of what was once the largest economy of the communist world.

Gaining the required assistance, not surprisingly, proved to be very difficult, and Russia's overall record was mixed at best. In June 1992, Russia was able to join the International Monetary Fund and the World Bank, which it saw as crucial for creating a market economy. By that time, Yeltsin's chief economic reformer, Yegor Gaidar, had already laid out an ambitious program, which had been predicated on the assistance of the IMF, WB, and European Bank of Reconstruction and Development (EBRD). IMF credits were essential for achieving macroeconomic stabilization and balancing the budget, but they did not (and could not) do much to assist Russia with integration into the world economy. Russia also managed to join the G-7 in July 1992, despite the opposition of both British prime minister John Major and German chancellor Helmut Kohl. Yet the membership did not change much in Russia's economic status. Even psychologically, progress was disappointing—Western leaders saw Russia as an aid recipient, not a donor, and did not treat the newcomer as an equal partner (figures on external aid and investment are shown in table 3.4).

Table 3.4. External Aid and Investment: Russia and Other Recipients, 1990–1995

	World Bank Lending Divided by GDP in 1990 (%)	Direct Investment Divided by GDP in 1990 (%)
Hungary	5.1	32.2
Czech Republic	2.0	12.6
Poland	6.6	11.0
Estonia	1.5	8.6
Turkmenistan	0.4	7.7
Kazakhstan	1.4	1.8
Azerbaijan	0.8	1.1
RUSSIA	0.8	0.6

Source: M. Steven Fish, "The Determinants of Economic Reform in the Post-Communist World," *East European Politics and Societies* 12, no. 1 (1998): 38.

The biggest gains resulted from Russia's emphasis on relationships with the United States. First, in the politically charged atmosphere of Russia's high expectations, Bush, supported by Kohl, announced a $24 billion package in April 1992. At the time, Yeltsin faced particularly strong opposition to his reform at home, as the Congress of People's Deputies revealed the commitments of many to fight privatization and land reform. U.S. president Bill Clinton was even more supportive of Yeltsin, arguing for a global alliance to support democracy and preventing a world "more dangerous in some respects than the dark years of the Cold War." As a result of the new American president's efforts to mobilize the West to support Russia, the Tokyo G-7 summit declared a $43.4 billion program of assistance for Russia.

Aside from that, the progress in either joining Western organizations or mobilizing them to assist Russia in its integration strategy was hardly satisfactory to the Kremlin leadership. With the assistance of the United States, Russia reached an agreement with the Paris Club about restructuring the Soviet debt of $70 million for which it had assumed liability. However, it failed to reach such an agreement with the London Club. Russia also did not manage to join those clubs, even as an observer, until much later. The reformers' efforts to gain broader access to the European Union market were also unsuccessful. Their attempts to dismantle the

Coordinating Committee for Multilateral Export Controls (COCOM) restrictions on trade bore fruit, but only in March 1994. In security affairs, Russia invited the peacekeeping forces of the United Nations and the OSCE into Europe to provide security in the former Soviet Union. Kozyrev wanted to rapidly integrate with European security institutions and even stated Russia's desire to gain membership in NATO. However, in dealing with new security challenges, Russia soon discovered the need to rely on its own army. I return to this point later in the chapter.

Supporting the West's International Security Agenda

Until approximately mid-1993, the new Russia's leaders also loyally supported the West's international security agenda. In Europe, Russia was working toward gaining full membership in all European security institutions, including NATO. Even when NATO announced its plans to expand east, Russia's new rulers initially raised no objections to the process.

Despite traditionally strong ties with Serbia, Russia's leaders also supported the West's agenda in the Balkans. Initially, they avoided even meeting with the leaders of Yugoslavia and sided with the West in condemning the Serbs for atrocities against the Muslims over the independent Bosnian state. In the spring and the summer of 1992, Russia also supported the United Nations' economic sanctions against Yugoslavia and suspension of the country's membership in the OSCE, although Russia's leaders had initially favored negotiations about the punishment of Yugoslavia. Furthermore, Moscow did not object to the United Nations security resolutions authorizing possible use of force against Yugoslavia, and it did not use its veto power when the UN General Assembly voted to expel the country from the United Nations. Later, Yeltsin also supported the Western plan, devised by U.S. secretary of state Cyrus Vance and British foreign secretary David Owen, for a weak confederation in Bosnia-Herzegovina.

The new Russian leaders also shared—even at the cost of the country's traditional ties—the West's arms control agenda. Yeltsin slashed strategic nuclear arsenals by half and also agreed to eliminate all land-based intercontinental ballistic missiles (ICBMs) armed with multiple warheads, while the United States retained such warheads in submarines. The terms of the new agreement, START II, were agreed upon at the June 1992 summit and signed in January 1993. This was an unprecedented move: for the first time in the history of the nuclear arms race, Russia abandoned the heart of its strategic arsenals, while the United States preserved its own. Even Russia's liberal commentators, such as Aleksei Arbatov, criticized the agreement as unbalanced.[29] Yeltsin acknowledged that Russia was sacrificing strategic parity with the United States, but stated that the parity was "ominous" and did not make any sense now that "the fundamental change in the political and economic relations between the United States of America and Russia"[30] had taken place. Until September 1993, Yeltsin also did not see the need to revise the Conventional Forces in Europe (CFE) treaty, which restricted the internal distribution of forces in Russia and gained strong opposition from the military establishment.

In its efforts to rapidly integrate with the West, Russia forfeited billions of dollars in arms sales by abandoning lucrative markets in the third world and supporting Western sanctions against Libya, Iraq, and Yugoslavia. On Iraq, Kozyrev even supported U.S. bombing, as well as UN sanctions. This policy stance began to change only in 1993 under the pressure of those arguing that Russia could not afford to lose Iraq's $7 billion debt to it. Kozyrev also went along with the United States' attempts to restrict Russia's military ties with China, Iran, and India. In the meantime, while Russia was going out of its way to persuade the West that it had been sincere in its integration drive, the West continued to play power politics and did not seem to care to reciprocate. In the arms markets, as the liberal *Izvestiya* noted, whereas Russia's share from 1991 to 1993 dropped from 38 to 17 percent, the U.S. share increased from 30 to 58 percent.[31]

The Neglect of Asia and the Muslim World

Russia's new Westernism had a clear zero-sum component, which was particularly visible in the attitude toward Asia and the Middle East. More partnership with the West meant less of a relationship with the non-Western regions. In the highly ideological mind-set of Kozyrev's team, the East was associated with "backwardness" and "authoritarianism" rather than the "prosperity" and "democracy" of the Western "civilized nations." Again, the identity argument was made: Russia had been too Asiatic already, and it was now time to move away "from its Asian roots of oriental despotism and toward the Western democratic camp."[32] Many in the Westernist camp believed that the non-Western systems, such as China and the Middle Eastern countries, would soon follow the Soviet and Eastern European example and collapse precisely because these systems were "nondemocratic." China was especially despised because of the Tiananmen massacre of Chinese democrats in 1989 and Beijing's support of the anti-Gorbachev coup in Moscow in August 1991.

Russia's relations with China are a clear example of the new leadership's passivity in the eastern direction. Although Gorbachev laid out preconditions for improving relations with China by signing two important joint communiqués and the border treaty, the progress in the relationship between the two sides was stalled by their growing ideological differences. In February 1992, the border treaty was ratified by Russia's Supreme Soviet, but Yeltsin and Kozyrev remained wary of China as anti-Western and critical of Russia's democratic development. The relationships were on hold until late 1992. Russia's leaders and politicians were avoiding even meeting Chinese officials. In March 1992, Kozyrev traveled to China in an attempt to stimulate economic cooperation between the two. However, the trip lasted only thirty hours, and the two sides disagreed on human rights issues by officially concluding that in Russia-China ties, "elements of considerable agreement coexist with different approaches to some quite significant questions."[33]

A similar pattern could be observed in Russia's relations with the Muslim world. Russia's leaders were initially dismissive of the region's significance. Yeltsin ordered the withdrawal of the CIS troops from Nagorno-Karabakh in the Caucasus and simultaneously asked for the deployment of NATO troops as a peacekeeping force there. Despite the growing instability in Afghanistan and central Asia, he also refrained from any serious involvement in the region, leaving the stage to Iran and Turkey. In April 1992 after the mujahideen takeover of Kabul, Kozyrev visited Afghanistan, but that visit, too, was a goodwill gesture more than an effort to develop the mutual relationship. Despite various complaints from the domestic opposition, Russia's officials had no problems with the increased activism of the United States in the region, evident, for instance, in the February 1992 visit of Secretary of State James Baker to central Asia.

Finally, Russia was slow to recognize the role of India and Korea in its foreign policy. Russia's Westernism meant a reduction of Russia-India trade, particularly in the military area. In the Korean Peninsula, Yeltsin and Kozyrev pursued the one-sided policy of favoring the South over the North. In 1992, both Russian leaders proposed signing a treaty of friendship with South Korea to cement their relationship, despite the assessments of Korea specialists that Russia's interests required balanced relations with the two. The ideological dichotomy between the "civilized" pro-Western South and the "barbaric" Stalinist North severely weakened the link to the North, while the anticipated economic benefits of a Moscow-Seoul relationship were not forthcoming. In June 1993, the North announced its first withdrawal from the Nuclear Non-Proliferation Treaty, and Moscow responded by supporting the United States–sponsored sanctions against North Korea.

The Westernizers insisted that relationships with the "barbaric" East were to be limited to those of issues of national security. When in March 1992 leading Statist Sergei Stankevich proposed that Russia reactivate its relations with the Muslim world, Kozyrev replied negatively. The foreign minister denied that Russia had any specific interests in Asia aside from those of maintaining security, and even those had to be addressed within the Western institutional framework. He singled out the need to put joint pressure on North Korea to relinquish its ambitious nuclear program. Later, when the Statist pressures on Kozyrev to view Russia as a "great power" in Eurasia had increased, he reframed his pro-American argument by linking Eurasia to the United States. Writing in *International Affairs* in early 1993, he asserted that Russia's Eurasian location is part of its status: "Anyone who looks at the map will see that the United States is our next-door neighbor in the East." To stress his point, Kozyrev added: "In the East, not the West."[34]

The Yeltsin-Kozyrev Course Backfires

The Yeltsin-Kozyrev course could not be sustained and began to backfire already in late 1992. The IMF-recommended "shock therapy" was introduced in January 1992 and led to severe economic hardship for ordinary people. Political opposition to reform had emerged and had become vocal. The general population was disillusioned with Western aid and disappointed in Yeltsin's overall reform design. Instead of gaining support at home, the reformers' strategy of integrating with the West resulted in public resentment toward the Western Other. A late 1993 poll showed, for example, that two-thirds of Russians were convinced that the West's economic advice represented a deliberate effort to weaken Russia[35]—precisely the message the hard-line opposition to reformers meant to convey to the larger society. In such a context opposition, particularly that of the Statists and conservative Civilizationists, was increasingly successful in challenging the Westernist foreign policies.

The first wake-up call came when Yeltsin had to cancel his trip to Japan to settle the old territorial dispute over the Kuril Islands. To Russia's leaders, Japan was a part of the West and therefore deserved the appropriate attention. The initial strategy was to embrace the 1956 Soviet-Japanese agreement as the basis for regulating the issue and to return two of the four northern islands, seized by Stalin at the close of World War II, to Japan. Yeltsin's visit was planned for September, yet—in a stunning reversal—he canceled the trip, scheduled to begin four days later. The argument about returning the islands provoked immediate negative reaction from Russia's parliament and the military-security lobby. The Supreme Soviet held a special hearing, and the Ministry of Defense openly insisted that geostrategic interests dictated against any military withdrawals from the Kurils. This was a serious blow to Russia's course that revealed that it had major limitations.

Yeltsin-Kozyrev's Balkan policy also came under heavy attack. The former Supreme Soviet emerged as especially active in criticizing the official policy toward the Balkans and even engaged in its own shuttle diplomacy with Belgrade. In December 1992, the Supreme Soviet passed a resolution calling for sanctions on all the warring sides and demanding that Russia use its veto in case of UN consideration of military intervention in the region. As a result of those pressures, Russia first abstained from a UN vote on additional sanctions against Yugoslavia and then refused to send its blue-helmet troops from Croatia into Sarajevo to help police a UN-brokered military agreement. The opposition's pressures on Russia's foreign policy in the Balkans further intensified in 1994 when NATO launched air strikes against the Bosnian Serbs.

In this increasingly politicized context, NATO made a decision to expand eastward by incorporating members of the former Soviet bloc in Eastern Europe. The decision provided domestic nationalist opposition with additional arguments and resources to mobilize against the Westernist course. If the West wanted to expand its military alliance without planning to include Russia in it, this could be and was interpreted by the opposition as a threat. Military and security services were especially active in arguing this position. Yevgeni Primakov, then director of Russia's Foreign Intelligence Service, issued a sharp criticism of the expansion, referring to the historical memory of Cold War hostilities and warning that it would result in a new isolation of Russia. The military responded by adopting in November 1993 a new doctrine, which now proclaimed Russia's immediate periphery the area of its geopolitical interests and most vital concerns. Russia's military, military industrialists, and security services also opposed concessions to the West in arms reductions and sales.

In mid-1993, largely in response to growing domestic criticism, the attitude of Russia's leaders began to change. The devastating December elections made it painfully clear that the sought-after Integration with the West was not meant to happen and that Westernizers needed to adjust to new realities. The elections brought many anti-Western forces into the parliament, partly the result of the state's uncompromisingly pro-Western policies. The victory of Vladimir Zhirinovski's extreme nationalist party reflected, in part, state neglect of the army and its needs. In response, Kozyrev spoke of a serious correction of his course. Immediately after the December elections, he announced changes in Russia's foreign policy according to the voters' preferences. Kozyrev proclaimed that these changes would include declaring the former Soviet region the sphere of Russia's vital interests, and the continuation of a military presence in regions where Russia had traditionally been dominant. Russia's leaders also refused to cooperate with NATO. Furthermore, faced with hard-line opposition at home, they had to reject the offer to join the Partnership for Peace program, which was designed to preserve cooperative military ties with the alliance.

The proclaimed change hardly meant the strategic reappraisal of the foreign policy course. Rather, it should be understood as a series of tactical concessions that reflected the changing balance of domestic power. Statists, such as presidential adviser Sergei Stankevich and Russia's ambassador to Washington, Vladimir Lukin, had formulated a "Eurasian" alternative to Kozyrev's "Atlanticist" foreign policy, and the overall pressures on the official course were considerable. The opposition pressed for more active policies toward Asia and the Middle East. By that time, Yeltsin had visited China in December 1992 and recovered some of the lost trade between the two countries. Kozyrev, too, had explicitly acknowledged the need for Russia to boost its foreign policy activities in China, India, and the East in general. None of these corrections, however, proceeded from principal reevaluation of the strategic beliefs that had underlain the Westernist course.

ISOLATIONISM IN THE FORMER SOVIET REGION

Yeltsin-Kozyrev's isolationism toward the former Soviet republics was an extension of their radical Westernist beliefs. Eager to integrate with the West, the new leaders had no time to wait for the republics to pursue similar policies. Nor did they feel responsible for assisting their neighbors in their transformation. Russia had to go West alone and, in order to overcome potential resistance from the ex-leaders of the republics, it had to erect nationalist economic, political, and security barriers against the former Soviet nations.

Isolationist Thinking

Westernizers justified the isolationist course on economic, political, and cultural grounds. Economically, they argued, Russia had been turned into an "internal colony" of the Soviet Union and, as a result, suffered from being a core of the Soviet empire even more than all other republics. As the largest and the wealthiest nation in the region, Russia had to subsidize the republics instead of selling its raw materials, such as oil and natural gas, at the world market's prices. Were Russia to continue to serve as an economic locomotive, the argument went, it would become the first victim of such generosity. The roots of this argument can be traced to Gorbachev's era when Yeltsin's umbrella organization, Democratic Russia, presented itself as an anti-imperial movement by emphasizing the autonomy of Russia and other republics and even openly calling for the dissolution of the Soviet Union. The Soviet Union was presented as an "empire" that was to be dismantled for the sake of Russian prosperity.

Throughout the political campaigns of 1990 and 1991, Yeltsin had advanced the "Russia-victim" argument, and it was his advisers who eventually wrote a scenario for dissolving the union. Ironically, the argument was borrowed from Russian anti-Western nationalists, who often complained about the Russian burden of providing for the rest of the union (although they never wanted to break up the union).

Furthermore, the post-Soviet Westernizers believed that during the Soviet era Russia also suffered politically and culturally, and it should now rebuild its identity in nonimperial or "civic" terms. Valeri Tishkov, the director of the Institute of Ethnology and Anthropology and the minister for nationalities in 1992, had provided the intellectual justification and first put forward the concept of a civic nation publicly in 1989. The central thrust of viewing Russia as a civic nation was its deethnification, or the removal of the categories of ethnicity and religion from the identity-building project. Tishkov argued that Russia should form a civic Russian (*rossiyskaya*) nation, or a community of all citizens of the Russian Federation regardless of their cultural and religious differences, rather than any form of ethnic Russian (*russkaya*) nation. Domestically, the new vision categorized Russia within its current post-Soviet borders as a political nation, and one of "co-citizenship."[36] Externally, it meant to relieve the new Russia of responsibility for the Soviet policies and their historical legacies in the region. In particular, Russia was not to be responsible for the well-being of twenty-five to thirty million ethnic Russians—about 30 percent of the homeland Russians—who resided in the former Soviet republics outside Russia.

The liberal foreign policy community supported the isolationist component in the country's national interest. For instance, one prominent report of the Foreign Ministry's Institute of International Relations warned against Russia's assuming the role of a new core in the Commonwealth of Independent States. It insisted that Russia's key interest was in entering the G-7 as a full-fledged participant, thereby moving from the periphery of the world economy to its core. The ambition of becoming the CIS's center would make it impossible to meet that key interest and therefore Russia had to be prepared to "give up the CIS in favor of orientation toward Europe."[37]

Political and Security Isolationism

Politically, Russia's isolationism aimed at separating from the ex-Soviet republics institutionally. Yeltsin and Kozyrev concentrated on strengthening sovereignty and independence from the former Soviet region and its transnational institutional umbrella, the CIS. The organization emerged to do away with the Soviet Union and initially—before it included all ex-republics except the Baltic ones—had had only Russia, Ukraine, and Belarus as members. Yeltsin, who had proposed the CIS mainly in order to defeat his political opponent Gorbachev, never meant for the organization to facilitate cooperation and interdependence in the region. Rather, he wanted it to complete the ex-Soviet republics' political and economic separation, and that vision permeated the organization's founding agreements and subsequent seminal documents, such as the CIS charter. In its practical policy, Russia preferred to deal with its neighbors on a bilateral, rather than multilateral, basis. It was also far from active in relations with the states of the region. Despite Kozyrev's rhetoric about the priority of the CIS in Russia's foreign policy, his first trips were to Western Europe, North America, and other regions of the world. Apart from a quick visit to Estonia, he first traveled to the former Soviet region only in April 1992. By July of the same year, Russia had opened only one embassy in the region, in Kiev. Moscow assumed that, even if some of the former states were to eventually gravitate toward Russia, this would happen much later and on a market basis. That attitude began to change in 1993 when Russia initiated the CIS Economic Union agreement, which was supposed to develop multilateral economic cooperation.

In security matters, Russia's isolationist policies reflected the desire to reduce to a minimum responsibility for maintaining order in the former Soviet region. The Russian analyst Alexander Pikayev captured four specific goals that the Kremlin sought to accomplish: the fastest possible withdrawal of Russian troops from outside Russia; tacit support of the control introduced by governments in the former Soviet republics on former Soviet troops; ignoring separatist tendencies within individual CIS states and maintaining relations with the central governments; and inviting foreign participation in settling conflicts in the post-Soviet region.[38]

Russia's officials tried to accomplish those goals until approximately mid-1992. Yeltsin ordered the withdrawal of troops from Nagorno-Karabakh, while simultaneously asking for the deployment of NATO troops as a peacekeeping force there. When Chechnya proclaimed independence in November 1991, he ruled out military intervention as a policy option. Yeltsin also did not initially oppose Ukraine, the largest CIS state outside Russia, taking control over the former Soviet troops located on the republic's territory. Furthermore, by establishing Russia's Ministry of Defense in April 1992, Yeltsin indicated his unwillingness to maintain the collective status of the former Soviet Armed Forces, which had been favored by the central Asian leaders. A signatory of the CIS collective security treaty (May 1992), Russia did little to activate the treaty, and over the year, it continued to seriously discuss the possibility of deploying the UN or NATO peacekeeping troops in the areas of ethnic conflict. Nor did it show serious concern over the status of ethnic Russians in the former Soviet states.

The leadership's position showed signs of change only when military conflicts in various parts of the former Soviet Union threatened to spill over to Russia. The first challenge came from Moldova in the spring of 1992. The intention of Moldova's leadership to reunite with Romania had provoked violent secessionism in the Transdniestr area, which gravitated to Russia economically and culturally. Moldova's efforts to involve the OSCE had failed to produce any results in a timely manner, and Russia intervened to stop widespread fighting. It put the fourteenth former Soviet division under its control, negotiated a cease-fire, and took on the task of maintaining peace in the region. Kozyrev at first condemned the army involvement and rejected the opportunity to establish ties with the separatist Transdniestr leaders. By late June, however, even he favored an intervention and deployment of Russia's military forces. This proved critical for preventing a further spread of violence and civil war in Moldova. It also established the precedent for further interventions in Tajikistan, Georgia, and elsewhere.

Economic Isolationism

In economic matters, Russia planned no coordination with the former republics. In the aftermath of the failed coup of August 1991, Yeltsin first formulated the idea of Russia going it alone as a matter of economic strategy. In his speech to the Russian Congress of People's Deputies, he committed himself to the strategy of shock therapy—or freeing up all prices by the end of the year, rapid privatization of both industry and land, large reductions in state spending, and a tough monetary policy. He argued that Russia must go first and that, by so doing, it would provide an example for other republics.[39] Yeltsin shared the widely held liberal convictions that the republics were nothing but a "burden [girya] on the Russian legs," and that Russia had little choice but to "break away" (uiti v otryv) from the former Soviet Union.

Acting on those convictions, Russia reformed its currency by unilaterally withdrawing from the ruble zone. In July 1993, it stopped money supplies to the ex-republics and withdrew old Soviet/Russian ruble notes from circulation in its territory. Russia had earlier pledged to consult with the republics in matters of economic policy, which had been written into the CIS founding principles in the Minsk agreement of December 1991. Yet, despite those obligations, it chose to proceed with the currency reform, as well as price deregulation, which immediately created a crisis for the republics relying on the ruble in their transactions. In addition, Russia began erecting trade barriers as soon as the Soviet Union fell apart, and maintained them at a relatively high level even after most-favored-nation and free-trade agreements with the republics were concluded. In part, those policies responded to relative trade disadvantages for Russia, since it had continued to export goods to the republics at prices considerably below those of the world market. Such policies also reflected Russian dissatisfaction with the state of payments by a number of republics in the aftermath of the Soviet disintegration. Both considerations further reinforced the leadership's belief that economic isolationism from the cash-stripped republics and extensive ties with the West would serve Russia's national interest best.

Cultural Isolationism

Finally, Russia acted on some of its cultural isolationist beliefs. Until 1993, the government subscribed to the civic identity policies as outlined by Minister of Nationalities Tishkov. Tishkov argued for understanding nationality as citizenship; for abolishing the principle of ethnic autonomies; and for giving priority to individual, rather than collective, rights. In November 1991, the government confirmed its commitment to the civic identity project by adopting the citizenship law. The law recognized all those living in the territory of the Russian Federation as citizens, regardless of their ethnic characteristics, and called a citizen of the Russian Federation *rossiyanin* (Russian defined in civic terms), not *russki* (ethnic Russian). In foreign relations the government denied any responsibility for ethnic Russians outside territorial Russia. Although Yeltsin had made some statements about the need to defend "our compatriots abroad," Kozyrev argued until the autumn of 1992 that ethnic Russians outside Russia did not constitute a special problem for the Russian government.

Many of Tishkov's principles were never implemented, however. The citizenship law was not fully consistent with the new vision of civic identity, as it allowed all citizens of the Soviet Union outside Russia to obtain Russian citizenship by a simple process of registration. The government never issued new nonethnic passports to all citizens of Russia. Nor did it ever redivide the country's regions along nonethnic principles or try to legally ban Russia's ethnically based parties.

The Opposition Challenges the Isolationist Course

The isolationist course found a formidable opposition. Partly as a result of new institutional channels that had become available under the new political system, Statists and conservative Civilizationists grew stronger over time. With the collapse of the communist authority structure, various agencies could more readily assert themselves.

Former Soviet managers and military industrialists with strong regional ties were the prime force opposing the government's economic isolationist policies. United by the Civic Union, they linked the isolationist course to disastrous outcomes, arguing for joint solutions and integration within the former Soviet region. The Civic Union and its Russian heir, the Union of Industrialists and Entrepreneurs, consolidated ties with trade unions and established branches throughout the entire post-Soviet space. It was impossible to ignore these groups' arguments because of collapsing economies in all the successor states. In the two years after 1991, all of these states experienced negative economic growth rates and a breakdown of their trade, production, labor, and energy ties. The non-Russian republics were hit particularly hard. Their trade structure was developed exclusively out of demands of the former Soviet "single economic complex," and they were forced to trade primarily with Russia and one another, rather than with countries outside the Soviet borders. The share of interrepublic trade comprised up to 85–90 percent of the republics' total trade. Furthermore, their industrial structure did not favor the establishment of full-fledged economies: some were primary-resource suppliers, while others specialized in manufacturing. Many were asymmetrically dependent on Russia's market, fuel, and supplies, and this dependence further complicated the task of creating independent economies. A number of the republics—such as Armenia, Belarus, Kazakhstan, Kyrgyzstan, and Tajikistan—were especially critical of Russia's isolationism. Russia, too, was hit hard, and its economy contracted severely (see table 3.5).

Table 3.5.   Post-Soviet Economic Decline: Russia Relative to Other Ex-Republics

	GNP Growth over Previous Year				
	1990	*1991*	*1992*	*1993*	*1994*
Armenia	−7	−11	−52	−15	5
Azerbaijan	−12	−1	−23	−23	−22
Belarus	−3	−1	−10	−12	−22
Estonia	−8	−11	−14	−7	6
Georgia	−12	−14	−40	−39	−35
Latvia	3	−8	−35	−15	2
Lithuania	−5	−13	−38	−24	2
Moldova	−2	−12	−29	−9	2
Kazakhstan	0	−13	−13	−12	−25
Kyrgyzstan	3	−5	−25	−16	−27
RUSSIA	−4	−13	−19	−12	−15
Tajikistan	−2	−7	−29	−11	−21
Turkmenistan	2	−5	−5	−10	−20
Ukraine	−3	−12	−17	−17	−23
Uzbekistan	2	−1	−11	−2	−3

Source: Bert Van Selm, *The Economics of the Soviet Break-up* (London: Routledge, 1997), 25.

The army grew especially prominent in opposing the Kremlin's security policies. Responding to growing pressures of instability in the post-Soviet area, some military branches openly challenged civilian authorities. Moldova is a case in point. When in May 1992 Yeltsin publicly announced the upcoming withdrawal of the Fourteenth Army, the defense minister, General Pavel Grachev, immediately corrected him, saying that the division could leave only after the conflict in the area had been defused. When in June of the same year Yeltsin appointed General Lebed to command the Fourteenth Army as a neutral peacekeeping force, Lebed did not hide that he saw his mandate differently. He likened Moldova's officials to "fascists" and defended ethnic Russians in the area. Within the political class, the position of defending Russians in the entire former Soviet region was strongly reinforced in both parliament and the executive branch. Parliament's International Affairs Committee, chaired by Yevgeni Ambartsumov and Vice President Aleksandr Rutskoi, was particularly vocal.

The larger population, too, opposed the isolationist policies. Ethnic autonomies resisted the civic nation project out of fear of losing their own identities. Many Russians also could not accept Russia's new national identity and continued to favor the preservation of strong cultural ties across the former Soviet region. Polls indicated that most Russians supported voluntary reunification of the ex-Soviet republics with Russia.[40] A powerful identification of many Russians outside Russia with their homeland, and vice versa, emboldened conservative Civilizationist thinking and organizations, such as the Congress of Russian Communities, to speak on the Civilizationists' behalf. Kozyrev attempted to protest against the growing influence of the military and nationalists on foreign policy, but without much effect. Yeltsin and Kozyrev therefore saw their agenda being taken away by the military, the Ministry of Defense, and conservative members of the political class.

Table 3.6 (on page 88) summarizes various dependencies and interdependencies between Russia and other former republics.

The Leadership Signals Change

All these developments made Yeltsin and Kozyrev depart from their initial isolationism and proclaim, at least rhetorically, their understanding of the priority relations with the ex-Soviet republics. The new emphasis was also explicitly acknowledged in the official Foreign Policy Concept of the Russian Federation, which was adopted in 1993. In response to pressures from the Statists, the officials spoke about Russia's "special responsibility" in the former Soviet Union. In June 1993, Yeltsin told a group of military officers that Russia must maintain and formalize its military presence in Moldova, Georgia, Armenia, and central Asia. Kozyrev echoed

Table 3.6. Russia and the Ex-Republics: Economic, Military, and Cultural Dependencies

	Share of Russia in a Republic's Trade in 1987	Russian Interrepublican Trade (% of Foreign Trade in 1990)	Ethnic Military Bases and Troops, 1993	Russians (% of Population in 1989)	Fluency in Russian by Titular Nationality (% of Population in 1989)
Armenia	49.7	90	5,000	1.6	44.3
Azerbaijan	52.7	88		5.6	31.7
Belarus	62.6	87	30,000	13.2	60.4
Estonia	58.3	92	5,000	30.3	33.6
Georgia	55.5	86	20,000	6.3	31.8
Latvia	53.5	89	18,000	33.9	65.7
Lithuania	64.9	90		9.4	37.4
Moldova	50.0	88	8,000	12.9	53.3
Kazakhstan	64.4	89		37.8	62.9
Kyrgyzstan	48.2	86		21.5	36.9
RUSSIA	—	61			
Tajikistan	45.0	87	23,000	7.6	30.0
Turkmenistan	45.2	93		9.5	27.6
Ukraine	72.9	82		22.1	59.5
Uzbekistan	51.4	89		8.4	22.2

Sources: Michael Bradshaw, *The Economic Effects of Soviet Dissolution* (London: Royal Institute of International Affairs, 1993), 27; Constantine Michalopoulos and David Tarr, *Trade and Payments Arrangements for States of the Former USSR* (Washington, DC: World Bank, 1992); *New York Times,* November 30, 1993, A12; Graham Smith, *Post-Soviet States* (London: Arnold, 1999), 36.

these sentiments by emphasizing the former Soviet region as a "zone of special responsibility and special interest."[41] The concept of involving international institutions, such as the OSCE or NATO, in solving conflicts in the region was also receding into the past. Convinced that Russia's troops would be most effective in maintaining security, Moscow also asked the UN to grant Russia special peacekeeping power in the region. In addition, Moscow no longer seemed to be as eager to predicate its policies upon the West's recognition. This was the case even once the champion of Westernist thinking, Kozyrev, complained about Western claims of Russian neoimperialism in the former Soviet region and insisted that Russia would not listen to the West's "lectures."[42]

The reevaluation of rhetorical policy had been completed in early 1994, when the foreign minister announced the need to follow the preferences of the voters after the nationalist victory in the December elections. The emphasis on the civic nation identity stance had changed, with Tishkov resigning and the government proclaiming its commitment to promoting dual citizenship in the former Soviet region. It looked as if the leadership indeed learned its lessons from the Statist coalition. Some of the former opponents, such as the parliamentarian Ambartsumov, even conceded that Kozyrev's approach had changed sufficiently to make him retract his call for the minister's resignation.[43]

ASSESSMENT

The new foreign policy project of Integration with the West proved to be a flawed one and was soon defeated by the opposing Statist coalition. The Statists acknowledged the need to cooperate with the West in creating a market economy and viable democratic institutions, but insisted that those goals should be subjected to the objective of strengthening Russia's great power status. Several developments assisted the Statists in defeating the Westernizers. First, the West itself did not satisfy Yeltsin's and Kozyrev's expectations when it treated Russia more as a dependent client than as a full participant in a coalition of Western nations. By not extending to Russia's leadership the sought-after recognition, the West contributed to the already growing feelings of public alienation from the new Westernist course. Second, the Russian domestic context greatly favored the revival of Statist thinking. The political culture was supportive of independent state and great power status, and new threats both inside (Chechnya, growing crime, and sharp decline in living standards) and outside the country (military conflicts in the periphery) created the environment permissive to the rise of Statist opposition. In challenging the Westernizers, the Statists also successfully exploited some cultural affinities of ethnic Russians, as well as institutional channels available in the new political system.

The departure during the second half of 1993 of Russia's leaders from their initially pro-Western foreign policy should not be understood as if their entire course was a calculation of strategic benefits. Nor does it mean, as some Western observers argue, that Russia had in mind to use the West in order to restore its weakened power capabilities and to rebuild its empire.[44] To argue this is to confuse the post-1993 tactical concessions and politically driven opportunism of Russia's leaders with their strategic beliefs. It is also to ascribe one's own realist viewpoint to policymakers, who made sense of the world in liberal categories of cooperation and integration. Russia's genuine beliefs had been revealed in these leaders' pre-1993 actions, and these beliefs unmistakably betray radical Western-ism and liberal institutionalism. After 1993, these beliefs were modified in response to opposition pressures, but this modification must not be equated with full acceptance of Statist or Civilizationist beliefs.

This section provides a more detailed analysis of the Westernizers' foreign policy record and summarizes lessons of their defeat.

The Record

The policy of Integration with the West was supposed to finally achieve Western recognition, by which Russia's new leaders meant full moral, political, and material support for their country as a new pro-Western democracy that broke away from anti-Western totalitarianism. Their highly inflated expectations were born in the political struggle with Gor-bachev, who they believed was much too conservative to achieve "true" recognition from the West. Since the West was skeptical of Gorbachev's socialist reform design, Russian Westernizers assumed it to be on their side and in full accord with their pro-Western policy course. Once they had arrived in power, they went as far as possible in proclaiming the convergence of Russia's interests and identity with those of the West. Their new concept of national interest, which emphasized rapid economic and political modernization, was designed to attract Western assistance and to prove that Russia was indeed a part of the West. The concept and the policy based on it proved to be a failure if we are to judge them by the earlier-specified criteria of security, welfare, autonomy, and identity. Too many eggs were put in one basket. Too many important national priori-ties were sacrificed in order to acquire the recognition of Western leaders, who were interested mainly in preventing a reemergence of Russia as a security threat.

Table 3.7 summarizes the record of Westernism.

Table 3.7.   The Record of the Westernist Course

Security	New threats in Moldova, central Asia, and the Caucasus
Welfare	Macroeconomic stabilization
	New poverty and collapsed social services
	Industrial stagnation
Autonomy	Dependence on Western lending agencies
	Dependence on Western security policies
Identity	Hurt Russian pride

Russia's Westernizers could hardly take credit for removing the external threat of the West as a result of their pro-Western foreign policy. By the time they assumed power, such a threat had already been eliminated thanks to Gorbachev's efforts. However, new security threats reemerged in the former Soviet region in the form of military conflicts in Moldova, central Asia (Tajikistan), and the Caucasus (Georgia and Chechnya), and Russia's leaders did little to preempt those threats or to react to them in a timely fashion. They acted under pressure from the opposition, which had little trust in the West as the ultimate peacemaker in the region or as the central object of Russia's foreign policy.

Nor could Westernizers convincingly defend their foreign policy record in social and economic welfare. Their hopes that a proclaimed commitment to Western values and shock therapy, as the strategy of marketization, would bring sufficient private investments and assistance to quickly revive the economy did not materialize. The heavy reliance on IMF and World Bank loans only allowed Russia to stabilize the economy in macroeconomic terms. However, the old economic structure remained in place, and the state did little to conduct an institutional reform or to assist former Soviet managers and workers in their difficult transition to a capitalist type of economy. High interest rates for repaying the borrowed money, collapsed social services, skyrocketed poverty, and stagnation in most economic sectors were the price of the shock therapy the Westernizers used as a method of bringing Russia into the family of rich Western nations. In the meantime, Western investments remained scarce. The radical policies alienated a considerable portion of the elites and the general public, and many Russians developed resentment toward Western nations, particularly the United States. For instance, during 1993–1995, the number of those viewing the United States as a threat increased from 26 to 44 percent among the general public and from 27 to 53 percent among elites.[45]

In addition, Russia developed a considerable dependency on Western lending agencies, with negative implications for its policy autonomy. The opposition charged that Russia's foreign policies were being made in

Washington, and the public increasingly believed that Russia was indeed ceding its autonomy to the West in economic and other affairs. In 1995, 44 percent of the elites and 75 percent of the population believed that the economy was essentially in foreign hands.[46] Additionally, the number of those viewing the West as seeking to weaken Russia also increased. The increased dependency on the West in economic affairs went hand in hand with a loss of autonomy in security affairs, as Washington was often dictating Moscow's foreign policy in such critical areas as the Balkans and Iraq. In the meantime, Russia was losing its traditional allies in Asia and the Middle East.

These developments indicated the pro-Western course's inability to alleviate Russian hurt pride and identity. Not only has the foreign policy course failed to provide the nation with security and welfare, but it also failed to engage the Statist component of Russia's identity. Collapse of the Soviet state, the Western encouragement of shock therapy in Russia's economic reform, and the decision to expand NATO toward Russia's borders prompted the Kremlin to reevaluate the course of integration with the West.

Lessons of the Failed Course

Much like Gorbachev's New Thinking, Yeltsin and Kozyrev's Integration with the West failed as a foreign policy course. Yet the lessons one can learn from its failure are somewhat different from those of the New Thinking failure.

First, much like Gorbachev's New Thinking course, the post-Soviet Westernism divorced itself from domestic and international power considerations and could not be successful in the face of the growing opposition from both Statists and conservative Civilizationists. However, Westernizers went much further in neglecting potential opposition to their course. Unlike Gorbachev, who had first emerged as a consensus builder with some support secured among military and party officials, Yeltsin and Kozyrev did little to reform the country "from the middle." Instead, their strategy was to seize the moment and impose their vision on the rest of the society, while it was not yet mobilized to respond.

Second, unlike Gorbachev, who had offered his country a culturally distinct perspective and an opportunity to reformulate its sense of national pride, the new Russia's leaders were astonishingly unimaginative in their vision of national identity. Ultimately, what were the odds that a country with centuries-old distinct economic, political, and cultural experiences would be satisfied merely with a status as a "part of the West"? The kind of Western recognition Russia's Westernizers sought was impossible to obtain, and it was naïve to predicate a foreign policy course on such recognition, often at the expense of national history and traditions. At the time when Russian society was desperately searching for self-definition after the end of the Soviet system, Westernizers gave little consideration to the country's past experience and, by offering it the "solution" of becoming a part of the West, they denied it the very legitimacy of a search for its own post-Soviet identity.

Not surprisingly, the course that was both politically and culturally insensitive could only lead to the strengthening of Russian nationalists, who were at most sanguine about the West. Russia's core perceptions of the West changed from those of a friend or a strategic partner to those of a potential threat. Hard-line opposition did not come to power, as Yeltsin and Kozyrev had feared. But the economic and political system that emerged was hardly reminiscent of those of the West and was far from the one the Westernizers had hoped for. In the economic realm, Russia built not a free-market model of capitalism, but rather what scholars call oligarchical capitalism. Under oligarchical capitalism, the economy is largely controlled by and divided among those with business interests in the West. In this environment, the Western assistance enriched the elites and provided support for the new regime that was evolving away from democracy. Oligarchs began to play the role of the new post-Soviet *nomenklatura* and influenced many key decisions of the state. In both Russia and the West, observers raised questions of the aid donors' responsibility for such developments.[47] In the realm of political and legal institutions, Russia developed a superpresidential system with few effective checks and balances. Under the 1993 constitution, the president gained enormous power and could exercise it to prevent a strongly integrated opposition from emerging.

Such was the irony of the radically pro-Western course that it could produce only non-Western, at times even anti-Western, economic and political outcomes.

NOTES

1. Andrei Kozyrev, "Rossiya v novom mire," *Mezhdunarodnaya zhizn'* 3–4, (1992): 92; Kozyrev, "The Lagging Partnership," *Foreign Affairs* 73, no. 3 (1994): 59.

2. Leonid Gordon and Leonid Fridman, "Rossiya—velikaya derzhava vtorogo ranga," *Nezavisimaya gazeta*, April 4, 1995.

3. Francis Fukuyama, "The End of History?," *National Interest* 16 (Summer 1989).

4. Timothy Garton Ash, *The Magic Lantern: The Revolution of '89 as Witnessed in Warsaw, Budapest, Berlin and Prague* (London: Vintage, 1989), 154.

5. The expression is that of U.S. president Jimmy Carter's former national security adviser Zbigniew Brzezinski. See his book *The Grand Failure: The Birth and*

Death of Communism in the Twentieth Century (New York: Charles Scribner's Sons, 1989).

6. William Pfaff, "Redefining World Power," *Foreign Affairs* 70, no. 1 (1991): 48.

7. Andrei Kozyrev, *Preobrazheniye* (Moscow: Mezhdunarodnye otnosheniya, 1995), 16.

8. Kozyrev, "Rossiya v novom mire," 93; Kozyrev, "Russia and Human Rights," *Slavic Review* 51, no. 2 (1992).

9. Kozyrev, "Rossiya v novom mire," 93.

10. As cited in George Breslauer, *Gorbachev and Yeltsin as Leaders* (Cambridge: Cambridge University Press, 2002), 157.

11. The terminology is that of Kozyrev. "Russia: A Chance for Survival," *Foreign Affairs* 71, no. 2 (1992): 9–10.

12. See, especially, Gennadi Zyuganov, *Drama vlasti* (Moscow: Paleya, 1993); *Rossiya i sovremennyi mir* (Moscow: "Obozrevatel," 1995); and *Geografiya pobedy* (Moscow, 1998).

13. Aleksandr Dugin, *Konservativnaya revolyutsiya* (Moscow: Arktogeya, 1994) and *Osnovy geopolitiki* (Moscow: Arktogeya, 1997).

14. Nikolai Fon Kreitor, "Stoletiye novogo mira," *Molodaya gvardiya* 6 (1998). See also Natalya Narochnitskaya, "Natsional'nyi interes Rossiyi," *Mezhdunarodnaya zhizn'* 3–4 (1992); Aleksandr Khatsankov, "Gorchakov—koshmar Kozyreva," *Den'*, August 8–14, 1992; El'giz Pozdnyakov, "Geopoliticheski kollaps i Rossiya," *Mezhdunarodnaya zhizn'* 8–9, 1992.

15. See, for example, Dmitri Furman, "Rossiiskiye demokraty i raspad soyuza," *Vek XX i mir* 1 (1992).

16. Boris Kapustin, "Rossiya i Zapad na puti k miru mirov," *Kentavr* 1, no. 2 (1993); Yuri Krasin, "O rossiyskikh natsional'nykh interesakh," *Svobodnaya mysl'* 3 (1996).

17. Vladimir Sogrin, "Zapadnyi liberalizm i rossiyskiye reformy," *Svobodnaya mysl'* 1 (1996): 32.

18. Andranik Migranyan, "Podlinnye i mnimye orientiry vo vneshnei politike," *Rossiyskaya gazeta*, August 2, 1992.

19. See "Rossiya v novom mire," *Mezhdunarodnaya zhizn'* 3–4 (1992).

20. See, especially, "Strategiya dlya Rossiyi," *Nezavisimaya gazeta*, August 1992, and "Strategiya—2," *Nezavisimaya gazeta*, May 27, 1994. The term "Near Abroad," coined to refer to Russia's former Soviet periphery, was introduced in one of the first statements of the organization.

21. Andrei Kozyrev, "Partnership with the West: A Test of Strength," *Moscow News*, October 25, 1992.

22. Cited in Richter, "Russian Foreign Policy and the Politics of National Identity," in *The Sources of Russian Foreign Policy after the Cold War*, ed. Celeste A. Wallander (Boulder, CO: Westview Press, 1996), 86. After the December 1993 elections, even leaders of Gaidar's radically pro-Western Russia's Choice Party, among them Sergei Blagovolin and Boris Fedorov, acknowledged in private that it was a mistake on their part not to present themselves as a patriotic/nationalist group concerned about Russia's great power status. Astrid Tuminez, "Russian Nationalism and the National Interest in Russian Foreign Policy," in *The Sources of Russian Foreign Policy*, 65.

23. Zbigniew Brzezinski, "The Premature Partnership," *Foreign Affairs* 73, no. 1 (1994).

24. Andrei Kozyrev, "The Lagging Partnership," *Foreign Affairs* 73, no. 3 (1994): 59.

25. Andrei Kozyrev, "Don't Threaten Us," *New York Times*, March 18, 1994, A28. In his book, Kozyrev writes about the evolution in his thinking toward Statism, acknowledging that by 1994, he "definitively had turned into a democrat-'Statist'" and "became convinced that Russia was doomed to remain a great power." Kozyrev, *Preobrazheniye*, 38–39.

26. This attitude was well reflected in the documents of Russian-U.S. summits in 1992 and 1993. In June 1992, for example, Yeltsin and Bush signed a Charter of Russian-American Partnership and Friendship, affirming "the indivisibility of the security of North America and Europe," which would "rest on lasting common values" and a common commitment to "democracy, the supremacy of law . . . and support for human rights." Leszek Buszynski, *Russian Foreign Policy after the Cold War* (New York: Praeger, 1996), 54.

27. Andrei Kozyrev, "Osnovnaya opasnost'—v nomenklaturnom revanshe," *Nezavisimaya gazeta*, October 8, 1992.

28. The figure of $100 billion was calculated as the equivalent per capita value of aid to Eastern Europe from 1989 to 1991. Nigel Gould-Davies and Ngaire Woods, "Russia and the IMF," *International Affairs* 75, no. 1 (1999): 5.

29. Buszynski, *Russian Foreign Policy*, 57.

30. Robert H. Donaldson and Joseph L. Nogee, *The Foreign Policy of Russia: Changing Systems, Enduring Interests* (Armonk, NY: M. E. Sharpe, 2002), 193.

31. Peter Shearman, "Russian Policy toward the United States," in *Russian Foreign Policy since 1990*, ed. Peter Shearman (Boulder, CO: Westview Press, 1995), 121.

32. Yevgeni Bazhanov, "Russian Policy toward China," in *Russian Foreign Policy*, 161.

33. Bazhanov, "Russian Policy toward China," 170.

34. Shearman, "Russian Policy toward the United States," 129.

35. Donaldson and Nogee, *The Foreign Policy of Russia*, 198.

36. Vera Tolz, *Russia: Inventing the Nation* (Oxford: Arnold, 2001), 250.

37. Andrei V. Zagorski et al., *Posle raspada SSSR: Rossiya v novom mire* (Moscow: MGIMO, 1992), 6–11, 15, 17.

38. Alexander A. Pikayev, "The Russian Domestic Debate on Policy towards the 'Near Abroad,'" in *Peacekeeping and the Role of Russia in Eurasia*, ed. Lena Jonson and Clive Archer (Boulder, CO: Westview Press, 1996), 52.

39. David Kotz and Fred Weir, *Revolution from Above: The Demise of the Soviet System* (London: Routledge, 1997), 167.

40. In 1994, the rate of approval among Russians outside Russia ranged from 84 percent in Ukraine and Belarus, the two Slavic states, to about 50 percent in four central Asian states, with Kazakhstan falling in between these two poles ("Opinion Poll of the Newly Independant States," United States Information Agency, September 1994, 1).

41. Astrid Tuminez, "Russian Nationalism and the National Interest," in *The Sources of Russian Foreign Policy*, 59.

42. Wynne Russell, "Russian Relations with the 'Near Abroad,'" in *Russian Foreign Policy* (Boulder, CO: Westview Press, 1995), 65.

43. Russell, "Russian Relations with the 'Near Abroad,'" 65.

44. The earliest case of such an interpretation of Russia's early post-Soviet foreign policy was made by Brzezinski, "The Premature Partnership." See also Allen C. Lynch, "The Realism of Russia's Foreign Policy," *Europe-Asia Studies* 53, no. 1 (2001): 140.

45. William Zimmerman, *The Russian People and Foreign Policy* (Princeton, NJ: Princeton University Press, 2002), 91.

46. Zimmerman, *The Russian People*, 92.

47. For Western scholarship, see especially Peter Rutland, "Mission Impossible? The IMF and the Failure of the Market Transition in Russia," *Review of International Studies* 25, no. 5 (1999); Janine Wedel, *Collision and Collusion: The Strange Case of Western Aid to Eastern Europe, 1990–1997* (London: Palgrave, 1998); Peter Reddaway and Dmitri Glinski, *The Tragedy of Russia's Reforms: Market Bolshevism against Democracy* (Washington, DC: United States Institute of Peace, 2001).

4

New Security
Challenges and
Great Power Balancing

Russia has been and remains a great power, and its policy toward the
outside world should correspond to that status.

Russia is both Europe and Asia, and this geopolitical location continues to play a tremendous role in formulation of its foreign policy. . . .
Geopolitical values are constants that cannot be abolished by historical
developments.

—Yevgeni Primakov[1]

The appointment of Primakov as Russia's foreign minister officially
completed Yeltsin and Kozyrev's early Westernist course. The new
appointment signaled a revival of Russia's most influential foreign policy
thinking, which put the key emphasis on statehood and great power status.

RUSSIA AS A GREAT POWER IN A MULTIPOLAR WORLD

The Grave New World and the Rise of Security Challenges

The revival of Statism as Russia's official foreign policy philosophy would
have been impossible without gathering security threats both inside and
outside the country. At home, Russia was confronted with the growing
challenge of secessionism and instability in one of its key southern regions,
Chechnya. Yeltsin's failure to respond to Chechnya's announcement of
independence in 1991, as well as the largely political nature of his decision
to intervene in late 1994, contributed to a long and bloody confrontation.
For Yeltsin, the decision was an attempt to shift the public attention away

from his own promises to improve or, at least, sustain the living standards of ordinary Russians. In the meantime, the actual income of ordinary Russians, most of whom were wage earners and pensioners, fell drastically, and the economy shrank considerably (see table 3.5 in the previous chapter). Partly as a reaction to Yeltsin's opportunism, the public remained largely skeptical of his military intervention. With little support at home, the army was unable to solve the conflict by force, as disorder and terrorism were increasingly spreading throughout Chechnya and outside.

Outside Russia, threats emerged from instabilities and ethnic conflicts in Moldova, central Asia, and the Caucasus. No less importantly, the West extended little recognition to Russia as one of its own, instead treating it increasingly as a potential threat. The Western decision to expand NATO despite Russia's opposition greatly contributed to the return of Statist thinking to the country. Statism assumes that respect and recognition can come only from strength, and weakness is not worthy of respect. The decision to expand NATO by excluding Russia from the process strengthened the Russian perception of the West as playing power games and attempting to take advantage of Russia's temporary weakness. Nationalists felt vindicated, whereas liberals were confused and at a loss for arguments. Many politicians and intellectuals, including those of a liberal orientation, saw NATO's expansion as a dangerous and threatening development.

As important as the decision to expand NATO was, it reflected the broader change in the West's perception of the world. From the rhetoric of victory in the Cold War and the "end of history," the Western political community moved to a feeling of anxiety over its growing inability to preserve peace and stability throughout the globe. The new ethnic conflicts in Europe and the former Soviet Union, the perceived threat from the undefeated regime of the Iraqi leader Saddam Hussein, and environmental and demographic pressures from Asia and Africa seemed to pose great risks. Various intellectual projects emerged to reflect the rising pessimism among U.S. policymakers about the future of the world order and to reject the early rosy perceptions of the world. With the growing awareness of new dangers came fear and suspicion of the non-Western world, which was best summarized by Samuel Huntington's thesis of the "clash of civilizations." Just as Fukuyama once expressed the West's optimism, even euphoria, about the future world order, Huntington expressed the growing feelings of anxiety and frustration. He insisted that instead of expanding globally, the West should go on the defensive and prepare to fight for its cultural values in coming clashes with non-Western "civilizations."[2] In this new intellectual context, Russia, with its authoritarian past and politically unstable present, was often viewed as a source of threat rather than as a "strategic partner." The once newly born liberal ally was now increasingly perceived to be driven by traditional imperial aspirations or as a failing state unable to govern itself.

The Statist Vision of Russia's Identity

In this context of growing security threats, the Statist insistence on viewing Russia as first and foremost a great power resonated with the elites and the broader public. Primakov and his supporters did not see the forces of international cooperation as shaping the nature of world politics. They appealed to the historical notion of Russia as a *Derzhava*, which can be loosely translated as a holder of international equilibrium of power. A *Derzhava* is capable of defending itself by relying on its own individual strength, and its main goal should be the preservation of that status. Although many Statists were former Westernizers, they no longer agreed that Russia was becoming a part of the West, and they argued that the country had its own interests to defend. Without implying a confrontation with the West, Statists sought to defend the image of Russia as a power holder striving to preserve its own geopolitical interests and areas of influence in the world. Geopolitical categories often used by Civilizationists— such as "national idea," "great power," and "Eurasia"—became intrinsic to Statist vocabulary.

To many Statists, the notion of Eurasia became symbolic in describing Russia's special geopolitical location and multiethnic nature. Taking issue with Westernizers, Statists pointed to the need to maintain a multicultural balance inside Russia. They also warned against Russia's unequivocally siding with Europe or the United States at the expense of relationships with key participants from the Eurasian continent, such as China, India, and the Islamic world. Committed to an essentialist vision of geography, Statists insisted that, by its geopolitical location, Russia was destined to act as a political bridge between Western and non-Western civilizations.

Unlike Civilizationists, however, Statists were more pragmatic and were prepared to cooperate with anyone defending the existing balance of international power and Russia's role in it. While viewing the world primarily in terms of disparities and competition among great powers, Statists were not anti-Western and did not see Russia as inherently hostile to the West. The school maintained that, although Russia's interests and values differed from those of the West, it had historically interacted with the West, and this limited interaction had not threatened Russian sovereignty. Although the school understood security as resulting more from the state's individual strength than from collective efforts, it saw the value of tactical coalitions and alliances. Statists were also different from conservative Civilizationists in their evaluation of Soviet foreign policy. Rather than putting all the blame on the West (as communists and Eurasianists did), Statists proceeded from the thesis of mutual and equal responsibility for the Cold War. Several Statists, including Primakov, were originally supportive of Gorbachev's New Thinking as it was emerging in 1986–1987.

The Statist worldview then was a familiar realist picture of power competition between sovereign states reminiscent of nineteenth-century European politics; that is, the world is not inherently hostile, but it does consist of selfish power-seeking state actors whose interests must be balanced in order to maximize peace and stability. Statists thought about the international system in terms of power poles and favored the United Nations as the key institution for maintaining a multipolar balance of power, particularly among great powers.[3]

The Statist coalition combined the military industries, army, and security services that saw the largely ignored potential for generating revenue through the development of new technologies and exportation of conventional weapons. In one of its documents, the Council for Foreign and Defense Policy, an influential nongovernmental organization, expressed the attitude typical of Statist circles when it described the military-industrial complex as "a key, possibly, the key factor of Russia's struggle for a dignified place in the twenty-first century."[4] Over time, the large Russian "security class" gained strength and was able to challenge the emerging and still nascent "commercial class" that promoted the Westernist image of Russia's identity. The Statist coalition greatly benefited from the 1993 and 1995 elections, in which nationalists and communists did well, compelling Yeltsin to modify the liberal agenda. Primakov's appointment was symbolic in this respect. As the *Financial Times* editorialized, of all the possible successors to Kozyrev, Primakov was "probably the least welcome in Washington. By selecting him, President Boris Yeltsin has signaled that he cares more about assuaging nationalism at home than soothing U.S. fears."[5] Primakov served as foreign minister from January 1996 through September 1998, and as prime minister he remained a guiding influence on foreign policy until May 1999. It was now up to the Statists to define and defend the country's national interests.

The Statist View of National Interest

Primakov and his team proposed two central elements for recovering Russia's status as a great power in a multipolar world: balancing the United States' unipolar ambitions in a coalition with other states and integrating the former Soviet region under tighter control from Moscow. Primakov understood that Russia was weak and had limited resources for foreign policy grandeur. Yet his thinking was, counterintuitively, that the country had to pursue "active" foreign policy (*aktivnaya vneshnyaya politika*)[6] in order to compensate for currently limited resources in reforming the economy and preserving territorial integrity. He believed that Russia was in a geopolitically dangerous environment and simply could not afford to concentrate on purely domestic issues (table 4.1 summarizes the Statist view of national interest).

Table 4.1.   Great Power Balancing (GPB): View of National Interest

What?	A great power in a multipolar world
How?	Flexible alliances Reintegration of the former Soviet region Economic reform

In relationships with the West, Primakov insisted that Russia be motivated primarily by its own interests, and he proclaimed the vision of a multipolar world. According to this perspective, Russia had a tendency to become dependent on the strongest and, to preserve its significant global geopolitical role, it had to pursue the goal of becoming an independent power pole. The Statist logic was simple: the power dictates its rules, and under the conditions of a unipolar world Russia would have no independent voice in international politics. The unipolar world was not going to be liberal or democratic, despite the American promises, and Russia should not succumb to the rhetoric of the strongest. Instead, it must use a combination of both cooperation and balancing policies for the purpose of undermining the unipolarity. Confrontation with the West was unnecessary; unlike the conservative Civilizationists, Primakov believed that a limited and pragmatic cooperation with either the "strongest" or the West was both feasible and important. Unlike the Westernizers, however, Primakov and his supporters insisted that the principle of absolute power equality must be honored in each instance of cooperation.

In addition to cooperating with the West, Statists believed that Russia also had to engage in balancing tactics against the strongest power, the United States. Because of Russia's presumed responsibility for maintaining world equilibrium and the balance of power, its cooperation with the West and the United States could not be as deep and far reaching as Westernizers saw it. In a multipolar world, which Russia wanted to see built, Russia had to be able to prevent the formation of an opposing coalition by using balancing tactics in relating to all its foreign partners—Western, Eastern, and Southern. When necessary, it had to capitalize on the potential conflicts that already existed in world politics, for example, those between the Western and Muslim or Asian countries or those within the West itself. Russia's policy orientation in the world then should have been multilateral, or "multivector," aiming to develop balanced relations with Western and non-Western countries. In Yevgeni Primakov's words, "Russia is both Europe and Asia, and this geopolitical location continues to play a tremendous role in formulation of its foreign policy. Its [geopolitical interests] include China, India, and Japan, and not just the United States or Europe. They also include the Middle East and the 'Third World.' Without such geopolitical scope, Russia cannot continue to be a great power and to play the positive role it has been destined to play. In building relationships with all these countries, one must remember that geopolitical values are constant and cannot be abolished by historical developments."[7]

Primakov made it explicit that his strategy was reminiscent of State Chancellor Alexander Gorchakov's "concentration" course after Russia's defeat in the Crimean War. After the March 1856 Paris peace treaty, which legitimized Russia's defeat, Gorchakov recommended to Czar Alexander II that, in facing the new conditions, Russia "will have to focus persistently on the realization of [its] internal development and the entire foreign policy will have to be subordinated to this main task."[8] Such a policy would be only temporary and, after rebuilding the domestic base, Russia would again be in a position to press for changes appropriate for its great power status. In combination with flexible alliance making, Russia at least partially achieved the goal: in 1870 it felt strong enough to act unilaterally and partially renounce the conditions of the Paris peace treaty. Primakov, too, was hoping that, after rebuilding the economy, Russia would "return" to world politics.

In the former Soviet Union, Statists defended the notion of a tightly integrated region with Russia's informal control over policies of the former republics. Primakov argued that Russian geopolitical needs stretched well beyond Russia, and it was only pragmatic to act on those needs. For him, the task of maintaining the world geopolitical equilibrium required that Russia remain a sovereign state with capabilities to organize and secure the post-Soviet space to resist hegemonic ambitions anywhere in the world. Unlike neocommunists or Eurasianists, the new foreign minister wanted no formal responsibility for the "postimperial space" and preferred to refer to Russia's relations with its post-Soviet neighbors as "multilateral integration."

Such thinking about Russia's national interests was adequately reflected in official documents. The country's National Security Concept of 1997 described "the new geopolitical and international situation" followed by "negative processes in the national economy" as key threats to Russia. It identified Russia as an "influential European and Asian power," and it invariably termed the country's relationships with "other great powers" as an "equal partnership." Furthermore, it recommended that Russia maintain equal distancing in relation to the "global European and Asian economic and political actors" and presented a positive program for the integration of the efforts of the Commonwealth of Independent States (CIS) in the security area. The government's official Foreign Policy Concept of 2000 referred to the Russian Federation as "a great power . . . [with a] responsibility for maintaining security in the world both on a global and on a regional level" and warned of a new threat of "a unipolar structure of the world under the economic and military domination of the United States."[9]

Although Primakov's perspective was definitely the closest to realist thinking, it is difficult to apply realism as an international relations theory for explaining Russia's turn to Great Power Balancing. Realists expect that policy change follows evolution in state material capabilities. Yet Russia's capabilities did not improve. As table 3.5 indicates, the country's economic decline continued, and there was hardly a material basis for developing a more assertive foreign policy. What changed, however, was the behavior of the West toward Russia and its local conditions; this contributed to an altered domestic perception and brought to power the identity coalition of Statists.

THE NATIONAL RECEPTION
OF GREAT POWER BALANCING

The new foreign policy vision found broad support in Russian society and, especially, among the political elites. After Kozyrev's departure, Yeltsin embraced the rhetoric of great power and multipolarity and pronounced the discussion of Russia's foreign policy priorities to be "completed" and the new foreign policy concept to be supported by a "consensus of various social and political forces."[10] Statists and many Social Democrats welcomed the new foreign policy course. Civilizationists, too, accepted some of Primakov's arguments while at the same time pushing him to adopt a more confrontational line in relations with the West. Finally, Westernizers got their act together and found some new arguments against aspirations for a great power and multipolar world order.

The Initial Support of Statists and Social Democrats

An overwhelming majority of Russia's political class welcomed the change in policy, defending Primakov's concept of the national interests on political, historical, and geopolitical grounds. Politically, the argument went, the new policy reflected a broad agreement of various social and political forces in Russia. Foreign policy was ceasing to be an exclusive domain of the president and had more chances to be corrected in a timely fashion. Historical parallels between the new course and the notion of Gorchakov's "concentration" were, too, widely accepted in scholarly and political circles. Since 1998, an annual Gorchakov conference for scholars and practitioners has been held at the Moscow Institute of International Relations for debating various issues of current foreign policy. And in 2001, Primakov was awarded the State Gorchakov Commemorative Medal for "outstanding service in strengthening peace and promoting international cooperation." Finally, the new course's pragmatic nature found a great deal of support. Although virtually all Statists wanted Russia to become one of the five great powers in the world—along with Germany, France, Japan, and China—most warned against attempts to organize foreign policy around resistance to the global influence of the United States. In fact, some questioned the notion of a multipolar world as the guiding vision of the international system.[11] Outside the Statist camp, some Social Democrats praised the new foreign policy for its proclaimed pragmatism, restraint, and sense of priorities.[12]

Conditional Criticism of Civilizationists

Many neocommunists and Eurasianists had long attacked Kozyrev for "betraying" Russia as a holder of the global balance of power, and they welcomed the new course and the concept of a multipolar world. Yet they challenged Primakov to go much further in resisting Western influences and to adopt a more radical notion of multipolarity. The new minister planned to pursue a moderate course and consolidate Russia's position by cooperating with the West, where possible, and by avoiding confrontation, where such cooperation was not an option. Aware of the scarcity of available resources, he saw a multipolar world as a desired objective, rather than a fact of life. To conservative Civilizationists, on the other hand, the notion of a great power implied the restoration of the Soviet Union, and multipolarity meant isolation from and competition with the West.[13]

Fear of the West and its global aspirations were the dominant obsessions of Civilizationist writers, such as the leader of Russian communists, Gennadi Zyuganov. For Zyuganov, Russia was a unique civilization that must be isolated from the West to survive and preserve its uniqueness. What Statists saw as Russia's special geographical and ethnic features, Zyuganov developed into the principal line of cultural confrontation with the West. The leader of the Russian communists never made his peace with the dissolution of the Soviet empire and insisted that the Soviet Union was a "natural" geopolitical form of "historic" Russia, whereas the current political boundaries of the country are "artificial" and imposed by the West through covert actions. To "return" to world politics and build a genuinely multipolar world, Russia must accomplish politicoeconomic autarchy (*samodostatochnost'*) and enter a strategic alliance with China.[14]

Other writers, too, presented the choice of Russia's survival as one between an independent Eurasian power and a virtual colony of the West, and they complained about the lack of radicalism in Primakov's vision.[15]

Opposition from Westernizers

Westernizers stood out from the rest of the political class in their most irreconcilable critique of the course of Great Power Balancing. They repeated the old Kozyrev argument that Russia's national interest is in building a competitive market economy and a vibrant democratic system, not in balancing against the West or integrating the former Soviet Union. In supporting this line of reasoning, Westernizers drew attention to the fact that ordinary Russians were concerned primarily with the state of the Russian economy and internal security, and not the issues of military capabilities and great power status. Insisting, as before, on Russia's politicoeconomic integration with European institutions, they saw as fundamentally misplaced Primakov's priorities of reviving the CIS as a vehicle of post-Soviet integration, resisting the eastern expansion of NATO, developing military cooperation with Iran, and trying to build the Russia-China-India security axis. Furthermore, they challenged the relevance of Gorchakov's "concentration" on contemporary foreign policy. In their view, Gorchakov's flexible alliances had deprived Russia of a chance to side firmly with democratic France and—ultimately—contributed to the rise of Germany and Russia's own revolution. They charged that, by not siding firmly with the West and trying to play Europe or China against the United States, Primakov's policy, too, was likely to result in failure.[16]

While echoing many of the old Westernist arguments, the new Westernizers became more pragmatic and less ideological in their reasoning. Increasingly, they were concentrating on various material benefits of Russia's pro-Western orientation. Some spoke of the need in "pragmatic liberalism" for successfully opposing Primakov's "pragmatic nationalism," whereas others acknowledged that the road to Europe would not be an easy or straightforward one.[17] Westernizers therefore learned the key lesson: ideology alone was a recipe for failure when not supported by interests and pragmatic reasoning.

Table 4.2 summarizes contending views on the Statist view of national interest.

Table 4.2. Great Power Balancing (GPB): Contending Views

Civilizationists:		Westernizers:
GPB must more decisively confront the West	vs.	GPB leads to confrontation with the West

CONTAINING WESTERN INFLUENCES

Thinking about the West and East

Primakov's strategy for dealing with the West included two central elements—upholding the power of the United Nations as the key agency for defining and enforcing rules of international conduct and developing close ties with influential states outside the Western Hemisphere, such as China and India. This emphasis on both power and institutions brought Russian thinking about international politics closer to the British International Society school, rather than American-style neorealism that does not see institutions as having particular significance in shaping the world order. Primakov was careful not to isolate Russia from mainstream international politics centered on the United Nations Security Council. As a permanent member of the Security Council, Russia planned to exercise its voting power as it saw fit, while at the same time contributing to world peace and stability as a member of the world "concert of great powers." The minister and his supporters saw these elements as critical in establishing a multipolar world order and containing the power of the West, particularly the United States. In practical terms, the new foreign policy strove to resist American hegemony by using the legitimate tools of diplomacy and power balancing, while avoiding confrontation with the United States. It sought to mobilize Russia's power resources to pursue that goal (for a summary of these resources relative to other nations, see table 4.3).

Table 4.3. Russia's Power Resources Relative to Other Powerful States (%)*

	United States	Japan	Germany	France	RUSSIA	China
Population (1995)	4.7	2.2	1.4	1.0	2.6	21.2
Territory (1994)	7.1	0.3	0.3	0.4	13.2	7.3
GNP (1995)	25.2	18.7	8.7	5.5	1.2	3.0
Manufacturing (1995)	22.6	25.4	11.7	5.9	3.1	5.3
Merchandise Exports (1995)	12.1	9.2	10.8	5.9	1.7	3.1
Nuclear Weapons (1996)	46.8	—	—	2.9	46.1	2.5
Military Expenditures (1993)	41.0	5.9	5.4	5.3	4.3	4.1
Military Personnel (1996)	6.7	1.4	1.6	1.8	5.7	13.2

*Share as a percentage of the world's total.
Source: Robert A. Pastor, ed., *A Century's Journey: How the Great Powers Shape the World* (New York: Basic Books, 2001), 19.

The East had a special role in this dual-track strategy. Unlike Westernizers, Primakov was a firm believer in special relations with Asian and

Middle Eastern countries. This belief firmed up during his long career as a Middle East specialist and policymaker. For many years, the future minister worked in several Middle Eastern countries as a correspondent for the leading communist newspaper *Pravda*. Primakov subsequently moved to academia to serve as director of the Institute of Oriental Studies and, later, of the prestigious Institute of World Economy and International Relations. He then began to work for Gorbachev. However, while advocating strong ties with Asia and the Muslim world, he differentiated sharply between the Islamic states and the Taliban's form of Islam, which he described as "Islamic extremism." Primakov wanted to engage the former for the sake of balancing against growing Western influences and isolate the latter.

Opposing NATO Expansion

The key focus of Primakov's policy was undoubtedly NATO's eastward expansion and Russia's adaptation to this new reality. The decision to expand the alliance was made in January 1994 in response to several security crises in the Balkans and pressures from the former Eastern European states. By the time Primakov had assumed his responsibilities, it became clear that NATO, rather than the Russia-desired Organization for Security and Co-operation in Europe (OSCE), was turning into the cornerstone of European security. It was also clear that, despite Russia's original hopes, it was not about to be considered for membership in the organization.

Many in Russia saw the expansion as the most serious foreign policy challenge and made their opposition to the process explicit.[18] The expansion was incomprehensible in light of Russia's historical commitments, its new relationships with the Western countries, and the West's own promises not to expand the alliance. Many Russians felt deceived, as the expansion followed Gorbachev's military withdrawals from Eastern Europe, Kozyrev's restriction of some profitable arms sales in order to comply with Western rules, and Russia's general commitment to developing a strategic partnership with the West. Overwhelmingly, the Russian foreign policy community perceived the expansion as a violation of the norm of reciprocity and the very spirit of the post–Cold War transformation. Eventually, even radical Westernizers, such as Kozyrev, announced their disappointment with the decision. The general public, too, expressed concerns, and those concerns only increased over time. As former U.S. defense secretary William Perry put it, Russian reaction to NATO expansion "ranged from being unhappy to being very unhappy. . . . This is a very widely and very deeply held view in Russia."[19]

Under these conditions, Primakov saw his task as limiting the potential damage of the expansion. His very appointment, in fact, served the purpose of ameliorating the anti-NATO backlash further because of his already-established reputation as a tough defender of Russia's national interests. Primakov soon recognized that the expansion of the alliance became inevitable and that Russia had to shift from the mode of resistance to that of adaptation. Although he was highly critical of the Western decision, he recognized the reality for what it was—"the expansion of NATO is not a military problem; it is a psychological one."[20] To narrow the gap of perception, Russia had little choice but to work on establishing closer diplomatic and political ties with the alliance. The result was the negotiated document signed by the two sides in May 1997 and titled "Founding Act on Mutual Relations, Cooperation and Security between Russia and NATO." Russia saw this as a quasi institutionalization of its relationship with NATO, and it also received the opportunity to join NATO in establishing a special body, the Permanent Joint Council, to consult about and—when appropriate—even join in decision making and joint action. In December 1997, in his speech to the State Duma, Primakov referred to the Founding Act as a major accomplishment and evidence of Russia's diplomacy in obtaining its own objectives.

Admittedly, the Founding Act did not give Russia the veto power it sought, and the subsequent intervention in the Balkans demonstrated this situation all too painfully. Domestic critics, such as the leader of the communists, Zyuganov, went as far as to compare the charter to a new Yalta, in which Russia was a defeated party signing its act of capitulation. Even some of Primakov's supporters felt he went too far in acquiescing to the West. Yet his strategy worked in terms of shifting Russia's focus to adaptation to the new reality and attempting to influence outcomes through diplomacy and bargaining from within. Despite the Kosovo crisis (described below), Russia was brought closer to NATO, and the question of the alliance's expansion was largely defused in domestic politics, depriving hard-line critics of the ability to pressure the government. Russia now had a mechanism for permanent consultations with the alliance. In addition, NATO reaffirmed in writing its commitment not to deploy nuclear weapons or substantial new forces on the territory of new member states. Russian diplomats extracted what they could given Russia's weak bargaining position.

Working to Improve Economic and Military Independence

A Statist, Primakov made an effort to improve Russia's economic and military capabilities, without which his strategy of containing Western influences could hardly have been sufficient. In economic affairs, rather than continuing with Kozyrev's policy of joining Western international organizations, he worked to restore a measure of Russia's independence.

He argued against a West-dependent economic recovery and entering the world economy as a supplier of raw materials, and he insisted on separating the economic issues from those related to politics and security. This attitude generally corresponded with how hard-line opposition felt about Russia's receiving financial assistance from the West's leading lending agencies. At the time, many of the government's critics charged that the assistance served to further corrupt the circles of the ruling elite and to entice them to "sell" Russia to the West.

Despite Primakov's efforts, there was little he could do to restore the country's economic independence. By the time of his arrival in office, Russia's foreign debt and domestic budget deficit figured prominently. The heaviest debt approached in 1999 when Russia had to pay $17.5 billion, at a time when its domestic budget was around $20 billion.[21] The budget deficit—which resulted mainly from the government's inability to collect taxes—had been consistently sizable since the beginning of Yeltsin's economic reform (see table 4.4). The government was desperate to find noninflationary ways to reduce the deficit and to restructure and reschedule the growing debt. The room for political maneuvering was severely limited, and the government continued the practice of borrowing from the International Monetary Fund (IMF). In turn, the IMF required a tight conditionality and secured a more politically compliant Russia. For all its talk about depoliticized relations with recipient countries, the political side of the IMF-Russia relationship was always visible. The 1995–1996 lending, for example, was conducted in the context of the approaching presidential elections, in which Yeltsin's victory was the number-one priority for the West. The Western intervention in Yugoslavia—against which Russia objected vehemently—took place as the Russian government was in the process of negotiating the restructuring of the approaching $17.5 billion payment.[22]

Table 4.4. Russia's Government Revenue and Expenditure, 1992–1998 (% of GDP)

	1992	1993	1994	1995	1996	1997	1998
Revenue	15.6	13.7	11.8	12.2	13.0	11.9	10.2
Expenditure	26	20.2	23.2	17.6	22.0	18.9	16.1

Source: Nigel Gould-Davies and Ngaire Woods, "Russia and the IMF," *International Affairs* 75, no. 1 (1999): 15.

After assuming the responsibilities of prime minister, Primakov realized ever more painfully the difficulties of maintaining the independence posture; even with what was considered to be a "leftist government," he had to submit to the State Duma a tight budget and fully comply with the IMF conditions.

In military affairs and arms control, the foreign minister turned prime minister sought to reduce the heavy economic burden of maintaining the largest nuclear arsenal in the world. Primakov believed in the political power of nuclear weapons, but advocated a relatively small arsenal. Against the hard-line opposition and even some of his supporters, he argued for ratification of START II, which had been signed in January 1993. Yet his efforts, accompanied by support from the Ministry of Defense, failed because of the United States' bombing of Iraq and, subsequently, NATO's military intervention in Yugoslavia. The events strengthened conservative Civilizationists and other hard-liners in the Duma, who feared U.S. intentions to develop a missile defense system and consequently blocked the ratification. START II, which promised to reduce the number of nuclear missiles to the new 3,000–3,500 threshold, remained formally dead until the arrival of Putin.

Resisting Military Solutions in Iraq

Primakov's principal opposition to what he viewed as imperialistic and hegemonic tendencies in world politics placed limits on his flexibility and pragmatism in dealing with the United States. However dependent Russia was on Western creditors, the minister could not support the United States–sanctioned military interventions, as did his predecessor. Intervention in Iraq emerged as one of the two key issues—the other being Yugoslavia—on which Primakov felt compelled to forcefully disagree with the American position. In his view, there were at least three major reasons why Russia could no longer limit its policy to supporting the U.S. bombings and opposing lifting the United Nations' sanctions in Iraq. First, because of his opposition to "unipolarity," he wanted to contribute to opposition to the United States–promoted military methods of dealing with Saddam Hussein. The second reason was a sizable debt—around $7 billion—of Iraq to Russia, which could not be repaid without lifting sanctions. Third, Russia's growing energy companies, such as Lukoil, were eager to acquire contracts in Iraq and the Arab markets in general.

It was this perception of Russia's interests that shaped Primakov's handling of two main crises in late 1997 and early 1998. In the first crisis, Primakov responded to the U.S. threat to attack Iraq following the latter's unwillingness to comply with the UN inspections and the inspectors' subsequent departure. In alliance with France, he negotiated a deal whereby all the inspectors were allowed to return in exchange for a vague promise to work for the lifting of sanctions. The deal did not last long, however, as sanctions were never lifted and Saddam Hussein made it difficult for inspectors to access "presidential sites," some of which were suspected of activities related to weapons of mass destruction. This time,

Russia seemed to have failed to produce a mutually acceptable agreement, and the UN secretary-general assumed the diplomatic initiative. Primakov, at least, felt satisfied that the issue was left to the United Nations, and not solved unilaterally by the United States. In the meantime, Saddam Hussein was playing his own game trying to pressure Moscow to be more aggressive on the issue of lifting sanctions.[23] During 1999, Russia—in part dissatisfied with Baghdad's uncooperative behavior, in part as a trade-off for the United States' not raising at the UN Security Council the issue of Russia's ruinous war in Chechnya, and in part having an insufficient number of options in the face of the U.S. military pressures—was less willing to work with Iraq. Much to Iraq's dismay, Russia eventually chose not to exercise its veto on Security Council Resolution 1284 (it abstained), which demanded Baghdad's compliance with the inspectors' ruling and promised lifting the sanctions on the importation of civilian goods to Iraq.

Primakov's approach appeared to have accomplished little. Sanctions remained in place, negotiations did not produce any visible results, and therefore Russia's economic interests were left unsatisfied. Yet, in one important respect Russia held its ground—the key political decisions with regard to Iraq remained the United Nations' prerogative, and those decisions were different from those favored by the United States. This remained so until the March 2003 decision of President George W. Bush to attack Iraq.

Confronting NATO's Intervention in Yugoslavia

Until the Western military intervention in the Balkans, Primakov followed the policy of pragmatic cooperation with NATO members. When he took over, the Dayton Accords of November 1995 had been signed with minimal input from Russia, and the hard-line opposition insisted on realignment with Serbia. The new foreign minister indeed moved to reevaluate the role of Belgrade in European security, but he did not go nearly as far as hard-liners wanted him to. While advocating pragmatism over Kozyrev's ideological commitment to the West, Primakov actively worked through the Contact Group, the framework for diplomatic coordination among Russia, the United States, France, Britain, and Germany created in response to Yeltsin's call in February 1994. Although Russia opposed NATO's command of peacekeeping and in some cases objected to specific acts of force against the Bosnian Serbs, in general it did not interfere with UN-sanctioned Western actions in Bosnia.[24]

NATO's decision to begin air strikes against Belgrade in March 1999 changed this framework of relationships. Despite a number of important disagreements between Russia and the West, the military intervention came as a shock to Russia's foreign policy community. This was illustrated by Prime Minister Yevgeni Primakov's decision to cancel the upcoming negotiations with the United States and the IMF in Washington on March 24, 1999. Although his airplane had already been approaching the United States, he ordered it to return home. Russia's official reaction was harsh and included issuing a statement on NATO's aggression in violation of the United Nations' jurisdiction and the Helsinki Act on the preservation of sovereignty, suspension of participation in the Founding Act agreement, withdrawal of the military mission from Brussels, and ordering NATO representatives to leave Russia.

Such reactions reflected the largely negative attitudes toward NATO within Russian society and its foreign policy community. The overwhelming majority believed that the Western actions were driven by power and hegemonic ambitions, rather than by concerns over Yugoslavian leader Slobodan Milošević's actions against Kosovo Albanians. Among the general public, about 90 percent opposed NATO's bombing of Belgrade and felt threatened by the alliance's actions.[25] It was the expansion of NATO, rather than the ethnic war in the Balkans, that shaped Russia's perception of the intervention in Yugoslavia. By that time, the Western alliance had already invited the Czech Republic, Poland, and Hungary to apply for membership. At the Madrid summit in the summer of 1997, the U.S. secretary of state Madeleine Albright specifically promised to extend the invitation to the Baltic states, which had been a part of the Soviet Union before 1991. Primakov's foreign ministry insisted again on the unacceptability of the alliance expansion. Despite the Founding Act agreement of May 1997, the post-Madrid atmosphere of Russia-West relationships was tense. The clash over Kosovo manifested the depth of the Russian fears. It brought in some elements of political escalation and, at times, came close to military confrontation. Russia's Duma, for instance, fell short by two or three votes of passing a resolution on accepting Yugoslavia into the Russia-Belarus Union, which would have made Russia a participant in the war.

Primakov had no plans to throw his support behind Serbia, as some conservative Civilizationists called on him to. Instead, he got involved in mediating the conflict. Using the West's interest in Russia's involvement, he formulated tough conditions for ending the war, which included guarantees for Yugoslavia's preserved sovereignty, a broad autonomy for Kosovo, and the UN's assuming leadership in the postwar settlement. Yet the peace was reached more on the West's than on Russia's terms. Out of fear of further Russia-West political escalation, Yeltsin dismissed Primakov as the key negotiator and replaced him with former prime minister Viktor Chernomyrdin, who was much too pro-Western and inexperienced in foreign affairs to negotiate the peace that Primakov had in mind. In early June, under pressure from Chernomyrdin, Serbia finally accepted the conditions for peace, but Russia's initial conditions had not been honored. As one Russian observer described the outcomes of the war, "Russia took part in Yugoslavia's acceptance of the same NATO conditions that it had previously called unacceptable."[26]

Statist Lessons from Engagement with the West

Primakov and the larger Statist community drew some tough lessons from Russia's engagement with the West. This engagement widened the gap between the two sides in perception and reinforced the sense of Russia's identity as distinct from that of the West. Russia's inability to stop NATO's expansion and Western military strikes on Iraq and Yugoslavia, as well as heavy economic dependence on Western lending organizations, reinforced the already-existing sense of isolation, at times even desperation, among the political class. Despite the dubious outcomes of the strategy to contain Western influences, many believed that Russia had no other choice but to develop capabilities for external balancing. Some saw the nation as already in the process of disintegration (Chechnya), and they insisted that breaking with the West was the only alternative to Russia's slavery or disintegration.[27] As one political scientist wrote, "The bombing of Yugoslavia became a turning point in the development of Russia's consciousness. Both authorities and common people begin to realize that . . . without Russia, the world can be turned into one big McDonald's, the road to which will be paved with missiles."[28]

To reduce what Statists saw as the country's external insecurity, they recommended a series of steps. First, the main external threat was perceived to be from NATO, even though previously many analysts had seen China as equally threatening. After the war in Yugoslavia, many now viewed Kosovo as a template of NATO's future strategy. This found its reflection in proposals to increase the defense budget, as well as in official documents. The new draft military doctrine emphasized that the threat of direct aggression against Russia and its allies could only be "deterred by conducting active foreign policy and maintaining high readiness of conventional and nuclear forces." The Security Council further proposed extending and updating strategic and tactical nuclear weapons, among other measures.[29] In this context, many argued against the ratification of START II. Second, Russian elites insisted on strengthening the UN Security Council in its decision-making and peacekeeping capacity at the expense of NATO. Third, many called for tightening the defense space in the former Soviet Union. Last but not least—and this had been an essential element of Primakov's strategy—Statists no longer saw as much of a threat coming from China and argued for stepping up strategic ties with

countries and regions outside the West. Indeed, while Yeltsin was trying
to broker peace in Yugoslavia, Primakov was proposing that Russia enter
into a tripartite partnership with China and India (which had long been
an agenda of neocommunists and Eurasianists). I now turn to Russia's
efforts to increase its ties with non-Western nations.

Capitalizing on Relations outside the West

The active foreign policy defended by Primakov meant the development
of geostrategic and economic ties outside the West. Both objectives were
designed to improve Russia's relative power position in the world at the
expense of Western nations, particularly the United States. An Arabist by
training, Primakov was notably more active in the Middle East than his
predecessor. In addition to expressing interest in playing a more active
role in the peace process, Primakov considerably increased Russian arms
sales in the region. Outside the Middle East, Russia was especially interested in the Asia-Pacific region, often describing the Association of Southeast Asian Nations (ASEAN) as an influential center of the developing
multipolar world. Everywhere he traveled the new minister spread his
message about the necessity of building a multipolar world order. However, three states played an especially important role in his vision—China,
Iran, and India.

China's significance for Russia is difficult to overestimate. China shared
a 4,300-kilometer-long border with Russia and demonstrated a very high
rate of economic development. China was also the main buyer of Russian
weapons; it purchased almost all of its arms and military equipment from
its northwestern neighbor. Politically, the two shared concerns about the
United States' global dominance and perceived as threatening developments NATO's expansion, the United States' plans to build a national
missile defense system, and interventions in Iraq and Kosovo. Finally,
both countries faced similar threats to internal security, with the separatist activities of the Chechens in Russia and the Muslim Uighur minority
in China's province of Xinjiang.

All of these factors brought the two countries closer together. In April
1996, the sides affirmed that they were entering into a new stage of partnership, and a year later the countries' leaders signed the "Joint Declaration on a Multipolar World and the Formation of a New International
Order," which reflected Primakov's vision of multipolarity as a work in
progress. The late 1998–1999 developments, such as U.S. military strikes
against Iraq, plans for the creation of a U.S.-Japanese theater of missile
defense, NATO expansion, and bombing of Yugoslavia again brought the
two together to actively coordinate their responses to what they saw as
threatening developments in world affairs. Economic relations between

Russia and China did not progress as fast as the countries had desired, but they did improve in areas of border trade and arms sales.

Yet despite pronounced progress, the Russia-China relationship did not go as far as Primakov would have wanted. His efforts met opposition across the political spectrum. China was leading Russia in GDP terms by a factor of five, and that worried both Westernizers and conservative Civilizationists, who sensed the danger of a Chinese encroachment in the Far East. Westernizers were particularly critical of Chinese authoritarianism, arguing that, sooner or later, it would translate into foreign policy expansionism. One prominent Westernizer provided the following chart to summarize the alarming picture of disparity in the two's economic and demographic indicators (see table 4.5). The strong Chinese gravitation to the global economic markets also complicated Primakov's geostrategic calculations. The full-fledged strategic partnership of Russia and China, therefore, remained only a possibility.

Table 4.5.   Russia and China: Demographic and Economic Disparities in the Far East, 1997

	Russian Far East (Southern Regions)	Northeast China
Population (millions)	5.0	104
Population Density (sq km)	3.8	132
Population Growth (%)	−40	1,000
Regional GDP Growth (%)	−8	13
Industrial/Agricultural Growth (%)	−12/−15	14/8

Source: Dmitri Trenin, *The End of Eurasia: Russia on the Border between Geopolitics and Globalization* (Washington, DC: Carnegie Endowment for International Peace, 2002), 209.

Another potentially strategic partner in Primakov's calculus was Iran. Politically, he saw the country as a regional ally in containing the influence of the Taliban regime in Afghanistan and Turkey, particularly on the states of central Asia and Azerbaijan. Globally, Iran was yet another potential ally in resisting the U.S.-controlled unipolarity. Economically, Russia was building nuclear reactors, supplying industrial equipment, and planning on forming a common policy in developing energy pipelines in the Caspian region. As with China, Primakov's record on Russia's cooperation with Iran was mixed. The two sides cooperated on economic matters and in arranging a cease-fire in Tajikistan and resisting the Taliban in Afghanistan. Despite objections from Washington that Iran was building a nuclear weapon in violation of the existing nonproliferation regime, Russia continued to cooperate with Iran while denying all the allegations.

Over time, however, Russian-Iranian relations demonstrated their limits. Politically, Russia did not want to see Iran emerging as a possible military threat in the region, and some officials publicly spoke against such a development. The issue subsequently became even more pronounced as Iran became the head of the Islamic Conference and emerged as more supportive of the Chechen rebels and Kosovo Muslims. Furthermore, while acting in concert with Russia in trying to block the Baku-Ceyhan and Trans-Caspian pipelines, Iran developed an interest in serving as an alternative export route for central Asian oil and gas. Finally, neither Yeltsin nor Primakov was willing to go too far with testing the United States' patience. The end result was what one scholar labeled a "minimax" policy, in which Russia tried to minimize the damage to U.S.-Russian relations while at the same time maintaining the maximum amount of influence in Iran.[30]

Finally, Primakov's diplomacy sought to engage India as a partner of strategic importance. The foreign minister was capitalizing on the old Soviet ties in trying to revive Russia as India's key rearmament agent. In 1997, the Indian prime minister announced that his country had purchased $3 billion in arms from Russia in the previous two years, and that the two sides had discussed potential contracts worth another $7 billion—a level that would move India ahead of China in the ranks of Moscow's arms customers.[31] Politically, Primakov was interested in building closer relations with Russia, India, and China to balance the power of the United States, which was a marked shift from the previous policy of balancing China through an alliance with India. In December 1998, Primakov spoke of the desirability of the three's alliance as a "new pole in world politics." This, however, remained wishful thinking, as neither India nor China had a similar interest.

On balance, Primakov's efforts to engage non-Western countries into strategic partnership with Russia for the purpose of balancing against the West hardly worked. Potential for developing bilateral ties with China, Iran, and India was there and likely to be more fully realized in the future. However, in the world of global economic interdependence, none of these countries was eager to enter into the Russia-sought balancing coalition. In addition, Russia's regional political interests proved to be too complex for it to fully commit to building such a coalition with explicitly articulated geostrategic objectives.

INTEGRATING THE FORMER SOVIET AREA

The Concept of Integration

Integration of the former Soviet area was another key pillar of Primakov's strategy of balancing Western power and resisting NATO expansion. The new foreign policymakers defined Russia's interests in terms of accumulating national power and sought to accomplish three objectives. First, being pressured by the new conflicts in the former Soviet Union, they wanted to maintain Russia's military presence in the area. Second, they wanted to protect the status of ethnic Russians living outside Russia. Furthermore, Moscow was interested in obtaining valuable economic assets and facilities in the post-Soviet world.

Using strong bargaining power in relations with the former republics, Russia was planning to obtain more informal control over their economic and security policies, without being overly responsible for the costs of such control. The country did possess considerable power to take a more assertive approach in the former Soviet Union. It had the most sophisticated weaponry, as well as the largest and the most experienced army in the region. Russia was also economically powerful due to the large size of its domestic market, rich endowment with natural resources, and more diversified commercial ties with countries beyond the former Soviet region. Politically, it was the only state in the region with the recognized reputation of a United Nations Security Council member, and it had also obtained membership in the prestigious G-8. Furthermore, it had a diversified linguistic diaspora of twenty-five million people, many of whom identified with their "homeland" and, therefore, could assist Russia in projecting its influence abroad. Some indicators of Russia's relative power in the post-Soviet region are summarized in tables 3.6 and 4.6.

Table 4.6. Russia's Power Capabilities Relative to Former Soviet States

Country	Population, 1989 (millions)	GNP, 1993 (billions)	Military Personnel
Armenia	3.4	1.9	60,000
Azerbaijan	7.5	4.4	86,700
Belarus	10.5	16	98,400
Estonia	1.6	1.7	3,500
Georgia	5.7	2.3	?
Latvia	2.6	1.6	6,950
Lithuania	3.8	2.9	8,900
Moldova	4.5	4.1	11,850
Kazakhstan	17.4	18.2	40,000
Kyrgyzstan	4.7	2.9	7,000
RUSSIA	148.9	1,160	1,520,000
Tajikistan	5.9	2.5	2–3,000
Turkmenistan	3.9	3.8	11,000
Ukraine	51.9	54.2	542,000
Uzbekistan	22.3	14	25,000

Source: Neil MacFarlane, "Realism and Russian Strategy after the Collapse of the USSR," in *Unipolar Politics*, ed. Ethan B. Kapstein and Michael Mastanduno (New York: Columbia University Press, 1999), 225–26.

The concept of integration was first clearly articulated on September 14, 1995, when Yeltsin issued a wide-ranging decree titled "The Establishment of the Strategic Course of the Russian Federation with Member States of the CIS." The eight-page document had been developed out of one of the Primakov-led Foreign Intelligence Service reports, and it was transformed into the CIS Concept of Economic Integrational Development adopted in March 1997. For the first time since the Soviet breakup, the Kremlin acknowledged the priority significance of the CIS for Russia's national interests and defined Russia as the leading power in the formation of a new system of interstate political and economic relations in the region. The proclaimed goal was to create "an economically and politically integrated alliance of states capable of achieving a worthy place in world society," which was similar to Primakov's own definition of integration as a Russia-led "policy aimed at bringing together the states formed on the territory of the former Soviet Union."[32]

In addition to the Primakov-led Foreign Intelligence Service, originators of the concept of integration included conservative Civilizationist and moderate Statist influences. Conservative Civilizationists defended the territorial unity of Russia and the former Soviet region on culturally essentialist grounds. Eurasianists advocated a cultural unity of Slavs and Muslims, whereas Russian ethnonationalists promoted the primacy of the Russian language and religion in the region. The Congress of Russian Communities, for example, proclaimed Russia responsible for Russian speakers in the former Soviet republics; this was the view Yeltsin himself later adopted. The Council for Foreign and Defense Policy (Sovet po Vneshnei i Oboronnoi Politike)—an influential nongovernmental organization that united industrialists, businessmen, intellectuals, and public opinion leaders—contributed greatly to the notion of integration by consistently challenging Gaidar's and Kozyrev's economic policies and advocating Russia's more region-sensitive actions. The notion was therefore a hybrid of hard-line and moderate influences. It sought to revive the social, economic, and political coherence of the former Soviet region, without reviving the empire.

The strategy of integration had a good portion of pragmatism in responding to the new challenges Russia was facing both in the region and outside. While a major departure from Kozyrev's early isolationism, integration could not be likened to a restoration of the empire or a revival of aggressive imperial nationalism. Certainly, Primakov's supporters did not see it that way. For instance, the influential Council for Foreign and Defense Policy, which was also close to Primakov, issued a report titled "Will the Union Be Revived?" in which it referred to the idea of the Soviet restoration as a "reactionary utopia."[33] At the same time, the report argued that a reasonable alternative to post-Soviet integration was not available and that Russia should assume the role of leader of such an integration.

For Primakov, the security context, particularly NATO's expansion, prompted the strategy's necessity. For the politically driven Yeltsin, however, the strategy was a way to neutralize his opposition and to restore the state-diminished capacity to conduct foreign policy. Yeltsin's opposition included members of the military, industrialists, and some hard-line nationalists who had ties with Russians outside Russia. In security affairs, the Primakov-recommended strategy helped to seize the initiative that the military had increasingly been taking away from civilian authorities. Under Primakov, the Ministry of Foreign Affairs took considerable power away from the Ministry of Defense. For instance, it led the resolution of the Tajik civil war and the Moldovan conflict, and in both cases it produced peace treaties. In economic and cultural affairs, integrationism meant promoting Russian state interests by taking the initiative away from nongovernmental organizations that sought to restore the Soviet Union. In response, in his February 1995 state of the nation address, Yeltsin unfavorably referred to some "forces abroad" who wanted to downgrade Russia's international role, arguing for a new integration of the CIS.[34] By late 1995, Russia had already undertaken a series of activities to intensify its relations with Belarus, Kazakhstan, and Ukraine, and in 1996, in attempting to further neutralize opposition to his policies, Yeltsin made a series of other new appointments. Among them was the appointment of Aman Tuleyev—a communist supporter and a defender of the CIS integration—as minister for cooperation with CIS states.

The new assertive course also had considerable social support at home. The general public was strongly supportive of Russia's closer economic, political, and cultural relations with the ex-Soviet states, although it did not favor the empire's restoration. For instance, in December 1997, 61 percent of Russian citizens were sorry that the Soviet Union had collapsed—up from 33 percent in December 1992. At the same time, most respondents did not approve of military interventionism to integrate the former Soviet region. Even more telling, in 1996 about 65 percent were convinced that the only way to regain the former great power status was through the successful development of the Russian economy.[35] Political elites, too, were supportive of the notion of integration. Even some observers of liberal orientation were now arguing the "inevitability" of integration within the former Soviet Union.

Political and Security Aspects

Integration of the post-Soviet area concerned first and foremost the political and security aspects. It was the new conflicts in the region that pushed the leadership to revise its originally isolationist stance with regard to the former Soviet Union. As early as the spring of 1992, Russia had to deal with ethnically based domestic and international military conflicts, particularly in the Caucasus, Moldova, and Tajikistan. Increasingly, Russia also faced threats of instability and terrorism in the south. It also had to confront the instability of borders with countries outside the former Soviet region and the issues of illegal immigration and narcotics trafficking that had emerged, especially on the Sino-Russian and Tajik-Afghan borders. It was in response to these threats that Moscow applied to the United Nations for special peacekeeping power in the region and began to see the region as an area of "special responsibility and special interest." It also began to advocate the CIS collective security forces and joint activities. Taking as a point of departure the 1992 Treaty on Collective Security, the Russia-led CIS members developed a fairly ambitious vision of military and defense coordination, which the CIS summit adopted in February 1995 as the Collective Security Concept. The concept, among other things, assumed the right to set up CIS peacekeeping forces.

Russia's leadership therefore effectively legitimized its security efforts, taking considerable power away from the military authorities. It saw its task in the region as twofold—first, to bring order and stability, and second, to preserve Russia's traditional powerful influences. In order to accomplish this, Yeltsin declared his intention to set up some thirty Russian military bases in the CIS states, and he envisioned the emergence of a common economic, political, and defense union in the area.[36] The new vision was based on the Foreign Intelligence Service's view of the security threat, which indicated a determination to prevent outsiders from filling a possible "power vacuum" in the region. The perceived security threats included especially the activities of Muslim states, such as Iran and Pakistan, in central Asia and the Caucasus. These threats resulted partly from Yeltsin's neglect of the area. The definition of the security threats also prominently included those from the United States and NATO's expansion.

Consistent with such a perception of threats, Russia sought to maintain its military presence in central Asia and the Caucasus. To keep away influences of Iran, China, and Afghanistan, it contributed greatly to guarding the borders of Turkmenistan, Kyrgyzstan, and Tajikistan. In the case of the last, Russia's presence was so extensive that Afghan border guards negotiated directly with Russian military commanders. Primakov's appointment led to the reestablishment of a balance between political and military tools of policy and helped to facilitate the end of the Tajik civil war and a peace treaty that was signed in June 1997 in Moscow. When it came to the Caucasus, however, Russia's stabilizing efforts were far less successful. Despite Primakov's more firmly established control of peacekeeping forces, he failed to stabilize the situation in Georgia. The earlier support by Russia's military of the Ab-khaz separatist movement backfired and contributed to Moscow's inability to mediate the conflict. It also resulted in Georgia's declining to support the CIS's collective security efforts. Finally, Russia intervened in Chechnya in order to respond to the republic's secessionism and to maintain a presence in the Caucasus. In addition to territorial integrity, Russia sought to defend the important Baku-Novorossiysk pipeline that runs through Chechnya. However, after the first Chechen war (1994–1996) and the May 1997 Chechen presidential elections, Moscow developed no specific policy in the republic, and Chechnya continued its slide into anarchy.

Russia's integration efforts on the western front differed from those in central Asia and the Caucasus. In the west, Moscow was especially eager to respond to the "threat" of NATO's expansion by normalizing and developing military ties with Belarus and Ukraine. Belarus, given its vital geostrategic location and pro-Russian orientation, emerged as particularly important. Ever since the two sides had signed the Treaty on the Formation of the Russia-Belarus Union State in April 1996, they had committed themselves to a far-reaching integration in political and military areas. They developed a common perception of security threats and a close coordination of foreign policies, and they pledged the establishment of a defense alliance. Under Primakov, Russia also activated political ties with Ukraine, which the new foreign minister saw as his first priority. The key issue here was the status of the Black Sea fleet, which Russia sought to preserve without jeopardizing its relations with Ukraine. Ukraine, on the other hand, was interested in legalizing the Russia-Ukraine post-Soviet borders by signing an appropriate treaty and therefore politically normalizing the two countries' relationship. As a result of Primakov's efforts, the two sides signed in May 1997 the so-called Big Treaty, which settled the fleet issue and legalized the borders. The treaty provoked some criticism on both sides, but Primakov's support was instrumental in its ratification in February 1999. Despite the hard-line domestic criticism, both Primakov and his successor Igor' Ivanov saw the political normalization with Ukraine as a step toward improving the two's relations, rather than as a concession to Ukrainian aspirations to join NATO. This attitude found broad social support at home, as 70 percent of Russians supported the "Big Treaty."[37] As for the policy toward the most pro-Western Baltic states, Russia sought to minimize the negative consequences of NATO's expansion by offering those states security guarantees, and by making explicit its position that Baltic membership in NATO would endanger Russia's good relations with NATO.

Economic Integration

Economic integration was another important aspect of Primakov's strategy. During the Soviet era, Russia and the former republics were tightly integrated economies (see table 3.6) and could not successfully break the multiple bonds of their mutual dependency. The initial opposition to Yeltsin's early policy of isolationism came from the former Soviet managers, who lobbied their views through the Civic Union. The appointment of Viktor Chernomyrdin as prime minister helped to further this group's agenda and signaled the change from the "West first" approach to the more region-sensitive approach. A former economic manager and the president of the largest gas company, Gazprom, Chernomyrdin lent Russia's regional policies more sensitivity with regard to its interdependence, rather than irreconcilable differences, with the former republics. His vision of relations in the former Soviet Union included manipulation of energy supplies for the purpose of making the energy-deficient former republics invest in Gazprom, as well as other large energy-related companies, such as Lukoil, Yukos, and Sidanko. Yeltsin endorsed this approach in his Decree No. 472, which was issued on May 7, 1995, and approved a new long-term energy strategy for Russia through 2010.

Primakov's own approach was different and more state oriented. Like Chernomyrdin, Primakov understood that what the Civic Union industrialists referred to as the "broken politicoeconomic ties" could not be easily repaired, and he, too, wanted to promote the interests of Russian businesses in the region. At the same time, the foreign minister wanted to actively practice "economic diplomacy"—the Kremlin's label for both negative and positive sanctions—to strengthen Russia's political interests in the region. He had in mind to capitalize on Russia's relative economic power (see table 4.4) in facilitating Russian-favored bilateral and multilateral political ties with the post-Soviet states. In the Statist spirit, Primakov reasoned that the state interests were superior to those of the private sector, and therefore one had to be prepared to invest in projects with the potential to facilitate the reintegration of the former republics.

This vision implied that integration of the former Soviet space would weigh heavily on the Russian state, rather than on the private sector—yet another indicator that the identity coalition behind the new vision in the region was at its core of a security nature. At the time such a vision had Yeltsin's support. The aforementioned presidential decree on the establishment of Russia's strategic course with the CIS members promised to draw the current members of the Economic Union into the Russia-dominant Customs Union based on "their deeply integrated economy and strategic political partnership."[38] It also proposed "the acceleration of practical steps toward the formation of a Payment Union," common foreign currency regulations, and, eventually, use of the Russian ruble as a reserve currency. Finally, the decree envisioned the creation of common "industrial, scientific-technical, and related structures," as well as "common interstate investment programs." While the decree mentioned the Interparliamentary Assembly of the CIS states as the preferred forum to develop the normative aspects of economic integration, the document also warned that a former republic's failure to adhere to "the model proposed by Russia" could have consequences in terms of "the scale of economic, political, and military support from Russia."

Yet the outlined strategy of multilateral integration remained largely unrealized, partly because of Russia's own economic difficulties and partly because some republics were eager to diversify their ties away from the former imperial core. These republics perceived the CIS economic integration projects as Russia's thinly veiled imperialism and therefore resisted even some commonsensical measures to coordinate economic policies. For instance, the Payment Union, as well as interstate investment cooperation, never materialized. Other economic agreements were not working effectively. The only major exception was the Customs Union, which was signed by Russia, Belarus, Kazakhstan, Kyrgyzstan, and Tajikistan in March 1995 and continued to function during Primakov's tenure. Russia made more progress in developing bilateral than multilateral relations in the region. In some cases, it successfully applied its economic power to achieve important political goals. In central Asia, for example, Russia used Turkmenistan's and Kazakhstan's dependence on Russia's energy pipelines to negotiate a more favorable treatment of ethnic Russians residing in these states. It also further consolidated its economic and political relations with Belarus.

With regard to Ukraine, Russia initiated and signed in February 1998 the ambitious Program of Economic Cooperation, which helped to revive the trade between the two countries and dealt with all major aspects of their economic relations from trade barriers to cooperation in various industries. The signing of the program became a part of the Russia-Ukraine treaty on economic cooperation for 1998–2007 and it followed the previously signed "Big Treaty" between the two. It helped to promote political normalization with the largest and most important of the post-Soviet states and therefore could be viewed as an achievement of the Kremlin's flexible economic diplomacy. Although it hardly promoted the integration originally envisioned by the Kremlin, it did defy the hard-line nationalist arguments on both sides and encouraged international cooperation in the region.

Cultural Aspects

The vision of post-Soviet integration also had a cultural component to it. Primakov felt that Russia had an obligation to respond to the political and cultural feelings of twenty-five million Russians who had found themselves outside their "homeland" and continued to identify with it. As early as in his sponsored 1994 Foreign Intelligence Report, Primakov directly linked the fate of the Russians in the former Soviet Union to the survival and prosperity of Russia. In addition to ethnic Russians, there were many who grew up speaking Russian as either their native or preferred language (see table 3.6). Combined, the Russian language–influenced community totaled about 30 percent of the entire population of the non-Russian post-Soviet states, which makes Russia, as one scholar acknowledged, "not simply a marginal national European state, but a potential center of a revived, distinct civilization."[39] The issue was closely related to preserving cultural balance inside Russia, which included by far the largest number of ethnic groups (some 140) with only five of its twenty-one ethnic republics having a clear majority of the titular nation (Chechnya, Chuvashia, Ingushetia, Tuva, and North Ossetia).

The challenge, as Primakov and Yeltsin saw it, was to find a way to revive the identity of the transnational community in the former Soviet area without giving ground to the hard-line Civilizationist opposition. Primakov's supporters cautioned against pushing the Russians-first vision too far and argued that such a vision could jeopardize Russia's own fragile multicultural balance. Although the leadership did not share the Civilizationist agenda and did not want to be led by it in its regional policies, it could no longer ignore close cultural ties in the region. The public opinion inside Russia seemed supportive of the government's efforts to find a middle ground between the earlier cultural isolationism and the hard-line ideas of imperial revival. Although most people consistently regretted the Soviet breakup, many did not see the Russian ethnicity or Orthodox religion as the key characteristics of the new "Russianness." Instead, 87 percent identified the obligatory features of a Russian as love for the country and perception of it as the motherland. In addition, most disagreed with the idea of Russia's political unification with adjacent territories populated mostly by Russians.[40] The solution, Primakov's supporters argued, was to embrace and to cautiously promote the idea of Eurasia as a multicultural, multiethnic, and multireligious community in place of the former Soviet Union.[41]

Russia's leadership seemed responsive to the idea. To promote it, the government first developed and began to promote the idea of dual citizenship in the former Soviet states, viewing it as an alternative to the direct support for Russians abroad advocated by the hard-line opposition.

The government also hoped to curb the uncontrolled flow of migrants to Russia by providing them with some security and peace of mind. Russia aggressively promoted dual citizenship, but by 1995 all the post-Soviet states, with the exception of Turkmenistan and Tajikistan, rejected the idea. In response, the Russian government began to advocate CIS citizenship. Both ideas meant to revive the identity of transnational community in the former Soviet area and would have given Russia the upper hand in shaping such a community. Yet none of these ideas was able to take strong root in the region.

The leadership was more successful in responding to the challenge of domestic multiculturalism. Rather than giving ethnic Russians "a leading role," it promoted what some political commentators interpreted as "hybrid, an eclectic mixture of values," while others viewed it as a Eurasian vision of multicultural federalism.[42] Most important in this respect was Presidential Decree No. 909, which was issued in June 1996 to approve the concept of the state nationalities policy of the Russian Federation. It stated the goal of a multiethnic Russia was to ensure "the cultural self-preservation and further development of national traditions and cooperation of Slavic, Turkic, Caucasian, Finno-Ugric, Mongolian and other peoples of Russia within the framework of Eurasian national-cultural space." The decree came close to Spain's model of offering autonomy to all interested constituent units by encouraging them to enter into power-sharing agreements with the center, rather than pursuing a path of complete independence. By March 1999, about fifty of Russia's eighty-nine constituent units had successfully negotiated various degrees of privileged status, with "work in progress" on a dozen or more. Although Chechnya was a notorious example of a violent deviation from the model of multicultural federalism, other Muslim republics, such as Dagestan, Ossetia, Tatarstan, and Bashkortostan, indicated their support for the project of Eurasian federalism.

To sum up, the foreign policy aspect of cultural integration did not materialize the way Yeltsin and Primakov had hoped. The issue of successfully bridging various ethnicities outside Russia remained largely unresolved partly because of Russia's low credibility in the former Soviet region, and partly because the cultural aspect of integration remained poorly defined. The leadership itself was far from clear as to what should replace the earlier ideas of the civic nation and cultural isolationism.

EVALUATING GREAT POWER BALANCING

The arrival of Primakov as the second foreign minister brought with it major changes in how the government perceived Russia's national interest and conducted international policies. The course of Great Power Balancing that had been advocated by the identity coalition of Statists did not mean to replicate the Soviet isolationist policies toward the West. The timing of Primakov's course, as well as domestic and international conditions, was fundamentally different. Yet the course that contained attempts to balance Western influences did bear some similarities to Soviet policies of containing the West, and to the extent that it did, it failed in accomplishing central foreign policy objectives. Trying to achieve the West's recognition through restoring a great power status had a limited effect under the conditions of Russia's increased economic and political dependence on Western nations. Russia had changed since Soviet rule, and the course of Great Power Balancing proved to have a mixed record in improving the country's international conditions.

The Record

Primakov's foreign policy had a number of successes, particularly in the realm of security. His attention to the former Soviet area and intense diplomatic involvement made a difference in negotiating peace in Moldova and Tajikistan (although not in Georgia). He also negotiated and pushed through ratification of the "Big Treaty" with Ukraine, which put the two countries' relations on a new security footing. The minister could also be credited for making progress in Russia's negotiations with NATO. Despite a number of setbacks in the two's relationship, Russia had developed a mechanism of permanent consultations with the alliance and obtained its written commitment not to deploy nuclear weapons or substantial new forces in the territory of new member states. In addition, the new minister worked hard to improve ties with the countries of Asia and the Asia-Pacific region.

Through his course, Primakov also restored some attributes of foreign policy autonomy. Although Russia continued to be highly dependent on the West in economic affairs, it made Washington more attentive to its national interests in the area of security issues. On such issues as arms sales and security in Yugoslavia, Primakov took a much tougher line than his predecessor, who, in the words of one journalist, "had corrupted Americans" by his willingness to follow in Washington's footsteps.[43] Both the elites and the general public expressed their strong support for the new course, welcoming its greater independence and concentration on solving security issues in the former Soviet Union. For example, on the issue of sending troops to the former Soviet republics, provided that Russia was asked to do so, the general public support grew from 35 to 56 percent during the 1993–1999 period. The elite's support on the same issue over the same period increased from 56 to 72 percent.[44]

Table 4.7 summarizes the foreign policy record of Great Power Balancing.

Table 4.7.   The Record of Great Power Balancing

Security	Peace agreements in the former Soviet region
	Mechanism of permanent consultations with NATO
	Improved ties with Asian world
Welfare	Failed economic union in the CIS
	Continued industrial stagnation at home
Autonomy	Less dependent decision making
Identity	Continued identity crisis

As analysts have acknowledged, Primakov accomplished these positive changes despite Russia's continuous decline in 1992–1997 and lack of balancing options. In the former Soviet region, one scholar noted, "Despite the sharp decline of its power, Russia has been far more successful and far less reticent in asserting its interests in the southern Near Abroad than is generally acknowledged."[45] Another realist scholar was surprised to note that the weakened Russia showed "a capacity to extract concessions"[46] in relations with the West. This policy activism from the position of weakness suggests yet again the limitations of realism as an international relations theory for understanding Primakov's foreign policy. Rather than being driven by material power alone, that policy was a response to a particular combination of international and domestic factors of a political and cultural nature.

However, Great Power Balancing had some major flaws as well. Primakov's failures to assert his vision in Iraq and Kosovo—as well as his uninspiring attempts to establish a strategic triangle of Russia, China, and India to contain the United States' global hegemony—are cases in point. Even more obvious were his failures to improve Russia's welfare, the issue for which dealing with the strategy of balancing Western influences had not been designed in the first place. Yet every foreign policy—especially that of a country during an economic depression—must have the welfare dimension as its central guiding criterion. The project of integrating the former Soviet region was especially misguided in this respect. Integration partly meant to respond to the imperative of improving life throughout the region, but it proved to be excessively geopolitically driven and not as founded on economic grounds. Most multilateral CIS-based economic agreements were not working properly, and the former Soviet states continued to drift separately. Most of them also rejected Russia's citizenship initiatives. Several regional initiatives emerged, including those without Russia as a participant. Faced with Primakov's state grandeur in the former Soviet region, the Russian private sector was not willing to invest in the relationships in the former Soviet Union. The energy companies, for example, grew strong by the time of the integration strategy, but often did not feel compelled to back up the state with their resources. While interested in expanding to the former Soviet space and maintaining stability there, the energy entrepreneurs did not want to subsidize the former republics or supply them at lower energy prices in exchange for their political loyalty to the Russian state. Despite some serious efforts on Russia's part to make integration work, its results left much to be desired. As far as the Russian economy was concerned, the post-Soviet integration did not provide the economy with new opportunities for growth. Nor did it bring any foreign investments or relieve the burden of foreign debt.

Nor did the new foreign policy strategy make serious progress in improving Russia's cultural well-being. The fact that Russia was going through an identity crisis was obvious to policymakers and observers alike. Symptomatic of the identity search was, for example, the discussion about Russia's new "national idea" that Yeltsin initiated immediately following his 1996 reelection as president. Primakov addressed the crisis by proposing a Eurasianist foreign policy orientation in building strategic relations with China, Iraq, and India. His cooperation with the West was merely pragmatic, as opposed to strategic, and NATO's intervention in Yugoslavia pushed Russia further away from the West. Yet the Westernist component of Russia's cultural identity had been confirmed by Russia's post-Soviet developments, and many Russians continued to identify with the West. The strategy of Eurasia-oriented Great Power Balancing was not successful in addressing this part of the Russian national psyche.

Lessons

What lessons can one learn from the foreign policy of Great Power Balancing? Undoubtedly, Primakov's diplomacy had important accomplishments, such as the already-discussed more democratic policymaking process, greater attention to the former Soviet region, the generally pragmatic nature of relationships with Western nations, and the aggressive search for new opportunities outside the West. Yet the central thrust of this diplomacy, rooted in Primakov's view of Russia's national interest as that of a contributor to balancing U.S. unipolar ambitions in the world, was a misguided one. If Russia would ever have to be preoccupied with the role assigned to it by its second foreign minister, it would have to take place in a different era and under different circumstances. Devoting valuable material and political resources to the task of building a multipolar world was hardly a worthy central task. Such preoccupation was hardly pragmatic and, despite Primakov's own convictions, bore only a superficial resemblance to Alexander Gorchakov's strategy of "concentration." Rather than "concentrating" on domestic economic and social revival, as that strategy had prescribed, Primakov's Russia occupied itself with balancing the West and integrating the periphery (also in the context of balancing the West). Two more specific lessons can be formulated.

First, during this difficult era of economic and geopolitical decline, Russia would have accomplished more by attempting to engage the West in cooperative projects than by trying to assemble a coalition of those unhappy with Western policies. Persistent thinking about the West as a "power pole" prevented Russia's foreign policymakers from probing and pursuing economic and security opportunities that might have been mutually beneficial.

Certainly, a great deal of blame for missing such opportunities lies with the Western side, which preferred to develop relationships with the narrow and corrupt ruling elite while simultaneously pursuing policies of containing Russia on security issues. Flawed Western financial assistance is an illustration of the overall narrow and self-serving strategy in working with Russia. Instead of encouraging social safety nets and rule of law in the process of fundamental structural transformation, Western assistance served merely to encourage a destruction of the previous economic system. The newly emerging system was far from socially or legally responsible. The fact that the West-sponsored reform strategy did not help to facilitate the transformation was reflected in, among other things, the figures of the overall capital flight during 1992–1999, which exceeded the amount of financial assistance. According to Russia's official statistics, the overall capital flight during that period was $182 billion, whereas the amount of foreign assistance constituted $174 billion.[47] The so-called reformers in Russia were well aware of the state of affairs and yet were unable to say no to Western "assistance."

While providing financial assistance, Western nations pursued policies that kept Russia safely at arm's length on security matters. First, there was the expansion of NATO, which even the liberal-minded Kozyrev saw as a "continuation, though by inertia, of a policy aimed at containment of Russia."[48] Many in Russia perceived the decision largely as an attempt to fill the existing security vacuum by taking advantage of Russia's weakness. In addition to NATO's expansion, Russia took a lot of heat for its "imperialist intentions" in the former Soviet region and "human rights violations" in Chechnya; other countries often ignored Russia's legitimate considerations of security and territorial integrity. Many in the West continued to mistrust the former "red menace," viewing it as threatening and barbaric. The United States, as the strongest Western power, bears prime responsibility for the inadequate policies toward Russia. European leaders, too, contributed to Russia's security isolation. Concerned with the country's lack of democracy and the conduct of the Chechen war, they suspended Russia's moves toward integration into Western European institutions. As a result, the Russian-sought "Common Strategy of the EU on Russia"—an elaborate document that formulated principles of relations with Russia and made its integration dependent on progress in building democratic and market institutions—was adopted only in June 1999.

Still, the West's flawed strategy was no excuse for giving up engagement in favor of limited cooperation. The lesson to draw is that, without sacrificing its interests, Russia should stay actively engaged with policies of Europe and the United States. This does not mean approval of every Western action (or acceptance of every criticism from the West), but it does mean that for the time being, resistance and condemnation should be restricted to political rhetoric. If anything, Russia's more modest economic capabilities, relative to those of Western nations (see table 4.3), should be a sober reminder to ambitious politicians. If one has no special tools to make an elephant move, trying to do it anyway is not a smart strategy.

The second lesson is that the state must look for economic opportunities more aggressively and work with the private sector to advance national interest. The Statist identity coalition of nonliberal origins proved sufficiently strong to challenge the initially isolationist policies in the former Soviet region, but it failed to rally sufficient support for economic integration. Neither the Russian state nor former republics had resources sufficient for reviving the economic ties in the region. A number of Primakov-outlined initiatives remained on paper only, and his efforts made many former republics wary of Russia's power intentions. The latter prompted them to create security groups of their own. Most prominently, in October 1997 a coalition of key states that had never signed the Russia-initiated Collective Security Concept—Georgia, Ukraine, Azerbaijan, and Moldova—established a regional group, GUAM, with an explicit purpose of containing Russia. If anything, this action was an indicator of a failure of multilateral integration. Multilateral arrangements cannot be forced and are not always superior to those concluded on a bilateral basis.[49] Working with the private sector and facilitating mutually beneficial bilateral agreements is a better means for accomplishing economic integration.

NOTES

1. Yevgeni Primakov as quoted at his first official press conference as foreign minister (Robert H. Donaldson and Joseph L. Nogee, *The Foreign Policy of Russia: Changing Systems, Enduring Interests* [Armonk, NY: M. E. Sharpe, 1998], 119) and at the conference "Preobrazhennaya Rossiya" held at Moscow Institute of International Relations in 1992 ("Preobrazhennaya Rossiya," *Mezhdunarodnaya zhizn'* 3–4 [1992]: 104).

2. Samuel Huntington, "The Clash of Civilizations?" *Foreign Affairs* 4, no. 72 (1993).

3. For elaboration, see especially Yevgeni Primakov, "Mezhdunarodniye otnosheniya nakanune XXI veka: Problemy, perspektivy," *Mezhdunarodnaya zhizn'* 10 (1996) and Yevgeni Primakov, "Rossiya v mirovoi politike," *Mezhdunarodnaya zhizn'* 5 (1998).

4. "Strategiya Rossiyi v XXI veke," *Nezavisimaya gazeta*, June 18, 1998.

5. "The Need for a New Ostpolitik," *Financial Times*, January 16, 1996.

6. Yevgeni Primakov, *Gody v bol'shoi politike* (Moscow: Sovershenno sekretno, 1999), 213, 217–21.

7. Primakov, presentation at the conference "Preobrazhennaya Rossiya," 104.

8. As cited in Primakov, "Rossiya v mirovoi politike." For a more extended analysis, see Flemming Splidsboel-Hansen, "Past and Future Meet: Aleksandr Gorchakov and Russian Foreign Policy," *Europe-Asia Studies* 54, no. 3 (2002).

9. National security concepts and foreign policy concepts are available in *Vneshnyaya politika i bezopasnost' sovremennoi Rossiyi*, ed. Tatyana Shakleyina (Moscow: ROSSPEN, 2002), 4:51–90, 110–11. For analysis, see Alla Kassianova, "Russia: Still Open to the West?," *Europe-Asia Studies* 6, no. 53 (2001).

10. Boris Yeltsin, "Mesto i rol' Rossiyi v period formiruyuschegosya mnogopolyarnogo mira," *Mezhdunarodnaya zhizn'* 6 (1998): 3.

11. For instance, Aleksei Bogaturov proposed viewing the post–Cold War international system as "pluralistic unipolarity," in which the unipolar center is a group of responsible states, rather than one state (the United States). Bogaturov saw Russia as a member of the group and argued for consolidation of its position within the global center, as well as for discouraging the formation of one-state unipolarity in the world. Aleksei Bogaturov, "Pluralisticheskaya odnopolyarnost' i interesy Rossiyi," *Svobodnaya mysl'* 2 (1996); "Amerika i Rossiya: Ot izbiratel'nogo partnerstva k izbiratel'nomu soprotivleniyu," *Mezhdunarodnaya zhizn'* 6 (1998).

12. For instance, Gorbachev's key foreign policy adviser, Georgi Shakhnazarov, prepared an analytical report on Russia's foreign priorities, in many respects sympathetic to Primakov's vision ("Vneshnepoiliticheskiye prioritety Rossiyi," *Politicheskaya mysl'* 1 [1998]).

13. For instance, the Ministry of Defense officials, such as General Leonid Ivashev, for quite some time dreamed of restoring Russia's superpower status ("Rossiya mozhet snova stat' sverkhderzhavoi," *Nezavisimaya gazeta*, March 7, 1995).

14. Gennadi Zyuganov, *Geografiya pobedy* (Moscow, 1998).

15. Aleksandr Dugin, "Yevraziyski proyekt," *Zavtra*, August 1996.

16. Yuri Fedorov, "Krizis vneshnei politiki Rossiyi," *Pro et Contra* 6, nos. 1–2 (2001).

17. Irina Kobrinskaya, "Pragmaticheski liberalizm vo vneshnei politike," *Otkrytaya politika* 7–8 (1997); Viktor Sheinis, "Rossiya i Yevropa: Interesy protiv mifov," *Nezavisimaya gazeta*, December 20, 2000.

18. For analysis of the decision to expand NATO and Russia's reaction to it, see James Goldgeier, *Not Whether, but When: The US Decision to Enlarge NATO* (Washington, DC: Brookings, 1999); and J. L. Black, *Russia Faces NATO Expansion: Bearing Gifts or Bearing Arms?* (Lanham, MD: Rowman & Littlefield, 2000), respectively.

132 Chapter 4

19. As cited in Neil MacFarlane, "Realism and Russian Strategy after the Collapse of the USSR," in *Unipolar Politics*, eds. Ethan B. Kapstein and Michael Mastanduno (New York: Columbia University Press, 1999), 242.

20. As cited in Leonid Mlechin, *Ministry inostrannykh del: Romantiki i tsiniki* (Moscow: Tsentrpoligraf, 2001), 620.

21. Richard Sakwa, *Russian Politics and Society*, 3rd ed. (London: Routledge, 2002), 294.

22. Some Statists linked the two events directly. See, for example, Aleksei Pushkov, "Otrezvlyayuschaya yasnost," *Nezavisimaya gazeta*, March 1999.

23. I draw here on Robert O. Freedman, *Russian Policy toward the Middle East since the Collapse of the Soviet Union* (Seattle: The Henry M. Jackson School of International Studies, University of Washington, 2001), 34–40; and Donaldson and Nogee, *The Foreign Policy of Russia*, 301–5.

24. Allen Lynch, "Realism of Russian Foreign Policy," *Europe-Asia Studies* 53 (2001): 15, 28.

25. Oksana Antonenko, "Russia, NATO and European Security after Kosovo," *Survival* 41, no. 4 (1999/2000): 143.

26. Aleksei Pushkov, "Sindrom Chernomyrdina," *Nezavisimaya gazeta*, June 11, 1999.

27. Aleksandr Belenski, "Mudrost' sily," *Sovetskaya Rossiya*, April 27, 1999; Gennadi Zyuganov, "Yugoslavski rubezh," *Sovetskaya Rossiya*, April 6, 1999.

28. Aleksandr Lukin, "Den' pobedy pod bombami," *Nezavisimaya gazeta*, May 27, 1999.

29. Antonenko, "Russia, NATO and European Security," 134–36.

30. Freedman, *Russian Policy toward the Middle East*, 23.

31. Donaldson and Nogee, *The Foreign Policy of Russia*, 316.

32. *Rossiyskaya gazeta*, September 23, 1995; Primakov, "Rossiya v mirovoi politike," *Mezhdunarodnaya zhizn'* 5 (1998): 11.

33. "Vozroditsya li soyuz? Buduscheye postsovetskogo prostranstva," *NG-Stsenariyi*, May 23, 1996.

34. *Rossiyskaya gazeta*, February 17, 1995, 5. Yeltsin's change of perception toward a more hegemonic role of Russia can be traced to an early-1994 television interview, in which he called Russia "the first among equals" in the post-Soviet region.

35. The poll data are from: Dimitri K. Simes, *After the Collapse* (New York: Simon & Schuster, 1999), 220; and Susan Birgerson, *After the Breakup of a Multi-Ethnic Empire* (New York: Praeger, 2002), 88.

36. Mark Webber, *CIS Integration Trends: Russia and the Former Soviet South* (London: Royal Institute of International Affairs, 1997), 13–14.

37. Georgi Shakhnazarov et al., "Vneshnepoliticheskiye prioritety Rossiyi."

38. *Rossiyskaya gazeta*, September 23, 1995.

39. Igor Zevelev, *Russia and Its New Diaspora* (Washington, DC: United States Institute of Peace, 2001), 175.

40. The poll data are from: Zevelev, *Russia and Its New Diaspora*, 61; Vera Tolz, *Russia: Inventing the Nation* (London: Arnold, 2001), 263.

41. Graham Smith, *Post-Soviet States* (London: Arnold, 1999), chap. 6; Tolz, *Russia: Inventing the Nation*, chap. 8.

42. Smith, *Post-Soviet States*, 143.

43. Izvestiya correspondent Stanislav Kondrashev, as quoted in Leonid Mlechin, *Ministry inostrannykh del*, 607.

44. William Zimmerman, *The Russian People and Foreign Policy* (Princeton, NJ: Princeton University Press, 2002), 91.

45. Rajan Menon, "After Empire: Russia and the Southern 'Near Abroad,'" in *The New Russian Foreign Policy*, ed. Michael Mandelbaum (New York: Council on Foreign Relations, 1998), 148.

46. MacFarlane, "Realism and Russian Strategy," 244.

47. Ivan Korolev, "Integratsiya Rossiyi v mirovuyu ekonomiku," *Pro et Contra* 6, nos. 1–2 (2001): 76.

48. Andrei Kozyrev, "Partnership or Cold Peace?," *Foreign Policy* 99 (Summer 1995): 13.

49. Primakov had a tendency to view bilateral ties in the former Soviet region as a "negative process" relative to those of a multilateral nature (see, for example, his *Gody v bol'shoi politike*, 387).

5

❦

The World after
September 11 and
Pragmatic Cooperation

Such a country as Russia can survive and develop within the existing
borders only if it stays as a great power. During all of its times of weakness . . . Russia was invariably confronted with the threat of disintegration.

We are a part of the Western European culture. No matter where our
people live, in the Far East or in the south, we are Europeans.

—Vladimir Putin[1]

With the arrival of Vladimir Putin and especially after the terrorist
attacks on the United States in September 2001, Russia's foreign
policy took yet another turn. This turn, while surprising, was not entirely
unexpected. The new course of Pragmatic Cooperation was both a continuation of and a departure from the previous Great Power Balancing.
Changed international and internal conditions brought to prominence a
new identity coalition, which helped to articulate a new vision of Russia's
national interest.

RUSSIA'S NEW PRAGMATISM

The Changed World Context

Two global developments were particularly important in leading to the
reformulation of Russia's foreign policy. The first was encouraging and of
an economic nature. It had to do with the relative recovery of the Russian
economy after the August 1998 financial crisis and new opportunities that

the recovery was promising for the country. The growth had been steady, and other indicators, too, had been encouraging (see table 5.1). Commercially, too, Russia was in a relatively advantageous position. Its foreign trade had been enjoying a structural surplus, and the economy was wide open for commercial operations. The share of foreign trade had been around 50 percent of the gross domestic product (GDP), making Russia's economy, on that measure, about as open as Germany's. The stock of foreign direct investment accumulated since 1989 remained low: about ten times less than in China and five times less than in Brazil.[2] Yet, the rising world oil prices further provided Russia with new opportunities to explore.

Table 5.1. Russia's Economic Recovery, 1998–2001 (% of 1998)

	GDP	Consumption	Government Investment	Capital Spending	Flight
1998	100	100	100	100	100
1999	105.4	87.2	104.6	105.4	94
2000	114.1	96.2	122.7	131.4	123.6
2001	120	101.3	131.1	133.7	73.6

Source: Philip Hanson, "The Russian Economic Recovery: Do Four Years of Growth Tell Us That the Fundamentals Have Changed?," *Europe-Asia Studies* 55, no. 3 (2003): 386.

The second development was negative and had to do with an intensification of terrorist activities in the Caucasus and worldwide. In Russia, the Kremlin's inaction in the aftermath of the 1996 peace agreement with Chechen rebels led to the further spread of anarchy inside the republic, not to political stabilization. The newly elected leader of Chechnya, Aslan Maskhadov, failed to maintain order, and mass kidnapping and extortion by local warlords continued. In August 1999, Chechen rebels led by Shamil Basayev and the Arab fighter Khattab had occupied parts of the neighboring republic Dagestan, in response to which the Kremlin resumed military operations in the region. Also in August, two bombs exploded in apartment buildings in Moscow, killing hundreds of civilians. The sheer magnitude of violence was unprecedented. Russians united behind Putin, who was running for president on the platform of "eradicating extremism" in Chechnya and reestablishing a "strong state" throughout the entire Russian territory. Initially, the popularity of then prime minister Putin was at the level of only 2 percent, but in two months it jumped to 26 percent, and as the war in Chechnya progressed, it reached the unprecedented 58 percent mark in January 2000.[3]

It was at this point that the domestic sense of insecurity was reinforced by the September 11, 2001, terrorist attacks on the United States. The horrific acts created a principally different social and political atmosphere inside Russia. President George W. Bush proclaimed terrorism to be "pure evil" directed at freedom-loving people throughout the world and argued the necessity to launch a strategy of preemption. Several leading intellectuals called for the capture or killing of Osama bin Laden and linked the violent attacks to Islam and the Middle Eastern region. In Russia, these developments provided Putin with a formidable opportunity to bolster his domestic and international posture and to vindicate his conception of security threats. Russia's new president wasted no time in taking advantage of September 11 to reshape Russia's relations with the United States and redefine the threats to Russia as being characterized by global terrorism.

New Identity Coalition

In response to these global developments, Putin put forward the ideology of pragmatism and self-concentration. The ideology articulated the vision of a new identity coalition, which combined both Westernist and Statist influences. With Westernizers, Putin came out critical of past practices of overextending foreign policy resources—a possible reference to both the Soviet and Primakov periods. However, he also committed himself to traditional values typically emphasized by Statists and Civilizationists. For instance, in his programmatic article "Russia at the Turn of the Millennium," which he addressed to his electorate, the future president emphasized patriotism, a strong state, and social solidarity as his country's key values. Unlike Gorbachev or Kozyrev, Putin was not eager to replicate Western social democratic or liberal values on Russian soil, and he made it clear that Russia would never become the "second edition of . . . the U.S. or Britain."[4] Rather, he saw his country as a modern great power capable of adapting to a changing world under state leadership. In the tradition of Statism, priority is given to governability and the state's ability to exercise its power, whereas democracy comes second.

Our state and its institutions have always played an exceptionally important role in the life of the country and its people. For Russians a strong state is not an anomaly that should be disposed of. Quite the contrary, they see it as a source of and guarantor of order and the initiator and main driving force of any change.[5]

Also in Primakov's Statist spirit, Putin spoke of the Eurasianist dimension of Russia's identity, and in late 1999–early 2000, he visited the key states of central Asia, China, India, Mongolia, North Korea, and Brunei. Furthermore, he was determined to continue the war in Chechnya as he saw fit, despite criticism from his Westernist opponents inside and outside the country. The Statist thinking therefore proved to be resilient in post-Primakov Russia.

Yet, unlike Primakov, who tended to view the world primarily in terms of new threats to Russia's security, Putin pointed to both threats and opportunities. In particular, he was keen on emphasizing the economic nature of the contemporary world and the need for Russia to be successful in its geoeconomic, rather than military, struggle. In the president's own words, "The norm of the international community and the modern world is a tough competition—for markets, investments, political, and economic influence . . . nobody is eager to help us. We have to fight for our place under the economic sun."[6] As far as security threats to the modern system of international relations were concerned, Putin saw them coming from terrorist activities, rather than state-organized military capabilities. In this, his Statism was also distinct from that of Primakov. Putin's "no one is going to war with us" was a reference to states, yet he was convinced that terrorism had interest in attacking Russia. His support for the Western countries and the United States' efforts in fighting international terrorism after September 11 was therefore not tactical, but came from his principal belief system.

This new vision was hardly an exclusive product of Putin's own imagination. Rather, it represented interests of the new mixed social coalition. Because commercial elites often defended Russia's Westernist identity, whereas military and security elites promoted Statism, the new coalition was sometimes referred to as the alliance of oligarchs and *siloviks*, or chekists (from the Russian CheKa, the original name of the Bolshevik security service). Liberal and commercially oriented Westernizers strongly supported Putin's election. Especially important were Russia's oligarchs, the group of superwealthy businessmen that had emerged as a powerful force in 1996. At that time they had managed to overcome their differences and pull together enough financial resources to reelect Boris Yeltsin, who was unpopular then. At the same time, many Statists and Civilizationists felt compelled to embrace Putin. Statists and various members of Russia's military elite supported him because of his background in the security service and his stated beliefs in strengthening the state and social order. Initially, even Aleksandr Prokhanov, the editor of the hard-line newspaper *Zavtra*, had written favorably about him, although a year later he returned to his typical "irreconcilable" opposition to the Kremlin. Although the members of the new coalition were committed to principally different worldviews, at this time they agreed on Putin as the preferred leader of the state. The new identity coalition rose to prominence in the post–1998 new domestic and external context. The relative recovery of the Russian economy improved the oligarchs' position, and the intensification of terrorist activities in the Caucasus and worldwide strengthened the *siloviks'* position. In the new world context of both threats and opportunities, the oligarchs and *siloviks* each hoped to increase their influence on the president.

In his turn, Putin was planning to take advantage of the unstable coalition's resources, while exercising his authority as he saw fit. He did not hide his preference for the state-dominant model of economic development and made known his lack of respect for how oligarchs emerged and enriched themselves. But he also expressed his readiness to honor the already-underway privatization and market reforms. In one of his private meetings with businessmen, Putin summed up his philosophy by telling businessmen that "they could keep what they had already stolen, but now they had to play clean, pay taxes, make investments and stay out of politics."[7] The president was being ruthless to those oligarchs, such as Boris Berezovski, Vladimir Gusinski, and Mikhail Khodorkovski, who he perceived as violating his new deal. The first two had to emigrate, and the third, the heir of the oil giant Yukos, was arrested on charges of multiple fraud and tax evasion. The president had more respect for security elites, especially the army, which had been much humiliated under Yeltsin. The first war in Chechnya taught the military, among other things, that it could not count on the civilian leadership for adequate financial assistance. Putin moved to change that by proposing a considerable reduction in the army's personnel—from 1.2 million in 2001 to between 800,000 and 850,000 by 2005[8]—along with modernization and a considerable increase in the military budget (see table 5.2 for details of the budget increase).

Table 5.2.   Russia's Increased Military Budget, 1999–2002

Year	1999	2000	2001	2002
Billions of Rubles	109.0	111.0	218.9	284.1

Source: Dale R. Herspring, "Putin and the Armed Forces," in *Putin's Russia: Past Imperfect, Future Uncertain*, ed. Dale R. Herspring (Lanham, MD: Rowman & Littlefield, 2003), 170.

The New Vision of National Interest—Pragmatic Westernism

Consistent with the new vision of Russia's identity, a new conceptualization of national interest was adopted. In the earlier period of his presidency, Putin had indicated that he was wary of U.S. policies and intentions, and he acted in ways that coincided with Primakov's Statist philosophy of multipolarity and Great Power Balancing. Yet Putin soon revealed his principal differences from his predecessors. For him, the most important national interest lay in Russia's modernization and economic growth, not balancing American influences in the world. Such a perspective assumed that in today's world, geoeconomics gained the upper hand over geopolitics, and thus Russia had to learn to defend its national interests by economic means. It also implied that Russia had to economize its resources and not overstretch itself in world political affairs. Balancing, therefore, needed to yield to pragmatic cooperation. Finally, it meant that any integration in the former Soviet area had to be open to and compatible with domestic private interests and the task of Russia's gradual integration with the world economy.

To substantiate his vision, Putin warned of the danger of turning into a third-world country. Ridiculing overly noisy great power rhetoric—"let us not recollect our national interests on those occasions when we have to make some loud statements"—Russia's new leader compared Russia to Portugal, the EU's poorest member. He then drew the uncomforting conclusion, "It would take us fifteen years and an eight percent annual growth of our GDP to reach the per capita GDP level of present-day Portugal."[9] The reality was that, despite Russia's economic recovery after the 1998 financial crisis, the size of its economy and purchasing power was less than one-fourth the size of the economies of China and Japan, and less than one-tenth the size of the economies of the United States and the European Union.[10] Putin's support for the concept of multipolarity was also muter, and the key emphasis of the new National Security Concept was on economic decline, organized crime, corruption, terrorism, and separatism. After September 11, his support for multipolarity continued to decline, and the focus was on pragmatism and self-concentration in foreign policy. Despite some common anti-Western sentiments among the members of Russia's political class, the president became far more active in promoting Russia's relationships with the United States and Europe, and more passive on the Eastern and Asian fronts.

Yet, it would be a mistake to cast Putin as a pro-Western liberal. It is true that he saw the first task as improving the state of the Russian economy by capitalizing on domestic oil reserves and increasing the ability to export to the West (provided that the West would invest more actively in the Russian petroleum industry). But at the same time, such economic improvement was seen as a way to confirm Russia's great power status and to preserve the required space to maneuver to defend Russia's political interests in world politics. Without antagonizing the West, and given the West's need to have Russia as an ally, Putin planned to promote its interests in relations with Chechnya, Iran, and Iraq as he saw fit. This vision of Russia as a defensive and pragmatically pro-Western power was different from the earlier described visions of integration with the West or balancing the West's global influences. So long as the new Russian leader was attempting to synthesize across Russia's political spectrum by incorporating both nationalist and Westernist perspectives, the new vision of national interest was culturally sustainable (table 5.3 summarizes Putin's view of national interest).

Table 5.3. Pragmatic Cooperation (PC): View of National Interest

What?	A great power in the West-centered world
How?	Counterterrorist cooperation with Europe and the United States Limited integration into the world economy Market-based principles in the former Soviet region

RESHAPING THE DEBATE ON NATIONAL INTEREST

Putin's decision to support the United States in the post–September 11 struggle against terrorism and his redefinition of national interest led to an important change in the Russian discourse. Although many representatives of Russian foreign policy elites supported his move, others offered their reservations and even hard-line criticisms. Many politicians and intellectuals were worried that U.S. policies might undermine, rather than strengthen, peace and stability in the world. They were therefore reminding the president that an unqualified support for the United States had the potential to damage Russia's relations with Europe, China, and Muslim countries.

Tentative Support of Liberal Westernizers and Social Democrats

Despite their criticism of Putin's early foreign policy, liberal Westernizers threw their support behind his post–September 11 vision. Yet they urged him to go beyond a tactical alliance with the West and toward forging a development of common identity and cultural values. A leader of the liberal Yabloko party, Grigori Yavlinski, in an article titled "A Temporary Friendship or an Eternal Alliance?," insisted that Putin's vision of national interest had to be viewed as a "choice in favor of a long-term unity with Western or European civilization, of which Russia is an organic part." In Russian, the word "alliance" (*soyuz*) is the same as the word "union," and this fact made the proposed rapprochement with the West sound similar to Kozyrev's strategy of integration. Without such a long-term strategic union with the West, argued Yavlinski, Russia was doomed to remain what he saw as an "oligarchic capitalism" without sufficient respect for human rights and freedoms of expression.[11]

Ideologists of another liberal party, the Union of Right-Wing Forces, went even further. Not unlike some Western politicians and commentators, they viewed the events of September 11 as a clash between "civilization" and "barbarians," who had yet to learn the "universal" rules of "civilization."[12] In a similar way, President George W. Bush and his defense secretary, Donald Rumsfeld, viewed the problem of terrorism in terms of pure evil against "freedom-loving people" throughout the world. Thomas Friedman, writing in the *New York Times*, specified the evil as not just Osama bin Laden, but "angry people" from "failing states in the Muslim and third world." For Friedman, the real war was between those with a modern and progressive outlook and those with a medieval one.[13] This group of Russian Westernizers also came out as critical of the pragmatic element in Putin's vision of national interest and insisted that Russia make a decisive choice in favor of "civilized nations." In addition to supporting the United States after September 11, many Westernizers also supported its military intervention in Iraq and argued that Russia had to side with the United States.

The attitude of the Social Democrats was a more complex and cautious one. Because Social Democrats viewed the world as culturally pluralist, rather than centered on the West, they were more inclined to search for solutions to September 11 by developing a global intercultural dialogue. This group, with supporters in the broader political center, was also supportive of Putin's new vision and generally sympathetic toward the West. At the same time, the group cautioned that, among other issues, the cause of the spread of terrorism was the United States' unilateral use of power and the narrowly chosen pro-American model of globalization. The quest for future policy choices for Russia, as the leader of Russia's Democratic Socialist Movement Aleksandr Buzgalin put it, "needs to be pursued in the context of looking for alternatives to the current model of globalization."[14]

The Social Democratic group also did not view the West as a culturally essentialist entity shaped by an American liberal capitalist outlook, as did the Russian Westernizers. Instead, Social Democrats perceived the West as an arena of competition between liberal capitalist and social democratic values, often represented by the American and European models, respectively. Accordingly, the choice for Russia was broader than merely joining the West versus remaining marginalized. As the group was less inclined to view the United States and Europe as culturally similar, some Social Democrats recommended that Putin explicitly side with Europe in the post–September 11 world. They urged Russia's president to choose in favor of the "social democratic" Europe of Tony Blair and Gerhard Schroeder, and not the American "neoconservatism" of George W. Bush. In their view, the former had a broad domestic appeal and would improve Russia's international standing, whereas the latter had the potential to isolate Russia from Europe and turn it into a raw-material appendage of the American economy. Social Democrats also cautioned against Russia's pro-American choice, which they feared would strengthen (and not weaken, as Yavlinski has argued) Russian nondemocratic tendencies.[15] Many other scholars in Russia and elsewhere called for the formation of a broad coalition of countries and cultures, including China and India, to respond to the global terrorist threat.[16]

In several respects, the views of this school of thought corresponded with those of President Putin. First, Putin also downplayed military interventions as a long-term solution to the problem of terrorism (which at the time contrasted with his choice of solutions in Chechnya). He did not commit Russian troops to the effort, and instead emphasized the relevance of international law and the United Nations. He was also careful to not cast his actions in a pro-American or an anti-Islamic light, and immediately after the terrorist attack, warned against framing the policy response as a war of civilizations. The latter is important given the afore-mentioned tendency of some of Russia's liberal Westernizers to character-ize 9/11 as a clash of Western "civilization" with a cultural "barbarianism." Second, and somewhat consistent with the Social Democrats' philosophy, Putin seemed to have differentiated between Europe and the United States, and indicated his interest in developing strategic relationships with Euro-pean countries. In his April 2002 state of the nation address, Putin strongly emphasized Russia's European priority, stating, "We have to firmly pro-claim our priorities on the European direction." He went on to define Russia's policy priorities in relations with Europe and the United States as those of "integration" and "maintenance of constant dialogue," respec-tively.[17] He also sided with France and Germany against military interven-tion in Iraq.

Criticism of Statists and Civilizationists

While Westernizers were critical of the new vision's pragmatism, Statists and Civilizationists were worried about its pro-Western component. The range of their reactions varied from moderate support for the idea of pragmatic cooperation against the "common enemy" of terrorism to an outright rejection of any association with the West.

Statists who were former supporters of Primakov's foreign policy course aimed to preserve Russia's independence and great power status in world politics. This school continued to view as Russia's main national priority the preservation of such status and the development of a multi-polar world. Primakov himself felt uneasy about Putin's post-9/11 strat-egy, referring to it as "justified, yet a big risk" and worrying about the American military presence in the Caucasus and central Asia.[18] Other Statists emphasized the "harmful" aspects of American military hege-mony and political unilateralism as one of the reasons for the attacks of September 11. One influential commentator argued: "Under the slogan of the struggle with terrorism, the United States achieved an important geopolitical victory, especially in central Asia and the Caucasus—regions that Russia viewed in the area of its vital interests. . . . As the result of the antiterrorist operation, Russia has lost important mechanisms of interna-tional influence related to the CIS Collective Security treaty and the "Shanghai Six"—these mechanisms have never been mobilized and are now falling apart."[19]

Many Statists saw the benefits of cooperation with the United States in some areas, including in central Asia, but insisted on the tactical, rather than strategic, nature of the cooperation. Strategically, Russia's pro-American and, more broadly, pro-Western choice had the effect of

worsening the country's relations with the Muslim and Asian regions
and irreparably damaging its moral, economic, and political standing. A
broad coalition of great powers, including Russia, China, and India, was
something that most Statists favored as the most appropriate response
to the threat of global terrorism.

Table 5.4 summarizes contending views on the new vision of national
interest.

Table 5.4.   Pragmatic Cooperation (PC): Contending Views

Civilizationists/Statists:		Westernizers:
PC is not sufficiently respectful of cultural and political independence	vs.	PC is not sufficiently pro-Western

The National Communists and Eurasianists went much further in criticizing Putin's vision and the response of the West to the events of September 11. Although this group also placed blame for the tragedy on Western
shoulders, its representatives conceptualized the role of the West differently. The problem, in the minds of the Communist/Eurasianist group,
was not merely the American strategy and hegemonic ambitions; such
strategy and ambitions themselves should be viewed as inevitable products of Western culture and its creature: modern civilization. For this
group, the politics of the West were inseparable from its culture and
economics. The tragedy of September 11 was seen as reflecting the spiritual program of modern history and the West (first and foremost, the
United States). The forces responsible for September 11 were of a transnational economic and military nature, and had little to do with developments in the third world.[20]

For this group, September 11 was nothing less than part of an epic
struggle for liberation from the unipolar/unicultural Western world, a
world in which Russia had a duty to side overtly with anti-Western and
especially anti-American forces. Much like President Bush, the hard-line
Civilizationists viewed the post–September 11 world in terms of a struggle
between "good" and "evil," except they found themselves on the other
side of the barricade. For their side to win in this struggle, they recommended building a broad coalition of anti-American cultures and civilizations. Among these cultures and civilizations, some saw an alliance of
Russia and Muslim countries as having the strongest potential to successfully resist Western modernity and hegemonic policies. Others added to
the alliance China and even, potentially, Germany.

Russian foreign policy perceptions are summarized in table 5.5.

Table 5.5.   Russia's Foreign Policy Discourse after September 11

	Liberal Westernizers	Social Democrats	Statists, Civilizationists
Causes of September 11	Non-West: "barbarism"	Both West and non-West	West: unilateralism and modernity
The necessary response	Spread Western values	Develop intercultural dialogue	Avert Western hegemony
Implications for Russia	Side with the West	Support the UN; integrate with Europe	Balance against the West

Adapted from: Andrei P. Tsygankov, *Whose World Order? Russia's Perception of American Ideas after the Cold War* (Notre Dame, IN: University of Notre Dame Press, 2004), 124.

The Wariness of the Broader Public

The political class's cautious reaction, described above, was broadly representative of the feelings within Russia's general public, which remained wary of Western intentions. The country's most traumatic postcommunist experience and the failure of Gorbachev's and Yeltsin's early attempts to develop a strategic partnership with the West made the Russian political class, military, media, and general public skeptical of the new efforts at rapprochement. At least three major issues drew public attention. First, many politicians and military officers pointed to the United States' unilateral decision to develop a national missile defense system and abandon the antiballistic missile (ABM) treaty, which the Russians continued to view as a cornerstone of strategic stability. Second, there was still the issue of NATO's expansion, often perceived as an essentially anti-Russian process that continued to follow the old maxim "Keep America in, Germany down, and Russia out." In addition, there was a concern over U.S. and NATO troops' presence in the central Asian states, which are in the immediate geographic proximity of Russia.

Because all these issues were in the spotlight, few factions in the Russian Duma initially supported Putin's decision to side with the United States after 9/11. Russia's Muslim leaders reacted critically to the American military campaigns in Afghanistan and Iraq. Of special importance was a series of published "open letters" signed by retired generals, including one of Yeltsin's former defense ministers, accusing Putin of "selling out" the country and "betraying" the nation's vital interests. Federal Border Guard Service head Konstantin Totski issued a characteristic statement maintaining that, if U.S. forces remained in central Asia after the counterterrorist operation in Afghanistan, "we are unlikely to remain friends."[21] Even the mainstream media described what they perceived as a sense of Russian "encirclement" by U.S. and NATO troops. For example, *Rossiyskaya gazeta*, the newspaper of the Russian government, rang the alarm with this statement: "One way or another Russia, the entire former USSR, remains encircled by a dense ring of military and intelligence-gathering installations belonging to the North Atlantic alliance." The American presence in the region, argued another source, resembled post–World War II events, when the Americans quickly turned from allies into enemies.[22] The Russian general public, although supportive of Putin's leadership, also showed signs of increased concern over American actions in the world. According to data from the Russian Center for the Study of Public Opinion, 63 percent of all Russians felt that the terrorist attack on the United States was a form of "retribution for American foreign policy."[23]

REENGAGING THE WORLD AFTER SEPTEMBER 11

With the introduction of the philosophy of pragmatic cooperation, the West remained at the center of Russia's foreign policy. The new policy was, however, to reengage the West in order to acquire its recognition of Russia as a great power. Therefore, while insisting on Russia's own interests in many areas of world politics, Putin sought to frame those interests as consistent with strategic commitments to Western values, such as international law, personal freedoms, and a market economy. His strategy of engaging the West was to propose a new agenda, the implications of which might be more far-reaching than those stemming from addressing the old issues of NATO expansion or the missile defense system. While not giving up on the old issues easily, Russia's leader did not want to be cornered on those issues. He therefore proposed some new areas in which Russia could develop some long-term advantages. Two of these areas were counterterrorism and energy cooperation. As a result, while preserving a large space in which to maneuver in dealing with his domestic critics, Putin has proven to be more efficient in engaging the West than was his most pro-Western predecessor, Kozyrev.

Reengaging the United States

Putin's efforts to engage the United States predate the September 11 attacks. The new leader wanted to start fresh after the Kosovo experience, which had considerably soured Russia-West relations, and he began to cultivate ties with the American administration soon after he came to office. Washington's initial reaction was cold. The new administration in the United States made it clear that it did not foresee any breakthroughs in relations with Russia. It made public the arrest of FBI agent Robert Hanssen, who had spied for the Russians, and it subsequently ordered fifty Russian diplomats to leave the United States. It threatened to end

any economic aid except for nonproliferation projects and—through Secretary of Defense Donald Rumsfeld—accused Russia of proliferating
nuclear materials and weapons technologies. As late as February 2001,
Bush's national security adviser Condoleezza Rice insisted that Russia
was a threat to the United States and its European allies. Putin persisted
and finally got his break when he met with the American president in
Ljubljana, Slovenia, in the summer of 2001. The relationship began to
change, largely thanks to personal chemistry between the two leaders. It
was after the summit that Bush made his famous remarks on Putin: "I was
able to get a sense of his soul."[24]

September 11 presented Putin with a unique opportunity to implement
his new vision of national interest. Soon after the terrorist attacks on the
United States, he offered that country's leaders broad support for antiterrorist operations in Afghanistan. The measures included intelligence
sharing, opening Russian airspace to relief missions, taking part in search-
and-rescue operations, rallying central Asian countries to the American
cause, and arming anti-Taliban forces inside Afghanistan. As our earlier
analysis indicates, the domestic public was wary of rapprochement with
the United States, and that constrained Putin's freedom of action. Determined, he pressed forward by stressing the positive potential of the new
Russia-U.S. relations. In particular, beginning with his interview in the
Wall Street Journal in February 2002, he emphasized Russia as a reliable
alternative to traditional Middle Eastern sources of oil and natural gas.
Russia was the world's single largest non-OPEC (Organization of Petroleum Exporting Countries) oil exporter, with 10 percent of the known oil
reserves and 9 percent of the world output. Yet this oil accounted for only
1 percent of American imports in 2001.[25] Putin projected for Russia to
increase production of crude oil at the rate of 9 percent per year, much of
it intended for export, with a considerable part for the United States. The
subsequent events demonstrated the existence of reinforcing interests in
this aspect of Russia-U.S. relations on both sides. In May of the same year
at their summit in Moscow, the U.S. and Russian presidents signed a joint
declaration on energy cooperation. Then followed the Houston "energy
summit" in October, where Russian officials said that they could export
as many as a million barrels a day to the United States within five years.
The *Economist* summed up all these efforts at the time: "America's relations with Russia are now better than at any time since the end of the
Second World War and are improving."[26]

Eager to engage the United States, Putin was careful not to overplay
his opposition on traditional issues, such as NATO, the Balkans, and the
ABM (Anti-Ballistic Missile) Treaty. Rather than insisting on Russia's
membership in NATO or the alliance's not admitting new members—both
demands being entirely unrealistic although not uncommon for previous

diplomacies—Putin moved to organize security relations with Western countries on the common basis of counterterrorism. After initial support for Slobodan Milošević, he opted to minimize involvement in the affairs of the post-Kosovo Balkans. In August 2003, Moscow withdrew its peace-keeping mission from Bosnia and Kosovo. And, despite formidable domestic resistance, Putin made little of his opposition to the U.S. desire to abandon the ABM Treaty, which had prohibited the unilateral building of a nuclear missile defense system. The United States' administration made it clear that it would be withdrawing from the treaty, regardless of the reaction from Russia. Putin's reaction was mute and nonthreatening, despite some expectations of a possible confrontational response. In his opinion, the United States' decision was a "mistake," but it presented no threat to the national security of the Russian Federation.

Capitalizing on Ties with Europe

In addition to developing the new relations with the United States, Putin put a new emphasis on ties with European partners, especially Germany, France, and Italy. Russia's energy markets were primarily in Europe—they accounted for 40 percent of Russia's foreign trade, relative to the United States accounting for a mere 5 percent of trade. In fact, if Europe is understood in the wider sense—as the one that includes the EU, Central and Eastern Europe, Norway, and Switzerland—then Europe's share of Russia's trade was up to 55 percent.[27] In June 2003, Putin also sealed a joint venture with British Petroleum worth over $6 billion. His vision of global security, too, proved to be quite compatible with those of large European nations. During the crisis over the American decision to go to war against Iraq, Russia joined the antiwar coalition and argued that the United Nations was the only legitimate body for sanctioning the use of force. In siding with the Europeans, Putin was firmly supported at home, but he was also careful not to present his views as anti-American, positioning himself instead as a voice of moderation and even reconciliation between the American and the European side in the West. Putin continued making efforts to bring Russia and Europe closer culturally. During the celebration of St. Petersburg's three-hundred-year anniversary, he went as far as to suggest that visas between EU countries and Russia be abandoned altogether by the year 2006.

As was the case with Russia's new relations with the United States, Putin's efforts to demonstrate his commitment to European values were unmistakably pragmatic. In those issues where the new leadership perceived European powers to be infringing upon Russia's interests, the Kremlin preferred to maintain a distance from Brussels. Most symptomatically, for all the rhetoric on developing closer relations with the EU, there was relatively little cooperation in the area of security. For instance,

Moscow continued to be mistrustful and rejected European ideas for joint peacekeeping missions in the former Soviet states, such as Moldova. It also shut down the OSCE mission in Chechnya. In addition, Putin's government decided to put an end to the activities of U.S. Peace Corps volunteers in Russia; this action became a source of irritation in relations with the United States. All this indicated that Russia continued to differ from its Western counterparts in its evaluation of national interest and security threats. Consistent with the earlier specified strategy of modernization, Russia continued to be interested primarily in economic cooperation with Europe, defined in terms of growing investments and sales of energy and weapons abroad.

In their turn, Europeans continued to be suspicious of Russia's often treating Europe, in the perception of Putin's adviser, as a "mischievous student in the school of democracy."[28] Some of these suspicions were visible in discussions about the issue of visas for Russian transit travelers to and from Kaliningrad. Kaliningrad was the Russian enclave that became surrounded by EU members after Lithuania's admission into the EU in May 2004. The Europeans were especially worried about corruption of the local administration in the Kaliningrad region as well as the miserable economic situation there. On that basis, they declined Russia's proposal to have a visa-free arrangement, but the two sides reached a compromise agreement in Luxembourg on April 2, 2004. The agreement spelled out measures aimed at ensuring the free transit of goods from Russia to Kaliningrad, and it ensured that Russian train travelers to the Kaliningrad enclave were to obtain a Lithuanian permit only. More broadly, the historical enlargement of the EU and the incorporation of ten new members on May 1, 2004, underscored the policy of constructing Europe without any meaningful role for Russia. As one observer put it, "A chagrined Russia finds itself not the architect of this new creation, or even a member, but an outcast relegated to a sideline role."[29]

Supporting the United States in Afghanistan, but Not in Iraq

The pragmatism in defining national interest helps to interpret Russia's divergent foreign policy responses toward two major military crises after September 11—Afghanistan and Iraq. Putin's support of the United States after 9/11, on the one hand, and his decision to oppose the war in Iraq, on the other, were both shaped by a sober calculation of payoffs in state power and autonomy.

The pragmatism of Putin's support for the United States' war against the Taliban regime in Afghanistan was quite obvious—for a long time, Russia supported the Northern Alliance and was eager to have its long-term rival removed from power without a single shot fired. While offering his support, Putin made it clear that he would not commit Russian troops to operations inside Afghanistan because the Russian constitution proscribed such operations and the United Nations had yet to authorize them. Another expected payoff from the extended intelligence cooperation was the American support for Putin's policies in Chechnya, the absence of which had been complicating Russia's efforts to develop a positive image in the eyes of the West. Other expectations were of an economic nature and related to Moscow's plans to increase energy sales abroad. Finally, Putin had in mind to eventually gain membership in the World Trade Organization (WTO), but on relatively favorable terms. On all these accounts, the president was counting on the support of the United States.

The war in Iraq was a different matter, however. Here, Putin decided to join the coalition of those opposing the war on American terms. Along with Russia's foreign policy officials, he warned against going over the head of the United Nations, which would authorize the use of force. The same vision of national interest underlined Putin's decision. As in Afghanistan, he wanted to reduce terrorist threats to Russia, and he wanted to provide his country with better conditions for economic modernization. Not convinced by arguments about the existence of a nuclear program in Iraq and links between Saddam Hussein's regime and the Al Qaeda terrorist network—both being the key arguments of the Bush administration—he saw the war as a deviation from the global war on terrorism. Along with many others in Russia's political circles, Putin believed that terrorism, as a stateless phenomenon, was a challenge to the very system of states. In his view, terrorism could be defeated only through the coordination of state efforts, and not through taking on relatively established states, such as Iraq.

The economic modernization consideration was also prominent in Putin's calculations. This consideration included Russia's ties with Europe and Iraq. The strategy of pragmatism assumed cooperation with the United States, but not at the expense of ties with Europe, the latter being far more extensive. In addition, Russia had important oil interests in Iraq, and Saddam Hussein skillfully exploited those by promising to Russian private companies more lucrative contracts. In the wake of the military intervention, many Russian experts forecasted a drastic fall in world oil prices in the near future—another nightmare for Russia, where a considerable part of revenue came from exporting natural resources. There was also the issue of Iraq's sizable debt to Russia—$7–8 billion, by different calculations—and Russia was worried it would never see the money as a result of the war.

The two divergent decisions found support at home. If Putin had lost any of his credibility for throwing his support behind American intervention in Afghanistan, he certainly regained it all during his opposition to the war in Iraq. Russian elites grew highly skeptical of the idea of siding with the United States. Even some of the Westernizers viewed the war in Iraq as a dangerous precedent of jeopardizing the role of the United Nations. Very few supported the war, insisting on the primacy of Russia's "strategic partnership" with the United States and Russia's future role in Iraq. Statists and Civilizationists, predictably, saw the war as George W. Bush's drive for global hegemony and warned of his appetite for Russia's resources and territory. For instance, a former defense minister, General Igor' Rodionov, in typical remarks referred to Russia as an "occupied country" defeated by the United States. At the conference marking the anniversary of the Nazi invasion of the Soviet Union, he went on to argue that "our geopolitical enemy has achieved what Hitler wanted to."[30]

As far as the general public was concerned, although many in Russia felt sympathy for the United States following the September 11 terrorist attacks and had little support for Saddam Hussein, Russian public opinion turned sharply against Washington's intervention in Iraq. In April 2003, only 2 percent approved of the U.S. military action, while 83 percent were opposed to it. This was a matter of anti-American, not pro-Iraqi, feeling. Only 45 percent sympathized with the Iraqis, whereas 46 percent were undecided and a mere 5 percent supported the Americans. And 71 percent of the Russian public felt threatened by the United States and was afraid of being next on the list of American targets for military intervention.[31] In addition, Putin's decision to oppose the war in Iraq rested on firm support abroad. In addition to France and Germany, the world outside Russia overwhelmingly—as the Pew Global Attitudes survey demonstrated—held a negative image of the United States and its actions in the post–September 11 era (table 5.6 demonstrates the degree to which different nations, including Russia, held negative views about the United States over time).

Table 5.6. Favorable View of the United States (%)

	1999/2000	*March 2002*	*March 2003*
Britain	83	75	48
France	62	63	31
Germany	78	61	25
Poland	86	79	50
RUSSIA	37	61	28
Turkey	52	30	12

The surveys were conducted among 38,000 respondents of forty-four nations. They found that "despite an initial outpouring of public sympathy for America following the September 11, 2001 terrorist attacks . . . images of the U.S. have been tarnished in all types of nations: among longtime NATO allies, in developing countries, in Eastern Europe, and most dramatically, in Muslim societies."
Source: Pew Research Center for the People and the Press, *What the World Thinks in 2002* (Washington, DC: Pew Research Center for the People and the Press, December 4, 2002); Pew Research Center for the People and the Press, *America's Image Further Erodes, Europeans Want Weaker Ties* (Washington, DC: Pew Research Center for the People and the Press, March 18, 2003), www.people-press.org.

Outside the West: Economic Modernization at Any Cost?

Putin's view of the world outside the West was shaped by the same belief that Russia must do everything in its power to conduct successful economic modernization. Like Primakov, he believed in the necessity for Russia to have a strong presence on the world political scene, but he chose a different method of achieving that goal. The issues that for Primakov had the political significance of balancing American power were reduced to considerations of economic recovery under Putin. Unlike his predecessor, Putin was not a committed Eurasianist and did not seem to have much trust in the East. In some ways, his thinking about Russia's Asian neighbors was similar to that of Westernizers and was marked by fear and defensiveness. For example, he shared the Westernizers' concern that if Moscow failed to improve the economic situation, neighboring nations could exploit Russia. In one of his speeches, the president issued an explicit warning, "I do not want to dramatize the situation, but if we do not make every real effort, even the indigenous Russian population will soon speak mostly Japanese, Chinese, and Korean."[32] Putin was also not particularly careful in some of his statements on Chechens; these statements further revealed his ethnocentric bias. Insistence on Russia's belongingness to Western European culture described his beliefs better than attempts to cast himself as a supporter of Eurasianist identity. In his own words, "Above all else Russia was, is and will, of course, be a major European power."[33]

Therefore, Putin's policies outside the West, as active as they were, are best understood as serving the purpose of modernizing Russia, rather than developing strategic diplomatic alliances or deep cultural affinities. In building ties with Asian neighbors, Russia was especially determined to win markets in arms and energy. It was interested in selling its arms in the West as well, but many Western forces dismissed Russian products as inferior. China and India, on the other hand, had emerged as Russia's largest buyers. Given that the two countries had been the world's largest and second-largest arms importers, the economic prospects of cooperating with them were quite promising. For Russia, additional incentive came from the military industrial complex's overcapacity relative to almost nonexistent domestic orders. As a result, arms exports rose dramatically, particularly in 2001 and 2002. During 1997–2001, Russia exported over $17 billion in arms, relative to the United States' share of almost $45 billion. Characteristically, while promoting weapons sales in Asia, at no point did Putin raise the issue of balancing the United States or creating some new strategic "axis" to serve this purpose. Even in the midst of signing a friendship treaty with China and knowing Russia's opposition to U.S. plans for a national missile defense, Putin stressed that

"Russia plans no joint actions with other states in this sphere, including China."[34]

While selling arms, Putin was typically dismissive of Western concerns about weapons proliferation. He argued that these concerns merely reflected commercial interests to drive Russia out of competitive markets. On a number of occasions, the president demonstrated that he was not willing to bow to Washington's pressures for Russia to stop cooperating with "dangerous regimes," such as Iran. Western officials and researchers argued that Russia was engaged in the proliferation of nuclear technology by helping India's nuclear program and building a nuclear reactor in Iran. However, Russia's president was convinced that his country's actions were perfectly legitimate. Russia pledged to build two more nuclear reactors in Iran and signed an $800 million deal with the Iranian government. The deal had been signed before Putin visited the United States in September 2003, and President Bush's efforts to change Putin's mind produced no results. In his interview with Western journalists, the Russian president stated, "according to our information, many western European and American companies cooperate with Iran—either directly or through intermediary organizations—in the nuclear sphere."[35] To substantiate the Kremlin's claims about the commercial nature of Washington's pressures, some Russian analysts argued that, in the absence of official contracts, the U.S.-Iranian trade turnover was around $1 billion, which was higher than that of Russia, despite the Russian-Iranian strategic partnership agreement. These analysts recalled that immediately before the Islamic revolution in Iran, Washington and Tehran had signed a $24 billion contract, which provided for U.S. assistance in constructing eight nuclear power plants in Iran within ten years.[36]

Another key area of concentration of Russia in Eurasia was energy and transportation projects. Here again, Russia was closely cooperating with China, Japan, Iran, and India. In the south, one key idea had been to build the so-called north-south transport corridor that would pave the way for the delivery of goods from India and the Arabian Peninsula through Iran and the Caspian region to Russia and Europe, and vice versa. In September 2000, Russia, India, and Iran signed the agreement, according to which all signatories would get relief from import tax and customs duties. The transportation route was expected to reduce transport costs by 20 percent and reduce delivery times by fifteen to twenty days compared with the old route via the Suez Canal. According to estimates by Mikhail Margelov, the head of the Federation Council's Foreign Relations Committee, Russia expected to make an additional $5–6 billion a year in transport revenues from the new route.[37]

In the east, Russia was planning to capitalize on rich Siberian oil reserves by building pipelines to the neighboring countries. During 2003–2004,

Russia's government was deciding between a shorter Chinese route and a longer route that would connect Siberian oil sources with Japanese markets. The Chinese Angarsk-Daqing project was agreed on by Russia's Yukos and China National Petroleum, and in May 2003, the twenty-five-year oil-supply deal was signed by the new Chinese president, Hu Jintao, on his first trip to Russia. The alternative project would connect East Siberia to Nakhodka and, from there, to Japan. It was extensively lobbied for by the Japanese side, which promised to finance the whole project if Russia agreed to it. The oil pipeline issue was being discussed along with the issue of northern territories and a possible peace treaty with Japan. Russian fears of China's gaining control over parts of Siberia continued to figure in Moscow's decision process, particularly since Beijing wanted the right to bring in tens of thousands of Chinese workers to build the pipeline. An additional complication for Russia was that China also wanted outright control over oil and gas, but offered to pay Russia only as much as Moscow sold gas for domestically.

PRAGMATIC COOPERATION IN THE FORMER SOVIET WORLD

Putin's approach to the former Soviet region was in line with his overall foreign policy philosophy of pragmatic modernization. Along with Primakov, he valued the region's political and geostrategic significance, but he placed the key emphasis on post-Soviet Eurasia's "advantage on the scale of global economic competition."[38] The new vision of the region assumed a more open, multilevel politicoeconomic space planned by the Russian state, but built with the close participation of the Russian private sector. In addition, Putin stepped up cooperation on issues of counterterrorism and attempted to assemble his own coalition of the willing in the region.

The New Westernist-Statist Consensus

The new vision rested on firm social support at home. Various media and political forces had long expressed their dissatisfaction with Primakov's grandiose foreign policy philosophy that had the "integration" of the former Soviet area as its key component. Westernizers were critical of the "integration" strategy for its underestimation of domestic business interests and for continuing what they saw as harmful practices of paying the former republics in exchange for their political loyalty to Russia. Boris Berezovski, a prominent oligarch and a one-time CIS executive secretary, attacked the Primakov-inspired vision for its "antimarket spirit." Scholars pointed to the prointegration efforts running in a fundamentally different direction from the real economic interests of most of the former Soviet republics.[39] Liberal politicians, such as Grigori Yavlinski, opposed the government's attempts to entice Ukraine and Belarus into a closer relationship by subsidizing their energy payments and being soft on their debts to Russia. As early as 1994, pro-Western reformers such as Economics Minister Yegor Gaidar and Finance Minister Boris Fedorov resigned, due partly to their opposition to the negotiations over an economic union with Belarus. To Westernizers, the former republics were unreliable partners—too corrupt and conservative to develop economic relationships with Russia.

Some of Primakov's Statist-oriented supporters, too, began to withdraw their support for the strategy of post-Soviet integration. Driven by nationalist, rather than free-market, considerations, they spoke against what they saw as Russia's one-sided concessions and unwarranted exploitation of its resources. For instance, Andranik Migranyan, once a prominent critic of Kozyrev's isolationism and a promoter of Russia's "Monroe Doctrine" in the former Soviet area, now saw the CIS-centered integration as too costly and argued against Russia's remaining a leader in such an integration. As he stated in his reevaluation, "During the last several years, it became absolutely clear that all the attempts to integrate the post-Soviet space have led to nothing. The CIS is barely able to function."[40]

The new liberal-nationalist consensus was summarized in the document of the influential Council for Foreign and Defense Policy titled "Strategy for Russia: Agenda for President—2000." Both Westernizers, such as Deputy Foreign Minister Anatoli Adamishin, and Statists, such as the chairman of the Duma's Committee on the CIS affairs Konstantin Zatulin, collaborated in writing the final draft of the document. They found Primakov's vision of a multipolar world to be outdated, expensive, and potentially confrontational. Instead, the authors proposed the concept of "selective engagement," which they compared with Russia's nineteenth-century policy of "self-concentration" after its defeat in the war in the Crimea and with China's policy since Deng Xiaoping. Regarding the former Soviet area, the authors recommended a "considerable revision" of policy, which would involve abandoning the "pseudointegration at Russia's expense" and "tough defense of our national economic interests." "We must begin by changing the very concept of integration. It should be built not from above, but from below—on the basis of supporting the integration of various markets of separate goods and services, creating transnational financial-industrial groups . . . exchanging debts for assets' ownership. The state policy of cooperation and integration should be directed at supporting exactly this kind of activities."[41]

The Russian public seemed to favor such a view: it supported measures to boost economic development and questioned military solutions in the region.[42] This is not to say that there were no groups within the Russian political class supportive of a far-reaching integration in the former Soviet region, including one that would have involved military intervention. Such groups continued to exist and advocate their views, but they had been effectively marginalized by the new consensus.

The Vision of Three-Level Ties in the Region

Consistent with the newly formed consensus, the new leadership adopted the rhetoric of pragmatism and self-concentration regarding the former Soviet area. In February 2001, the secretary of the Security Council, Sergei Ivanov, publicly announced the new course, acknowledging that it would mean a serious rethinking of Russia's previous policies in the region. Almost repeating the lines of Primakov's critics, he announced that previous attempts to integrate the CIS had come at a very high price and that Russia must now abandon the integration project in favor of a "pragmatic" course of bilateral relations. By the time of this announcement, the debt of the CIS states to Russia had reached $5.5 billion.[43] Vice Premier Viktor Khristenko clarified the new approach by emphasizing its reciprocal nature: "The essence of the current policy of Russia toward the CIS states is an energetic bilateral cooperation based on pragmatism and a reciprocal account of interests. We develop multilateral contacts only in those spheres that received support from the parties. Based on such an approach, we move to more advanced forms of cooperation mainly with those partners who express a genuine interest in a tighter integration."[44]

In the words of the parliament's CIS committee member Igor Glukhovski, Russia's relations with the former Soviet states would now exist on three separate levels—bilateral, subregional, and regional. In addition to bilateral relations, Russia would participate in subregional arrangements, such as the Collective Security treaty signed by Russia, Belarus, Armenia, Kazakhstan, Kyrgyzstan, and Tajikistan. Another subregional arrangement was the Eurasian Economic Union, which was formed by Russia, Belarus, Kazakhstan, and Kyrgyzstan, with Ukraine joining in October 2003. Finally, Russia would develop regional forms of participation, particularly when it came to defending the region from international terrorist threats.[45]

New Bilateral Relations

Putin's objective of strengthening Russia's economic presence in the region materialized in aggressively asserting control over the ex-republics' strategic property and transportation. For example, in Georgia, Russia's state electric company obtained the right to be the main electricity provider, which provided it with a formidable opportunity to influence Georgian economic development. In Armenia, Russia obtained several strategic assets, such as an atomic electric station, to offset a debt of $40 million. Outside the Caucasus, Russia was covering 30 percent of the energy needs in Belarus, and the head of Russia's state electric company, Anatoli Chubais, also expressed an interest in participating in energy privatization in Ukraine and other states of the former Soviet region. Chubais went on to announce that Russia's main goal in the twenty-first century should be to develop "liberal capitalism" and to build up a "liberal empire" through strengthening its position in the former Soviet Union.[46] Empire or not, Russia continued to press for control of oil pipelines in the Caucasus, central Asia, Ukraine, and the Baltics. Its most important achievement was a strategic energy accord with Turkmenistan, under which virtually all of Turkmenistan's gas fell into Russia's sphere of influence for the following twenty-five years. The accord effectively eliminated the plans to utilize Turkmenistan's gas fields for laying pipelines through Afghanistan with the assistance of the United States.

This strategy of economic domination also implied Russia's cultivation of relationships with the already-existing political regimes in the former Soviet Union, however democratic or authoritarian they were. In the fall of 2003, Russia quickly endorsed elections in Azerbaijan and Armenia, despite their questionably democratic nature. The transformation in relations with Azerbaijan was especially interesting given that previously Russia had perceived it with suspicion for developing ties with NATO and GUUAM. Putin's emphasis on economic ties assisted here as well. In late September 2003, he visited Azerbaijan to sign an agreement dividing the two countries' rights to Caspian oil and gas, which mattered greatly to Azerbaijan. Russia also secured continued use of the Gabala radar station, which was located in Azerbaijan and which Russian media speculated Moscow was using to monitor the United States–led war on Iraq. In Georgia, Russia chose not to comment on another fraudulent parliamentary election that eventually caused President Eduard Shevardnadze to resign, and it quickly moved to start afresh with the newly elected president, Mikhail Saakashvili. Here, in addition to its economic interests, Russia wanted to secure the border with Chechnya and, especially, the Pankisi Gorge, which was long recognized as a transit point for terrorists.

In central Asia, Putin actively coordinated counterterrorist efforts with the local regimes, and he provided them with substantial military assistance in exchange for Russia's expanded military presence. He secured a strategic partnership with Kazakhstan, in part through the division of Caspian resources. As a part of the gas deal with Turkmenistan, he also promised President Sapurmurat Niyazov some unspecified extra security services "to combat international terrorism." In Ukraine, Putin decisively supported the incumbent president Leonid Kuchma in his conflicts with the opposition. Here, too, the expectation was that the next president would continue Kuchma's policies of cooperation with Russia, and Russia would therefore continue to expand its economic presence in the country. In his turn, Kuchma agreed to sell Russia parts of Ukraine's natural gas transit system to offset the debt of roughly $2 billion to Moscow for energy deliveries. Finally, in Belarus, Russia continued to support President Aleksandr Lukashenko and supply energy at a discounted rate, but raised new demands regarding further steps in developing the Russia-Belarus union.

In addition to developing its economic presence in the region, Moscow sought to offset the growing geoeconomic influences of the West. Joint U.S.-British companies controlled 27 percent of the Caspian's oil reserves and 40 percent of its gas reserves. The United States also supported the Baku-Ceyhan oil pipeline, which passed through Georgia and Turkey to Europe and bypassed Russia. It provided resources for GUUAM, an economic and security group of five former Soviet states—Georgia, Ukraine, Uzbekistan, Azerbaijan, and Moldova—established in 1998 as a counterweight to Russian influence. And after September 11, it opened military bases in several central Asian states. Russia responded to these developments by preserving and strengthening its military presence in the Caucasus, central Asia, and Belarus through bilateral and multilateral efforts. Bilaterally, it negotiated the establishment of a new air force base in Kyrgyzstan and a base in Tajikistan, in addition to the already-existing other arrangements, such as the Baikonur Cosmodrome, the ballistic-missile testing range in Kazakhstan, and a major early-warning radar in Tajikistan. Russia also moved to consolidate its naval supremacy on the Caspian Sea with the planned induction of dozens of new warships in its Caspian flotilla over the next few years.

Pragmatic Multilateralism

Although Putin abandoned the Primakov-like effort to revive the CIS, he did not give up multilateralism as a way to strengthen Russia's position in the region. Through both economic and security multilateralism, Putin was patiently assembling his own coalition of the willing. In the economic area, a notable development was the creation of an economic agreement with Belarus, Kazakhstan, and Ukraine, which aimed at eliminating trade barriers and devising shared energy-transport policies. In the security realm, Russia concentrated on counterterrorist activities by developing the Shanghai Five, with China as a prominent member, and rebuilding the old Tashkent Collective Security Treaty. The Shanghai Five, or the Shanghai Cooperation Organization (SCO), emerged out of a Russia-China treaty on significant reduction of the number of border troops. The treaty was signed in 1997 along with Kazakhstan, Tajikistan, and Kyrgyzstan. After September 11, both Russia and China reactivated the SCO to address terrorism and a security vacuum in central Asia. A perceived threat of Islamic separatism was a matter of concern for Beijing, due to outbreaks of unrest among the Muslim Uighur minority—a Turkic-speaking group in China's Xinjiang region, which borders central Asia, Afghanistan, and Pakistan. Even Uzbekistan, once the central Asian state most interested in reducing Moscow's power in the region, was now more inclined to cooperate with Russia. Uzbekistan joined the Moscow-created center to fight terrorism and called Russia "not only the guarantor of our security, but also a reliable strategic partner." Uzbekistan joined the SCO in late 2001, and in June 2004, it went so far as to sign a strategic cooperation agreement with Russia that included some important economic and military dimensions.

In addition, Russia's long-advocated collective security action to deal with perceived threats in central Asia found its expression in transforming the old Tashkent treaty into a full-fledged regional defense pact. In April 2003, six states—Russia, Belarus, Kazakhstan, Kyrgyzstan, Tajikistan, and Armenia—formed the Collective Security Treaty Organization (CSTO), pledging to pool their resources to fight terrorism in the area. The organization sought to mimic the Cold War–era Warsaw Pact in Eastern Europe, complete with a joint headquarters and armed forces and a written commitment to respond to aggression against any member state.

Transportation Initiatives

Accelerating the development of a transportation system through transnational and transregional projects was an especially prominent focus of Putin's activities in the post-Soviet region. Most of these projects involved transporting oil and gas, of which Russia is one of the world's largest producers. In response to the rising oil prices, Russia stepped up its production considerably and, some analysts speculated, was on a course to pose a rivalry to Saudi Arabia by the end of the decade.[47] The Caspian Sea was a particularly prominent area of attention from the Russian state. Here, the idea was to quickly establish a gas supply network to Turkey and Europe in order to undermine some Russia-competitive pipelines in the region. One such pipeline—from Baku to Ceyhan—was completed in May 2005, and by connecting northern Caspian structures to the Russian oil pipeline system, Russia would emerge as more competitive. Another pipeline was under discussion. It was of a trans-Caspian nature, and it was meant to bring oil underwater from Aktau in Kazakhstan to Baku and then to outside markets via the Baku-Ceyhan line. In February 2002, the Russian president also proposed an ambitious "gas OPEC" project that would involve Russia's pooling its natural gas resources with those of the central Asian states for the purpose of dominating the world markets.

Russian policymakers have been actively promoting transregional projects besides those related to the Caspian Sea. One of these projects is the Trans-Siberian Railroad, both an east-west route and a north-south one. The Russian Transportation Ministry has strongly lobbied for the Trans-Siberian project, which involves a completion of the 8,500 miles of railroad for transporting up to 100 million tons of cargo a year. While developing the project, the Russian government sought to be globally competitive, with potential competition coming from TRASEKA, the Brussels-planned international transportation corridor for connecting Europe, the Caucasus, and Asia. In addition to the Trans-Siberian route, Moscow's plans included developing a China–Kazakhstan–Russia–Europe route (east-west) and one that would connect Russia with India, Iran, Kazakhstan, Turkmenistan, and other Persian Gulf states (the north-south route). More recent initiatives included the April 2005 agreement between Russia and Germany on a project to deliver Russian gas directly to Germany by a pipeline under the Baltic Sea, bypassing the Baltic states and Poland.[48]

Many of Putin's efforts were improvisations, and it remains to be seen whether they will be more successful than previous policies of disengagement and integration in the region. In the meantime, some critics raised concerns that these efforts were of an ad hoc nature and not very well thought out, and that they overestimated the power of the Russian private sector. These critics feared that the new policy of pragmatism was about to repeat Kozyrev's errors of disengagement, which might eventually cost Russia its dominant presence in the region. Furthermore, they urged Putin not to give up the CIS as a vehicle for preserving Russia's influences.[49]

Yet the new vision was hardly an example of disengagement. It assumed that post-Soviet Eurasia is a relatively economically open region, but one in which Russia occupies a central role and derives considerable economic, as well as political, benefits. The Russian foreign policy community had been debating the benefits of such geoeconomic thinking for quite some time. For instance, in his Eurasian Strategy for Russia, Sergei Rogov proposed that Russia focus on building the "communicational bridge" linking its southern, western, and eastern peripheries through the development of ground, air, and electronic transportation routes.[50] Economically, the project could, in the author's view, decrease by half the length of networks of communication that were linking Europe and East Asia, and this would be mutually beneficial for all participants. In addition, Eurasia was meant to be preserved as a politically stable and cohesive region. Although market oriented, this vision meant to preserve Russia's leadership in the region and was broadly supported by various political movements, as well as a regionally oriented private sector. It bore little resemblance to Kozyrev's philosophy of integration with the West at the expense of Asian and former Soviet partners.

NEW CHALLENGES FOR PRAGMATIC COOPERATION

Soon after his reelection in March 2004, Putin was confronted with a series of new challenges. An intensification of terrorist activities in the northern Caucasus, the Orange Revolution in Ukraine, destabilization of central Asia, and refusal by some European states to celebrate the sixtieth anniversary of the victory over fascism in Moscow became important tests for the survival of Pragmatic Cooperation. The course defended the enhancement of Russia's influences in the world by cooperating with Western nations on a variety of economic and security issues. Putin's Russia wanted to be a normal great power or the one recognized by the outside world. As the country faced new challenges, the course came under criticism at home. Some Statists insisted that cooperation with the West was not paying off, and that Russia had to defend its interests more aggressively because its own survival was at stake. On the other side of the spectrum, liberal Westernizers argued the need to give up great power ambitions and pursue greater economic and political liberalization. In addition, the domestically questioned course had to be defended in the context of intensified efforts by Western nations, particularly the United States, to influence developments in the former Soviet region.

Washington's Regime-Change Strategy in the Former Soviet Region

Although many in Russia saw the American invasion of Iraq as driven by an appetite for Middle Eastern oil, Washington also had the objective of democratizing the region by establishing a new pro-Western regime at its heart. Soon, it became apparent that the strategy of changing regimes and expanding liberty was not limited to the Middle East. President Bush's inaugural address in January 2005 made the spread of freedom and democracy the center of the United States' political strategy in the "war on terror," and his State of the Union speech in February continued the theme: "The attack on freedom in our world has reaffirmed our confidence in freedom's power to change the world."[51] The so-called Rose Revolution in Georgia in November 2003 replaced the old regime by popular protest over a rigged parliamentary election and emboldened Washington to apply the strategy in the former Soviet region as well. While the military option was excluded, the emphasis was still on providing opposition with relevant training and financial resources for challenging the old regimes in power.[52]

The Kremlin's reaction to the new strategy was consistent with that to the intervention in Iraq. Moscow did not view terrorism as a state-based phenomenon, and it wanted interstate cooperation, not regime change, to be the basis for solving the problem. It therefore perceived the new American effort to reshape the post-Soviet space with suspicion, as a threat to Russia's own influence in the region.[53] For example, when the United States and other Western nations stepped up their support for the opposition in the October 2004 Ukrainian presidential election, the Kremlin threw all its weight behind the candidate of the ruling regime. Russia also maintained close relationships with existing leaderships in Belarus, Armenia, and the central Asian countries, despite growing criticism of them by the United States and the EU. Few were willing to question the Kremlin's reaction or to lend support for the regime-change strategy adopted by Washington. The majority of the political class and general public remained wary of Western intentions, and this made it easier for the Kremlin to articulate its concerns and pursue the chosen course.

Moscow's response to Washington's regime-change strategy was therefore domestically sustainable. Two additional considerations reinforced the reaction by the Kremlin. First, supporting the opposition in those countries where existing regimes remained fully in control was hardly a viable option. Second, the Kremlin had reasons to suspect geopolitical motivations behind the regime-change strategy, which included a long-term geostrategic presence and greater control over natural resources in the region.[54] Russia therefore continued to defend its distinct interests, while developing relationships with Western nations in the areas of mutual concern. Despite some serious setbacks, this course survived tests of new challenges.

Beslan and Terrorism in the Northern Caucasus

Domestically, the most serious challenge to Pragmatic Cooperation came in September 2004 when, after downing two civilian airliners, terrorists took more than a thousand people hostage in a school in Beslan, North Ossetia. Chechen field commander Shamil Basayev took responsibility for the incident, demanding the withdrawal of Russian troops from the territory of Chechnya. Ultimately, as the terrorists were in the process of releasing hostages, hundreds of women and children died. In the long list of terrorist attacks on Russian civilians, this was the worst. It also came in the middle of the Kremlin's efforts to stabilize the situation in Chechnya and to present it as considerable progress in fighting terrorism. The attacks seemed to have been spreading across the greater northern Caucasus, and people felt increasingly less, not more, protected from the threat. This reaction was a major blow to Putin's promises to "eradicate terrorism," which had helped him to win the March 2000 presidential election.

The Kremlin's initial reaction was hardly in line with the pragmatic Westernist course. In his first public statement, Putin admitted that Russia had inadequate defenses, but also he relegated partial responsibility for the Beslan incident to some unspecified foreign forces. In a thinly veiled reference to the West, Russia's president said, "Some want to tear off a big chunk of our country and others are helping them. They are helping them in the belief that Russia, as one of the greatest nuclear powers of the world, still poses a threat to them and, therefore, this threat has to be eliminated. Terrorism is their only tool."[55] Soon, Putin came under heavy attacks at home from both nationalist and liberal forces for not being able to prevent the terrorist attack and for choosing "wrong" ways of dealing with the threat. Nationalists blamed him for not building a more strongly centralized power, while liberals faulted Putin for missing a chance to negotiate with some elements within the Chechen separatist movement. Liberals also insisted that only international involvement similar to the involvement that stopped the escalation of violence in Northern Ireland would bring an end to violence.[56]

Gradually, the Kremlin gained composure and proposed a series of steps which included a far-reaching reform of the political system. At the heart of the proposed reform was the idea of further centralization of decision making. Local governors were no longer to be elected; instead, they were to be nominated by the president and confirmed by local legislative bodies. In addition, the Kremlin stepped up its counterterrorist activities and promised to hold new parliamentary elections in Chechnya. Finally, although suspicions of the international role persisted, Russia made efforts to reengage the West. After the September hostage taking in North Ossetia, Russia asked for a special session of the UN Security Council. It also provided an opening for a more positive Western role in the region by informing German chancellor Gerhard Schroeder of its desire for active Western involvement in the economic development of the North Caucasus region.[57] It remains to be seen, however, whether these measures will prevent terrorism from spreading across the northern Caucasus and other Russian territories.

Velvet Revolutions and the Test of Ukraine

Georgia's peaceful change of power following the fraudulent parliamentary election was not the only velvet revolution in the former Soviet region. The next and most important one took place in Ukraine. In November 2004 under pressure from both the Ukrainian opposition and the West, the results of the rigged presidential elections were renounced. The Kremlin's favored candidate, Viktor Yanukovich, was subsequently defeated. Putin lost his sought-after political influence, but found a way to retreat and to remain engaged with Ukrainian leadership and the West.

Putin's support for Yanukovich never amounted to an effort to build a new empire or to incorporate Ukraine into Russia. The Kremlin did not seek to incorporate Ukraine, just as previously Putin had not sought to incorporate Armenia, Azerbaijan, or Belarus, countries that had held similarly flawed elections. Although the Russian president badly miscalculated Yanukovich's chances of winning, and although he provided strong support for Yanukovich's election,[58] Putin was never willing to sacrifice his relations with the West over the crisis in Ukraine, and he did not let his readiness to stand for Russia's strategic interests be turned into confrontation. This behavior was consistent with past experiences that showed that Russia's president was not a poor loser and usually had an exit strategy prepared. For instance, he had no confrontational response when the Bush administration made it clear that it would be withdrawing from the ABM Treaty. Putin's reaction was muted and nonthreatening. In his opinion, the United States' decision was a "mistake," but presented no threat to the national security of the Russian Federation.

In handling the crisis and developing relationships with the new Ukrainian leadership, the Kremlin did not follow the advice of hard-line Statists who recommended applying economic sanctions or supporting separatism in Ukraine.[59] Although the general public in Russia overwhelmingly supported Yanukovich and many members of the political class felt cheated and betrayed by the West,[60] Putin sought an asymmetrical response. Immediately before the anticipated victory of Viktor Yushchenko, he issued a statement welcoming any winner in Ukraine's rerun of its presidential election and asserted that Russia had no objections to Ukraine's joining the European Union. Rather than coercing and applying pressures, the Kremlin planned to co-opt Yushchenko by mobilizing Russia's soft power and the two nations' economic, cultural, and institutional interdependence.[61]

At the same time, Putin did not accept the advice of liberal Westernizers to side with Yushchenko in the disputed election. He supported a candidate whom he perceived as pro-Russian, and he challenged Western leaders not to "meddle" in Ukrainian elections. He attributed the crisis to the West's heavy involvement in the elections and he is likely to continue to protect Russia's interests in Ukraine by exerting great power influence in that country. The presence of the Russian fleet in the Crimea, conditions for ethnic Russians and for Russian business, and Ukraine's foreign policy orientation will continue to be of great concern to Russia. Although a pragmatist in his beliefs, Putin may opt to respond to domestic nationalist pressures as a way to maintain his legitimacy and power base. If the Ukrainian leadership proves unwilling to meet the Kremlin halfway, applying pressure cannot be entirely excluded. Russia's way of handling Georgia is a case in point. Putin assisted the new Georgian leadership in negotiating a way out of the elections crisis and in ending separatism in Adjaria. In return, he expected Russia's interests in the Caucasus to be honored and not to be rushed in dismantling Russia's two military bases on Georgian soil. When Putin had seen what he perceived as a lack of reciprocity on the Georgian side, he changed tactics. After Tbilisi had attempted to subjugate the separatist South Ossetia by force and pressured Russia to withdraw, Putin retaliated. He stopped short of formally recognizing the separatist South Ossetia and Abkhazia, but extended some support to them[62] and kept a visa regime on the border with Georgia.

The Destabilization of Central Asia

The next challenge to Russia's new foreign policy came with the destabilization of central Asia. In March 2005, Kyrgyzstan went through a change of power that involved mass protest. Similarly to what already had happened in Georgia and Ukraine, the opposition in Kyrgyzstan challenged the regime of Askar Akayev over the process and results of the parliamentary election by forcing Akayev to leave office. Unlike in Georgia and Ukraine, however, the Kyrgyz "revolution" was not "velvet." Although the regime refused to apply force, the protests were far from orderly and were accompanied by violence and looting. An even worse development occurred in Uzbekistan in May 2005, when thousands of demonstrators challenged the state decision to imprison several prominent businessmen in Andijan and used force to help them escape. The government, too, used force, justifying it as needed to confront the growing threat of Islamic extremism in the region. Several hundred protesters died.

Both events had the potential to spread greater violence in the region. In both countries, Russia had a considerable military presence and well-established relations with the ruling regimes. In response to the crises, the Kremlin emphasized the importance of preserving legality and order in Kyrgyzstan, and it backed Uzbekistan's president in handling the crisis. Foreign Minister Sergei Lavrov blamed the involvement of "outside extremist forces" from Afghanistan, including the neo-Taliban, and supported the use of force to suppress the protests.[63] Although there was little opposition to the Kremlin's policies in Kyrgyzstan, the Russian public actively discussed Moscow's response to the violence in Uzbekistan. Comments by politicians and analysts ranged from unconditional support to strong criticism of the Uzbek crackdown on protesters in Andijan. Civilizationists and some Statists blamed the protest on the U.S. military presence in the region and fully supported the crackdown. Liberal Westernizers, however, warned against Russian support for the Karimov regime, which could trigger civil war in Uzbekistan. For instance, Boris Nemtsov, of the Union of Right Forces, argued that the Karimov regime was doomed and that by supporting Karimov the Kremlin had picked a losing scenario, as it had in Ukraine.[64]

At least in the short run, Russia's response to the central Asian crises was warranted and within the framework of Pragmatic Cooperation. In Kyrgyzstan, Moscow abstained from interference and quickly established relations with the new leadership by providing continuity in policy. In Uzbekistan, Russia did not have the option to not lend some support to Karimov. While exercising considerable influence in the region, the Kremlin did not have the ability to change regimes in the region and viewed such an approach as revolutionary and destructive. In the absence of policy leverage, it had little choice but to maintain relationships with the ruling regimes even when such regimes were mired in corruption and resorted to force and nondemocratic practices. Although building relationships with the entire political spectrum of neighboring countries may be desirable, as the Orange Revolution demonstrated, central Asia was no Georgia or Ukraine. As one Western expert commented, in Uzbekistan "there is no Saakashvili or Yushchenko waiting in the wings,"[65] and therefore a change could come only from inside the regime. Not unimportantly, Russia's reaction to the central Asian developments was not fundamentally at odds with that of the West. The Western nations called for an investigation of the events in Andijan, but refrained from calling for Karimov's resignation. Looking out for its interests in the region and cooperating with the West in the areas of mutual concern seem to have continued to work for Russia.

A Contested Victory Celebration and Relations with the New Europe

Finally, Russia's strategy of developing relations with Western nations while preserving its own vision of national interests was challenged by some of the former Eastern European nations. When the Kremlin invited more than fifty foreign leaders to come to Moscow on May 9, 2005, to celebrate the victory over fascism, several nations refused. Among them were two Baltic states, Lithuania and Estonia, which saw the end of World War II as the beginning of their occupation by the Soviets. Separating the victory over fascism and the occupation by the Soviets, for which many in Russia called, did not turn out to be possible for the small East European nations.

Russia's officials and political elites, as well as many common people, viewed the perception by new European nations as an insult and an attempt to undermine Soviet Russia's paramount role in destroying Hitler's regime. For instance, the nationalist Duma faction Rodina decided to boycott the official ceremonies in Moscow, protesting statements about the end of the war made by Latvia's president Vaira Vike-Freiberga and officials of other Baltic states.[66] The insistence by new European leaders on their version of history presented Russia as unable to relinquish its "imperial ambitions" and called into question Russia's policies of improving relationships with the European Union. The United States exerted additional pressures on Russia by supporting these claims. For instance, the American president, while traveling to the region and visiting Latvia, strongly condemned the Soviet annexation and occupation of the Baltic republics as a result of World War II.

The Kremlin stood firm and did not yield to pressures to frame the issue in terms of responsibility for Stalin's occupation of the Baltic states. Overall, despite the clashing interpretations of the end of World War II, Russia reached its two most important objectives. It reconfirmed its role in liberating the world from fascism, and it did so in the presence of fifty foreign leaders, including U.S. president George W. Bush, UN secretary-general Kofi Annan, Japanese prime minister Junichiro Koizumi, German chancellor Gerhard Schroeder, Italian prime minister Silvio Berlusconi, and Israeli president Moshe Katsav. Symbolically, the event assisted Russia in legitimizing its status as a Westernizing great power.

PUTIN'S LESSONS FOR THE FUTURE

Russia's Pragmatic Cooperation continued and changed the previous course of Great Power Balancing. Putin picked up where Primakov left off and remained focused on the objective of preserving great power status. Yet, the new leader abandoned the old strategy for achieving the objective. A multipolar world and post-Soviet integration—key tenets of Primakov's thinking—were replaced by more pragmatic means of asserting Russia's interests in global politics. This foreign policy transformation became possible due to a reshaped structure of domestic interest groups and their favored identity visions, as well as changes that had taken place in the international arena. The political context for foreign policymaking had been principally altered, and the new president took advantage of it. This section offers an evaluation of Russia's foreign policy record based on developments up to June 2005. I also briefly speculate on some foreign policy dilemmas that the course of Pragmatic Cooperation is likely to encounter in the future.

An Evaluation of Putin's Foreign Policy

Vladimir Putin's first four years showed his commitment to the newly chosen course. Having started as a Primakovite, the new leader quickly evolved in the direction of engaging the West in a new global project. His strategy bore some similarity to that of Mikhail Gorbachev. What Gorbachev saw as a crisis of human civilization that had resulted from arms races, poverty, and environmental destruction during the Cold War, Putin sought to frame as the global threat of terrorism. Both politicians attempted to engage the West in a commonly shared understanding in order to achieve better recognition and open a way to a joint search for solutions to the world's problems. Yet both sought to preserve what they saw as Russian national interest and special characteristics. Gorbachev defined such interest in terms of preserving "socialist values," while Putin demonstrated his commitment to the idea of great power. While Gorbachev lost his battle, Putin seems to have learned to be aware of the dangers of making too many concessions to the West.

The overall record of Pragmatic Cooperation is generally positive and registered considerable progress in terms of meeting the foreign policy criteria of security, welfare, autonomy, and identity. The new course was encouraging in terms of addressing its welfare dimension. Relative to the pre-1999 period, the country's economic and social standing improved considerably. Critics argued that this improvement reflected the increased world oil prices. This, however, was only one part of the story; the other part had to do with having the leadership ability to make the best of the favorable global conditions. In order to press forward with economic reforms at home and gain membership in vital international institutions, such as the WTO, and to increase Russian market share in the world economy, leadership was crucial. Capitalizing on new economic opportunities, Putin managed to considerably improve relations with the United States, Europe, and the former Soviet states. Some examples of this include the energy summit in Houston, where Russia pledged to radically increase its oil supplies to the United States, and where it forged a joint venture with British Petroleum worth $6 billion. In 2003, Russia increased its oil production 11 percent and—in order to improve its bargaining position—it entered into a deal with Saudi Arabia. The five-year deal pledged cooperation between the Russian and Saudi energy sectors and in setting the international price of oil. As some observers noted, Russia was a net beneficiary of the deal because of its ability to further enhance its market power.[67] Renewed activism in winning energy and transportation markets in the former Soviet region added to the impression that the government was serious about economic modernization as its key foreign policy objective.

Table 5.7 summarizes the record of Putin's pragmatism.

Table 5.7.   The Record of Pragmatic Cooperation

Security	Remaining problems with terrorism
Welfare	Improved economic and social standing
Autonomy	No external assistance needed
Identity	Engaged Western and Statist dimensions of Russia's values

The new foreign policy course also improved Russia's decision-making autonomy. Partly as a result of Russia's changed economic standing, its improved relations with Western nations did not come with strings attached. Russia was able to pay its debt obligations on time and was no longer in need of additional external assistance. New engagement of the West on counterterrorism and energy issues did not mean that Russia's power to defend its own perceived interests at home and in the region was to be seriously curtailed.

Did Russians appreciate the foreign policy shift toward state pragmatism and economic modernization? Most polls indicated so, although there was still an expectation of greater improvement. Many supported Putin's efforts to improve the economy and strengthen Russia's position in the world. No less importantly, the Russian public seemed to back Putin's emphasis on state-driven modernization, which is one policy that would have preserved independence and not resulted in a loss of policy autonomy to the West or domestic commercial groups. For instance, in November 2001—immediately after the terrorist attacks on the United States and at a time when Russians felt a strong sympathy toward Americans—only 30 percent agreed with the statement that cooperation with the West was the main condition of Russia's economic prosperity. At the same time, 61 percent supported the idea that it was necessary to first develop the economy and only then to improve ties with the West.[68]

Putin's record in responding to Russia's security needs was weaker. The president made the correct decision by supporting the U.S. military operation against the Taliban regime in Afghanistan. For years, Russia had been supporting the Northern Alliance without particular success, and it would have been unwise to pass on the opportunity to remove a key cause of instability in the region. Also in order to fight terrorism, Putin had been patiently assembling a coalition of the willing from the former Soviet states. Working both bilaterally and multilaterally, he made progress in pooling available military and intelligence resources in the region. However, he was much less successful in defusing a key source of terrorism on his own territory, in Chechnya. Granted, he had been left with a tough legacy after the years of lawlessness in the republic and had little choice but to apply military force. But the improvement of the situation remained marginal, with terrorist attacks continuing and the Russian public expressing reservations about the effectiveness of Putin's policies. Although people continued to have trust in the president, many increasingly felt that he failed to deliver on his promise to eliminate the resistance in Chechnya. For instance, in December 2003, one poll registered as many as 68 percent expressing their frustration with the situation.[69]

Finally, the record of Pragmatic Cooperation in addressing the Russian people's identity needs was both positive and ambivalent. The new course was successful in engaging both the Westernist and the Statist components of Russian national psychology. It did not neglect the relevance of national experience, as did Kozyrev's Westernism. Nor did it encourage anti-Western themes in national consciousness, which had been a result of Primakov's foreign policy. The new course therefore provided the space necessary for reformulating Russia's national identity and moving beyond the post-Soviet identity crisis. Yet that space was yet to be filled with some creatively defined national idea, and the government was yet to engage some of the Russians' key cultural concerns. For instance, polls consistently demonstrated that Russians supported the need to maintain strong ties with the former Soviet republics. Previous efforts to maintain such ties by encouraging the post-Soviet states to adopt dual-citizenship policies with regard to ethnic Russians had been a failure, but no other initiatives came to replace those policies.

Can Pragmatic Cooperation Be Sustained?

Although the effort to seize the middle ground between the old-style Statism and Westernism has been generally successful in responding to the nation's foreign policy challenges, the course of Pragmatic Cooperation is bound to face some critical dilemmas in the future.

One such dilemma is how to improve Russia's security without becoming overly dependent on traditional Statist tools, such as buying political supporters, using force against opponents, and maintaining relationships with dictatorial regimes. In the past, Russia tried these tactics in the former Soviet region with only limited success. Fighting terrorism using the same tactics has its limitations. Use of force can no longer solve the Chechnya problem. Nor can it stabilize Georgia, Moldova, Uzbekistan, or other neighboring states. Offering money to leaders in central Asia or the Caucasus in exchange for a more extended military presence can help only in the short run. Extending support to regimes that violate their citizens' rights is an extreme measure, and it should not become a common policy practice. More robust solutions would require the development of greater leverage for influencing neighboring states in the region. Such solutions might include the mobilization of ties with societies, rather than states only, through greater use of Russia's soft power and establishment of contacts with the entire political spectrum in the neighboring nations. They might also include adopting similar standards of behavior across the region and building international security institutions to deal with terrorist challenges.

Another dilemma has to do with the need to deepen cooperation with Western nations. Westernization has its costs, as Kozyrev's foreign policy has shown all too well, and it is important to preserve the ability to defend Russia's own interests. Yet without moving in this direction, Russia will remain provincial in economic and political dimensions. Russia has had to constantly maneuver between its military deals with China, Saudi Arabia, or former Soviet states, on the one hand, and chances to develop a better image or institutional presence in the West, on the other. In the past, Putin's unprecedented policy activism was helpful in squaring this circle. But preserving this policy line in the future may prove to be more difficult if Russia's partners outside the West continue to be autocratic and if the West grows less patient with Russia's pragmatism. Some symptoms of a growing rift between Russia and the West include geopolitical rivalries in the former Soviet region and Putin's reluctance to travel abroad to meet his Western European "partners" in 2004. For instance, he put off important visits to the EU in 2004 in favor of summits with the leaders of Brazil, China, and India. In addition, Europeans themselves continue to be wary of strengthening ties with Russia, despite some obvious gains from doing so.[70] Without consistent policy engagement from both sides, the course of Pragmatic Cooperation is likely to degenerate into the old-style Great Power Balancing.

Furthermore, Pragmatic Cooperation has been supported by a delicate domestic coalition that, absent strong leadership, may fall apart. Putin's way of dealing with Khodorkovski and other oligarchs alienated many Westernizers from his course. On the other hand, his military reform and removal of some key generals strained his relations with the military. The more he presses forward with the military reform the less likely he is to lose the support of elites. While state capacity and autonomy are important in foreign policymaking, losing such support should not be equated with it. At home, Pragmatic Cooperation is likely to run into difficulties with the political elites, and it will need, more than ever, the support of the general public.

Finally, Russia's continuing identity crisis may yet again pose the question of how to assist the nation in improving its sense of cultural confidence without resorting to some hard-line ideology. Many Russians continue to feel the identity void, yet the course of Pragmatic Cooperation has not done enough to address it. Putin will have to find a way to respond to Russia's need to see itself as a civilization, not just as a great power, if he wants to defuse the appeal of hard-line Civilizationists. It would be important to take into consideration the recent failure of the civilizational vision of "Eurasia" and reemphasize the European quality of Russia's cultural roots.[71] The European and great power components of Putin's vision must be bridged more forcefully, not separated from one another. Ukraine's 2004 presidential elections showed, among other things, the danger of separating the two. If Russia is going to develop a viable civilizational identification, it should reconfirm its commitment to democratic and institutional, rather than merely geopolitical, objectives of its foreign policy. Although Russia's success is also predicated on Europe, in the absence of renewed democratic commitment, its civilizational perspective is in danger of becoming a hostage of a narrowly defined and state-driven modernization.

NOTES

1. Vladimir Putin, "Poslaniye Federal'nomu Sobraniyu Rossiyskoi Federatsiyi," Kremlin.ru, March 16, 2003; Vladimir Putin, *First Person: An Astonishingly Frank Self-Portrait by Russia's President* (New York: Public Affairs, 2000), 169.

2. Philip Hanson, "Joining but Not Signing Up? Russia's Economic 'Integration' into Europe," *Russian and Eurasia Review* 2, no. 6 (March 18, 2003); Julien Vercuil, "Opening Russia? Contemporary Foreign Trade," *Russian and Eurasia Review* 2, no. 4 (February 18, 2003), www.jamestown.org.

3. Richard Rose, "How Floating Parties Frustrate Democratic Accountability," in *Contemporary Russian Politics*, ed. Archie Brown (Oxford: Oxford University Press, 2001), 221–22.

4. Vladimir Putin, "Rossiya na rubezhe tysyacheletiy," *Nezavisimaya gazeta*, December 1999.

5. Putin, "Rossiya na rubezhe tysyacheletiy." In Putin's most revealing words, "If by democracy one means the dissolution of the state, then we do not need such democracy" (interview, *Washington Post*, September 26, 2003).

6. Vladimir Putin, "Poslaniye Prezidenta Federal'nomu Sobraniyu Rossiyskoi Federatsiyi," *Mezhdunarodnaya zhizn'* 5 (2002): 4–5.

7. Peter Rutland, "Putin and the Oligarchs," in *Putin's Russia: Past Imperfect, Future Uncertain*, ed. Dale R. Herspring (Lanham, MD: Rowman & Littlefield, 2003), 148.

8. Dale R. Herspring, "Putin and the Armed Forces," in *Putin's Russia*, 170.

9. Putin, "Rossiya na rubezhe tysyacheletiy."

10. William Wohlforth, "Russia," in *Strategic Asia 2002–03: Asian Aftershocks*, ed. Richard J. Ellings and Aaron L. Friedberg (Washington, DC: The National Bureau of Asian Research, 2003), 199.

11. Grigori Yavlinski, "Druzhba na vremya ili soyuz navsegda?," *Obschaya gazeta*, January 24, 2002; Grigori Yavlinski, "Dver' v Yevropu nakhoditsya v Vashingtone," *Obschaya gazeta*, May 16, 2002.

12. Aleksei Kara-Murza, "Na perekrestke politiki i nauki," *Polis* 6 (2001).

13. Thomas Friedman, "World War Three," *New York Times*, September 19, 2001. For similar arguments made by Western conservatives, see Francis Fukuyama, "Their Target: The Modern World," *Newsweek*, December 17, 2001; Margaret Thatcher, "Advice to a Superpower," *New York Times*, February 11, 2002.

14. A. Buzgalin, "Russia and America: A New Twist in the Confrontation?," *Prism* 8, no. 2 (2002), www.jamestown.org (accessed April 2, 2002).

15. Valeri Fedorov, "Vpered, k ideologiyi?," *Nezavisimaya gazeta*, February 18, 2002. Dmitri Furman argued that Putin's pro-Western choice might help to preserve the essentially nondemocratic regime in Russia, just as an American alliance with the central Asian states and Pakistan does not mean to make these states more friendly to human rights (Dmitri Furman, "Polyet dvuglavogo orla," *Obschaya gazeta*, May 30, 2002).

16. See, for example, Graham Allison, Karl Kaiser, and Sergei Karaganov, "The World Needs a Global Alliance for Security," *International Herald Tribune*, November 21, 2001.

17. Putin, "Poslaniye Prezidenta," 18. The European emphasis was made the key theme of Putin's address to the Federation Council in April 2005.

18. Yevgeni Primakov, *Mir posle 11 sentyabrya* (Moscow: "Mysl'," 2002), 106–7.

19. Sergei Kortunov, "Rossiysko-Amerikanskoye partnerstvo?," *Mezhdunarodnaya zhizn'* 4 (2002): 69.

20. See, for example, Aleksandr Panarin, "Ontologiya terrora," in *Geopolitika terrora* (Moscow: Arktogeya, 2002), 46; Aleksandr Prokhanov, "Ameriku potseloval angel smerti," *Zavtra*, September 18, 2001; Dugin, "Terakty 11 Sentyabrya: Ekonomicheski smysl," in *Geopolitika terrora*.

21. RFE/RL Newsline, January 16, 2002; Katrina Vanden Heuvel and Stephen F. Cohen, "Endangering US Security," *Nation*, April 15, 2002.

22. Sergey Ptichkin and Aleksei Chichkin, "From Where Russia Is Clearly Visible," *Rossiyskaya gazeta*, January 22, 2002; Evgeny Mikhilov, "The Art of Wiping Things Out," *Versty*, January 24, 2002 (as translated by *CDI Russia Weekly* 190, January 25, 2002).

23. A. Oslon, ed., *Amerika: Vzglyad iz Rossiyi* (Moscow: Institut Fonda "Obschestvennoye mneniye," 2001), 27. Another 64 percent of respondents perceived Washington's military activities in Afghanistan as dangerous for Russia (*Amerika: Vzglyad iz Rossiyi*, 124). At the same time, Russians continued to show strong support for Putin's decision to side with the West (*Amerika: Vzglyad iz Rossiyi*, 34, 124; "Rossiyani podderzhivayut sozdaniye soyuza RF i SshA v bor'be s mezhdunarodnym terrorizmom," *Nega-Set*, November 18, 2001).

24. As cited in Dale R. Herspring and Peter Rutland, "Putin and Russian Foreign Policy," in *Putin's Russia*, 237.

25. Leon Aron, "Russian Oil and U.S. Security," *New York Times*, May 5, 2002.

26. "Bush's Russian Romance," *Economist*, May 22, 2002.

27. Hanson, "Joining but Not Signing Up?"

28. Sergei Yastrzhembsky, "Russophobia Still Rampant," *New York Times*, April 24, 2002.

29. Stephen Foye, "The EU's Enlargement; Russia Plays Bridesmaid," *Eurasia Daily Monitor*, May 3, 2004, www.jamestown.org.

30. Associated Press, "Ex-defense Minister Accuses US of Seeking to Dominate Russia," June 19, 2003 (as cited by *CDI Russia Weekly* 262, June 2003).

31. A poll taken in April by the All-Russian Center for Public Opinion Studies (VTsIOM), as quoted in Nikolai Petrov, "The War in Iraq and the Myth of Putin," *Russia and Eurasia Review* 2, no. 8 (April 15, 2003), www.jamestown.org; Pew Research Center for the People and the Press, September 2003, www.people -press.org.

32. Vladimir Putin, "Vystupleniye na soveschaniyi 'O perspektivakh razvitiya Dal'nego Vostoka i Zabaikalya,'" *Blagoveschensk*, July 21, 2000, www.kremlin.ru.

33. Vladimir Putin, "Annual Address to the Federal Assembly," The Kremlin, Moscow, April 25, 2005, www.cdi.org/russia/johnson/9130-1.cfm.

34. Wohlforth, "Russia," 201–2.

35. Interview with Putin, *Washington Post*, September 26, 2003.

36. Marianna Belenkaya, "America's Iranian Policy and Russia's Interests," Russia's Information Agency, as cited by the *Center of Defense Information* 259, no. 6 (May 29, 2003), www.cdi.org/russia/259.cfm.

37. RFE/RL Newsline, February 28, 2002, www.rferl.org.

38. Vladimir Putin, "Vistupleniye Prezidenta na rasshirennom zasedaniyi s uchastiyem poslov Rossiyskoi Federatsiyi v MID Rossiyi," Kremlin.ru, July 12, 2002.

39. Boris Berezovski, "SNG: Ot razvala k sotrudnichestvu," *Nezavisimaya gazeta*, November 13, 1998. For a representative summary of Westernist scholarship on the subject, see *Blizhneye i dal'neye zarubezh'e v geoekonomicheskoi strategiyi Rossiyi*, ed. Yuri V. Shishkov (Moscow: IMEMO, 1997). Already in 1994, Andrei Zagorski argued that the diverging economic interests of Russia and other former republics would prevent Primakov's integrational efforts from becoming permanent. See his *SNG: Ot dezintegratsiyi k reintegratsiyi?* (Moscow: MGIMO, 1994).

40. Andranik Migranyan, "Rasstavaniye s illuziyami," *Nezavisimaya gazeta*, October 27, 2000.

41. *Strategiya dlya Rossiyi: Povestka dlya prezidenta—2000* (Moscow: Sovet po vneshnei i oboronnoi politike, 2000), www.svop.edu.

42. Susan Birgerson, *After the Breakup of a Multi-Ethnic Empire* (New York: Praeger, 2002), 89.

43. Alan Kasaiev, "Sovet Bezopasnosti Rossiyi reshil zakryt' SNG," *Nezavisimaya gazeta*, February 7, 2001.

44. As cited in Yekaterina Tesyemnikova, "Preimuschestva sodruzhestva dlya Rossiyi ochevidny," *Nezavisimaya gazeta*, August 2, 2001.

45. Igor' Glukhovski, "Mnogovektornaya integratsiya kak otvet novym vyzovam," *Nezavisimaya gazeta*, February 13, 2001.

46. Anatoli Chubais, "Missiya Rossiyi v XXI veke," *Nezavisimaya gazeta*, October 1, 2003.

47. Edward L. Morse and James Richard, "The Battle for Energy Dominance," *Foreign Affairs* 81, no. 2 (2002).

48. Vladimir Socor, "Schroeder-Putin Gas Deal Undercuts Both New and Old EU Member Countries," *Eurasia Daily Monitor*, April 13, 2005, www.jamestown.org.

49. Kasaiev, "Sovet Bezopasnosti Rossiyi reshil zakryt' SNG."

50. Sergei Rogov, *Yevraziyskaya strategiya dlya Rossiyi* (Moscow: Institut SshA i Kanady, 1998); also, Rogov, "Izolyatsiya ot integratsiyi," *NG-Dipkuryer*, December 7, 2000.

51. As quoted in Anatol Lieven, "Bush's Choice: Messianism or Pragmatism," OpenDemocracy.net, February 22, 2005, www.carnegieendowment.org.

52. For some evidence of and discourse on such strategic calculations, see, for example, Stephen Blank, "Georgia: A Study in Democracy Exportation," *Asia Times*, December 6, 2003, atimes.com; Graeme P. Herd, "Colorful Revolutions and the CIS," *Problems of Post-Communism* 52, no. 2 (2005).

53. Igor Torbakov, "Different Understanding of Democracy May Put Bush and Putin on Collision Course," *Eurasia Daily Monitor*, February 25, 2005, www.jamestown.org.

54. See, for example, Anatoli Gordienko et al., "Zastolbili Kaspi," *Nezavisimaya gazeta*, April 15, 2005.

55. "Putin Says Russia Faces 'Total War' with Terrorism," RFE/RL Newsline, September 7, 2004, www.rferl.org.

56. Charles Gurin, "Observers Say Terror Attacks Eroding Putin's Legitimacy," *Eurasia Daily Monitor*, September 7, 2004, www.jamestown.org; Robert Coalson, "Russia Girds Itself for War," RFE/RL Newsline, September 3, 2004, www.rferl.org.

57. Fiona Hill, Anatol Lieven, and Thomas de Waal, *A Spreading Danger: Time for a New Policy toward Chechnya* (Washington, DC: Carnegie Endowment for International Peace, March 2005), 2.

58. Europe and the United States, in their turn, did not limit themselves to political statements about the "unacceptability" of the election's results—a step in itself unprecedented in light of their previously much calmer reaction to considerably less fair elections in central Asia and the Caucasus. Through the activities of various NGOs, the West also provided considerable financial assistance for Yushchenko's campaign.

59. The eastern regions of Ukraine, particularly Donetsk, Luhansk, and Crimea, vowed to pursue greater autonomy from Kiev after the nullification of Yanukovich's victory in the first presidential election. In Russia, nationalist State Duma members and Moscow mayor Yuri Luzhkov visited eastern Ukraine to express their support for Yanukovich and for regional autonomy. It is not difficult to imagine how such autonomy claims might be manipulated to become a factor in Russian-Ukrainian high politics.

60. Levada-Tsentr, "Ukrainskiye sobytiya glazami rossiyan," December 16, 2004, www.levada.ru/press/2004121601.html; Igor Torbakov, "After Ukraine Debacle, Kremlin Strategists Warn of Serious Rift with the West," *Eurasia Daily Monitor*, December 17, 2004, www.jamestown.org.

61. Russian-Ukrainian interdependence has been well documented. See, for instance, Paul J. D'Anieri, *Economic Interdependence in Ukrainian-Russian Relations* (Albany: State University of New York Press, 1999); Andrei P. Tsygankov, *Pathways after Empire: National Identity and Foreign Economic Policy in the Post-Soviet World* (Lanham, MD: Rowman & Littlefield, 2001); Mikhail A. Molchanov, *Political*

Culture and National Identity in Russian-Ukrainian Relations (Austin: University of Texas Press, 2002).

62. For instance, Russia extended its citizenship to many residents of South Ossetia and Abkhazia. Some analysts recommended that the Kremlin go much further and formally recognize the independence of the separatist republics (see, for example, Stanislav Belkovski, "Poslye imperii," *Komsomol'skaya pravda*, May 18, 2004).

63. "Moscow Accuses 'Outside Extremists,'" RFE/RL Newsline, May 16, 2005, www.rferl.org.

64. Sergei Blagov, "Uzbekistan's Riots Yield Mixed Response in Russia," *Eurasia Daily Monitor*, May 19, 2005, www.jamestown.org.

65. Martha Olcott, United States Helsinki Commission briefing on Uzbekistan, May 19, 2005, www.carnegieendowment.org.

66. "Nationalist Duma Faction Boycotts the Ceremonies," RFE/RL Newsline, May 16, 2005, www.rferl.org.

67. Stephen Blank, "Moscow's Cozy Saudi Connection," *Asia Times*, September 13, 2003.

68. Vladimir A. Kolossov and Natalya A. Borodullina, "Rossiya i Zapad: Mneniye rossiyan," *Russia in Global Affairs* 1 (2003).

69. The poll of VTSIOM, as cited in "Support for Putin's Policies Is Weak, but He Is Still Popular," RFE/RL Newsline, December 2, 2003.

70. On this point, see, for instance, Alexander Rahr and Nicolai N. Petro, "Our Man in Moscow," *The Fletcher Forum of World Affairs* (Summer 2005), fletcher.tufts.edu/forum.

71. Putin has attempted to move in this direction, as is seen in his 2005 presidential address to the Federal Assembly. Vladimir Putin, "Annual Address to the Federal Assembly," The Kremlin, Moscow, April 25, 2005, www.cdi.org/russia/johnson/91301.cfm.

6

❧

U.S. Regime Change Strategy and Great Power Assertiveness

One state and, of course, first and foremost the United States, has over-stepped its national borders in every way. This is visible in the economic, political, cultural and educational policies it imposes on other nations. Well, who likes this? Who is happy about this?

... Russia is a country with a history that spans more than a thousand years and has practically always used the privilege to carry out an independent foreign policy. We are not going to change this tradition today.

—Vladimir Putin, the Munich Conference on Security Policy,
February 2007[1]

Soon after the colored revolutions in the former Soviet region, Putin's Great Power Pragmatism obtained a new dimension—assertiveness. Russia's foreign policy has not returned to the era of Primakov's balancing the United States' power in the world. Instead, Russia has sought to capitalize on its new economic recovery and energy competitiveness and break into Western economic markets, while maintaining political stability and an essentially defensive security posture. Putin's speech at the Munich Conference on Security Policy became a high point in Russia's new assertiveness and was extremely critical of the U.S. "unilateralism," yet it only meant to preserve and deepen achievements of cooperation with the West. It sent a strong signal to the Western nations that in the Kremlin's perception, the course of Russia's integration with the West was in jeopardy because of highly destabilizing policies of the United States.

RUSSIA'S NEW CONDITIONS AND WORLDVIEW

Washington's Regime Change Strategy and Russia's Security Vulnerabilities

The colored revolutions that took place in Georgia, Ukraine, and Kyrgyzstan during 2003–2005 did not improve cooperation between Russia and Western countries in what had become a key international objective after September 11, 2001—fighting terrorism. Indeed, there was a connection between Washington's strategy of regime change and growing terrorist violence and political instability in the world. After the U.S. invasion of Iraq terrorism became more, not less, active in the Middle East. Iraq was in a stage of civil war with hundreds of thousands of people killed and misplaced and millions leaving the country.[2] Afghanistan, recently considered a successful antiterrorist operation, also showed multiple signs of growing destabilization and was quickly turning into a new safe haven for terrorists and members of the overthrown Taliban regime. Yet Washington seemed determined to press ahead with its strategy and even showed signs of preparing to attack Iran unilaterally. A number of policymakers believed in "an attempt to revive the concept of spreading democracy in the Middle East by creating one new model state."[3] The United States pulled military forces in the Persian Gulf, including aircraft carriers, and it increased the number of troops in Iraq by 20,000. Washington also warned Tehran not to "meddle" in Iraq. In addition to perceiving Iran as building a nuclear bomb, Washington viewed it as a regime that harbored terrorists and obstructed U.S. efforts to stabilize Iraq.

Russia also became more vulnerable because of the spread of political instability in its periphery. The so-called colored revolutions were strongly supported by the Western nations, but have been viewed as destabilizing by Russia and directed against the Kremlin's power and security. Georgia, Ukraine, and Kyrgyzstan failed to address the root causes of the revolution, such as poor living conditions and unpopular leadership. In dealing with separatist South Ossetia, Tbilisi increasingly relied on force, while pressuring Russia out of the region. In addition, Georgia and Ukraine expressed their desire to join NATO, which added to Russia's sense of strategic insecurity. In the aftermath of the NATO summit in April 2008, President Putin stated, "We view the appearance of a powerful military bloc on our borders . . . as a direct threat to the security of our country. The claim that this process is not directed against Russia will not suffice. National security is not based on promises."[4] The public, too, reacted overwhelmingly negatively to the alliance's expansion. Seventy-four percent of Russians polled in March 2008 said that

Ukraine's possible accession to NATO posed a threat to the national security of the Russian Federation, and 77 percent expressed a similar attitude toward Georgia's possible membership in the organization.[5]

Moscow also feared a revolution inside Russia. In addition to growing instability in the region, the colored revolutions added to the perception within the Kremlin that Washington's chief objective was in fact to change the regime in Russia. Although the public support for a revolution was weak, the Kremlin's political technologists took the threat seriously, knowing that less than 1 percent of the population was really involved in the recent capitals-centered colored revolutions and that influential elites in the United States maintained contacts with some radical organizations in Russia. For instance, in April 2007, the U.S. State Department issued a report highly critical of Russia's political system and pledging various assistance to "democratic organizations" inside the country. In response, the Kremlin took a number of defensive steps. It trained its own youth organizations to defend what it saw as Russia's indigenous democracy, restricted activities of Western NGOs and radical opposition inside the country, and warned the United States against interference with Russia's domestic developments.

Finally, Russia felt vulnerable to the radicalization of Islam in response to the U.S. style of fighting a war on terror. Although the situation in the Chechen Republic became more stable, North Ossetia, Ingushetia, Kabardino-Balkaria, and Dagestan were experiencing a growing number of terrorist attacks. Some of it, undoubtedly, could be attributed to Russia's own errors. A growing influence of radical Islamist ideologies, rising immigration from Muslim ex-Soviet republics, and attempts by some of Russia's authorities to address the problem by closing local mosques created a politically explosive environment. However, the other part had to do with the U.S. style of fighting a war on terror that was increasingly perceived in the Muslim world as a war of civilizations. What began as a counterterrorist operation in Afghanistan with relatively broad international support has increasingly turned into a "war of civilizations," or a U.S. crusade against Muslims and their style of living. Instead of engaging moderate Muslims, U.S. policies tended to isolate them and give the cards to radicals. In a global world, this translated into greater support for Islamic radicals inside Russia.

Russia's Growing Domestic Strength

After the years of the post-Soviet depression, Russia's domestic conditions have changed dramatically. During 1999–2007, the economy caught up with the level of 1990 and continued to grow at the annual pace of about 7 percent (Russia's basic economic indicators are summarized in table 6.1 [on facing page]). The overall size of the economy increased about six times in current dollars—from $200 billion to $1.3 trillion. Russia's per-capita GDP has quadrupled to nearly $7,000, and about twenty million people have been lifted out of poverty.[6] Russia's middle class now constituted about 25 percent of the population.[7] Over 2000–2005, the average Russian saw a 26 percent annual growth in income, relative to only a 10 percent rise in that of the average Chinese.[8] Direct foreign investments to the Russian economy skyrocketed, making it first in the world among developing economies.[9] Although much of the economic recovery was due to high oil prices, the government continued to work to reduce reliance on energy exports. In early 2008, for example, industrial production rose an annual 9.2 percent.[10] As a result, the number of Russians who thought that the chosen development course in Russia was correct had been growing year on year.[11] The economic recovery provided conditions for Russia's active business promotion in Europe, which accounts for 50 percent of Russia's foreign trade. The Kremlin insisted on long-term contracts with Europeans and greater integration with European markets in order to avoid a repetition of the 1985–1986 scenario, when sharp decline in energy prices had considerably contributed to the breakup of the Soviet economy.

The Changed Identity Coalition

The persistent security vulnerabilities and improved economic conditions led to changes in Russia's identity coalitions. Security threats strengthened the position of the security class. As a result, in the coalition of oligarchs and *siloviks*, the latter gained a considerable prominence over the former. The security class did not become dominant, as some have suggested,[12] but it was affecting state decisions more than it had previously, and it gained a greater presence in commercial companies, especially energy-related companies. The state was not consolidated enough to isolate powerful security influences, yet it did not become a hostage to those influences. Liberals, such as Aleksei Kudrin and German Gref, stayed in the government and continued to make a case for more aggressive liberal economic policies. Members of the security class were unable to assert greater isolationism in economic matters by protecting large companies from international competition and in politics by forcing Putin to stay for the third presidential term.

Rather than staying for the third term, Putin designated Dmitri Medvedev—not known for his ties with members of the security class—as his successor. Despite predictions of a third term and assessments of Russia's political system as fundamentally unstable, the power transition went

Table 6.1. Russia's Basic Economic Indicators, 1999–2007 (% annual change)

	1998	1999	2000	2001	2002	2003	2004	2005	2006	2007
Real GDP growth	−5.3	6.3	10.0	5.1	4.3	7.7	7.2	6.4	6.7	7.3
Real wages	−10	−22	18	20	16	11	11	13	13	16
Budget surplus (% of GDP)	−5.3	0.5	3.5	3.0	1.4	1.7	4.5	8.1	8.5	5.5
Urals oil prices ($/barrel)	12.0	17.0	27.0	23.0	24.0	27.0	34.0	50.0	61.0	69.0

Source: Peter Rutland, "Putin's Economic Record: Is the Oil Boom Sustainable?," *Europe-Asia Studies* 60, no. 6 (2008): 1052.

generally smoothly. With Putin's support, Medvedev decisively defeated his three rivals—the Communist Party's Gennadi Zyuganov, Vladimir Zhirinovski of the Liberal Democratic Party, and the Democratic Party's Andrei Bogdanov—winning the overwhelming majority of the popular vote in the first round of voting. Western media and election-monitoring organizations, such as the OSCE, were critical of the elections, citing the lack of public debate among the candidates and harassment of the opposition.[13] Yet the United States and European governments preferred to work with the Kremlin and expressed cautious support for Medvedev. The elections testified yet again that the state was not a hostage to ideologies of security-driven isolationism or liberal-minded openness and was in charge when deciding between them.

In economic matters, the state position has been to stake a middle ground between the two approaches by acquiring a greater prominence in economic affairs, yet using it for making Russia more open, not closed, to international competition. Ever since most of the powerful oligarchs, such as Boris Berezovski, Vladimir Gusinski, and Mikhail Khodorkovski, were stripped of their economic empires, the state has consistently asserted itself in other key areas. It increased its share in leading energy companies, such as Gazprom and Rosneft. It has renegotiated production-sharing agreements with Western companies in the most lucrative oil fields in Siberia and the Far East. Foreign energy giants, such as Royal Dutch Shell and British Petroleum, now had to play by different rules, as introduced by the more assertive Russian state. In addition to the energy industry and military-industrial complex, the state announced plans to create "national champions" or state-supported companies in the banking, aerospace, automobile, and heavy machinery industries. Yet the state also argued that creation of such companies was necessary to position them for successful international competition.[14] Russian officials also insisted on expediting the country's entrance into the WTO. Furthermore, Putin's strategy of a state-dominant capitalism recognized the vital need of foreign investments for continuing high economic growth, particularly coming from Western nations.

The state assertiveness in the nation's political economy reshaped the previously loose coalition of oligarchs and *siloviks*, creating a more stable alliance that shared Putin's pragmatic vision of Russia as a "normal great power"—a strong state playing by internationally accepted rules and norms of behavior.

The Refined Vision of National Interest

The overall objectives of Russia's foreign policy stayed the same as they had been outlined in Putin's early programmatic speech "Russia at the

Turn of the Millennium"—economic modernization, political stability, and enhancement of security.[15] Yet the context in which Russia had to act changed considerably, and that modified methods of pursuing foreign policy objectives.

In his response to new challenges and security vulnerabilities, Putin sought to reaffirm Russia's commitments to European values. In his programmatic speech delivered to the Federation Council in March 2005, Putin declared that he saw Russia moving toward the same values that are shared by others in the European continent—"the ideals of freedom, human rights, justice and democracy."[16] In the former Soviet region, this translated into the doctrine of "continuing the civilizational role of the Russian nation in Eurasia." Responding to charges of "imperialism" toward post-Soviet nations in the wake of the colored revolutions, Putin insisted that Russia seeks not the post-Soviet states' territory or natural resources, but the human dignity and quality of life of its citizens, whom it regards as its own cultural compatriots.

Putin was clear, however, that while moving in the same direction of freedom and democracy with Europeans, Russia does so at its own pace and given its own conditions. In the same speech, referring to the Western role in the colored revolutions in Georgia and Ukraine, Putin insisted on Russia's right to "decide for itself the pace, terms and conditions of moving towards democracy," and he warned against attempts to destabilize the political system by "any unlawful methods of struggle."[17] The motive of noninterference in Russia's domestic developments from outside only became stronger over time, and in his addresses to the Federation Council in May 2006 and April 2007, Putin put an even greater emphasis on values of sovereignty and strong national defense.[18]

Putin's supporters interpreted his vision of Russia's identity using the idea of "Euro-Eastern" civilization, which should be differentiated from the earlier discussed "West" and "Eurasia."[19] Intellectuals and political consultants, such as Gleb Pavlovski, articulated three components of the new civilizational idea. First, the countries of Euro-East, such as Russia, Ukraine, and Kazakhstan, shared with Europe values of the market economy and a growing middle class. Second, because of their preoccupation with domestic economic and social modernization, the Euro-Eastern area had a special need for maintaining political stability. A growing middle class and political stability should not be viewed, however, as in conflict with development of democratic institutions. Rather, according to Pavlovski, each nation in the region should be given a right to experiment with its own democratic model that fits its national and international conditions. To him, Kazakhstan, a country that was typically viewed as lacking democracy, was also in the process of finding its model of democratic development.[20] Third, domestic transformation of the Euro-Eastern nations requires preservation of political sovereignty and defense from attempts by outsiders to exploit internal resources of the nation or the region. Russia—by virtue of its size and capabilities—is in a special position to greatly contribute to providing the collective goods of security, sovereignty, and stability in the region.

The Kremlin's ideologists and theorists sympathetic to the official agenda have developed concepts of "sovereign democracy" and "sovereign economy,"[21] insisting on the need for Russia to protect its path of development and natural resources. "Sovereign democracy" implied a desire to defend an internally determined path of political development.[22] "Sovereign economy" indicated that the state was determined to have an upper hand in deciding the conditions through which Western companies were to participate in Russia's economic development. In the world of growing energy prices, the emphasis shifted from providing a macroeconomic discipline and tough fiscal policies toward a desire to capitalize on Russia's reserves of natural gas and oil. In addition, Russia insisted that a more assertive foreign policy would better protect its national security. Putin's speech in Munich[23] and a strong criticism of the U.S. "unilateralism" in world politics was especially noteworthy, serving as another reminder that Russia was not about to tolerate policies that it viewed as interfering with its sovereignty and security. Importantly, the speech was delivered to a European audience, and Putin's supporters had long argued that insistence on sovereignty and security was not inconsistent with European values. In their perspective, by upholding values of sovereignty Russia was in fact preserving European values that Europe itself could not always sustain when confronted with political pressures from the United States.[24]

Overall, a new foreign policy consensus emerged that an assertive style of achieving the objectives of development, stability, and security suited Russia well at the moment. The new Foreign Ministry report titled "A Review of the Russian Federation's Foreign Policy," commissioned by the Kremlin and released on March 27, 2007, further elaborated on the new face of Russia's Great Power Pragmatism. It indicated an important change in Russia's thinking since the 2000 Foreign Policy Concept. The report embraced the notion of multipolarity based on "a more equitable distribution of resources for influence and economic growth,"[25] which it said laid the foundation for a more self-confident and assertive Russia. The document presented Russia as ready to actively shape international relations by challenging the actions of others, particularly the United States, if they were "unilateral" and disrespectful of international law. At the same time, the report was not anti-American and did not call for any concerted effort to undermine the U.S. global position. Instead, it defended the notion of collective leadership and multilateral diplomacy as the alternative to unilateralism and hegemony in international relations.

Russia's new president, Dmitri Medvedev, amplified Putin's assertive vision, seeking to position Russia as a global player and a maker of new global rules. Speaking in Berlin in June 2008 he proposed a broad perspective on Europe "from Vancouver to Vladivostok" and proposed a new all-European treaty to establish a new security architecture by moving beyond NATO expansion and the conflict over Kosovo.[26] In addition to expressing his dissatisfaction with the U.S. role in European security, Medvedev blamed the United States for generating the global financial crisis by trying to substitute for the global commodities and financial markets, and he proposed an overhaul of the international economic order.[27] By these criticisms Russia did not mean to pursue an anti-Western policy. On the contrary, it sought to reengage the West on terms the Kremlin viewed comfortable—by strengthening membership within a U.S.-EU-Russia alliance, developing ties with growing powers, such as China and India, and sharing the world's economic benefits with poor non-Western nations (table 6.2 summarizes the new vision of national interest).

Table 6.2. Great Power Assertiveness (GPA): View of National Interest

What?	A great power in the West-centered world
How?	Multilateralism among great powers Energy power Indigenous democracy

DOMESTIC DEBATE ON NATIONAL INTEREST

Advocates of Assertive Foreign Policy

The changed vision of Russia's identity remained consistent with Putin's overall foreign policy philosophy. Throughout his presidency, he advocated a greater integration with Western nations, while insisting on Russia's great power status and viewing such status as a necessary geopolitical condition for domestic economic and political development. While emphasizing Russia's own interests in many areas of world politics, Putin sought to frame those interests as fully compatible with strategic commitments to Western values, such as international law, personal freedoms, and a market economy. A great power status was not a goal in itself for Putin; rather, the role of the great power status was to create a necessary condition for Russia's more advanced engagement with the world. The term "normal" signaled support for Westernizers, whereas the concept "great power" spoke to the need to protect Russia's territorial integrity. Such a vision was not principally new. For instance, in the late nineteenth–early twentieth century, the so-called new liberals, such as Pyetr Struve, Pavel Novgorodtsev, and Sergei Gessen, saw Russia as both a European and a distinctively strong socially responsible state. This vision differed from the one defended by the old liberals of primarily constitutionalist orientation, such as Boris Chicherin and Pavel Milyukov.[28]

As Russia was moving closer to its economic and social recovery, a new version of assertiveness made itself heard in political circles. Louder than before, some influential politicians and intellectuals voiced their support for a more expansionist foreign policy that would seek gains in power, not merely status quo maintenance. Such a policy, they believed, was warranted by Russia's full restoration to great power status. For instance, Minister of Defense Sergei Ivanov publicly proclaimed, "Russia has now completely recovered the status of a great power that bears global responsibility for the situation on the planet and the future of human civilization."[29] His article sought to justify the need for greater military expenditures, yet it also served to embolden those advocating greater separation from the West in areas such as energy supplies and relations with the former Soviet states. Energy analysts and geopoliticians insisted that Russia would be better off sharply redirecting its oil and gas supplies toward Eurasian countries, such as China and India, because it would assist the country in developing "energy-intensive goods" and in transforming its current status as a raw-materials appendage of Europe.[30] Supporters of more aggressive policies in the former Soviet region proposed that Russia increase its power by recognizing separatist territories in "politically disloyal" Georgia, Moldova, and Azerbaijan and demanding a greater independence of Crimea in Ukraine.[31]

This kind of assertiveness was more than a difference in style compared to Putin's foreign policy. Putin's perspective was still pragmatically focused on internal modernization, rather than directly challenging interests of the West, and the United States in particular, in the world. Increased toughness on the United States' "unipolar" actions, as indicated by the Kremlin's numerous public statements, did not mean to promote Russia's unilateralism or crude accumulation of power instead. Rather, it meant to draw attention to nonaddressed critical challenges of the post–Cold War world, such as terrorism, weapons of mass destruction, poverty, and political instability. It also meant to convey Russia's desire to be more integrated with the Western economy, and for these reasons, it was hardly a return to Primakov's policy of balancing the United States. Although a chance of moving in Primakov's direction remained, the policy course stayed focused on strengthening economic relations with the world, especially Europe,[32] not on building a strong security alliance with China and India or tightening the CIS under the Kremlin's leadership.

Pro-Western Critics

Russia's liberal Westernizers criticized Putin for his insistence on advancing a great power status. In their mind, there existed only two fundamental paths—pro-Western or great power nationalistic. Accustomed to viewing reality in terms of dichotomies, they followed the line of some Western analysts, insisting that if Russia is not a Western-style democracy, then it must be an empire,[33] or if it is a great power, then it must be an anti-Western one. Despite Putin's efforts to integrate with Western nations economically and in terms of addressing common security threats, Westernizers charged the Kremlin was becoming increasingly anti-Western in various aspects of its foreign policy. They blamed Putin for his lack of commitment to institutional integration with the West, and they insisted that Russia was becoming (1) increasingly imperialist toward its neighbors, (2) unnecessarily confrontational toward the West, and (3) obsessed with restoring great power at the expense of domestic modernization needs.

For instance, Liliya Shevtsova of Carnegie Moscow Center expressed a typical liberal view that the Kremlin became obsessed with insecurity and control over economic assets, as the situation was growing increasingly unpredictable. Rather than building a pluralistic political system and improving relations with the West, she argued, "the Kremlin's policies have in fact become a tool for the elite, composed of representatives of energy companies and force structures, to pursue its own interests—and this in turn has led to a worsening in Russia's relations with the West and with the new independent states, including its closest allies."[34] Energy-dependent nations, such as Ukraine, Moldova, and even the loyal ally Belarus, were now eager to escape Russia's embrace and look for alternative international ties. Members of the European Union, too, showed their reluctance to develop economic relations with Moscow. According to Shevtsova, the Kremlin also abandoned domestic modernization in favor of becoming a petrostate that "transforms market relations into affairs of state, and economic resources into political tools."[35] For these reasons, liberals believed, a sharp decline in oil prices would do Russia good, as it would push it toward modernization and democratization.

Table 6.3 summarizes contending views on Assertive Pragmatism.

Table 6.3.   Great Power Assertiveness (GPA): Contending Views

Civilizationists/Statists:		Westernizers:
GPA is insufficient to achieve political and cultural independence	vs.	GPA provokes confrontation with the West

Civilizationists and Social Democrats

Civilizationists showed their ambivalence toward the new, more assertive foreign policy advanced by the Kremlin. On the one hand, a greater assertiveness is what they had been advocating since the 1990s, challenging Russia to restore its hegemony in the former Soviet region and strong ties with the Soviet allies (see chapter 4). On the other hand, the assertiveness they defended served entirely different purposes and meant to support Russia's break with the West, not an appropriate place within the West-centered economic and political structures. For instance, Russian imperialists advocated a restoration of a "fortress Russia" able to resist powerful pressures from both Western and Eastern directions.[36]

A different group, Eurasianists, advocated a close alliance with China or Iran in order for Russia to return to its "cultural roots" and defend itself against influences from the West, seen as the most dangerous.[37] According to Eurasianists, if Russia had indeed fully recovered as a great power, it did not need to seek the West's approval of its actions and intentions. Russia had to create energy cartels and exclusive military alliances, and push arrogant Americans out of Eurasia once and for all. As a member in the Eurasian coalition, Russia would grow much faster, thereby creating a meaningful counterbalance to the West. Eurasianists also frequently argued against Russia's preoccupation with ethnonationalist ideas that were perceived as prone to violence and disruption of the region's ethno-religious balance. Although Eurasianists kept a relatively low profile, their influence in the Kremlin and Russia's media space grew. Their philosophy was often shared by Putin's powerful deputy head administrator, Igor Sechin, who was in control of the state-owned oil company Rosneft, the second-largest in the country, and who had numerous allies in the media and political circles. Putin was not invulnerable to the group's pressures, and its members insisted on the president's third term, hoping to continue consolidating their influence in his shadow.

All groups within the Civilizationist school of thinking agreed that Putin's foreign policy was lacking a "civilizational mission" or an "image of a future." Their criticism of the Kremlin's ideology of a sovereign state was not a criticism of sovereignty as an outdated concept—something that a number of Westernizers were likely to agree with—but an argument that sovereignty itself must not be equated with state bureaucracy and its assets. Rather, Civilizationists argued, sovereignty is a tool of advancing a national sense of purpose, and before asserting its sovereignty Russia had to know first what it was culturally and spiritually.[38] In their assessment, the Kremlin's policies of energy independence and raising prices for Russia's neighbors and "loyal allies," such as Armenia and Belarus, were harmful to Russia's status as spiritual leader and protector of the region.[39]

Social democrats, too, were critical of the potentially bureaucratic nature of Russia's new foreign policy assertiveness and preoccupation with sovereignty. Unlike Civilizationists, however, this group concentrated on development of human potential, stronger social programs, and improvement of people's lives rather than cultural mission as a key foreign policy objective.[40] Alternatively, at least some Eurasianists showed themselves to be mainly concerned with rebuilding Russia's power, not living standards. Sergei Pereslegin, for instance, defended a destruction of the newly emerged middle class and stimulation of social inequality in order to expedite economic growth and become an internationally powerful state. If Putin were serious in his critique of unipolarity, he had to bid farewell to the "hypocritical and stagnating" middle-class Europeans and embrace economic tigers in Asia and growing powers in the Middle East.[41]

Table 6.4 (on the following page) summarizes Russia's foreign policy discourse.

Support from the Larger Society

Overall, despite the diversity of elite perspectives on Russia's foreign policy, the larger society was very supportive of its official ideology and new assertive methods of advancing international objectives. Russians strongly supported Putin and his outlined foreign policy objectives—economic development, political stability, and security from threats. Multiple polls demonstrated that society was well aware of the considerable financial and political costs of embarking on imperial projects. Most respondents were convinced that the only way to regain the former great power status was through a successful development of the Russian economy and had no illusions about restoring the Soviet system. In a typical poll, about 60 percent expressed nostalgia about the system, yet only about 12 percent considered its restoration realistic, and 31 percent were against such a restoration.[42] In addition, only 34 percent wanted Russia to become a world power, while about 47 percent would have been content to see their country among the world's ten to fifteen most advanced economies and politically influential countries.[43]

Table 6.4. Russia's Foreign Policy Discourse

	Kremlin	Westernizers	Civilizationists	Social Democrats
Main objective	Great power normalization	Westernization	Advancement of cultural values	Improvement of human capital and living standards
Geopolitical orientation	Euro-East	West	Independence or Eurasia	Europe
Foreign policy methods	Pragmatic assertiveness	Cooperation with Western nations	Independent assertiveness; cooperation with Eurasian nations	Cooperation with European nations

Russians also valued political order and stability as a result of a successful foreign policy by expressing strong condemnation of revolutionary prospects in the country. One poll revealed, for instance, that Russians
are most positive about such word symbols as "order" (58 percent),
"justice" (49 percent), and "stability" (38 percent). In the same poll, the
word "revolution" was among the least popular ones, with 22 percent
viewing it in a negative light.[44]

In addition, Russians showed their lack of strong identification with
Europe or Asia—a disappointment for both liberal Westernist and Eurasianist hopes. In March 2007, only 38 percent saw Russia as a part of
Europe, while 45 percent claimed Russia was a particular Eurasian civilization with interests in moving the East in the future. The poll should not
be read as anti-European, however, as the notion "Europe" brought positive emotions from 77 percent of Russians, relative to 56 percent being
favorably predisposed to the notion "Asia."[45]

Finally, although the registered feelings hardly qualified the society as
supportive of various Civilizationist projects, Russians showed their support for assertive tactics for advancing national interests in the world.
One poll indicated that most of them approve of Putin's tough approach
and "welcome the readiness of the authorities to discuss energy matters
with the neighbors from the position of strength." About 61 percent
viewed Putin's course as "well-considered and well-balanced," and only
about 40 percent felt that another Cold War with the West was possible,
while 48 percent did not think so.[46]

THE UNITED STATES AND EUROPE

Cooperation and Rivalry with the United States

In a number of areas, Russia's cooperation with the United States had
remained strong since establishment of the post-9/11 partnership. Both
sides were committed to solving issues of nuclear proliferation and joined
forces in encouraging North Korea and Iran to halt their movements
toward producing nuclear bombs. The United States supported Russia's
proposal to reprocess spent nuclear fuel outside Iran as a way for the
country to continue with its nuclear program for peaceful purposes. The
two sides also coordinated numerous antiterrorist activities. For instance,
in December 2006 U.S. intelligence alerted Russia to a potential terrorist
threat of an explosion in the Moscow metro, which helped the Kremlin to
adequately respond to the threat.

Despite these positive developments, tensions between the two countries
grew dramatically and concerned at least five issues—Iran, arms sales

abroad, China, energy resources, and expansion of American military infrastructure toward Russia's borders. Elections of new presidents in both
countries during 2008 did not eliminate the tensions over these issues. On
Iran, Russia was against putting additional pressures on the Middle Eastern nation, favoring continuing negotiations. The Kremlin was not willing
to support tough sanctions for two main reasons—its own interests and
fear of U.S. unilateralism and potential use of force. First, it viewed the
issue in a broader context of Russia's multiple economic, political, and
security ties and what it viewed as an important neighbor. No other United
Nations Security Council (UNSC) member has relations with Iran as deep
and as extensive as those of Russia, and the Kremlin assumed that Mahmoud Ahmadinejad, with his regime and irresponsible policies, was temporary, while Iran was here to stay. Russia wanted to find the right balance
between pressuring the top leaders of Iran and not disrupting important
ties between Russian and Iranian societies, and such an approach was sure
to dictate a foreign policy that would differ from those adopted by the
United States, the EU, and China. Second, Russia's leadership signaled it
was not optimistic about resolving the issue in the face of the U.S. policy to
continue with threats to use force, while abstaining from initiating any
nuclear reductions.[47] The Kremlin's leadership did not want to be seen as
responsible for moving the issue down to the path of military confrontation
and therefore participating in what it saw as another immoral act of aggression similar to those against Yugoslavia and Iraq.

An additional area of tension was Russia's sharply growing arms sales,
including to regions of potential concern to the United States in the Middle
East, China, and Latin America. In 2006 sales of arms and military hard-
ware were up 20 percent over 2005, for a total value of $6.5 billion.[48]
Although the United States protested against sales to such U.S.-unfriendly
states as Iran, Syria, and Venezuela, Russia's response was that those
weapons systems were commercially important and of a defensive
nature. By selling them, the Kremlin therefore did not violate any international agreements and only did what the United States was doing by
selling its own weapons worldwide, including to areas of Russia's concern, such as Georgia and Azerbaijan.

Related to weapons sales was the issue of China, as the country was the
single largest buyer of Russia's arms. Russia-China ties, however, were of
concern to the United States for a host of other reasons, first and foremost
geopolitical ones. Russia-China cooperation, particularly in addressing
security issues in central Asia, was viewed in the light of the two nations'
growing ambitions to challenge American interests. That could be
achieved by creating a regional alliance of several countries that would
make rules for its members but exclude the United States from participating. For example, the Shanghai Cooperation Organization, established by

Russia, China, and central Asian states, added India and Iran as its associate members, yet refused to consider such status for the United States. The Kremlin remained suspicious, however, viewing the geographic region through the lens of competition rather than potential cooperation. It felt that the United States was mainly interested in the region's abundant energy resources and geostrategic presence and was about to use Trojan Horse tactics: move in first and conquer second.

Another issue was that of Russia's energy interests in the former Soviet region and Europe. Russia's energy strategy—increasing state share in energy companies, often at the expense of Western capital; building pipelines in all geographic directions; raising energy prices for its oil- and gas-dependent neighbors; moving to control transportation networks in the former USSR; and coordinating its activities with other energy producers—generated anxiety in the American political class. Its members, such as Senator John McCain and Vice President Dick Cheney, issued multiple statements that indicated their concerns about Russia's new "imperialism" and energy "blackmail." The United States built the alternative Baku-Ceyhan pipeline and worked hard on persuading potential investors and central Asian nations to build the Trans-Caspian route under the Caspian Sea, circumventing Russia. In May 2007, Putin secured a commitment from Kazakhstan, Turkmenistan, and Uzbekistan to increase exports of central Asian energy via Russia's pipelines, which only served to heighten U.S. concerns. President Barack Obama's administration created the position of special envoy for Eurasian energy to support the United States' energy goals in the Eurasian region.

In Russia's perception, its actions were perfectly legitimate and only reflected its desire to capitalize on its energy reserves and improve its chances to serve as a reliable oil and gas supplier of the EU. Despite its increased state share in energy companies, Russia indicated it was still very interested in Western investments and technology. As for its attempts to control transportation networks and gain greater presence in European markets, these meant to ensure reliability of supplies and greater integration with the West. Finally, raising energy prices was necessary for commercial reasons, as a preparation for future membership in the WTO and as a practice fully consistent with market economy rules.

Finally, there was the issue of expanding American military infrastructure closer to Russia's borders, which was taking place within and outside NATO. The United States continued contacts with former Soviet states, such as Azerbaijan, Georgia, and Ukraine, who expressed their intent to join NATO. Outside NATO, Washington announced plans to deploy elements of a missile defense system against Iran and other unspecified dangerous states to the territory of Poland, the Czech Republic, and, possibly, Georgia and Ukraine. Russia saw these developments as threatening its national security and indicated it was not satisfied with the United States' explanation.[49] At the summit in Bucharest in April 2008, Russia managed to block issuing Georgia and Ukraine Membership Action Plans (MAPs), and it further expressed a strong criticism of an OSCE/NATO-based security system in Europe, arguing against new "lines of division" between nations with a common history.[50] In addition, President Medvedev said Russia was "extremely disappointed" that the United States signed a deal to deploy part of a missile defense system in the Czech Republic and would respond appropriately.[51] By then, the Kremlin had already tested new missiles capable of penetrating the missile defense system (MDS) and announced plans to reequip its new single-warhead intercontinental ballistic missile (ICBM) Topol-M (SS-27) with multiple warheads.[52] In early 2009, the United States signaled its willingness to reconsider the issue of the missile defense system in exchange for Russia's cooperation on Iran, but the Kremlin reacted with a counteroffer of not delivering short-range missiles (Iskander) if the United States abandoned its MDS plans.[53]

Despite all these disagreements, Russia and the United States were not moving toward another Cold War. The newly elected leaders of the countries, Dmitri Medvedev and Barack Obama, remained interested in working together, which was further demonstrated by the U.S.-Russia summit in Moscow in July 2009. No less importantly, there was no ideological line dividing the two nations—they agreed on some issues while sharply disagreeing on others. Russia's new assertiveness expressed by Putin's Munich speech indicated frustration with the lack of progress in developing ties with the West, not with the principle of Westernization as a foreign policy objective.

Russia's Energy Strategy and Relations with Europe

In relations with European countries, Russia's main focus was greater integration with the EU's economy, and it has concluded a number of important agreements to this effect. Russia's largest natural gas company, Gazprom, agreed to build a direct pipeline to Germany underneath the Baltic Sea. It also negotiated an agreement with Hungary to extend Russia's Blue Stream pipeline from Turkey to Hungary via Bulgaria and Romania. Another important development was a new oil pipeline to Bulgaria and Greece projected to be built by 2010, with Russia owning 50.5 percent and the other two countries 24.5 percent each. In case of the latter, the oil supplies from Russia would be shipped through the Black Sea, bypassing the crowded Bosphorus.[54] Russia also managed to achieve greater integration with European economies by exchanging some companies' shares. Russia also made progress in political relations with the EU nations by developing a common understanding on solving the Middle Eastern conflict and the issue of Iran's nuclear program. Many Europeans shared the Kremlin's commitment to multilateralism and negotiations, rather than sanctions and force.

Still, the strategy of integration with European countries faced important obstacles. Economically, Russia and the EU disagreed on what defines economic security. The EU perceived Russia's energy disputes with former Soviet republics as a threat to its own interests, insisting that Russia ratify the Energy Charter. The charter had been signed by Boris Yeltsin during the 1990s and stipulated access of third parties to Russia's energy pipelines. The EU also saw the issue in terms of market diversification principles and wanted to have room for changing energy partners should such an opportunity present itself. However, Russia was an energy producer, not a consumer, and it wanted to sign long-term contracts with Europeans, resisting access to its pipelines. Given the significance of high energy prices for its economic development, Russia wanted to avoid a repetition of the 1985–1986 scenario, when a sharp decline in prices had undermined the Soviet economy. In addition, Russia was wary of European efforts to negotiate separate energy agreements with Azerbaijan, Turkey, and the countries of central Asia. Russia also had limited success in gaining greater access to the EU retail markets and distribution networks, as well as shares in prominent European companies.

Other difficult issues with Europeans included the role of the OSCE in the former Soviet region and bilateral disputes with some Eastern European nations concerning, among other things, their decision to work with the United States in deploying elements of an antimissile system on their territory. Russia saw the OSCE as deviating from its main mission of solving security conflicts and concentrating instead on pushing a particular version of democracy in the region. The Kremlin indicated to the organization that it would withdraw its financial contribution should the practice continue. Russia also took a hard line on the antimissile defense system, claiming that in response it was considering withdrawing from the Intermediate Nuclear Missile Treaty and aiming some of its missiles at Poland and the Czech Republic, the nations that agreed to host the system on their territory. In addition, Russia refused to yield to pressures from Eastern European states to acknowledge responsibility for their post–World War II occupation or transport energy to Western European countries through their territory. Russia-EU summits in Samara (May 2007), Khanty-Mansiysk (June 2008), and Khabarovsk (May 2009) failed to secure a "strategic partnership" pact or produce any substantive agreements.

THE MIDDLE EAST AND ASIA

Opposing the "War of Civilizations" in the Middle East

Russia also demonstrated a renewed activism in the Middle East and the larger Muslim world. Aside from ambitious economic projects and weapons sales to India, Iran, Syria, and Palestine, the Kremlin encouraged an international conference on Iraq accompanied by American phased withdrawal from the country. In order to address growing suspicions of Iran's intent to obtain a nuclear bomb, it also encouraged Tehran to send its spent nuclear fuel to Russia. Acting independently from the UN-U.S.-EU-Russia quartet, the Kremlin also opened political dialogue with leaders of Hamas, who won the Palestinian elections but continued to refuse to renounce violence against Israel or recognize its right to exist as an independent state. In addition, Russia strongly condemned the publication in Denmark and some other European nations of cartoons satirizing the Prophet Muhammad as an "inadmissible" provocation against Muslims.

Russia's Middle East assertiveness had roots in both global and domestic developments. Globally, the Kremlin was reevaluating its relations with the United States. Many of Russia's post–September 11, 2001, expectations have not materialized. Military cooperation in central Asia and Afghanistan was now replaced by rivalry over controlling security space and energy resources. Instead of rebuilding Afghanistan, the United States launched a war in Iraq. The Kremlin no longer viewed Russia-U.S. cooperation in central Asia and the Middle East as primarily beneficial, and it thought the U.S. presence there invited terrorism rather than eradicated it. Russia's perception of the U.S. role in the region as destructive corresponded with perceptions by many Muslims across the world, who viewed the U.S. "war on terror" as a war on them.

For Russia's well-being, the implications of the "war of civilizations" were fundamental. For a country with 20 million to 25 million Muslims, involvement in such a war would mean inviting fire to its own home. Russia's domestic intercultural ties were far from balanced. A growing influence of radical Islamist ideologies, rising immigration from Muslim ex-Soviet republics, and the poorly conceived actions of some of Russia's local authorities in failing to build ties with Muslims created a politically explosive environment. Although the situation in Chechnya was much more stable, Islamic radicals were spreading violence and extremist ideology across the larger Northern Caucasus.

Although Russia's Eastern initiatives were not anti-Western, they signaled that the "war of civilizations" between Western nations and Islam was intensifying, as well as an understanding that Russia had no business participating in that war. Just as it was a tragic mistake to get involved in

World War I in 1914, Russia felt it would be tragic to have a fully hardened Western-Islamic front today and to see Russia joining it. Russia's willingness to engage Iran and Hamas sought to compensate for blunders of Western policies in the region, such as calls to boycott elections in Iran or clumsy attempts to pressure Palestinian voters, and to find a way out of a developing intercivilizational confrontation. Implicitly, the new Kremlin initiatives also fully recognized that the threat of Islamic radicalism in Russia cannot be successfully confronted without reaching out to the Muslim world. The notion of a dialogue with the Muslim world was strongly endorsed by Russia's political class. Russia called for an "intercivilizational alliance" and "compromise" involving countries in the Middle East. For example, in March 2008 President Putin sent a message to the Organization of the Islamic Conference meeting in Senegal in which he said that "deeper relations of friendship and cooperation with the Islamic world are Russia's strategic course" and that "we share concerns about the danger of the world splitting along religious and civilizational lines."[55] Other officials presented Russia as a country "which is on the junction of Europe and Asia and is a natural inter-civilization bridge" and expressed desire to have closer ties with the Islamic world.[56]

Imperatives of Modernization and Security in Asia

Although Russia saw itself as a country of European identity, it sought to take advantage of its strategic proximity to Asia for the purpose of modernizing the economy. It was highly symbolic that after being elected Russia's new president, Medvedev chose China and central Asia as the first regions to visit. China and the Asia-Pacific region were important because of their potential for becoming a gateway for Russia's entrance into the global economy. With half of the population and one-fifth of global trade, the region was viewed by many as a success story of modernization/globalization. Rich in natural resources, Russia was poised to contribute to satisfying the region's growing demand for energy and modernizing its own domestic economy along the way. Russia moved from a primitive accumulation of capital to the stage of generating a stable flow of investments in the economy, and it was turning its forward-looking vision and growing resources into a more aggressive foreign policy. In addition, the region faced some long-standing security challenges, such as the nuclear ambitions of North Korea and China's relations with Taiwan.

Russia's first interest was in increasing its role in solving vital security issues in East Asia. For years, Russia's officials argued for the development of a multilateral security framework in the region and outside. The

Kremlin insisted that security problems could only be solved through systematic coordination of state efforts, and not through use of force by ad hoc coalitions. For instance, it developed the Shanghai Cooperation Organization (SCO), with China and four central Asian states, for addressing threats from terrorism and the security vacuum in the area. In East Asia, Moscow advocated multilateral solutions to the nuclear crisis with North Korea and contributed considerably to creating the six-party format for dealing with the crisis.

Russia's most important priority remained economic modernization, and that required determination to win markets in arms and energy. China and India remained Russia's largest buyers, purchasing more than 90 percent of Russia's annual arms exports. While promoting weapons sales in Asia, Putin did so mainly for commercial reasons, not out of desire to create some new strategic "axis" against the United States. Russia viewed itself as connected with Asia in an economically open region, in which Russia, due to its richness of natural resources, occupies an appropriately important role and reaps considerable economic, as well as political, benefits. Although its energy markets remained primarily in Europe and accounted for about 50 percent of its foreign trade, Russia continued to aggressively promote itself as an energy pipeline hub connecting Asia, Europe, and North America. Russia's energy strategy estimated that by 2020, 30 percent of the country's oil exports would go to Asia, compared with 3 percent in 2005.

Russia's other priorities in the region include nuclear security and political stability. Seeking a nonnuclear status for North Korea, Moscow has worked to develop its ties with North Korea, and it stayed engaged with Pyongyang during nuclear crises. Close relationships with North Korea helped Russia to increase its participation in security negotiations, and it was ultimately Pyongyang that demanded that Moscow join the six-party format. It was critical for Russia that changes in the region, such as reunification of the two Koreas, were orderly and not destabilizing in nature. On several occasions, Putin extended his support for unification of the two Koreas if it takes place in an orderly fashion and on the basis of inter-Korean dialogue. Russian analysts considered a unified Korea a potential strategic partner, provided that the shape of unification was not overly determined by the United States. For these reasons, Russia insisted on preserving special and evenhanded relations with both Koreas.

Of course, none of this meant that Russia faced no constraints on advancing its greater influence in the region. One such constraint had to do with progressive power differentials. As Russia continued to supply China with energy and weapons and China continued to grow at a considerably higher rate than its northern neighbor, the risk of Moscow's becoming a junior partner in a Beijing-led coalition increased. However, a way out of this "relative gains" dilemma was not to reduce bilateral interactions, but rather to continue strengthening multilateral security institutions in the region. In addition, it was important to be versatile in developing economic relations by strengthening relations with the United States and promoting trilateral cooperation with South Korea and North Korea in anticipation of a future unification of Korea. Russia could only reap economic and security benefits through development of multiple ties in the region with all the sides involved—China, South Korea, North Korea, the United States, and Japan.[57]

THE FORMER SOVIET WORLD

The same commitment to economic development, political stability, and security delivered in assertive style was visible in Russia's foreign policy toward the former Soviet world.

"No More Energy Subsidies"

Consistent with the new vision, Russia moved to strengthen its energy position in world markets. In addition to increasing Russian shares in foreign companies abroad and coordinating its activities with other energy producers, Russia's energy strategy included building pipelines in all geographic directions, raising energy prices for its oil- and gas-dependent neighbors, and moving to control transportation networks in the former USSR. Although many interpreted Gazprom's energy dispute with Ukraine in December 2005 as an attempt by the Kremlin to punish the new leadership of Ukraine for the Orange Revolution, the dispute also aimed to economically normalize relations with Kiev by moving in the direction of establishing market-based prices for energy supplies. Moscow worked to reduce the amount of subsidies to the Ukrainian economy, and Kiev, understandably, resisted the effort. Russia's decision reflected the Kremlin's long-articulated pragmatic modernization approach in the former Soviet region. Already in February 2001, then secretary of the Security Council, Sergei Ivanov, announced that previous attempts to integrate the region of the CIS had come at a very high price and that Russia had to abandon the integration project in favor of a "pragmatic" course of bilateral relations. By the time this announcement was made, the CIS states' debt to Russia had reached $5.5 billion.[58]

Russia's decision also reflected a policy adjustment in the post-Soviet world following the colored revolutions. As Ukraine, Georgia, and Moldova moved to challenge Moscow by questioning the Russia-controlled CIS, the Kremlin was determined to secure economic gains in the region.

As explained by Putin, "Over the last fifteen years Russia subsidized the Ukrainian economy by a sum that amounted to $3 to 5 billion each year," and "each year we raised the issue of whether we should change to the European regime for determining prices."[59] The fact that Russia's close allies in the region, such as Armenia and Belarus, were also presented with the same deal of tripled gas prices further indicated that the Kremlin's energy strategy reflected imperatives of economic modernization. In an energy dispute with Belarus during late 2006–early 2007, Russia's Gazprom canceled a preferential price, doubling it to $100 per 1,000 cubic meters and acquiring a 50 percent stake in the Belarusian state gas pipeline company, Beltransgaz. On oil, Russia imposed a new export duty, increasing domestic revenue and reducing Belarus's chances of reexporting Russian oil. The net gain from both deals for Russia, according to some calculations, amounted to around $4 billion, or over 2 percent of the overall budget.[60]

Importantly, the Kremlin also renegotiated price arrangements with the oil- and gas-rich Turkmenistan and Kazakhstan, leaving them with less incentive to sell to Europe and China.[61] With attractive prices and an energy transportation system in place, the Caspian states would be less likely to construct new pipelines that are favored by non-Russian nations. In addition, the autocratic regimes in central Asia appreciate that Russia does not aim to "democratize" them.

Russia's energy policy was pursued against objections from various directions. Western countries expressed concerns over the Kremlin's use of energy as a "political weapon" against its neighbors. Belarusian president Aleksandr Lukashenko accused Moscow of trying to incorporate his country into Russia.[62] At home, Russia's Civilizationists attacked Putin's policies as betraying the notion of "Slavic unity" and pushing Belarus into the arms of the "hostile" West.[63] Yet the Kremlin remained firm, insisting that its policies of ending energy subsidies were perfectly legitimate and indeed necessary for Russia to join the WTO and remain a reliable energy supplier to European markets. If anything, the story reaffirmed that Russia remained pragmatically focused on selfish considerations of national recovery, not empire.

In Search of Stability and Security

As Russia's economic recovery required preservation of the international status quo, the Kremlin sought to insulate the region from what it saw as politically destabilizing activities. It took different approaches to different parts of the region. In central Asia, the Kremlin chose to work independently from the West and in partnership with China to address a challenge of destabilization from local and foreign Islamic radicals. This was a departure from the original policy of working with the West and allowing U.S. and NATO troops' presence in the central Asian states in order to launch a counterterrorist operation in Afghanistan. In Ukraine, Russia signaled a desire to move beyond the Orange Revolution and work with a broad range of political forces in the country.[64] In Georgia, the Kremlin took a hard-line approach, imposing sanctions, strengthening ties with separatist territories, and practicing containment toward Tbilisi. After President Mikhail Saakashvili's arrests of four of Russia's intelligence officers in September 2006, Moscow reacted with a heavy package of economic and political sanctions that stayed in place even after the officers had returned to Russia.

Even this hard-line approach did not work, and on August 8, 2008, Georgia attacked the South Ossetian capital Tskhinvali in attempting to restore control over the rebellious province. Georgian troops killed ten Russian peacekeepers and, by attacking the city with heavy artillery, Georgia inflicted heavy civilian casualties on South Ossetia. Russia responded with overwhelming force that included several armored battalions, air power, and marines, defeating and destroying much of the Georgian military. Russia also recognized the independence of South Ossetia and Abkhazia and imposed areas of security control throughout Georgia. Despite Saakashvili's efforts to present his offensive as a response to Russia's aggression, sources as diverse as intelligence agencies, human rights organizations, the Georgian exiled leader Irakli Okruashvili, and various government analysts agreed that the aggression came from Tbilisi, not Moscow.[65]

Much of Russia's reaction can be explained by its perception of threat stemming from the expansion of NATO. The West's geopolitical advances into what Russia has traditionally viewed as its sphere of interests and the desire expressed by the postrevolutionary Georgia and Ukraine to join NATO exacerbated Russia's sense of vulnerability and isolation by the West. Following the summit of NATO in Bucharest, Russia reiterated that it would do everything in its power to prevent expansion of the alliance and extension of its membership to Georgia and Ukraine.[66] The so-called frozen conflicts were merely leverage in the Kremlin's hands, and until the war in the Caucasus in August 2008, the Kremlin had planned to keep them frozen until NATO bore out its plans to continue its march to the East. In the aftermath of the summit, to signal its dissatisfaction to Georgia, the Kremlin extended additional assistance to the secessionist South Ossetia and Abkhazia.[67] Some Russian analysts argued that if membership in NATO is most important to Georgia, then Tbilisi is likely to obtain it at the cost of its territorial integrity.[68] South Ossetia and Abkhazia continued to oppose Georgia's membership in the Western alliance and to press for integrating with Russia. Such integration came a few steps closer after the United States' recognition of the independence of Kosovo and the Kremlin's recognition of South Ossetia and Abkhazia's independence in the wake of the Caucasus crisis. At the same time, Moscow expedited negotiations with Moldova over incorporation of Transdniestr provided that Kishinev stays a neutral state and does not join NATO.[69] Moscow may be signaling that the "no NATO membership in exchange for territorial integrity" deal may still be possible to conclude with other republics outside Georgia, such as Ukraine and Azerbaijan.

EVALUATION OF GREAT POWER ASSERTIVENESS

Balance Sheet

On balance, the shift toward foreign policy assertiveness has been successful in defending Russia's objectives. Apart from the conflict with Georgia, Russia did not experience any major threats to its security, from either terrorist attacks or elsewhere. While pressing for preserving and strengthening security ties with Western countries, Russia managed to sustain good relations with Iran and other Middle Eastern nations. The latter often had complicated relationships with the United States and the EU and, no less importantly, had potential to undermine Russia's security through funding religious extremist activities. The Kremlin's effort to reach out to the Muslim world by initiating contacts with its multilateral organizations and developing bilateral ties served Russia well. The overall situation improved in Chechnya, although terrorism in the Caucasus remained an important issue. In the former USSR, Russia strengthened its security standing by maintaining evenhanded relations with other states in central Asia and the Caucasus. The exception was Georgia, against which the Kremlin applied sanctions and then military force.

Russia's foreign policy was also relatively successful in meeting the objective of economic development. The Kremlin's strategy of capitalizing on the country's energy reserves added revenue without alienating potential foreign investors. Russia's drastic decisions to cut energy supplies for some of its neighbors, as well as some other components of its energy strategy, raised concerns among Western countries and former Soviet republics but on balance did not do any irreparable damage. More importantly, Russians themselves were strongly behind the course of foreign policy assertiveness. For example, in March 2007, 61 percent of respondents evaluated the Kremlin's international actions as well considered and well balanced. Indeed, 16 percent felt that the foreign policy course was too pro-Western for their taste, relative to only 8 percent who believed it was hard-line and uncompromising with regard to the West.[70]

Table 6.5 summarizes the record of Assertive Pragmatism.

Table 6.5.   The Record of Great Power Assertiveness

Security	Remaining problems with terrorism in the Caucasus
Welfare	Improved economic and social standards
Autonomy	Increased ability to influence international affairs
Identity	Continued efforts to bridge Westernist and Statist values

Challenges

This assessment, of course, is subject to how well Russia is going to meet future foreign policy challenges. One can identify at least two groups of such challenges—external and internal.

Russia's main external challenge is to preserve the international status quo in order to continue with the vital program of domestic economic and social modernization. Major economic disturbances, such as world economic recession or a sharp decline in oil prices, are bound to complicate the process. The international financial crisis has made itself felt in Russia and may continue to negatively affect its economic development. If those experts who project growing demand for energy among both developed and developing nations, such as China and India, are correct, then in the midterm perspective Russia should still be able to take advantage of the situation if it is successful in developing its own reserves. Another danger might be related to further destabilization of the Middle East and continued expansion of the Western military presence to Russia's borders. The U.S. withdrawal of its troops from Iraq without leaving an adequate security framework in place or a military confrontation with Iran would be sure to create a large flow of refugees, in which case the region will be destabilized further. The effects of such destabilization are likely to be felt in the Caucasus and central Asia and therefore, at least indirectly, in Russia. No less dangerous could be NATO's decision to extend membership to Georgia and Ukraine, or American attempts to deliver elements of an antimissile defense system in close proximity to Russia. These kinds of international disturbances may provide ammunition to those inside Russia's political class who resent Putin's Great Power Pragmatism and want to push the assertive style to the edge of radically anti-Western policies.

The internal challenge remains to overcome the split within the political class over how to deal with Western pressures. Too many in Russia have become emboldened by its recent economic recovery to the point of forgetting the country's lingering problems. Yet Russia, as the old saying goes, while never as weak as it seems, is also never as strong as it says. The country is strong in its growing international presence and energy power, yet it remains weak in such critical respects as population health, demographic dynamics, and the size of its middle class. Indicators of poverty, HIV infection, and demographic crisis are plentiful enough to make a convincing case for the nation's continuing weakness. Despite all the trumpets of great power revival, Russia remains a vulnerable country in an increasingly volatile environment. At least for the next ten to fifteen years, Russia will do well to think hard about the linkage between external war and internal instability. Its own experience speaks volumes about the linkage.

NOTES

1. "Speech at the Munich Conference on Security Policy," Munich, February 10, 2007, Kremlin.ru.

2. Charles Recknagel, "Iraq: U.S. Plans to Take in 7,000 Refugees," *RFE/RL Research Report*, February 15, 2007, www.rferl.org.

3. Seymour M. Hersh, "The Next Act," *New Yorker*, November 27, 2006, www.newyorker.com/archive/2006/11/27/061127fa_fact?printable=true.

4. Vladimir Putin, "Press Statement and Answers to Journalists' Questions Following a Meeting of the Russia-NATO Council," Bucharest, April 4, 2008, Kremlin.ru.

5. "Poll Shows Russians See NATO Membership for Ukraine, Georgia as Threat," *Interfax*, April 1, 2008.

6. "Russia's Economy under Vladimir Putin: Achievements and Failures," *RIA Novosti*, March 1, 2008.

7. "Middle Class Grows Atop," *Kommersant*, February 27, 2008.

8. Andrea Crandall, "Invest in China? Invest in Russia," *Johnson's Russia List* 22, April 19, 2006, www.cdi.org/russia/johnson.

9. "Russia Is Most Attractive Emerging Economy for Investors," *Kommersant*, February 14, 2008.

10. Paul Abelsky, "Russia Industrial Output Rises 9.2%, Nine-Month High," *Bloomberg*, May 20, 2008.

11. "Russians Think Chosen Development Course Correct—Poll," *Interfax*, June 18, 2008.

12. Both Russian and Western analysts speculated that security class became omnipresent in policymaking. See, for example, O. Kryshtanovskaya and S. White, "Putin's Militocracy," *Post-Soviet Affairs* 19, no. 4 (2003); Daniel Treisman, "Putin's Silovarchs," *Orbis*, Winter 2007.

13. See, for example, "A Potemkin Election," editorial, *Washington Post*, January 30, 2008; "Kicking Democracy's Corpse in Russia," *New York Times*, editorial, January 30, 2008; Alvaro Vargas Llosa, "Eternal Putin," *New Republic*, March 5, 2008; "Putin's Mini-Me (or Not?)," *New York Times*, editorial, March 4, 2008.

14. Dmitri Medvedev, "Dlya protsvetaniya vsekh nado uchityvat' interesy kazhdogo," *Ekspert* 28 (522), July 24, 2006, expert.ru.

15. Vladimir Putin, "Rossiya na rubezhe tysyacheletiy," *Nezavisimaya gazeta,* December 1999.

16. Vladimir Putin, "Poslaniye Federal'nomu Sobraniyu Rossiyskoy Federatsiyi," March 2005, Kremlin.ru.

17. Putin, "Poslaniye."

18. Vladimir Putin, "Poslaniye Federal'nomu Sobraniyu Rossiyskoy Federatsiyi," May 10, 2006, April 26, 2007, Kremlin.ru.

19. For development of this comparison, see Andrei P. Tsygankov, "Finding a Civilizational Idea: 'West,' 'Eurasia' and 'Euro-East' in Russia's Foreign Policy," *Geopolitics,* 12, no. 3 (2007).

20. Gleb Pavlovski, "O politike Rossiyi na postsovetskom prostranstve," America-Russia.net, April 28, 2005; "Zapad—eto antiyevropeyskoye ponyatiye," *Izvestiya,* July 14, 2006.

21. Vladislav Surkov, "Suverenitet—eto politicheski sinonim konkurentnosposobnosti," *Moscow News,* March 3, 2006; Aleksandr Tsipko, "Obratno puti net," *Literaturnaya Gazeta* 19 (May 2006).

22. Not all in the Kremlin shared the concept of "sovereign democracy." For a different view, see Medvedev, "Dlya protsvetaniya vsekh nado uchityvat' interesy kazhdogo."

23. Putin, "Speech at the Munich Conference."

24. Vlad Sobel, "A Resurgent Russia, or Triumphalist West?," *Johnson's Russia List* 249, November 6, 2006. In attempting to emphasize Europe's independence, Pavlovski has criticized the concept of "West," viewing it as "anti-European" and only relevant for understanding the Cold War ("Zapad—eto antiyevropeyskoye ponyatiye").

25. "Obzor vneshnei politiki Rossiyskoi federatsiyi," March 27, 2007, www.mid.ru.

26. Dmitri Medvedev, speech at meeting with Russian ambassadors and permanent representatives to international organizations, Russian Foreign Ministry, Moscow, July 15, 2008, and speech at the World Policy Conference, Evian, France, October 8, 2008, Kremlin.ru. Also see the article by Russia's foreign minister Sergei Lavrov, "A Strategic Relationship: From Rivalry to Partnership," *Russia beyond the Headlines,* May 28, 2008, www.rbth.rg.ru/.

27. Dmitr Medvedev, speech at the 12th Petersburg International Economic Forum, St. Petersburg, June 7, 2008, www.kremlin.ru.

28. For analyses of Russia's liberal currents, see especially G. Fisher, *Russian Liberalism: From Gentry to Intelligentsia* (Cambridge, MA: Harvard University Press, 1958); Andrzej Walicki, *Legal Philosophies of Russian Liberalism* (South Bend, IN: University of Notre Dame Press, 1992); Marsha Wiedle, *Russia's Liberal Project* (University Park: Pennsylvania State University Press, 2000).

29. Sergei Ivanov, "Triada natsional'nykh tsennostei," *Izvestia,* July 14, 2006.

30. See, for example, Sergei Pereslegin, "Rossiya sosredorochilas'," *Russki zhurnal,* February 1, 2007, www.russ.ru.

31. Moscow Mayor Yuri Luzhkov and a number of State Duma deputies, in particular, have been active in advancing this kind of goal.

32. Putin's special representative to the European Union Sergei Yastrzhembsky suggested that Putin's Munich speech was a "cold shower [and not a return] to a

Cold War." Yastrzhembsky added that Putin's remarks were aimed primarily at a European public and also sought to draw attention to a variety of world issues. Pointing out that Putin challenged the concept of what he called a U.S.-dominated "unipolar world," the aide said that an unspecified recent poll showed that at least 60 percent of German respondents agreed with Putin's remarks (RFE/RL Newsline, February 23, 2007). In a different interview, Yastrzhembsky drew attention to Russia's desire to integrate with Europe economically. "The Russian business elite wants to go into a massive investment offensive, shall I say, in the best meaning of this word, in the European market. One of the goals of the state is to create conditions for such activities of Russian entrepreneurs" (press conference with presidential aide Sergei Yastrzhembsky on RF-EU relations, January 30, 2007, www.fednews.ru).

33. For an early statement of this viewpoint, see Zbigniew Brzezinski, "The Premature Partnership," *Foreign Affairs* 73, no. 2 (March/April 1994).

34. Liliya Shevstova, "Rossiya-2007: Vlast' gotova k samovosproizvodstvu, ili ob opredelennosti neopredelennosti," Carnegie Moscow Center Briefing 1, January 2007, www.carnegie.ru.

35. Ibid. For similar statements by Russian liberals, see Vladimir Milov, "Bratya imperialisty," *Vedomosti*, February 7, 2007; Grigori Yavlinski, "Present-Day Russia in an Autocracy," *Gazeta*, March 16–18, 2007, www.gazeta.ru.

36. Mikhail Yuryev, *Tretya imperiya* (St. Petersburg, Russia: Limbus Press, 2007).

37. Den'ga Khalidov, "Myunkhen: rasstavaniye s illuziyami," *Russki zhurnal*, February 27, 2007, www.russ.ru.

38. Oleg Matveychev, "Dukhovkyi suverenitet," *Russki zhurnal*, February 17, 2006, www.russ.ru.

39. Aleksandr Prokhanov, "Belarus, ty prava!," *Zavtra* 3 (687), January 17, 2007.

40. See, for example, Vladislav Inozemtsev, "Rossiya i mirovyye tsentry sily," *Publichnyie lektsiyi*, Polit.ru, www.polit.ru.

41. Pereslegin, "Rossiya sosredorochilas'."

42. *Nezavisimaya gazeta*, April 7, 2006.

43. "Poll Suggests Russians Unimpressed By 'Imperialist Ambitions,'" RFE/RL Newsline, January 24, 2007.

44. "Russians Like Order and Justice," *RosBusinessConsulting*, March 28, 2007.

45. "Russian Interests to Move to Asia in Future—Poll," *Interfax*, March 17, 2007.

46. "Poll Suggests Russians Favor Tough Foreign Policy," RFE/RL Newsline, March 14, 2007.

47. "Moscow Warns U.S. Iran Policy May Spark 'Clash of Civilizations,'" *RIA Novosti*, March 27, 2007.

48. "Russian Arms Business Breaks New Records," RFE/RL Newsline, March 22, 2007.

49. Kristin Roberts, "Gates Gets Cool Russian Welcome over Missile Plan," Reuters, April 23, 2007.

50. "Medvedev Doubts Effectiveness of OSCE/NATO-based Security System," ITAR-TASS, June 11, 2008; Dmitry Rogozin, "Global Security and Propaganda," *International Herald Tribune*, July 1, 2008.

51. Henry Meyer and Sebastian Alison, "Medvedev Says Russia to Respond to U.S. Missile Deal," *Bloomberg*, July 9, 2008.

52. "Russia to Re-equip Its New Mobile ICBMs with Multiple Warheads," *RIA Novosti*, December 15, 2007.

53. "Iskander Plans if U.S. Scraps Missile Shield," *RIA Novosti*, March 3, 2009.

54. Andrew E. Kramer, "New Pipeline Will Bypass the Bosporus but Involve Russia," *New York Times*, March 16, 2007.

55. "Putin Wants 'Deeper Friendship' with Islamic World." RFE/RL Newsline, March 14, 2008.

56. "Russia Ready to Contribute to Alliance of Civilizations Potential," ITAR-TASS, January 16, 2008; "Minister Hails Ties to Muslim World," RFE/RL Newsline, January 11, 2008.

57. For development of these points, see Gil Rozman, Kazuhiko Togo, and Joseph Ferguson, eds., *Russian Strategic Thought toward Asia* (New York: Palgrave, 2006), especially the chapter by Aleksandr Lukin.

58. *Nezavisimaya gazeta*, February 7, 2001.

59. Vladimir Putin, transcript of meeting with the leaders of the news agencies of G-8 member countries, June 2, 2006, Novo-Ogaryovo, Kremlin.ru.

60. Andrei P. Tsygankov, "The Test of Belarus," *Johnson's Russia List* 14, January 19, 2007.

61. Max Delany, "Energy Ties Take Medvedev Eastward," *Moscow Times*, July 2, 2008.

62. "Belarusian President Rejects Russia's 'Imperial' Approach," RFE/RL Newsline, February 6, 2007.

63. Prokhanov, "Belarus', ty prava!"

64. However, in August 2009, President Medvedev delayed sending a new Russian ambassador to Ukraine, blaming Ukrainian president Viktor Yushchenko for conducting anti-Russian policies. Medvedev's letter to the Ukrainian president was widely interpreted as Russia's attempt to influence Ukrainian presidential elections by undermining the position of Yushchenko and his political supporters (for Medvedev's letter, see Dmitri Medvedev, address to the President of Ukraine Victor Yushchenko, Kremlin.ru, August 11, 2009).

65. See, for example, "A Month after the War: Violations of Human Rights and Norms of Humanitarian Law in the Conflict Zone in South Ossetia," special press release by Memorial Human Rights Center, September 16, 2008; Patrick Armstrong, "The War He Actually Got," *Johnson's Russia List*, September 17, 2008; Brian Rohan, "Saakashvili 'Planned S. Ossetia Invasion': Ex-Minister," Reuters, September 15, 2008; "Did Saakashvili Lie?," *Der Spiegel*, September 15, 2008.

66. "Russia Again Vows to Block NATO Enlargement," RFE/RL Newsline, April 9, 2008.

67. C. J. Chivers, "Russia Expands Support for Breakaway Regions in Georgia," *New York Times*, April 17, 2008.

68. Anatoly Tsyganok, "On the Consequences of Georgia's NATO Entry," Fondsk.ru, January 2, 2008, www.fondsk.ru/article.php?id=1148.

69. "Moldovan President, Transdniester Leader Hold Landmark Talks," RFE/RL Newsline, April 14, 2008.

70. Leonti Byzov, "Narodnyye imperialisty," *Vremya Novostei*, March 13, 2007.

7

❧

Global Instability
and Russia's Vision
of Modernization

We must be more effective in our use of foreign policy instruments
specifically for pursuing domestic objectives, for modernising our
country, its economy, its social life and, to some degree, its political
system, in order to resolve various challenges facing our society.

—Dmitri Medvedev[1]

We are ready for mutually beneficial cooperation and open dialogue
with all our foreign partners. We aim to understand and take into
account the interests of our partners, and we ask that our own interests
be respected as well.

—Vladimir Putin[2]

Around the fall of 2009, Russia's foreign policy began to depart from
the assertive course that had culminated in the war with Georgia in
August 2008. Russia's assertiveness had generally solved the key tasks
the Kremlin had articulated around 2005. The country revived its status
as a great power and defended its international prestige using available
economic, military, and diplomatic means. Russia exploited its energy
clout to expand its relations abroad and cemented its military presence in
the strategic area of the Southern Caucasus by defeating Georgia and
recognizing South Ossetia and Abkhazia's independence. Under the
presidency of Dmitri Medvedev, the country gradually adopted a more
nuanced approach to the outside world—one which was dictated by the
need to modernize the domestic economy. Having established itself as a

major power, Russia was now turning to domestic modernization and inviting the outside world to contribute to it.

The new approach did not mean that Russia was returning to its pro-Western course of the early 1990s or attempting to build special ties with the United States in the manner that followed 9/11. Not only did Russia become stronger, but the international context in which Russia had to defend its interests changed dramatically. The world was no longer West-centered. The global financial crisis revealed the United States' and Europe's economic vulnerability; the Russia-Georgia war undermined the West's monopoly in the use of force in world politics. In the meantime, China and India kept growing during the crisis by consolidating new regional centers of power and establishing politicoeconomic interdependence outside the West.[3] Under these new conditions, Russia has worked to broaden its existing ties with countries across the world, from Europe and the United States to Asia and Afghanistan. The Kremlin has also mobilized its soft power to reverse the colored revolutions in Kyrgyzstan and Ukraine and strengthen Russia's influence in the former Soviet region. Finally, Russia remained critical of the United States' proposal to develop an MDS jointly with Europeans but separately from Russia.

This chapter documents the new policy shift away from the Kremlin's assertive foreign policy, explaining it by Russia's revealed vulnerabilities and new international opportunities. Contrary to some common views that attribute Russia's foreign policy to the nation's traditionally imperialist and anti-Western political culture, the primary drivers in the Kremlin's foreign policy have remained contemporary and domestic. They include new opportunities for economic growth and stability, as well as the need to address increasing security threats. Being seriously hit by the global financial crisis, Russia remains keenly interested in developing economic and technological ties with the Western nations. At the same time, the Kremlin's priorities have begun to shift. Initially the country's leadership was hoping to develop a grand strategy by engaging Western nations, in particular the United States, into projects of common significance, such as counterterrorism and energy security. However, as Russia grew stronger and the West began to decline relative to the rising powers in Asia and Latin America, the Kremlin made important adjustments to its policy.

CHANGED INTERNATIONAL CONDITIONS

Three factors—the global financial crisis, new relations with the United States, and revolutions in the Middle East—served as global conditions that affected Russia's identity and shaped its foreign policy perspective.

During 2008, Russia's economy was hit by the global financial crisis. The crisis ended an era of unprecedented growth which lasted nine years (1999–2008) and during which the economy not only caught up with 1990 levels, but continued to grow at an annual pace of about 7 percent. The global economic crisis revealed the tenuous nature of Russia's recovery and the remaining weaknesses of its power base. During the crisis, Russia, which is heavily dependent on energy, including exports, was hit particularly hard and its GDP fell by around 9 percent in 2009, while China and India continued to grow, albeit at a slower pace. Russia had to spend a considerable portion of its reserves to bail out domestic enterprises, including noncompetitive ones, and to scale down its activist foreign policy in central Asia and the Caucasus.[4] The crisis revealed that Russia has met some of its economic and security challenges, but it has also perpetuated an insufficiently diversified economic structure and has failed to address some serious gaps in its social infrastructure.

Another important factor that affected Russia's foreign policy was the United States' decision to improve relations with the country. Despite Russia's war with Georgia in August 2008, the newly elected president Barack Obama quickly moved to "reset" relations with Russia and establish strong ties with Russia's president, Dmitri Medvedev. The "reset" diplomacy alleviated the Kremlin's fear of NATO expansion and the region's destabilization in response to Washington's strategy of global regime change. For several reasons, Russia had previously condemned both policies. First, it viewed the liberalizing and democratizing instincts coming from the United States as directed against the Kremlin's power and security. Second, the so-called colored revolutions in Georgia, Ukraine, and Kyrgyzstan during 2003–2005 failed to bring greater stability and prosperity, but greatly politicized the international environment in the region. Georgia and Ukraine expressed their desire to join NATO, which added to Russia's sense of strategic insecurity. In the aftermath of the NATO summit in April 2008, President Putin stated, "We view the appearance of a powerful military bloc on our borders . . . as a direct threat to the security of our country. The claim that this process is not directed against Russia will not suffice. National security is not based on promises."[5] Third, Russia felt vulnerable to the radicalization of Islam in response to the U.S. methods of fighting a war on terror. Although some of Russia's problems with Islamic terrorism could be attributed to its own errors, such as attempts by some of its authorities to close local mosques, other aspects were related to U.S. policies that tended to isolate moderate Muslims and give the cards to radicals. In a global world, this translated into a greater support for Islamic radicals inside Russia.

Finally, Russia was affected by transformations in the Middle East from regime changes in Egypt, Tunisia, and Libya to rising instability in Syria.

From Russia's perspective, the Middle Eastern changes had the potential to destabilize the region and contribute to growing terrorist violence, including inside Russia. Russia's domestic ties with 20 million to 25 million Muslims were far from balanced, constantly testing the relationships between ethnic Russians and residents from the Islamic republics of the Northern Caucasus.

RUSSIA'S WORLDVIEW

The Vision of Modernization

It took Russia's leadership some time to adjust its foreign policy perspective to the new global conditions. Until the fall of 2009, the country's officials refused to fully acknowledge the debilitating effects of the global financial crisis and continued to issue generally optimistic assessments. For example, the new National Security Strategy to the year 2020 provided a long list of potential threats to the country's security, but stated in its preamble confidence in the country's ability "to reliably prevent internal and external threats to national security and to dynamically develop the Russian Federation and to turn it into a leading power in terms of technological progress, people's quality of life and influence on global processes."[6] As time was passing, Russia had begun to draw fundamental lessons from the crisis. In September 2009, Medvedev published the article "Go, Russia!" with a highly critical assessment of the country's domestic conditions. By pointing to "a primitive economy based on raw materials and endemic corruption," "semi-Soviet social sphere, fragile democracy, harmful demographic trends, and unstable Caucasus," the new president posed a rhetorical question: "if Russia cannot relieve itself from these burdens, can it really find its own path for the future?"[7] His proposed solutions included the modernization of the economic and the political system, technological changes, and strengthening the judiciary to fight corruption. In his address to the Federation Council in November 2009, Medvedev further insisted that the effectiveness of foreign policy must be "judged by a simple criterion: Does it improve living standards in our country?"[8] Finally, in his meeting with Russia's ambassadors in July 2010, he further highlighted the need to establish "modernization alliances" with the United States and other Western nations.[9] Official documents, too, began to reflect the new vision. The Foreign Ministry document prepared for the president in February 2010 sought to strengthen Russia's economic position. By reflecting the realities of the global financial crisis, the document builds on Medvedev's notion of "modernization alliances" and provides detailed recommendations for attracting Western investments and creating favorable conditions for Russia's technological modernization.[10] (Table 7.1 summarizes the new vision of national interest).

Table 7.1. Alliances for Modernization (AM): View of National Interest

What?	A modernizing state
How?	Exploiting economic opportunities with Western and non-Western powers
	Improving domestic institutions
	Remaining tough in defending security interests

The new vision responded to the new realities without undermining the established foreign policy consensus in Russia. Such consensus assumes that the currently "unipolar" structure of the international system diminishes Russia's global influence and that its leadership must work to revive the country's status and remain tough in defending its national interests.[11] In addition, both Putin and Medvedev advocated essentially economic means for achieving Russia's international objectives. Both sought to position their country for successful competition in the world economy, including by capitalizing on Russia's rich energy reserves. Both were pragmatically focused on exploiting opportunities outside the West and building flexible coalitions with members of BRICS, members of SCO, and other non-Western countries to promote Russia's global interests. Finally, both were concerned that political changes in the Middle East and elsewhere might further complicate the already painful global economic recovery.

The Domestic Reception

Medvedev's foreign policy vision was met with a mixed reaction at home. The group of Westernizers emerged hopeful that the new leader would move in the pro-Western direction. The initially skeptical members of the business community became increasingly supportive of the president's priorities, which included new incentives for investment from the private sector.[12] Critical of what they viewed as an excessively centralized and energy-oriented model of development, members of the business class supported Medvedev's emphasis on modernization as essential for the country's integration with the world economy and Western institutions. In particular, the Institute of Contemporary Development (INSOR), led by the head of Russia's Union of Industrialists and Entrepreneurs Igor' Yurgens, published a number of reports and statements supportive of Medvedev's domestic and foreign policy agenda. One such report described Russia's future aspirations in the twenty-first century, presenting the country as bound to the European Union by shared values, security interests, and visions of world order and a system of treaties on strategic partnerships in military, energy, political, and cultural areas.[13] Foreign policy analysts with ties to the West also supported Medvedev and encouraged him to go further in developing Russia's pro-Western orientation. For example, Director of the Moscow Carnegie Center Dmitri Trenin argued that "Russia is not a distinct civilization or a world unto itself," and therefore "Russia's noninclusion into the European security architecture is a problem, while China's absence from the U.S.-led system of security arrangements in Asia is not."[14]

More critical was the reaction from those groups within the political class who read Medvedev's policies as excessively pro-Western and detrimental to the nation's sovereignty. Those with strong ties to the defense and security establishment shared the Statist identity and demonstrated that their foreign policy priorities differed from those with commercial and political relations to the West. By highlighting Russia's obligations to preserve global strategic balance and influence in Europe, Eurasia, and other regions, these groups defended a more muscular and assertive foreign policy, and not the one "judged by a simple criterion: Does it improve living standards in our country?" These groups' modernization priorities also differed from those of Medvedev. Those supported by Deputy Prime Minister Igor Sechin prioritized the development of the energy and military sectors, as opposed to the diversification highlighted by Medvedev. Importantly, Putin, too, was often sympathetic to the group's ideas.[15] The Middle Eastern changes had the effect of deepening fears that similar developments could take place inside Russia and destabilize the existing political structure. As the presidential election was approaching, foreign investors, too, were divided, with some showing signs of nervousness about political stability and leaving the country's markets.[16] Outside the Kremlin, the divide widened between successful professionals in large cities and those dependent on additional state assistance for survival during the economic crisis.

Table 7.2 summarizes contending views on Alliances for Modernization.

Table 7.2. Alliances for Modernization (AM): Contending Views

Westernizers:		Statists:
AM should move further in the pro-Western direction	vs.	AM is too pro-Western and not respectful of Russia's security and energy independence

In September 2011, Putin responded to the growing divide by making public his decision to run for the presidency. Quite possibly, the decision reflected Putin's skepticism regarding his protégé's vision and ability to act on his perspectives on the country's future. On March 4, 2012, after running an aggressive and populist campaign, Putin was elected in the first round with an impressive 64 percent of the vote. The Medvedev project therefore remained half completed. The system was again stabilized on Putin's terms. However, the cities-based middle class, which was critical of Putin's system, grew restless and increasingly ready for political protest. The elections to Duma on December 4, 2011, amply demonstrated the public fatigue with the system, which worked to promote the ruling party, United Russia (UR), at the expense of other parties and movements. Even the official count recognized that UR gained 49 percent of the vote by losing 15 percent of what it obtained in 2007. In addition, the vote was widely contested across the country, especially in large cities. The new power structure assumed the need to incorporate Medvedev's supporters, to which Putin responded by appointing Medvedev prime minister.

RELATIONS WITH THE WEST

"Reset" with the United States

Russia's ties with the United States began to improve soon after Washington's proclaimed desire to "reset" relations with Moscow and President Obama's trip to Russia in July 2009. The two sides were now cooperating in several areas. They signed and ultimately ratified the new START by replacing the old treaty of 1991. Signed in Prague on April 8, 2010, the new agreement further limited the number of strategic nuclear missiles to the level of 1,500, renewed a verification mechanism, and banned the deployment of strategic weapons outside the national territories. Russia also cooperated with the Western nations on Iran. The United States had earlier supported Russia's proposal to reprocess spent nuclear fuel outside Iran as a way for the country to continue with its nuclear program for peaceful purposes. However, Tehran refused to go along with the Russian proposal, and Moscow opted to support the United Nations' resolution on Iran. In addition, U.S.-Russia relations notably improved in the area of stabilizing Afghanistan. Russia agreed to U.S. military overflights and overland transportation of nonmilitary cargo. The two countries jointly raided several opium laboratories in Afghanistan, destroying more than two thousand pounds of heroin.[17] In March 2012, the Kremlin went as far as approving NATO use of an airport in Ulyanovsk as a transit point for moving soldiers and cargo to and from Afghanistan.[18] Finally, Russia renewed a strong interest in developing economic relations with the United States. Medvedev stressed the importance of investments in the information technology sector. Russia also completed negotiations over its membership in the World Trade Organization—the end of the road that began in 1993. In addition, Russia's state oil company, Rosneft, concluded with ExxonMobil to explore and develop Russia's Arctic Basin.[19] The deal's success depends on Moscow's commitment and approval by the U.S. Congress.

The progress in relations with the United States did not overshadow a number of unresolved issues between the two countries. The Kremlin remained critical of the U.S. proposal to develop an MDS jointly with the Europeans. Russia was worried about being isolated from Western security developments and viewed as potentially threatening the expansion of American military infrastructure closer to Russia's borders, which had been taking place within and outside NATO. Even after Obama's election, the United States continued to develop programs of military cooperation with the former Soviet states and remained supportive of their bids for NATO membership.[20] Russia maintained its right to protect its interests in Georgia and elsewhere in the former Soviet region, whereas the United States continued to demand that the Kremlin withdraw its military from Northern Ossetia, Abkhazia, and Moldova. The two sides also competed, rather than cooperated, on energy transportation issues. As Russia worked to increase the exports of central Asian energy via Russia's pipelines, the United States tried to persuade potential investors and former Soviet nations to build alternative transportation routes, such as the trans-Caspian route under the Caspian Sea.

Outside Europe and Eurasia, Russia remained concerned about the United States' foreign policy interventions, which became evident from Moscow's decision to abstain in the UNSC resolution that authorized airstrikes against Libya.[21] The tensions between Russia and the Western nations became especially acute over a growing crisis in Syria. By spring 2012, a military confrontation within the country between government and opposition turned into a civil war claiming many thousands of civilian lives. The list of unresolved issues between the two countries also included Russia's arms sales to non-Western countries, the Soviet-era Jackson-Vanik amendment that blocked development of bilateral economic ties, and human rights. In particular, against objections from the Russian government, the U.S. Congress considered a bill that would impose visa bans and asset freezes on human rights violators in Russia. The bill was named after Russian lawyer Sergei Magnitsky, who was defending a foreign firm but was arrested and died while in detention.[22]

Relations with Europe

The attempts to "reset" U.S.-Russia ties assisted the development of Russian ties with European countries. Speaking in Berlin in June 2008, Russia's president, Dmitri Medvedev, articulated a broad perspective on Europe "from Vancouver to Vladivostok" and proposed a new all-European treaty to establish a new security architecture by moving beyond NATO expansion and the conflict over Kosovo.[23] He cited the need to strengthen international law and urged moving beyond Atlanticism by developing an equal partnership between the European Union, the United States, and Russia. Medvedev further suggested that, if the West and Russia were able to sign the Helsinki Act of the Conference on Security and Cooperation in Europe in 1975, then they would be in an even better position to negotiate a new security treaty after the end of the Cold War.

Moscow's intervention in Georgia's conflict with South Ossetia of August 2008 created new tensions in Russia-West relations, yet Medvedev saw the conflict as an opportunity to strengthen his case. According to him, the fact that neither NATO nor the OSCE was able to prevent the military confrontation indicated the need for an improved security framework in Europe. The two organizations, Medvedev argued, were important yet insufficient for filling the existing security vacuum. Comparing the significance of the Caucasus conflict to Russia to that of September 11, 2001, to the United States, Russia's president insisted that "We simply have to create a new security system, otherwise there will be no guarantees that someone like Saakashvili could not . . . try something similar to what happened in August."[24] In November 2009, Russia published its proposal for a new security treaty by pledging to legally restrict its unilateral use of force in exchange for European nations and the United States doing the same. The Kremlin presented the draft as the document that would "finally do away with the legacy of the Cold War."[25]

In the economic area, Russia remained focused on greater integration with the EU's economy, and the two sides concluded a number of important agreements to this effect. Russia's largest natural gas company, Gazprom, built a direct pipeline to Germany underneath the Baltic Sea. It also negotiated an agreement with Southern European nations to build a new oil pipeline to Bulgaria and Greece by bypassing the crowded Bosphorus. Russia also managed to achieve greater integration with European economies by exchanging some companies' shares. In addition, it began to negotiate deals with European companies over joint development of the Arctics. Furthermore, Russia made progress in political relations with EU nations by seeking to develop a common understanding on solving the Middle Eastern conflict and the issue of Iran's nuclear program. Many Europeans shared the Kremlin's commitment to multilateralism and negotiations, rather than sanctions and force. Finally, Russia worked on improving bilateral relations with Eastern European states, such as Poland and Latvia.

Still, the development of relations with European countries faced important obstacles. Despite sufficient backing at home, the idea of a new security pact did not receive the outside support Russia was looking for. Although some Western nations welcomed Russia's efforts to reach out to Europe, they offered only general support and remained wary of Medvedev's initiative. Germany and France responded by proposing to establish the EU-Russia Political and Security Committee as an institution to consult on strategic issues on the continent.[26] They agreed with the need to address the vacuum of European security, but did not find Russia's proposal satisfactory. NATO secretary-general Anders Fogh Rasmussen said he saw no need for the new legally binding security treaty "because we do have a framework already."[27] The United States was equally dismissive. U.S. secretary of state Hillary Clinton found a new European treaty unnecessary—the position that Medvedev described as reflecting "a certain envy" among "our American partners."[28] Washington expressed full confidence in the NATO-centered security system in Europe and proposed that any revisions should be discussed in the OSCE context.[29] Finally, the Eastern European nations were concerned that Russia's initiative was about recognizing Russia's sphere of interests and giving Moscow a veto over NATO's international operations. They shared the perspective of Georgia and viewed Russia as the most important threat to their security.[30] At the end of 2010 Medvedev expressed disappointment with the lack of international support and acknowledged that two and half years of discussions did not lead to any breakthrough. Citing the power of stereotypes, he said his initiative may have appeared ahead of its time and would have to wait before being considered in the future.[31]

Progress was also slow regarding Western plans for an MDS in Europe and the handling of the Middle Eastern crisis. Moscow threatened to develop new intercontinental ballistic missiles that could spark a new arms race. The Kremlin maintained that NATO's missile defense plans could undermine Russia's security as soon as 2020, when the system's fourth phase would be deployed. Russia also took issues with the West going after regime change and Libya's Muammar Gaddafi personally. Although Moscow had originally not vetoed the UNSC resolution on the use of force against him, it later criticized the implementation of the resolution and then vetoed a much weaker resolution on Syria. The problem lay in the divergent perception of interests by Russia and the West. Russia, through its initiatives—from merging the two missile defense systems to negotiating a new pan-European security treaty—demonstrated a desire to have strong cooperative relationships, whereas Western nations wanted more favors from Moscow—from allowing transit routes to Afghanistan to pressuring Iran into nuclear compliance and negotiating a political exit for Middle Eastern leaders.

Economically, Russia and the EU continued to disagree over what defines economic security. The EU perceived Russia's energy disputes with former Soviet republics as a threat to its own interests, insisting that Russia ratify the Energy Charter. The charter had been signed by Boris Yeltsin during the 1990s, and stipulated the access of third parties to Russia's energy pipelines. The EU also saw the issue in terms of market diversification principles and wanted to have room for changing energy partners should such an opportunity present itself. However, Russia was an energy producer, not a consumer, and it wanted to sign long-term contracts with Europeans, resisting access to its pipelines. Given the significance of high energy prices for its economic development, Russia wanted to avoid repetition of the 1986 scenario, when a sharp decline in prices undermined the Soviet economy. In addition, Russia was wary of European efforts to negotiate separate energy agreements with Azerbaijan, Turkey, and the countries of central Asia. Russia also had limited success in gaining greater access to the EU retail markets and distribution networks, as well as shares in prominent European companies.

CHINA AND THE MIDDLE EAST

Russia improved its standing in the non-Western world by participating in international coalitions, such as the SCO (Shanghai Cooperation Organization) and BRIC (Brazil, Russia, India, and China), and fostering bilateral ties. Relations with China, Russia's largest neighbor, obtained a strategic dimension in the areas of commerce and regional security, and the two demonstrated an increased convergence in perceiving global priorities and proposing solutions to existing issues in world politics.

Turning to the Asia-Pacific Region

Considerations of economic modernization and security reinforced Russia's determination to develop ties with Asia and the Asia-Pacific region. In particular, the Asian and Pacific Economic Council (APEC) organization combines twenty-one countries and accounts for 55 percent of global GDP and 44 percent of global trade.[32] Over the past decade, Russia's trade share in that region increased from 16 percent to 24 percent—largely due to China—and continues to grow.[33] The region is also important in terms of meeting Russia's security interests in Siberia, East Asia, and the Korean peninsula.

Russian officials made clear their priority in building strong ties with the region. After being elected president, Putin visited China, among several other states. By September 2012, he had already hosted an APEC summit in Vladivostok, asserting Russia's status as "an intrinsic part of the Asia-Pacific region"[34] and offering new policies to strengthen his country's Pacific identity. Rather than viewing this priority as "a reorientation from West to East," the Kremlin sees it in terms of Russia's ability to develop a global capacity by strengthening relations with Asia. Russia's recent proposal to build a new Eurasian Union among the CIS states also fits this global design to become influential in connecting Europe and Asia. In Putin's words, the idea is to "become a bridge between the European Union and the Asia-Pacific region" by pursuing "closer integration of economic models, regulation and technical standards among the EU, APEC and the Eurasian Economic Union," which "would offer businesses the ability to operate seamlessly across a vast area."[35]

To facilitate such developments in Asia, Putin emphasized Russia's energy and transit potential. Given that Asia is resources poor, Russia has much to offer and has worked toward this goal. For instance, in September 2010, Russia completed an oil pipeline connecting to northeastern China and also planned two gas pipelines.[36] Although Russia's sales of weapons and energy to China decreased, the two nations' economic and political interests are compatible, and it is certain their cooperation will continue to grow in the future.

The second proposed direction involves transportation logistics. "Russia's logistical possibilities are enormous because two-thirds of Russian territory is located in Asia, and a third is in Europe. From the economic point of view, it is beneficial to use these routes," Putin said.[37] One transportation initiative includes unification of the Trans-Siberian and Trans-Korean railways, which Russia also views as a contribution to security of the Korean Peninsula. The Kremlin has worked to promote trilateral cooperation with South Korea and North Korea. In August 2011, Moscow hosted a trip by North Korea's leader Kim Jong Il. Kim and then president Medvedev agreed to create a bilateral commission to investigate the possibility of constructing a trans-Korean pipeline.[38] Another logistical initiative is to utilize the Northern route to transport goods from Asia to Europe via the Arctic. The route is much shorter than via the Suez channel, although the route is open only four months per year.

In attempting to strengthen ties with the Asia-Pacific region, Russia is mainly motivated by considerations of developing Siberia and East Asia. After the Soviet disintegration, these parts of Russia became severely depressed, especially when compared with China's booming growth. With declining population and deteriorating infrastructure in Siberia and East Asia, Russia needs to secure foreign investments, especially from China, South Korea, and Japan. This explains why the Kremlin has not supported the United States' proposal to build a trans-Pacific free-trade zone. Russia views the proposed Trans-Pacific Partnership as potentially diverting trade and investments from Siberia and East Asia, should China choose to join it and move outside of APEC.[39]

Finally, in all economic initiatives, Russia is concerned for its sovereignty and security, especially in light of China's rise. By facilitating trans-Korean integration and investments in the East Asian region, Russia seeks to increase its cumulative power to offset China's growing influences. In preparation for the summit in Vladivostok, the Russian government invested around $9 billion in the city's infrastructure, with private investors contributing an additional $13 billion. Vladivostok is the home port of Russia's Pacific Fleet, which also suffered from the post-Soviet decline and needs new investments.[40] Moscow's decision to order heavy investments in the disputed Kuril Islands' defense and to send two new warships to patrol access to the Pacific Ocean may also reflect Russia's desire to strengthen its naval presence in the region.

Relations with the Middle East

In the Middle East, Russia has worked to develop relations across the region and sustain its influence on Iran and has considerably expanded ties with Turkey, Israel, and Afghanistan. Although Moscow failed to persuade Tehran to send its spent nuclear fuel to Russia, the Kremlin continued a dialogue with Iranian leaders. Russia sought to restrain Western leaders from military intervention or imposing additional sanctions on Iran, while welcoming negotiations. In February 2012, Putin warned that the consequences of a military strike on Iran "will be truly catastrophic."[41] In Afghanistan, Russia attempted to introduce its own policy by appointing a presidential special representative for the country, fostering ties with its official leadership and establishing separate lines of communication to the Taliban leadership.[42] Despite Russia's traditionally strong ties with Syria, Palestine, and other Arab states, the Kremlin also managed to deepen its relations with Israel. For example, the two sides signed the $100 million deal for Israel to provide Russia with unmanned aerial vehicles, thereby enabling the Russian security forces to tighten surveillance over Georgia.[43] In addition, Turkey has emerged as especially important to Russia, with the two converging on perceptions of world order, developing ambitious energy plans, and cooperating on improving security in the Black Sea area. In May 2010, the two countries signed an agreement to carry Russian oil from the Black Sea to the Mediterranean. The two nations were also connected by important gas projects such as a pipeline from Russia to Greece, Italy, and Israel and from Russia to Southern Europe—both through Turkey or the Turkish sector of the Black Sea waters.[44]

Finally, the pragmatic, nonideological orientation of Russia's leadership assisted it in making adjustments to the postrevolutionary realities in the Middle East. For example, the Kremlin sought to distance itself from the old leaders, such as Libya's Muammar Gaddafi, by not vetoing the UNSC resolution on the use of force against him.[45] At the same time, Russia was worried about the potential strengthening of extremist forces in the Middle East following revolutions in the region. Russia's officials continued to voice concern about the possible radicalization of Middle Eastern states. Acting jointly with China, Russia vetoed the United States and Europe–sponsored UNSC resolutions regarding Syria. Fearful that such resolutions would lead to a military intervention and regime change in Syria, as had happened in Libya, the Kremlin instead pushed for negotiations between Bashar al-Assad and the military opposition. The BRICS summit held in April 2012 in India then further supported negotiations in Syria. In May, the Kremlin moved closer to accepting a possible removal of Assad, but not at the cost of dismantling the Syrian regime or losing Russia's influence over it.[46] In June 2012, when the presidents of Russia and the United States met in Mexico, Obama further pressed Putin on Syria and Assad's departure as a condition for peace. However, Putin was concerned with preserving stability in the country and the wider region after Assad.[47]

Russia's Middle East activism had roots in both global and domestic developments. Globally, the Kremlin was seeking to increase political influence and commercial gains. Domestically, Russia remained concerned about the potential reverberations of the Middle Eastern destabilization. A growing influence of radical Islamist ideologies, rising immigration from Muslim ex-Soviet republics, and insufficient state policy on the Northern Caucasus economic and political integration created an explosive environment. During 2010–2012, Russia was confronted with terrorist violence. Previously contained in Chechnya, terrorism spread throughout other parts of the region—Dagestan, Ingushetia, Kabardino-Balkaria, and North Ossetia. Since the October 2002 seizure of a Moscow movie theater, Chechen jihadists have worked to stage violent actions in Russia's capital. On March 29, 2010, two female suicide bombers trained by the Caucasus-centered Doku Umarov detonated their explosives inside a Metro train, killing forty people and injuring many more. Another major attack came in March 2011, when a bomb detonated in the largest Moscow airport, Domodedovo, killing thirty-six and injuring 180 people. The Kremlin responded by outlining a new antiterrorism strategy for the region,[48] but the violence was far from curtailed. In summer 2012, the violence spread to Tatarstan, where terrorists assassinated two moderate Muslim leaders. Perhaps most significantly, on August 29, 2012, a female suicide bomber killed a leading moderate Muslim cleric in Dagestan, Sheikh Said Atsayev, who had been engaged in negotiations with radical Islamists.[49]

THE FORMER SOVIET REGION

"Privileged Interests" and Regional Aspirations

In the former Soviet region Russia insisted on its own sphere of influence. The regional component of Russia's policy was supposed to reinforce the global one, moving Russia on the path of becoming an independent center of power and influence in the world. Russia's foreign policy consensus assumed the importance of domination in the region by remaining "pragmatic" and avoiding the use of brute force in achieving its objectives. Although the Kremlin was unapologetic about using force against Georgia and recognizing the independence of South Ossetia and Abkhazia in August 2008, both Putin and Medvedev viewed regional dominance in terms of soft power, rather than direct control over Russia's neighbors' domestic and international priorities. They assumed that Russia has sufficient economic, diplomatic, institutional, and cultural capacity to regionally negotiate the preferred international postures of the former Soviet states.

Medvedev's concept of "privileged interests" served to reinforce this thinking after the war with Georgia. Russia sought to downplay the use of force in the Caucasus and obtain international recognition of its regional vision. Immediately following the war, the president set out five principles in conducting foreign relations: the primacy of international law; multipolarity as a basis of global stability; nonconfrontational relations and active development of ties with Europe, the United States, and other nations; protection of Russia's citizens and business needs; and special ties with close neighbors.[50] It is the fifth principle that Medvedev articulated using the term "privileged interests." Following Russia's earlier expressed position,[51] the president sought to clarify that his country did not want an area of geopolitically exclusive influence. Rather, Medvedev was referring to a common historical experience, and spoke of "countries with which we have been living side by side for decades, centuries, now, and with which we share the same roots . . . countries where Russian is spoken, and that have a similar economic system and share much in terms of culture."[52]

Following the idea of strengthening Russia's ties with its neighbors, Putin proposed to build a new Eurasian Union among the CIS states.[53] Similarly to Medvedev, Putin emphasized an open nature of the proposed union and laid out economic incentives for joining it, including increase in trade, common modernization projects, and improved standards of living.

Aiming at a Low-Cost Political Stabilization

Following the outlined vision, Russia sought to strengthen its influence in the former Soviet region by relying on diplomatic, economic, and cultural tools. By capitalizing on high oil prices, it strengthened its presence in neighboring economies and contributed to reversing the colored revolutions in Ukraine and Kyrgyzstan, which the Kremlin viewed as dangerous for Russia and destabilizing for the larger region. In both countries, anti-Kremlin governments were replaced with those in favor of stronger ties with Russia. Following a change in government, Russia negotiated new terms for its political influence. In Ukraine, the two sides agreed in April 2010 to extend the lease on Russia's Black Sea Fleet for twenty-five more years in exchange for the reduction of gas prices by 30 percent.[54] In 2011, Russia invited Ukraine to join the Customs Union, promising another major discount for gas prices.[55] While the former deal meant to close NATO's door for Ukraine, the purpose of the latter was to keep Ukraine within the area of Russia's economic influence. The Customs Union was created in 2010 and includes Russia, Belarus, and Kazakhstan. In Kyrgyzstan, following the revolution that the Kremlin had helped to foment,[56] Russia sought to bring to power a pro-Russian coalition and establish a political system with a strong central authority.[57] In early November, the pro-Russian candidate, Almazbek Atambayev, was elected the new president in the first round of elections. Even in Georgia, the Kremlin was now finding a way to influence events without relying on force by developing ties with Georgian opposition to President Mikhail Saakashvili.[58]

The Kremlin also wanted to consolidate its military presence in the region. In Kyrgyzstan, Russia sought to create a new antiterrorism center under CSTO auspices in the southern part of the country.[59] In Tajikistan, Moscow negotiated redeployment of six thousand troops to patrol the border with Afghanistan in exchange for a promise to rearm the Tajik army. Finally, the Russia-controlled CSTO, which also includes Armenia, Belarus, Uzbekistan, Tajikistan, Kazakhstan, and Kyrgyzstan, amended its mission by pledging to defend its members from internal "unconstitutional disturbances." In an apparent response to Arab-like uprisings, the CSTO also conducted an ambitious military exercise by imitating the defeat of an attempted coup in Tajikistan.

The preservation of Russia's influence in the region would have not come without the country's attempts to act globally and win at least some support for its policies from established powers in the West and rising non-Western powers. For example, the Kremlin would not have been as successful in its offensive against the United States' "unilateralism" were it not for France and Germany's tacit support, which had resulted from the three's opposition to the invasion of Iraq. Were the two Western European states to have supported NATO membership for Ukraine and Georgia, it would have taken longer for the colored revolutions to run out of steam. In addition, Russia probably could not have been as successful in its war against Georgia were China to have taken a strong critical stance toward it. Although Beijing refused to endorse Russia's recognition of Abkhazia and South Ossetia's independence, the Chinese informally supported Russia during the crisis in the Caucasus, and the issue has not complicated the two nations' relations.[60]

The problem for Russia is that the non-Russian states in the region often perceive its policies as excessively selfish and its influence as hegemonic. For example, in order to balance against Russia's power, central Asian states increasingly seek to strengthen their ties with China and the United States. In June 2012, Uzbekistan went as far as to withdraw its membership in the CSTO—in part to signal its dissatisfaction with Russia.

That the post-Soviet states remain wary of Russia's unilateral interventions complicates searches for security and stability in the region. Perception of Russia as a hegemonic power partly explains why its increased influence has not translated into stability in the region. The reversal of the colored revolutions has yet to bring more order to Eurasia. Evidence of instability has included the tense atmosphere in the Caucasus following the war with Georgia, renewed terrorist attacks, the persistent failure of Western forces to stabilize Afghanistan, the inability of central Asian rulers to reign in local clans and drug lords, and the weakness of legitimately elected bodies of power in Moldova and Ukraine. Kyrgyzstan may serve as another example of instability in the region. When the second violent round of power struggles occurred in Kyrgyzstan in June 2010, the new interim government in Bishkek failed to gain control over the country, and the southern part—a stronghold of the ousted president Kurmanbek Bakiev—became de facto independent.[61] Yet the crisis elicited little serious response from key powers or international organizations in the region. Despite its perception as a hegemonic power, Russia is not eager to act single-handedly to stabilize and pacify the region. At best, the Kremlin defends its core interests in regional settings and addresses its economic interests.

Maximizing Economic Opportunities

Having reversed the colored revolutions in Eurasia, Russia sought to gain economically from it. Not in the position to become the regional center, Russia instead emphasized "pragmatic" bilateral ties and issue-specific multilateral contacts. Energy remained its main card. In addition to gaining control over the most valuable assets abroad and increasing Russian shares in foreign companies, the Kremlin's general economic objective remained strengthening its energy position in world markets by coordinating its activities with other energy producers, building pipelines in all geographic directions, raising energy prices for its oil- and gas-dependent neighbors, and moving to control transportation networks in the former USSR.

In Ukraine, Russia was primarily interested in gaining control over energy infrastructure. In order to overcome the dependence on Ukrainian transit in transporting natural gas to European markets, the Kremlin developed a dual-track approach. It worked with Turkey and Southern European states in order to obtain their permission to build the Southern pipeline that would deliver Russian energy to Europe via the Black Sea by circumventing Ukraine. On the other hand, Moscow continued to pressure Kiev to agree to a joint ownership of Naftogas,[62] Ukraine's state-controlled gas company. The Kremlin wanted to avoid additional energy disputes with Ukraine similar to those in 2005 and 2006 by purchasing controlling stakes in Naftogas. As articulated by Konstantin Kosachyev, chairman of the International Affairs Committee of the State Duma, the idea was for Ukraine and Russia to "become a single transit space between Europe and China, between European and Asian markets."[63] In 2011 Russia invited Ukraine to join the Customs Union, promising another major discount on gas prices. The Customs Union was created in 2010 and includes Russia, Belarus, and Kazakhstan. Ukrainian leaders declined the Customs Union offer, but indicated willingness to accommodate Russia in strengthening its presence in the Ukrainian economy.

In central Asia and the Caucasus, Russia sought to obtain valuable assets and renegotiate price arrangements with the oil- and gas-rich states, such as Azerbaijan, Turkmenistan, and Kazakhstan, leaving them with less incentive to sell to Europe and China. With attractive prices and an energy transportation system in place, the Caspian states would be less likely to construct new pipelines that are favored by non-Russian nations. In the energy-poor Kyrgyzstan, the Kremlin worked to gain controlling stakes in valuable companies, such as the enterprise that has supplied the United States' military base with energy and the Dustan torpedo plant on the shore of the country's mountain lake.[64]

RECORD

Under Medvedev's presidency the Kremlin preserved influence in a number of key areas. Following the difficult months after its military assertiveness in the Caucasus, Russia has revived its relations with the Western nations. Not only has Russia preserved the existing level of ties with France, Germany, and other Western European nations, but Moscow has worked to strengthen these ties. European leaders have reciprocated by proposing to establish the EU-Russia Political and Security Committee as an institution to consult on strategic issues on the continent. The United

States' attempts to "reset" relations with Moscow have further assisted the continuous development of Russian ties with Europe. With respect to Asia and the Middle East, Russia has continued to develop economic and political ties across the two regions by prioritizing relations with China, Turkey, and Israel. The record on the Middle Eastern transformation is mixed. By rhetorically opposing the West's intervention in Libya and by diverging from the Western nations on Syria, Russia demonstrated its relevance and strengthened its prestige in international politics. On the other hand, regime changes in Libya and Syria damaged Russia's economic and security interests and it remains to be seen how the Kremlin will work to rebuild its influence in the region.

In the former Soviet world, the Kremlin has found new partners in the postrevolutionary governments of Ukraine and Kyrgyzstan. Uzbekistan's departure from the CSTO was a setback for Russia's efforts to stabilize central Asia, indicating the importance of new efforts to strengthen a collective security system in the region. In the economic area, Russia has made some advancement in reviving the old Kremlin's initiative, the Customs Union. This became possible due to high oil prices and "pragmatic" economy-driven ties with the non-Russian states in the region.

The new course, which combined elements of pragmatic cooperation and assertiveness was not fully consolidated at home and abroad. During 2011–2012, the course began to unravel in response to new domestic and international challenges. Russian elites remained divided on how to move forward, and the country's leadership showed sensitivity with respect to possible rise of protest politics. Soon after Putin's inauguration as president, the State Duma passed several laws allowing for election of regional governors and registration of new political parties, but also strengthening control over activities of radical opposition politicians.[65] Russia also had to respond to a changed international environment that included the West's continued international expansion and rise of non-Western nations. The next chapter returns to these points.

Table 7.3 summarizes the record of Russia's international course to the summer of 2012.

Table 7.3.   The Record of Alliances for Modernization

Security	Remaining problems with terrorism in the Caucasus
	Instability in Afghanistan and the Middle East
	New tensions with NATO over MDS
Welfare	Economic decline and oil-based recovery
Autonomy	New vulnerability to international influences
Identity	Renewed efforts to engage the Westernist dimension of Russian values

NOTES

1. Speech at meeting with Russian ambassadors and permanent representatives in international organizations, Kremlin.ru, July 12, 2010.

2. "Russia and the Changing World," *Moskovskiye novosti*, February 26, 2012.

3. Some observers pointed to the importance of these trends before the crisis (Naazneen Barma, Ely Ratner, and Steven Weber, "The World without the West," *National Interest* 90, no. 4 [2007]).

4. Jeffrey Mankoff, "Internal and External Impact of Russia's Economic Crisis," *Proliferation Papers* 48, March 2010.

5. Vladimir Putin, "Press Statement and Answers to Journalists' Questions Following a Meeting of the Russia-NATO Council," Bucharest, April 4, 2008, Kremlin.ru.

6. *Interfax-AVN*, May 13, 2009. The full Russian text of the strategy is published on the website of the Russian Security Council at the address www.scrf.gov.ru.

7. Dmitri Medvedev, "Go Russia!" Kremlin.ru, September 10, 2009.

8. Dmitri Medvedev, address to the Federation Council of the Russian Federation, Kremlin.ru, November 12, 2009.

9. Dmitri Medvedev, speech at meeting with Russian ambassadors and permanent representatives in international organizations, Kremlin.ru, July 12, 2010.

10. *Programma effektivnogo ispol'zovaniya vneshnepoliticheskikh faktorov v tselyakh dolgosrochnogo razvitiya Rossiyskoi Federatsiyi* (Program of effective use of foreign policy factors to assist long-term development of the Russian Federation), February 10, 2010, www.runewsweek.ru/country/34184.

11. For a more detailed description of Russia's global strategy, see Andrei P. Tsygankov, "Preserving Influence in a Changing World: Russia's Grand Strategy," *Problems of PostCommunism* 58, no. 1 (2011).

12. See, for example, Medvedev's speech in Magnitogorsk, which stressed the need to improve the business climate (Dmitri Medvedev, meeting of the Commission for Modernization and Technological Development of Russia's Economy, Magnitogorsk, March 30, 2011, eng.kremlin.ru/news/1981).

13. *Rossiya XXI veka* (Moscow: Institut sovremennogo razvitiya, 2010) 44–45.

14. Dmitri Trenin, "Blowing Both Hot and Cold," *Moscow Times*, March 24, 2009.

15. Vladimir Putin, speech at meeting with deputies of State Duma, April 20, 2011, premier.gov.ru/events/news/14898/.

16. Tai Adelaja, "Competitive Constraints: A New Report Says Russia Is Losing the Global Battle for the Hearts and Minds of Investors," *Russia Profile*, September 8, 2011.

17. Michael Schwartz, "Russia Joins Drug Raid in Afghanistan, Marking Advance in Relations with U.S.," *New York Times*, October 29, 2011.

18. "NATO Base in Russia 'Pragmatic Decision'—Analysts," *RIA Novosti*, March 21, 2012.

19. Roland Nash, "Rosneft and Exxon—a Big Deal," *Business New Europe*, September 7, 2011, www.bne.eu.

20. Arshad Mohammed, "Hillary Clinton Tells Ukraine Door to NATO Open," Reuters, July 2, 2010; Yuri Paniyev, "NATO prosit Moskvu pomoch' Afghani-

stanu," *Nezavisimaya gazeta*, May 23, 2012; Geogri Dvali, "SshA moderniziruyut PVO Gruziyi," *Kommersant*, June 15, 2012.

21. Indeed, Putin criticized the resolution as "defective and flawed" and resembling "medieval calls for crusades." Medvedev rebuked Putin's criticism (Alexei Anishchuk, "Russia's Medvedev Raps Putin's Libya 'Crusade' Jibe," Reuters, March 21, 2011).

22. For a discussion, see Cory Welt, "Russia, Trade, and Human Rights: Thinking through U.S. Policies," *American Progress*, April 30, 2012, www.americanprogress .org/issues/2012/04/us_russia_magnitsky.html.

23. Dmitri Medvedev, speech in Berlin, *Izvestiya*, June 6, 2008.

24. Dmitri Medvedev, meeting with the participants in the International Club Valdai, Moscow, Kremlin.ru, September 12, 2008; Dmitri Medvedev, interview of the president to the Spanish media, Kremlin.ru, March 1, 2009.

25. Conor Humphries, "Russia Drafts 'Post–Cold War' East-West Security Pact," Reuters, November 29, 2009.

26. Judy Dempsey, "Russia Wants to Formalize Relation with E.U.," *New York Times*, October 18, 2010.

27. Robert Bridge, "Moscow Looking for European 'Re-think' at Munich Security Conference," *Russia Today*, October 21, 2010, www.russiatoday.com.

28. "Europe Will Need European Security Treaty Sooner or Later—Medvedev," *RIA Novosti*, December 1, 2010.

29. For a more detailed analysis of the United States' position from a conservative perspective, see Sally McNamara, "Russia's Proposed New European Security Treaty: A Non-Starter for the U.S. and Europe," Heritage Foundation, Backgrounder 2463, September 16, 2010.

30. For documentation that the Baltics and Poland wanted NATO to develop secret contingency plans in response to the war in the Caucasus, see Ivo Daalder, "Action Request: Baltic Contingency Planning," October 18, 2009, wikileaks.ch/cable/2009/10/09USNATO464.html.

31. *RIA Novosti*, December 1, 2010.

32. Alexey Eremenko, "Russia's APEC Integration 'Just Beginning,'" *RIA Novosti*, September 2, 2012.

33. Sergei Strokan, "Strana voskhodyashchego Vostoka," *Kommersant*, September 25, 2012.

34. Vladimir Putin, "An Asia-Pacific Growth Agenda," *Wall Street Journal*, September 6, 2012.

35. Putin, "An Asia-Pacific Growth Agenda."

36. Gillian Wong, "Russia Wants to Supply All of China's Gas Needs," *AP*, September 27, 2010.

37. "Putin Explains Benefits of Trans-Siberian, BAM, Northern Sea Routes to APEC Leaders," *Interfax*, September 10, 2012.

38. Russia pledged an annual supply of 10 billion cubic meters of gas for the projected pipeline, two-thirds of which would go through North Korea (Khristina Narizhnaya, "Kim Endorses Trans-Korean Pipeline," *Moscow Times*, August 25, 2011).

39. Ben Aris, "Russia Looks East for Business; Cool on US-led Asia Trade Group," *Business New Europe*, August 30, 2012.

40. Vlad Sobell, "Russia and APEC: Increased Cooperation Will Aid Russia's Modernization," us-russia.org, September 4, 2012.

41. Vladimir Putin, "Russia and the Changing World," *Moskovskiye novosti*, February 26, 2012.

42. M. K. Bhadrakumar, "Mullah Omar Gets a Russian Visitor," *Asia Times*, March 23, 2011.

43. M. K. Bhadrakumar, "Israel Joins Russian Ballet School," *Asia Times*, September 11, 2011.

44. Anna Smolchenko, "Medvedev Hails 'Strategic' Turkey Ties," *AFP*, May 12, 2010.

45. The Kremlin also recalled Russia's Libya ambassador for criticizing Moscow's decision ("Former Russian Ambassador to Libya Chamov on Dismissal, Situation There, UN Vote," *Zavtra*, March 30, 2011, www.zavtra.ru).

46. Simon Tisdall, "Syria: Why Russia Changed Tack," *Guardian*, May 28, 2012.

47. Helene Cooper, "Face to Face, Obama Tries to Persuade Putin on Syria," *New York Times*, June 19, 2012.

48. "Medvedev Outlines Anti-terrorism Strategy for North Caucasus," *RIA Novosti*, April 1, 2010.

49. James Brooke, "'Civil War' among Muslims Shakes Russia's South," *Voice of America*, August 30, 2012.

50. Paul Reynolds, "New Russian World Order: The Five Principles," BBC News, September 2, 2008.

51. For example, see Putin's insistence that Russia seeks not the post-Soviet states' territory or natural resources, but the human dignity and the quality of life of their citizens, whom it regards as its own cultural compatriots (Vladimir Putin, address to the Federation Council of the Russian Federation, March 2005, Kremlin.ru).

52. Dmitri Medvedev, meeting with members of the Council on Foreign Relations, Washington, DC, November 15, 2008, Kremlin.ru.

53. Vladimir Putin, "The New Integration Project for Eurasia," *Izvestia*, October 3, 2011.

54. Lyubov Pronina, "Russia Gas Deal Shuts NATO Door for Ukraine, Opens Asset Access," *Bloomberg*, April 23, 2010.

55. *Kommersant*, April 7, 2011.

56. Philip P. Pan, "Russia Helped Fuel Unrest in Kyrgyzstan," *Washington Post*, April 12, 2010. One element of Russia's pressures concerned export duties for gasoline and diesel fuel. By shifting from selling fuel duty-free to raising duties for dependent neighbors, the Kremlin could achieve impressive results. In the second half of 2010, Russia also tried the approach in Tajikistan by seeking its permission to install a military base there. Russia supplies 93 percent of the country's petroleum products ("Russia Ends Fuel Duties for Kyrgyz, Raises Them for Tajiks," CentralAsiaOnline.com, March 25, 2011).

57. Steve Gutterman, "Russia, U.S. at Odds on Kyrgyzstan's Future," Reuters, October 6, 2010.

58. Yuri Simonyan, "Nino Burdzhanadze obyavili 'predatelem Guziyi'" (Nino Burdzhanadze is pronounced a traitor of Georgia), *Nezavisimaya gazeta*, April 3, 2010.

59. Bruce Pannier, "Russia's Star on Rise Again in Kyrgyzstan," RFE/RL News-line, April 8, 2011.

60. As Elizabeth Wishnick writes, "Prior to the recognition, Chinese media coverage largely echoed Russian positions, and, even afterwards, Chinese experts sympathized with Russian opposition to NATO's expansion" (Elizabeth Wish-nick, *Russia, China, and the United States in Central Asia* [Carlisle, PA: Strategic Studies Institute, U.S. Army War College, February 2009], 41).

61. Andrew Higgins, "In Central Asia, a New Headache for U.S. Policy," *Washington Post*, September 1, 2010.

62. Tatyana Ivzhenko, "Ukrayina i Rossiya mogut izmenit' gazovo-flotski dogovor" (Ukraine and Russia may change the gas-fleet treaty), *Nezavisimaya gazeta*, March 15, 2011.

63. "Moscow to Counteract 'anti-Russian' Form of Ukraine's Integration with EU," *Interfax*, March 4, 2011.

64. Aleksandr Gabuyev, "Rossiysko-kirgizskiye otnosheniya smazali i zapravili" (Russia-Kyrgyzstan relations have been oiled and added new energy), *Kommersant*, March 22, 2011.

65. Darya Garmonenko, "Pod silovym kolpakom" (Under control of the security agencies), *Nezavisimaya gazeta*, July 3, 2012; Aleksandra Samarina, "Novyi ritm possiyskoi politiki" (The new rhythm of Russian politics), *Nezavisimaya gazeta*, August 14, 2012.

8

❧

The West, the Non-West, and Russia's "Civilizational" Turn

> [P]rimitive borrowing and attempts to civilize Russia from abroad were not accepted by an absolute majority of our people. This is because the desire for independence and sovereignty in spiritual, ideological and foreign policy spheres is an integral part of our national character. . . . The 21st century promises to become the century of major changes, the era of the formation of major geopolitical zones, as well as financial and economic, cultural, civilisational, and military and political areas.
>
> —Vladimir Putin, December 2014[1]

The return of Vladimir Putin as Russia's president in March 2012 signaled a critically important change in foreign policy since the presidency of Dmitri Medvedev. Russia revived the assertive course that had culminated in the war with Georgia in August 2008 and was then reassessed by Medvedev. Under Medvedev, the country's approach to the outside world was dictated by need to modernize the domestic economy and reach a new understanding with the Western nations. Because Russia was seriously affected by the global financial crisis, it was keenly interested in developing economic and technological ties with the Western nations.

This chapter documents the new policy shift away from the Kremlin's rapprochement with the West, explaining it by its renewed pressures on Russia's political system by Western nations and Putin's perception of those pressures as threatening his power. Contrary to some common views that attribute Russia's foreign policy to the nation's traditionally imperialist and anti-Western political culture, the primary drivers in the

Kremlin's foreign policy have remained contemporary and domestic. Confronted with new challenges to his rule, Putin reached out to nationalist constituencies at home and sought to strengthen Russia's position in the former Soviet region. The crisis in Ukraine resulted in part from Russia and the European Union and the United States' attempts to pull Kiev in their own areas of influence by further straining Russia's relations with the West. The Kremlin also sought to capitalize on new international opportunities by establishing stronger ties with non-Western countries.

Global and Local Conditions

The West's continued global assertion of its values, the rise of non-Western nations, and Russia's ongoing domestic crisis have defined Putin's foreign policy since his return to presidency.

The United States and the European Union were uncomfortable with Putin's return and increased their criticism of Russia's domestic system and human rights record. Previously, members of Obama's administration were rarely engaged in criticism of Russia under Medvedev during 2009–2011, as the United States worked to strengthen relations with him at the expense of Putin.[2] Europeans too were hopeful that they would be able to rebuild their ties with Russia although they were well-aware that Medvedev's actions had Putin's full support.[3] In addition to the shift of power to Putin, this was a response to new policies by the Kremlin that Washington found difficult to accept. In particular, Western nations also reacted critically to Putin's attempts to reassert power domestically. Western leaders voiced their disagreement with handling of protesters by the Kremlin following demonstrations following fraudulent elections to State Duma in November 2011. The West also condemned corruption in Russia and imposed visa bans and asset freezes on those it linked to the case of Russian lawyer Sergei Magnitsky who was arrested and died while in detention. In addition, the U.S. and the EU leaders criticized Russia's policies of restricting rights of minorities and opposition.

In the meantime, Russia and the West seriously diverged on foreign policy issues. The policy of reset initiated by president Obama during Medvedev's presidency helped to solve some important issues in the two countries' relations, yet failed to address root causes of their disagreements (please see chapter 7). Increasingly, the Western nations expected more cooperation from Russia, as the Kremlin expressed growing frustration with what it saw as insufficient cooperation on part of the West. The two sides disagreed on Western plans regarding the Missile Defense System (MDS) in Europe, and policies in the Middle East and Eurasia. Russia proposed to build MDS jointly and was frustrated with lack of progress in the area. The Kremlin's proposal of a new security treaty in Europe was not supported by the Western partners. There were also growing disagreements over addressing the issue of instability in Syria and the wider Middle Eastern region. In June 2013, Moscow and Washington also had to confront the problem caused by defection of the former CIA employee Edward Snowden to Russia, as the Kremlin refused to comply with the U.S. demand to turn him over.[4]

Finally, Western leaders expressed concerns over the Kremlin's attempts to build the Eurasian Union. Even though Putin emphasized an open nature of the proposed union and laid out economic incentives for joining it,[5] American and European leaders perceived the idea as threatening. They were especially concerned about Ukraine being pulled in the Russia-centered union and worked against it by presenting the proposed arrangement as anti-European and offering Kiev an opportunity to sign an Association Agreement with the European Union. Following the revolutionary change of power in Ukraine and the Kremlin's annexation of Crimea and support for Donetsk and Luhansk, the Western nations condemned Russia, imposed sanctions against the Russian economy, and moved to strengthen NATO's military readiness in Eastern Europe.

Another important factor that influenced Russia's international behavior was the notable economic and political rise of non-Western nations. Economically, the world witnessed emergence of a coalition of non-Western powers seeking to diversify global commercial and monetary transactions. The rising economies of China, India, Brazil, and others have challenged the dominant position of the West by establishing institutional venues including annual meetings of BRICS (Brazil, Russia, India, China, and South Africa) and SCO (Shanghai Cooperation Organization), pooling financial resources and producing around 30 percent of the world GDP.[6] During its sixth summit in Fortaleza, Brazil, held in July 2014 the BRICS' members have agreed to establish a new development bank and pool of reserve currency, and have proposed formation of an alternative energy association.[7]

The U.S. military decline is evident in growing proliferation of nuclear weapons and emerged incidents of unsanctioned use of conventional weapons in non-Western regions. Its economic decline is no less obvious with rise of China and the Asia-Pacific region as new centers of the world's gravity. Instead of relying on the protection and welfare of Western hegemony, nations increasingly seek refuge in reformulating their interests to better protect their societies and readjust to their regional environments. Failure of the United States to successfully complete its military operations in Afghanistan and Iraq, stabilize the Middle East, impose its rules on Russia in Eurasia, and maintain a viable international economic order indicate that the world is departing from its politically unipolar state of the 1990s. The idea of Western-style democracy, while still attractive, no longer commands the same attention. In part decline of the idea's attractiveness is related to the fact that democratization and democracy promotion outside the West are not infrequently accompanied by state weakness, lawlessness, and ethnic violence. In the meantime, observers have noted intensification of processes of cultural reformulations and rise of alternative soft power projects which develop both within and outside the legitimizing language of democracy.[8]

Overall, the unipolar moment known for dominance of the United States' values and interests in world affairs is challenged in a most fundamental way. Structurally, it is still the familiar world of American domination with the country's superiority in military, political, economic, and cultural dimensions. But dynamically the world is moving away from its West-centeredness[9] even though the exact direction and result of the identified trajectory remains unclear. In sum, the world is entering its post-American[10] and—to the extent that America has shaped the West—a post-Western stage. The altered position of the only superpower in the international system is likely to affect the world for many years to come. Today, the G-20, rather than the G-8, is increasingly successful in representing and articulating positions required for stabilizing the international order.

Finally ongoing weaknesses of Russia's domestic economic and political system continued to affect the country's foreign policy. Following the Soviet breakup Russia is yet to establish a coherent post-communist identity, an effective state capable of strategic planning and allocation of resources, and a viable diversified economy. Although by 2011 the Russian economy recovered from the financial crisis that resulted in a 9 percent decline of its GDP by 2009, the core economic problems such as excessive dependence on exports of raw materials, corruption, and lack of rule of law were not addressed. Russia's economic competitiveness remains relatively low and the technological gap with the West wide. The ineffectiveness of the economic system was revealed in the devaluation of the ruble in the fall of 2014 when the Russian currency lost about 50 percent of its value due to the cumulative impact of declining oil prices and Western economic sanctions. Following the West's economic pressures, Russia had to urgently look for alternative foreign economic ties reorienting its economy toward Asia and China. It remains to be seen whether the need in such reorientation will serve as the incentive for reforming Putin's political and economic system. This system that is centered on informal economic deals between the state and oligarchs, and the Kremlin-controlled elections, has demonstrated its limitations. The mechanism for sustainable engagement with society is lacking and, as a result, Russia's foreign policy is rarely discussed or influenced by broad social groups.

Russia as a Civilization

The situation of cultural ambivalence amid global uncertainty has stimulated a resurgence of civilizational thinking in non-Western cultures including Russia. Several schools or perspectives have emerged to define their civilizational status and to determine its appropriate goals and international strategy. Pro-Western elites argue that integration with the West is the only available option and that, in itself, it constitutes a viable civilizational project. Others caution that such integration cannot be realized without considerable sacrifices at the expense of indigenous values that include religion, moral economy, and local traditions.[11] This debate has deep intellectual and historical roots, and it delineates what may be seen as a civilizational dilemma: how can a civilization culturally connect with the outside world, while preserving its own self?

The Vision of Russia as a Civilization

Partly in response to the U.S. criticism, since Putin's return to presidency, Russia's foreign policy has obtained an ideological justification. Before Putin's third term as Russia's president, the Kremlin's discourse was largely shaped by ideas of adjustment to the international community and protecting national interests. Throughout the 2000s, Putin was commonly dismissive of calls for a "Russian idea" by instead filling his speeches with indicators of Russia's economic and political successes. In his 2007 address to the Federation Council, Putin even ridiculed searches for a national idea as a Russian "old-style entertainment" (*starinnaya russkaya zabava*) by comparing them to searches for a meaning of life.

Beginning with his election campaign, Putin has promoted the vision of Russia as a culturally distinct power, committed to defending particular values and principles relative to those of the West and other civilizations. In July 2012, in his meeting with Russia's ambassadors he called to actively influence international relations by relying on the tools of lobbying and soft power.[12] In his 2012 address to the Federation Council, Putin spoke of new demographic and moral threats that must be overcome if the nation is to "be preserved and reproduced."[13] He further stated that "[i]n the 21st century amid a new balance of economic, civilizational and military forces Russia must be a sovereign and influential country . . . We must be and remain Russia."

Putin's return to the Kremlin meant a continuation of the effort to carve out a new role for Russia in the international system by challenging the established position of Western nations. The 2008 Foreign Policy Concept already recommended that Russia remain true to a "balanced multi-vector approach" in light of the West's gradual departure from the world's economic center.[14] In February 2013, Russia released a new Foreign Policy Concept that further developed the ideas of transition toward a multipolar structure of the international system and the emergence of new threats outside of those connected to nuclear weapons. The Concept began by stating that "[t]he capabilities of the historically established West to dominate the global economy and politics continue to decline" and "[t]he global potential of strength and growth is dispersing and shifting eastwards, particularly towards the Asia Pacific region."[15] The document also emphasized global economic competition, in which different "values and development models" would be tested and "civilization identity" would obtain a new importance. In this context civilization was understood to be a distinct cultural entity, not a universal phenomenon. Russia was beginning to see itself as culturally and politically independent from the West.

Relative to Medvedev, Putin's priorities inside the country included strengthening Russia's traditional values and articulating a new idea uniting Russians and non-Russian nationalities. Since early 2012, he advanced the idea of state-civilization by recognizing ethnic Russians as "the core (*sterzhen'*) that binds the fabric" of Russia as a culture and a state.[16] While proposing to unite the country around Russian values, Putin also argued against "attempts to preach the ideas of building a Russian 'national,' mono-ethnic state" as "contrary to our entire thousand-year history" and "the shortest path to the destruction of the Russian people and the Russian state system."[17] Another theme developed by the president in the 2012 inaugural address to the Federation Council and other speeches is the theme of a strong state capable of addressing "corruption" and "flaws of the law enforcement system" as root causes of ethnic violence. Finally, being especially concerned with national unity, Putin pointed to "deficit of spiritual values" and recommended strengthening "the institutions that are the carriers of traditional values" especially family and schools. In multiple statements, he further criticized what he saw as Europe's departure from traditional religious and family values. In his Valdai Club speech, he quoted Russian traditionalist thinkers and declared "the desire for independence and sovereignty in spiritual, ideological and foreign policy spheres" as an "integral part of our national character."[18] In his 2013 address to the Federation Council, Putin further positioned Russia as a "conservative" power and the worldwide defender of traditional values.[19] Finally, in his address to the same institution in December 2014, Putin elaborated on his vision of conservatism and justified incorporation of Crimea in terms of consolidating Russia's centuries-old "civilizational and sacred significance."[20]

Moscow's new civilizational discourse is not exclusively focused on distinctiveness from the outside world. Putin remains interested in strengthening Russia's relations with the European Union and the United States in a global world. Importantly, the Foreign Policy Concept signed by Putin into law in February 2013 describes the world in terms of a "rivalry of values and development models within the framework of the universal principles of democracy and the market economy."[21] Although Putin feels threatened by the West's human rights rhetoric and international policy, he continues to value their contribution to global civilization and Russia's development.

Table 8.1 summarizes the vision of Russia as a state-civilization.

Table 8.1.   State-Civilization (SC): View of National Interest

What?	Distinct civilizational values
How?	Domestic consolidation Strategic cooperation with non-Western nations Pragmatic cooperation with the West

The Domestic Reaction

Putin's civilizational turn resonated domestically. The global uncertainty and Western pressures have stimulated a resurgence of nationalist thinking in Russia. Pro-Western elites that argued for modernization and integration with the West grew progressively weaker. Until Putin's return to the presidency, the discourse of modernization was actively promoted by then president Medvedev and supported by the middle class and the business community groups. The latter were critical of what they viewed as an excessively centralized and energy-oriented model of development and favored the country's integration with the world economy and Western institutions. Foreign policy analysts with ties to the West also supported this thinking and encouraged the Russian state to strengthen a pro-Western orientation. Experts working at leading foundations and universities, such as the Carnegie Moscow Center, Higher School of Economics, and Moscow State Institute of International Relations, frequently argue that Russia is not a distinct civilization and must align itself with European and the U.S.-led security institutions.

In contrast to those favoring modernization, those viewing foreign policy in terms of defending Russia's sovereignty and cultural distinctiveness have grown increasingly influential in political and policy circles. Officials, such as Vladimir Yakunin, Minister of Railroad Transportation advanced the notion of Russian civilization in their speeches and public writing.[22] A number of Orthodox priests, including Patriarch Kirill, endorsed the idea of Russia's religion-centered civilizational distinctiveness. Politicians from the relatively marginal to the well-established, such as the Communist Party leader Gennadi Zyuganov regularly spoke on issues of Russia's national interests as tied to Eurasian geopolitics and self-sufficiency. Several clubs were established to promote the idea of Russia's distinct civilizational values. For example, on September 8, 2012, the Izborsky club was founded to serve as an umbrella organization that combines intellectuals, experts, and politicians of Eurasianist, neo-Soviet, and Slavophile convictions affiliated with the ROC (Russian Orthodox Church) and various nationalist media and think tanks. The Minister of Culture, Vladimir Medinsky, was present at the inaugural meeting of the club, and executive secretary at the Eurasian Economic/Customs Union Commission, Sergei Glazyev, holds membership.

Putin's own views have been closer to those promoting the state's ability to respond to external threats to Russia's security and equated successful foreign policy with that of a strong independent state. Although Statists frequently emphasize the importance of cross-cultural dialogue for the purpose of preserving political stability, they are ambivalent with respect to Russia's cultural or civilizational affinities. Some of them advocate stronger ties with the West, whereas others call for bandwagoning with non-Western countries, such as China. Those with strong ties to the defense and security establishment tend to read modernization-based priorities as insufficient, potentially excessively pro-Western, and detrimental to the nation's sovereignty. Their foreign policy priorities differ from those with commercial and political ties to the West and include the preservation of a global strategic balance and influence in Europe, Eurasia, and other regions. Statist modernization priorities are also distinct and include the development of the energy and military sectors, as opposed to the diversification highlighted by Medvedev. Beyond the Kremlin, those living outside large cities and/or dependent on state assistance for survival are supportive of Statist views.

Consistently with his statist priorities, Putin used the ideas of civilization instrumentally, as a rhetorical tool for shaping Russia's values in the Kremlin's desired direction. These ideas assist Putin in forging a greater loyalty among elites by serving as an additional source of legitimation and loyalty to the state. The language of national unity appeals to various elite strata, in particular Statists and supporters of Russia's cultural distinctiveness. It helps to deflect the domestic appeal of ethnic nationalism, appear supportive of a dialogue with Islam, and remain critical of Western human rights pressures at the same time. It also strengthens the Kremlin's bond with the masses by identifying the conservative majority sympathetic with the notion of Russia's distinct values, as opposed to the more cosmopolitan and West-leaning middle class.

Table 8.2 summarizes contending views on state-civilization.

Table 8.2.   State-Civilization (SC): Contending Views

Westernizers:		Ethnic Nationalists:
SC implies confrontation with the West	vs.	SC is not sufficiently sensitive to needs of ethnic Russians

Conflict and Cooperation with the West

Conflicts with the Liberal West

The developments since Putin's return to the presidency revealed the extreme fragility of Russia's relations with the West. On major issues, Russia and the Western nations had little to agree on. Russia's newly stated commitment to "conservative" values of national unity, sovereignty, and traditional family put it at odds with the liberal Western priorities of minority rights, democratization, and responsibility to protect people from abuses by their own governments. The value-based conflict served to exacerbate disagreements generated by different understanding of national interests. As the world power balance began to shift away from the West, the Kremlin was no longer motivated by the same vision of a normal great power articulated by Putin in the early 2000s. The Kremlin now expected the Western nations to coordinate their policies with other powers and recognize them as equal participants in shaping world order. The Kremlin was prepared to exercise its options independently, should the West choose to ignore Russia's new international ambitions.

With respect to Russia's domestic politics, Western leaders voiced their disagreement with the handling of protesters by the Kremlin. For example, a Russian court sentenced members of the punk band Pussy Riot to two years in jail for hooliganism. Three members of the group danced near the altar of Russia's main cathedral by calling Mother of God to "chase Putin away." Western governments expressed their strong disagreement with the decision almost immediately after the verdict. The U.S. State Department called the punishment "disproportionate" and urged the Russian authorities to "ensure that the right to freedom of expression is upheld." Strong criticisms were also issued by heads of European governments.[23] Another expression of U.S.-Russia disagreement concerned the case of Magnitsky, whom the United States viewed as an anticorruption fighter. In December 2012, the U.S. Congress, while normalizing trade relations with Russia, passed the bill named after Magnitsky that imposed sanctions against human rights violators in Russia. The Russian State Duma retaliated by passing the "Anti-Magnitsky Act," which targets U.S. citizens who Russia considers to be violators of human rights, and banning the adoption of Russian children by U.S. citizens. The crisis provoked speculation of a new Cold War in the making, with U.S.-Russia relations being jeopardized by a weak presidency in Washington.[24] Obama did not initially support the Magnitsky Act, but signed it because the repeal of the Jackson-Vanik amendment was attached to it and because there was so much support in both chambers of Congress for the bill.

The United States also expressed disappointment with Russia's new law against "propaganda of non-traditional sexual relations among minors" passed in June 2013. According to the Kremlin, the law does not seek to police adults but aims to protect children from information that rejects "traditional family values." Eighty-eight percent of Russians supported the law.[25] However, many human rights activists in the United States and Europe saw it as "anti-gay law" by calling to boycott Russian vodka and the Winter Olympics in Sochi. President Obama, too, publicly spoke against the new legislation and declared that he has "no patience for countries that try to treat gays, lesbians or transgender persons in ways that intimidate them or are harmful to them."[26] Overall, the issue added to the Western image of Russia as disrespectful of minority rights. The Kremlin, however, continued the policies of restricting the political space for radical pro-Western opposition,[27] while U.S. and EU officials continued to be highly critical of the Kremlin's domestic policies and propaganda following the Ukraine crisis.[28]

Russia and the West also disagreed sharply on Syria. As Western nations supported the military opposition, the Kremlin expressed concerns about instability in the country and the wider region after Bashar al-Assad, and strengthened ties with those within the Syrian opposition interested in working with Russia. Putin blamed European and American leaders for spreading instability in the Middle East, "Our partners . . . have already created chaos in many territories, and now they are continuing the same policy in other countries, including Syria. . . . We did warn that prudent action was needed and that it would be wrong to try to achieve anything by force, otherwise chaos would ensue. And what do we see today? Chaos prevails."[29] As the United States accused Bashar al-Assad's regime of using chemical weapons against military opposition, Russian officials responded by rejecting such accusations and characterizing them as an effort to derail a planned peace conference on Syria.[30] Since the appointment of John Kerry as the new Secretary of State, the United States and Russia tried to organize such a conference. However, the attempts at negotiations in Geneva in February 2014 proved unsuccessful in part due to lack of a unified approach of the United States and Russia. Washington again raised the issue of regime change by refusing to recognize Assad, whereas Moscow insisted on negotiations between Syria's existing government and opposition. The situation began to change only in May 2015 when Kerry arrived in Moscow to acknowledge the United States' "catastrophic errors" in handling the Middle East and to seek Russia's cooperation in isolating Islamic extremists in Syria and other parts of the region.[31] In late September 2015, Putin intervened in Syria by sending military aircraft to bomb terrorist organizations and support the Assad government. The decision in part reflected the Kremlin's desire to repair the broken relations with the West, yet its consequences are yet to be clarified.[32]

There was also no progress on nuclear issues. The United States indicated that it was interested in further nuclear reductions, but not in establishing the joint MDS preferred by Russia. President Obama wrote a long letter to the Kremlin explaining his interest in reducing strategic nuclear warheads in the United States by an additional one-third beyond the START treaty. Russia, however, did not want to consider any further cuts, viewing nuclear force as the basis of national defense and international stability. In the words of Russia's deputy foreign minister, Sergei Ryabkov, "Before discussing the necessity of a further reduction of nuclear weapons we need to arrive at an acceptable solution of the ABM [antiballistic missile] problem."[33]

In June 2013 Russia and the West had to confront yet another problem caused by the defection of the former CIA employee Edward Snowden to Russia. In the eyes of the U.S. political class, Snowden was a traitor for making public the surveillance activities by the U.S. government over its citizens because of its importance in the fight against terrorism. Washington therefore expected Moscow to turn Snowden over to the United States, not grant him political asylum.[34] When Putin refused to comply, members of the American political class threatened a full range of retaliatory steps, from cancelling Barack Obama's trip to Moscow to expanding the Magnitsky list and severing economic and military ties with Russia. The effect was the opposite, as on August 7 the Kremlin granted Snowden asylum. Soon afterwards, Obama expressed his disappointment with the decision and cancelled a bilateral summit with Putin scheduled for September in Moscow. Russia also continued to disagree with the European Union on multiple issues from energy to sanctions against the Russian economy and ways of building relations with East European countries.[35]

A major example of Russia-West disagreements concerned the situation in Ukraine where the Kremlin interfered in February 2014 out of fear of a broadening political and military destabilization in the country. According to Putin, Western nations were behind the revolutionary change of power in Ukraine without understanding their destabilizing consequences. In justifying his intervention in Crimea, Russia's president said that he acted on behalf of overthrown but still legitimate president of Ukraine Viktor Yanukovich, and that the action was necessary to safeguard Russia's military fleet in the Black Sea and prevent violence and violation of human rights in the region by the "rampage of Nazi, nationalist, and anti-Semitic forces."[36]

However, Western nations did not view themselves as meddling in Ukraine. Instead, they condemned what they saw as Russia's "imperialism" and violation of neighbors' sovereignty. In response to Putin's initiative to build a new union among the CIS states, U.S. secretary of state Hillary Clinton referred to it as "re-Sovietization" and promised to find "effective ways to slow down or prevent it."[37] Speaking for many in the U.S. political class, Republican senator John McCain called the proposed Eurasian Union "an old idea that the Russians have had dating back to the days of the tsars."[38] European leaders too were worried that Russia was aiming to pull Ukraine into the Russia-centered Eurasian Union and away from the European Union and its values. The EU officials characterized the proposed arrangement as anti-European and offered Kiev an opportunity to sign an Association Agreement with the European Union.

Thus, values intertwined with geopolitics by pushing the Western leaders to support a change of power in Ukraine in February 2014 and recognize the new government in Kiev despite Russia's objections against what it saw as an anti-constitutional coup by radical nationalists. When Putin intervened in Crimea by sending additional troops to the region on February 28, 2014, the United States and Canada threatened to apply a broad range of sanctions against the country and its officials and to expel Russia from G-8. President Obama referred to Russia's intervention as a clear violation of the independence and sovereignty of Ukraine that was "deeply destabilizing" and would incur "costs."[39] European governments at first found sanctions to be unnecessary and potentially counterproductive,[40] but in April, following Russia's growing involvement in Ukraine and the downing of a Malaysian civilian airplane with 286 passengers on board, the EU, too, implemented sanctions against the Russian economy.

Areas of Cooperation

Despite disagreements, the Kremlin was keenly interested in cooperating with Western nations on issues of stabilizing Afghanistan, counterterrorism, and economic development. The Russian leadership remained concerned that the U.S. military withdrawal from Afghanistan could mean grave consequences for the security of the country and the broader Central Asian region. For its part, Russia helped Afghanistan with training its military, police, and antidrug specialists, as well as offering economic aid. On counterterrorism, Russia provided intelligence for Western nations.

In particular, Russian intelligence services warned the FBI and the CIA about the radicalization of Tamerlan Tsarnaev, who became involved in the Boston Marathon bombing in April 2013. Tsarnaev sought ties with radical Islamists in Russia and became further radicalized upon his return to the United States.[41] That counterterrorism remained a key area for cooperation was further confirmed by the U.S. interest to jointly address the threat of Islamic State (IS) in the Middle East as demonstrated during the Secretary of State's visit to Moscow in May 2015. Also in May Vice President Joe Biden publicly stated the U.S. interest in cooperating with Russia on containing the IS fighters in Syria and nuclear nonproliferation in Iran.[42]

Russia also maintained intelligence contacts with Western countries over developments in the Syrian civil war. Despite its sharp disagreement with the West's understanding of the conflict, the Kremlin kept looking for ways to engage it in a joint process of stabilizing the region. In August 2013, the United States accused Assad of using chemical weapons against the opposition on a mass scale—with 1,400 casualties including women and children—and announced its preparedness for a military intervention in Syria. In explaining the decision, Secretary of State Kerry remarked that intervention was necessary to prevent future use of chemical weapons by Damascus because Assad was not about to do what was necessary and destroy his weapons. In response, Russia proposed to develop an international process of monitoring and eliminating Syrian chemical weapons. The Kremlin disagreed that it was Assad who used the weapons, but it wanted to initiate a new dialogue with Western nations on the Middle East. In September 2013, Kerry and Russian foreign minister Sergey Lavrov reached an agreement on phased elimination of Syria's chemical weapons. Russia also supported the UN Security Council binding resolution demanding that Syria abandon its weapons stockpile and that chemical weapons experts be given full access to their sites.[43] Another major example of cooperation with the West concerned the Iranian nuclear program. In July 2015, sustained joint efforts by the United States, United Kingdom, France, Russia, China, and Iran produced a nuclear agreement on limiting the Iranian nuclear program in exchange for the lifting of international sanctions.[44]

In addition, Russia continued to be interested in the development of economic relations with Western nations. The Russian economy was in need of foreign investment, and the Kremlin was well aware of the negative perception of Russia's business climate by Western investors. Indeed, in Putin's view, problems in political relations with the West were strongly influenced by weak economic cooperation: "the main problem is that bilateral political dialogue and cooperation do not rest on a solid economic foundation. The current level of bilateral trade falls far short of the potential of our economies. The same is true of mutual investments. We have yet to create a safety net that would protect our relations against ups and downs. We should work on this."[45] To improve the situation, the Kremlin hired PR agencies in the West, funded radio and TV programs with pro-Russian news coverage, and established organizations and rating agencies to combat the negative perception of Russia. Putin ordered the government to improve Russia's ranking in the World Bank's Doing Business Index from 120th in 2011 to 20th by 2018. Russia also hired the U.S. banking company Goldman Sachs to strengthen the image of the country's investment potential abroad. In addition, Russia's role as a successful host of the Sochi Olympics in February 2014 and the excellent performance of Russian athletes in the games were meant to improve the country's international reputation. Even sanctions imposed by the West against the Russian economy in response to the Kremlin's annexation of Crimea did not principally change Russia's desire to preserve strong economic ties with Western nations. While developing plans to adapt to the sanctions, Russia's officials continued to hope that such sanctions would be lifted within a short-term perspective.[46] In July 2015, the Kremlin also chose not to provide any financial support for Greece when the latter was presented with the choice to comply with the EU creditors' demands or leave the European Union.[47]

Despite these expectations and examples of cooperation, the Kremlin stood firm on issues it saw vital to Russia's national security and domestic values. Immediately after being elected as president, Putin indicated his displeasure with the United States' stance on the Missile Defense System by cancelling his trip to the NATO summit in Chicago. He insisted on Russia's distinct position on Syria and the Middle East by refusing to support the West-sponsored UNSC resolutions. He further placed the emphasis on Russia's insecurity as a result of the West's nuclear policies. For example, he refused to renew the Nunn-Lugar Cooperative Threat Reduction Program, which experts viewed as a response to the U.S. insistence on continuing with its MDS program. Although Putin expressed willingness to cooperate on nonproliferation issues, he said that a more pressing priority was to address the United States' MDS plans in Europe.[48] When the United States cancelled the bilateral summit with Russia over Snowden, Moscow expressed a formal readiness to continue dialogue but showed few signs of being disappointed. The Kremlin also seemed unaffected by Western criticisms of Russia's political system and human rights record, pressing ahead with the "Anti-Magnitsky Act" and restrictions on the activities of Western NGOs and radical opposition inside the country. The decision to provide the defector with asylum reflected Putin's preparedness to accept the consequences of worsening relations with the United States. Finally, the Kremlin was defiant on its rights to intervene in Ukraine. As the United States and the European Union were considering various steps to isolate Russia internationally in response to its intervention in Ukraine, Putin was defiant that his action was fully legitimate and that," if we see such uncontrolled crime spreading to the eastern regions of the country, and if the people ask us for help, while we already have the official request from the legitimate President, we retain the right to use all available means to protect those people."[49]

In addition to pragmatic cooperation with the liberal West, the Kremlin launched a PR offensive to win support from conservatively minded government and various political constituencies in Europe. In order to appeal to both left and right, here Russia's message was couched in broad terms of condemning Western interventionist policies, "fascism" in Ukraine, sanctions against the Russian economy, secularism, and the EU lack of independence in face of the U.S. political pressures. Among those supportive of Russia's conservative approach were the governments of Greece, Serbia, and Hungary, as well as political movements and politicians in Austria, Britain, France, Germany, Greece, and other countries.[50] The least supportive were the Baltics and other East European nations, as well as Sweden. Critics of Russia argued that the Kremlin's message was not effective, while its political campaign was accompanied by financial support for some of European politicians—something that the U.S. vice president Biden condemned as a "new foreign policy weapon" of "corruption and oligarchs as tools of coercion."[51]

Growing Cooperation with the Non-West

Russia's newly discovered civilizational identity assumed the need to protect it from the West's pressures by developing relations with the non-West. In one of his presidential addresses, Putin defended preservation of a "new balance of economic, civilizational and military forces" in global politics. He further insisted on Russia's "geopolitical relevance," which the country must increase further: "Russia must not only preserve its geopolitical relevance—it must multiply it, it must generate demand among our neighbors and partners. I emphasize that this is in our own interest. This applies to our economy, culture, science and education, as well as our diplomacy, particularly the ability to mobilize collective actions at the international level. Last but not least it applies to our military might that guarantees Russia's security and independence."[52] In September 2014 speaking at the Valdai international expert forum Putin, again, was critical of the United States' "destabilizing" role in world affairs and stressed Russia's significance and "special responsibility for maintaining peace, stability, and prosperity" in the world.[53]

Consistently with such worldview, Putin not only continued bilateral pressures on Ukraine and other former Soviet states in attempting to build upon Russia's influence in Eurasia, but also worked on strengthening its relations with China, Iran, and India, and to exploit non-Western institutional vehicles, such as BRICS (Brazil, Russia, India, China, and South Africa) and SCO (Shanghai Cooperation Organization). In the summer of 2015, Russia hosted summits of both organizations in the city of Ufa. The BRICS members pledged $100 billion as a reserve currency pool and additional resources for development projects,[54] while the SCO began the process of admitting India and Pakistan as a members. Positions of Russia and non-Western nations on various international issues were increasingly close. BRICS countries did not publicly condemn Russia's incorporation of Crimea, did not join Western sanctions, and did not support the campaign to isolate Russia politically. According to the Russian Foreign Ministry, a "top priority" for Russia's presidency in BRICS is to transform the assembly into "a full-scale mechanism of strategic interaction on key issues of global policy and economics."[55] Other agenda items include plans to strengthen strategic stability and international information security, reinforce the nonproliferation regime, and combat international terrorism.[56]

Relations with China, Russia's largest neighbor, obtained a strategic dimension, as the two nations demonstrated an increased convergence in global priorities and solutions to existing issues in world politics. Although Beijing did not recognize Russia's annexation of Crimea, the two nations had multiple complementary interests in the areas of commerce and regional security. Their energy-related ties continued to progress. In May 2014, Putin traveled to Beijing to sign a $400 billion-agreement about exporting almost 40 billion cubic meters (bcm) of gas annually to China thereby further diversifying Russia's trade away from Europe. In November 2014, Russia signed another massive gas deal by pledging to supply an additional 30 bcm starting in 2019.[57] Other important agreements were signed in Moscow, in May 2015 on the eve of a military parade on the Red Square marking the end of World War II. The parade also featured China's president Xi Jinping and Putin presiding over the ceremony in the front row while observing the marching of Russian, Chinese, and Indian soldiers. Western leaders were invited but chose not to attend due to disagreement with the Kremlin over Ukraine.[58]

Russia's main priority in Asia remained focused on development of Siberia and the Far East. China was an essential partner not only in assisting Russia with diversification of economic relations under Western sanctions, but also in bringing jobs and investments to Russia's non-European regions. To offset a potentially excessive dependence on one partner, the Kremlin continued earlier developed policies of building relations with non-Chinese countries and strengthening regional integration in Asia. In 2014, Moscow wrote off $10 billion of North Korean debt on the condition of building a gas pipe and rail link into the south.[59] Russia also increased diplomatic contacts with Japan in order to eventually solve the territorial issue and open a new page of economic relations with the eastern power. In the fall of 2013, Putin visited Japan to make progress on the issue and sign a number of investment and trade agreements. Moscow also increased its level of participation in regional arrangements and forums such as the APEC summits in June 2012 and November 2014. In May 2015, Russia and other members of the Eurasian Union signed a free trade agreement with Vietnam pledging reduction of tariffs from 10 percent to 1 percent.[60]

In comparison with the West, non-Western nations largely shared Russia's values and priorities. China, India, Brazil, and the Middle Eastern nations have never been critical of human rights violations or the domestic political system in Russia. On the Middle East and Syria, Russia frequently acted jointly with China by vetoing Syria resolutions introduced in the UNSC by the Western nations. Moscow and Beijing were concerned that such resolutions would pave the way for a military intervention and regime change in Syria, as happened in Libya. By building on non-Western resentment toward U.S. hegemony and military interventions, Putin strengthened his global reputation as an advocate for sovereignty, national unity, and cultural values. While meeting with Barack Obama during the G-20 summit in St. Petersburg, Putin obtained support of most non-Western leaders present for his position on Assad and the Middle East. In addition, the Kremlin was able to take advantage of the Snowden affair. The former CIA employee Edward Snowden defected to Russia in June 2013. In the eyes of the U.S. political class, he was a traitor for making public the surveillance activities by the U.S. government over its citizens because of its importance in the fight against terrorism. Washington therefore expected Moscow to turn Snowden over to the United States. By granting Snowden asylum, Moscow again positioned itself as a defender of national sovereignty and protector against global interferences from hegemonic power.

In the Middle East, Russia continued to advocate negotiations with Iran by discouraging the West from threats and military solutions. In 2014, following Western attempts to impose sanctions on Russia over its annexation of Crimea and position on the Ukraine's crisis, Moscow and Tehran increased their level of economic relations. In particular, they discussed an energy deal worth of $10 billion that would involve a barter trade of oil in exchange for building electricity stations in Iran.[61] As the United States intensified its diplomacy to assure Iran's compliance with the nuclear nonproliferation treaty, the Kremlin was supportive of the diplomacy, but had its own priorities in mind. Among them were the strengthening of bilateral commercial and political ties with Tehran and its membership in non-Western institutions such as the SCO. In April 2015, to further revitalize relations with Iran Putin removed the ban for delivering the S-300 (advanced military system for air defense). Previously, Russia signed but then cancelled the delivery agreement.[62]

Outside Iran, Russia focused on regional stability by encouraging negotiations between Syria's Assad and moderate elements of opposition. Here too Russia worked jointly with its non-Western partners. The BRICS summits supported negotiations in Syria such as those that started in Geneva in February 2014. In addition, with continued destabilization of Syria and Iraq by Islamic radicals, the focus by Russia and other powers was on shifting to countering the region-wide threats posed by the self-proclaimed Islamic State (IS). By early 2015, the IS emerged to be the leading force with capacity to topple Assad and secure important territorial gains in Iraq. In particular, the IS militants conquered western Iraq and eastern Syria claiming to control territory with six and half million residents.[63] In June 2014, they took control of Mosul, Iraq's second-largest city, and in May 2015, they seized the ancient and UNESCO-protected town of Palmyra in Syria. To contain and defeat the IS, Russia consulted both Western and non-Western nations, especially Iran. Moscow continued to strengthen economic and political relations with Tehran, in part for the purpose of jointly assisting stabilization in Syria and Iraq. Increasingly, Moscow was also reviving strong ties with Egypt[64] and, disagreements on Syria and Iran notwithstanding, sought to strengthen relations with Saudi Arabia.[65]

Another important partner of Russia in the Middle East was Turkey. Although the two nations supported different sides in the Syrian conflict, they were both critical of the Western role in the region and shared a desire to stabilize it by local powers. Russian-Turkish relations were also made easier by shared values of a civilizational identity and strong modernizing state able to overcome pressures from domestic and foreign influences.[66] In addition to similarity of values, their interests were compatible. In particular, Moscow and Istanbul continued cooperation on energy issues. As Russia sought to circumvent Ukraine in developing an alternative transportation route to European markets, Turkey wanted to position itself as a major energy hub. In January 2015, Putin traveled to Istanbul to propose the building of a gas pipeline through Turkish territory to Europe's borders. The European Union objected to the development in part because of the need to build the required infrastructure.[67] Previously, due to disagreements with Ukraine, Russia cut gas supplies for European customers to pressure Kiev into paying negotiated fees.

The Ukraine Crisis and Eurasia

Finally, Russia's priorities were supported by its policies in the former Soviet region. In addition to economic benefits, Russia sought to increase its influence in the former Soviet region by promoting its newly articulated values of state-centered national unity, traditional religious ties, and respect for cross-cultural relations, and sovereignty/noninterference from large powers in the region. In October 2011, Putin proposed building a new Eurasian Union among the CIS states and laid out economic incentives for joining it, including increase in trade, common modernization projects, and improved standards of living.[68] In December 2014, speaking at the Valdai forum of international experts, Putin further stated that

> integrating with our neighbors is our absolute priority. The future Eurasian Economic Union, which we have declared and which we have discussed extensively as of late, is not just a collection of mutually beneficial agreements. The Eurasian Union is a project for maintaining the identity of nations in the historical Eurasian space in a new century and in a new world. Eurasian integration is a chance for the entire post-Soviet space to become an independent center for global development, rather than remaining on the outskirts of Europe and Asia.[69]

The Eurasian Union initiative continued Russia's other regional integration efforts. In 2010, Russia initiated a Customs Union that also included Belarus and Kazakhstan. In the following year, Russia also invited Ukraine to join a Customs Union, promising a major discount for gas prices. Armenia and Kyrgyzstan too are being considered for membership in the Eurasian Union. In Belarus and Ukraine, Russia's civilizational arguments have to do with the three's Slavic and Orthodox Christian values. With respect to Muslim states of the region, the Kremlin advocates the notion of cross-cultural ties and similarity of political systems with highly concentrated authority. By capitalizing on high oil prices, the Kremlin hoped to reverse the pro-Western revolutions in Ukraine and Kyrgyzstan by supporting those governments in favor of stronger ties with Russia.

However, the development of the Eurasian Union did not go the way Russia expected. Moscow's regional initiatives have met with opposition from those outside the former Soviet region who perceive the Kremlin's promoted values as threatening. In addition, there was evidence of instability in the region which included the tense atmosphere in the Caucasus following the war with Georgia, renewed terrorist attacks, the persistent failure of Western forces to stabilize Afghanistan, the inability of Central Asian rulers to reign in local clans and drug lords, and the weakness of bodies of power in Moldova and Ukraine.

The Ukrainian revolution served as a powerful testament that Russia's influence had not translated into stability in the region. In November 2013, following President Victor Yanukovich's decision not to sign an Association Agreement with the European Union, mass protests took place in Kiev pressuring Yanukovich to reverse his decision. Russia and the European Union pulled Ukraine in different directions by promising benefits from joining their political-economy arrangements. With the Ukrainian economy in recession, Yanukovich declined the EU offer because Putin gave Ukraine a major discount in energy prices and pledged $15 billion in aid. In the meantime, the Ukrainian protest was gathering momentum and reached an unprecedented proportion. Opposition was critical of Yanukovich's policies at home and favored the country's pro-European development. On February 21, 2014, the compromise agreement between president and opposition brokered by the European Union collapsed. For unknown reasons, Yanukovich left the office, moved to the east of Ukraine and then to Russia.

Since the revolution and removal of the president from power, the situation in Ukraine continued to worsen by evolving in the direction of civil war, with Russia and the Western nations providing support and assistance for different sides of the conflict. Residents of the east and south of Ukraine did not trust Kiev's rule and demanded more autonomy. Assisted by Russia, activists in several key regions (Donetsk, Luhansk, Nikolayev, Khar'kiv, and Odessa) refused to cooperate with the central government, while the latter launched "anti-terrorist" operations against the protestors, thereby exacerbating tensions. Russia blamed the Western governments for collapse of the compromise agreement and demanded that Kiev refrain from using force and initiate new constitutional changes, guarantee protection of Russian speakers, and conduct a decentralization reform in the country. Russia also annexed Crimea, provided various forms of assistance for protesters in the eastern Ukraine, amassed troops on Ukraine's border, and raised prices for natural gas deliveries to Kiev.[70]

As violence and instability in the eastern and southern parts of Ukraine proliferated, attempts to negotiate peace brought limited results. The Geneva accord negotiated on April 17, 2014, did not hold, as radicals on both sides refused to abide by it. On May 2, forty people were burned alive in Odessa. The summer saw especially intense fighting between the eastern rebels and the Ukrainian army. A new military escalation in eastern Ukraine in August resulted in Kiev's defeat and a new cease-fire agreement was negotiated in Minsk on September 3, 2014. However, in October of the same year heavy fighting resumed with thousands of people killed and over a million refugees fleeing the eastern part of the country. On February 11, 2015, the leaders of Ukraine, Russia, France, and Germany with presence of the East's representatives met to formulate new conditions for peace in the Minsk-II agreement. The conditions were to be observed by the Organization for Security and Cooperation in Europe and included removal of heavy weapons by the fighting sides, amnesty and exchange of prisoners, decentralization reform and passing of the law on self-governance in Donetsk and Luhansk, restoration of pensions and services for residents of the East by Kiev, and control of the border with Russia.[71]

The reality, again, proved different. Although the fighting was not as intense as before the agreement, violence did not stop and the two sides failed to implement the signed conditions. Rather than working in concert, Russian and Western powers blamed each other for not putting sufficient pressures on their patrons and engaged in mutual sanctions against each other's economies. Despite the formal peace, the situation remained highly unstable. By the early summer, many analysts speculated that full war could resume at any moment. The position by leading powers, as well as Ukraine's deep cultural divide between West, Center, and the East-South, continued to challenge the government's job of building a nation. In addition, the post-Soviet years have led to degradation of the economy with the super rich controlling its various parts and the majority of the population living in poverty with little prospect to improve its living standards.

The situation in Ukraine radically changed prospects for the Eurasian Union. Without Ukraine, the union was set to be Russia-centered with former Soviet nations and the outside world viewing it as a hegemonic project. Aware of such perception, Russian experts were proposing ideas of the union's diversification even before the Ukraine crisis. For example, in October 2013 the editor of *Russia in Global Affairs* Fyodor Lukyanov suggested that the Kremlin should consider developing the Eurasian region jointly with Turkey and China.[72] China was especially active in promoting its vision for development of Eurasia and offering itself in building the region. Increasingly, Beijing acted on its economic ambitions by inviting former Soviet states to join a larger China-centered trade and transportation arrangement titled the Silk Road Economic Belt.[73] In this scheme the Eurasian Union would become an integrated part of an economic and transportation project advanced by China. On May 8, 2015, the vision obtained a major support with endorsement of it by leaders of Russia and China. During President Xi Jinping's visit to Moscow, the two nations signed an agreement on cooperation between the Eurasian Union and the Silk Road.[74] Among the objectives were the establishment of the network of land and sea routes to connect the western regions of China with the main markets of Central Asia and Europe via the territories of Kazakhstan and Russia.[75]

The new vision and practice of Russia-initiated Eurasian Union and China-advocated Silk Road's convergence encouraged those who viewed the two nations' cooperation in terms of being a value alternative to the European Union.[76] The fact that the United States and the European Union have worked to keep Ukraine away from the Russia-dominant Eurasian Union may have contributed to the Kremlin motivation to develop Russia's own civilizational ideology. The West's sanctions against the Russian economy in response to the Kremlin's annexation of Crimea and support for eastern fighters in the Ukrainian civil war served to strengthen Russia's reorientation away from Western nations and towards China.[77] Such foreign pressures also emboldened those defending the objective of Russia's development in isolation from Europe.[78] Although China's system of values is distinct from that of Russia, the two systems may be compatible, especially relative to the West's system.[79] Therefore the cultural pillar may strengthen the rapidly progressing economic and political partnership between the two nations.

Assessment

Russia's foreign policy continues to evolve. Despite serious tensions and areas of disagreement with Western nations, the Kremlin preserved working relations with those nations particularly on the issues of counterterrorism and nuclear nonproliferation. In relations with non-Western nations, Russia has had important accomplishments. Partly in response to the West's sanctions against the Russian economy, Moscow has prioritized and strengthened economic and political ties with China and Turkey, as well as other nations in Asia and the Middle East. In the former Soviet world, the Kremlin capitalized on "pragmatic" economy-driven ties and made important advancements in developing the Eurasian Union in partnership with China's Silk Road initiative.

Since the return of Putin to the presidency and especially since Ukraine's revolution, Russia has also embarked on risky policies of asserting its interests. As Ukraine was descending into a civil war, soft power was no longer an option to Russia. To defend its core interests in Ukraine, Moscow now had to rely on various forms of political, economic, and military pressures on Kiev. The Ukraine crisis challenged Russia's foreign policy in the former Soviet region in a fundamental way. It remains to be seen whether a robust resolution of the crisis can be found. In the meantime, the Eurasian Union is set to develop without Ukraine. The Kremlin's ties with Western nations have declined to an unprecedentedly low level. The crisis in relations with the West led to sanctions against the Russian economy and had negative effects on the European part of Russia's national identity. Although Russia's relations outside the West grew stronger, the Kremlin now had to be careful to not develop an excessive economic and political dependence on China. The Western sanctions presented Russia with opportunities to diversify its economy, but the authorities are yet to make a choice between continued maneuvering and building a developmental state with a strong state role in planning and mobilization of resources.

Overall, Russia's foreign policy has moved in an uncertain, possibly unsustainable direction and may need to be corrected in a not-so-distant future. The new course, which combines elements of cooperation and assertiveness in various geographic directions, is yet to be consolidated. In the meantime, the country needs to concentrate on solving its formidable institutional problems including reforming education and healthcare systems. Externally, Russia's new course depends on favorable developments in the global political and economic system. Russian relations with the West need to be predictable, reciprocal, and developed in the direction of strengthening mutual trust. Lack of progress with issues such as MDS in Europe, or coordination of policies toward Ukraine and other former Soviet states, Afghanistan, and the Middle East may encourage the Kremlin to further advance a risky policy in relations with the West. Development of the global economy is another critical factor. A global recovery and stable energy prices may facilitate Russia's engagement with the world, whereas major disturbances, such as a recession or a sharp decline in oil prices, are bound to undermine the process.

Table 8.3 provides a tentative summary assessment of Russia's "civilizational" foreign policy.

Table 8.3.   The Record of State-Civilization

Security	Confrontation with the West and Ukraine
Welfare	Economic crisis
Autonomy	New vulnerability to international influences
Identity	Undermined Westernist dimension of Russia's identity

NOTES

1. Vladimir Putin, Address to the Valdai International Discussion Club, October 24, 2014, http://eng.kremlin.ru/news/23137.

2. Paul J. Saunders, "Another Setback for the Reset," *The National Interest,* March 6, 2012, http://nationalinterest.org.

3. As three European analysts concluded about the Russian discourse, "Although there is a lively debate between different factions around the Kremlin . . . it is important to understand that this is a competition within the wider 'Putin consensus'," Ivan Krastev, Mark Leonard, and Andrew Wilson, eds., *What Does Russia Think?* (London: European Council on Foreign Relations, 2009).

4. For background, see Cory Welt, "What the Snowden Affair Says About U.S.-Russian Relations," *The Center for American Progress*, July 17, 2013.

5. Vladimir Putin, "The New Integration Project for Eurasia," *Izvestia*, October 3, 2011.

6. "BRICS pomeryayetsya siloi s MVF," Editorial, *Nezavisimaya gazeta*, 02.04.2015, http://www.ng.ru/editorial/2015-04-02/2_red.html.

7. "BRICS establish $100bn bank and currency pool to cut out Western dominance," July 15, 2014, http://rt.com/business/173008-brics-bank-currency-pool/.

8. For example, despite their differences from the West, both Russia and China present their grand visions as consistent with the idea of democracy. Islamists, however, promote Islamic caliphate and do not hide despisement for secular democratic ideals.

9. I follow here a conventional institutional definition of the West as an area that includes the United States and European nations. These nations share pluralistic political institutions, market economy, and basic geopolitical objectives of advancing their values and institutions across the globe and defeating their ideological and politico-economic opponents.

10. Fareed Zakaria, *The Post-American World* (New York: Public Affairs, 2008). Russian analysts too have envisioned a relative decline of the U.S. position in the new international system, describing it as "pluralistic" rather than one-state "unipolarity" and presenting Russia as a member of the unipolar center or a group of states. See for example, Aleksei D. Bogaturov, "Sovremennyi mezhdunarodnyi poryadok" [The contemporary international order], *Mezhdunarodnyye protsessy* 1, 1, 2003, http://www.intertrends.ru.

11. For details of this debate in Russia, see Andrei Tsygankov and Pavel Tsygankov, "National Ideology and IR Theory: Three Reincarnations of the 'Russian Idea'," *European Journal of International Relations* 16, 4, 2010.

12. Vladimir Putin, "Meeting with the Russian Federation Ambassadors," Moscow, Foreign Ministry, July 9, 2012.

13. Vladimir Putin, "Poslaniye Prezidenta Federal'nomu Sobraniyu Rossiyskoy Federatsii," December 15, 2012, http://president.kremlin.ru.

14. *The Foreign Policy Concept of the Russian Federation*, kremlin.ru, July 12, 2008.

15. *The Foreign Policy Concept of the Russian Federation*, kremlin.ru, February 18, 2013, http://www.mid.ru/bdomp/ns-osndoc.nsf/e2f289bea62097f9c325787a0034c255/c32577ca0017434944257b160051bf7f.

16. Vladimir Putin, "Samoopredeleniye russkogo naroda—eto polietnicheskaya tsivilizatsiya, skreplennaya russkim kul'turnym yadrom," *Nezavisimaya gazeta*, January 23, 2012.

17. Putin, "Samoopredeleniye russkogo naroda." Along these lines, the new official nationalities strategy until 2025 signed by Putin in December 2012 reintroduced Russia as a "unique socio-cultural civilization entity formed of the multi-people Russian nation" and, under pressures of Muslim constituencies, removed the reference to ethnic Russians as the core of the state (*Kommersant*, December 19, 2012).

18. Vladimir Putin, "Meeting of the Valdai International Discussion Club," September 2013.

19. Vladimir Putin, "Poslaniye Prezidenta Federal'nomu Sobraniyu Rossiyskoy Federatsii," December 13, 2013, http://president.kremlin.ru.

20. Vladimir Putin, "Poslaniye Prezidenta Federal'nomu Sobraniyu Rossiyskoy Federatsii," December, 2014, http://president.kremlin.ru.

21. *Kontseptsiya vneshnei politiki Rossiyskoi Federatsiyi*, Moscow: Foreign Ministry, February 18, 2013, http://www.mid.ru/bdomp/ns-osndoc.nsf/e2f289bea62 097f9c325787a0034c255/c32577ca0017434944257b160051bf7f.

22. Vladimir Yakunin, "Dialog tsivilizatsiy dlya postroyeniya mirnykh i inkluzivnykh obshchestv," *Polis* 5 (131), 2012; Vladimir Yakunin, "Politicheskaya tektonika sovremennogo mira," *Polis* 4 (136), 2013.

23. Howard Amos, "Guilty Verdict Puts the Heat on Putin," *Moscow Times*, August 20, 2012.

24. Stephen F. Cohen, "America's New Cold War With Russia," *The Nation*, February 4, 2013.

25. "Moscow Dismisses Western Criticism of Gay Propaganda Law," *RIA Novosti*, August 7, 2013.

26. Christi Parsons, "Obama criticizes Russia's new anti-gay law in Leno interview," *Los Angeles Times*, August 7, 2013.

27. On May 23, 2015 Putin signed Law on "Undesirable" Organizations giving prosecutors the power to shut down international organizations ("Putin Signs Russian Law to Shut 'Undesirable' Organizations," *Associated Press*, May 23, 2015, http://abcnews.go.com/International/wireStory/putin-signs-russian-law-shut -undesirable-organizations-31258166).

28. For example, see Assistant Secretary of State for Democracy, Human Rights, and Labor Tom Malinowski's interview in Russian newspaper *Kommersant* on March 3, 2015, "Vesti dielo stalo ochen' slozhno," http://www.kommersant .ru/doc/2678676.

29. "Putin blames West for global chaos," *Russia Today*, 27 September, 2012.

30. Fred Weir, "Chemical weapons in Syria: How Russia views the debate," *Christian Science Monitor*, August 22, 2013.

31. Andrei Kolesnikov, "Na poltona blizhe," *Kommersant*, May 12, 2015, http:// www.kommersant.ru/doc/2725130.

32. For some discussion, see Pavel Koshkin, "Is there any way to reconcile the interests of the US, Russia in Syria?" *Russia Direct*, October 5, 2015, http://www .russia-direct.org/debates/there-any-way-reconcile-interests-us-and-russia-syria; Andrei Tsygankov, "The Kremlin's Syria gamble is risky, but could have a big payoff," *Russia Direct*, October 3, 2015.

33. Sergei L. Loiko, "Russia reacts coolly to Obama's nuclear proposals," *Los Angeles Times*, June 19, 2013.

34. For background, see Cory Welt, "What the Snowden Affair Says About U.S.-Russian Relations," *The Center for American Progress*, July 17, 2013.

35. Philipp Casula, "Russia's and Europe's Borderlands," *Problems of Post-Communism* 61, 6, 2014; Hiski Haukkala, "From Cooperative to Contested Europe? The Conflict in Ukraine as a Culmination of a Long-Term Crisis in EU–Russia Relations," *Journal of Contemporary European Studies* 23, 1, 2015.

36. Vladimir Putin's Press-Conference, kremlin.ru, March 4, 2014, http://eng .kremlin.ru/news/6763.

37. Charles Clover, "Clinton Vows to Thwart New Soviet Union," *Financial Times*, December 7, 2012.

38. "Should the West be afraid of Moscow's plans for a Eurasian Union?" Expert panel edited by Vlad Sobell, *us-russia.org*, July 12, 2013.

39. Statement by the President on Ukraine, White House, February 28, 2014, http://www.whitehouse.gov/the-press-office/2014/02/28/statement-president -ukraine.

40. Kirill Belyaninov, "Yevropa ne prisoyedinilas' k SshA," *Kommersant*, March 5, 2014.

41. Scott Shane, "A Homemade Style of Terror: Jihadists Push New Tactics," *The New York Times*, May 5, 2013.

42. Joe Biden, "Remarks on the Russia-Ukraine Conflict." Washington, D.C., The Brookings Institution, www.brookings.edu, May 27, 2015.

43. "Syria chemical weapons: UN adopts binding resolution," *BBC News*, 28 September 2013.

44. "Iran nuclear talks: 'Historic' agreement struck," *BBC News*, 14 July 2015, http://www.bbc.com/news/world-middle-east-33518524.

45. Vladimir Putin, "Russia and the changing world," *Moskovskiye novosti*, February 26, 2012.

46. Alexey Timofeychev, "'We need to find a way out' of sanctions, says Putin on visit to Rome," *Russia Beyond the Headlines*, June 11, 2015, www.rbth.ru.

47. Aleksandr Baunov, "Pochemu spaseniye Gretsiya ne stalo polem bitvy Rossiyi i Ameriki," Moscow Carnegie Center, July 13, 2015, http://carnegie.ru/2015/07/12/ru-60675/id9u.

48. David M. Herszenhorn, "Russia Won't Renew Pact on Weapons With U.S.," *The New York Times*, October 12, 2012.

49. Ibid.

50. Greg Simons, "Aspects of Putin's appeal to international publics," *Global Affairs*, DOI: 10.1080/23340460.2015.1020727.

51. Biden, "Remarks on the Russia-Ukraine Conflict."

52. Putin further insisted on preservation of a "new balance of economic, civilizational and military forces" and instructed the government to pay more attention to development of patriotic and military education. See his Annual Address to the Federal Assembly, Moscow, the Kremlin, December 12, 2012, www.kremlin.ru.

53. Vladimir Putin, "Meeting of the Valdai International Discussion Club," September 19, 2013.

54. Katya Golubkova, "New BRICS bank to look at local, international borrowing," *Reuters*, July 9, 2015.

55. Aleksey Nikolsky, "Russia charts new course for BRICS nations as presidency begins," *TASS*, April 1, 2015.

56. Ibid.

57. Aleksey Nikolsky, "Russia-China Gas Deal Requires Moscow's Reconciliation With US, EU," *Sputnik*, November 10, 2014.

58. Vladimir Soldatkin and Timothy Heritage, "Russia and China deepen ties with new economic deals," *Reuters*, May 8, 2015.

59. Chris Weafer, "Russia Needs to Pivot East and West," *Moscow Times*, May 8, 2014.

60. Tatyana Yedovina, "K Evraez prisoyedinili vyetnamsky rynok," *Kommersant*, May 30, 2015, http://www.kommersant.ru/doc/2738346.

61. Yeveniya Novikova, "Moskva i Tegeran soprotivlyayutsya sanktsiyam," *Nezavisimaya gazeta*, April 30, 2014.

62. For details of Russia-Iranian relations, see Nikolay Kozhanov, "Understanding the Revitalization of Russian-Iranian Relations," Moscow Carnegie Center, May 5, 2015.

63. Zachary Laub and Jonathan Masters, "The Islamic State," Council on Foreign Relations, May 18, 2015, http://www.cfr.org/iraq/islamic-state/p14811.

64. Yelena Suponina, "Kak Yegipet opyat' stal luchshim drugom Rossiyi na Blizhnem Vostoke," *Nezavisimaya gazeta*, June 10, 2015.

65. Simeon Kerr and Kathrin Hille, "Saudi defence minister to meet Vladimir Putin for talks on Syria," *Financial Times*, June 17, 2015.

66. P. Bilgin and A. Bilgiç, "Turkey's 'new' foreign policy toward Eurasia," *Eurasian Geography and Economics* 52, 2, 2011.

67. Ben Aris, "The Riga summit of disappointment," *Business New Europe*, May 21, 2015.

68. Vladimir Putin, "The New Integration Project for Eurasia," *Izvestia*, October 3, 2011.

69. Vladimir Putin, "Meeting of the Valdai International Discussion Club," September 19, 2013.

70. For details, see Tsygankov, "Vladimir Putin's Last Stand: The Sources of Russia's Ukraine Policy," *Post-Soviet Affairs* 31, 4, 2015.

71. "The Minsk ceasefire deal, point by point," *Russia Today*, February 12, 2015.

72. Feodor Lukyanov, "Nastoyaschaya Yevraziya," *gazeta.ru*, October 23, 2013, http://www.gazeta.ru/comments/column/lukyanov/5721721.shtml.

73. Yuri Tavrovsky, "Pekin sobirayet gory i morya [Beijing collects mountains and seas]," *Nezavisimiaya gazeta*, November 15, 2013, http://www.ng.ru/ideas/2013-11-15/5_china.html.

74. "Rossiya i Kitai podpisali dogovor o 'Shelkovom puti'," *BBC*, May 8, 2015 http://www.bbc.com/russian/rolling_news/2015/05/150508_rn_china_putin_jingping_silk_route.

75. For detailed proposals by Russian experts of Russia-China cooperation in Eurasia, see The Valdai Club's Report "Toward the Great Ocean—3: Creating Central Eurasia (Moscow, June 2015), http://valdaiclub.com/publication/77920.html.

76. Alexander Lukin, "What the Kremlin Is Thinking: Putin's Vision for Eurasia," *Foreign Affairs*, July-August, 2014.

77. Dmitry Trenin, *From Greater Europe to Greater Asia? The Sino-Russian Entente* (Washington, DC: The Carnegie Endowment for International Peace, 2015).

78. Sergei Glazyev, "Moment istiny: Rossiya i sanktsiyi Zapada," Moscow: the Izborsky Club, 26 June accessed July 15, 2014, http://www.dynacon.ru/content/articles/3397.

79. Gilbert Rozman, *The Sino-Russian Challenge to the World Order: National Identities, Bilateral Relations, and East versus West in the 2010s* (Stanford: Stanford University Press, 2014).

9

Conclusions and Lessons

All healthy human action . . . must establish a balance between utopia
and reality, between free will and determinism.

—E. H. Carr[1]

This final chapter summarizes the approach taken in this book to
understanding change and continuity in Russian foreign policy. It
also suggests several lessons that Russian and Western policymakers can
learn from the past thirty years of their interaction if they wish to improve
their communication and security in the world. If Russia and the West are
to become partners in the twenty-first century, learning these lessons is
essential.

CHANGE AND CONTINUITY IN RUSSIA'S FOREIGN POLICY

Seven Visions of National Interest

Despite what realists and liberals often assume, nations rarely have once
and forever established visions of their fundamental external interests.
More typically, national interests fluctuate with changes on the domestic
and international political scene. This book identifies seven distinct visions
of national interest that Russia has developed and pursued throughout the
last twenty years.

Mikhail Gorbachev's vision of his country's interest, New Thinking, was
a part of his perestroika project, which meant to revive socialist values at

home and achieve a fundamentally new level of cooperation abroad. New Thinking saw the world as socially diverse and yet united by common human values, as well as by fundamental threats. In particular, the new leadership pointed to threats of nuclear catastrophe, ecological devastation, and poverty. National interests were to be pursued in close coordination with other members of the global society, and, for the Soviet Union, this meant the need to give up the old ideological vision and to acknowledge positive contributions by the West to the world's development.

Despite growing resistance from various domestic opponents, the leader of New Thinking acted consistently with his beliefs. He made disproportionately large cuts in conventional and nuclear arsenals and proposed to eliminate all nuclear weapons by 2000. He also withdrew from Afghanistan and other third world countries. Furthermore, Gorbachev abandoned the "Brezhnev doctrine" of limited sovereignty in Eastern Europe and made it possible to tear down the Berlin Wall. Finally, the new Soviet leader committed himself to the idea of principally reforming the United Nations and supporting it with greater resources, so the organization would be capable of meeting new world challenges. At home, Gorbachev—admittedly belatedly—recognized the need to give up the old imperial principles of maintaining Soviet unity, and he offered a vision that combined elements of federation and confederation. The new union treaty was to be renegotiated and approved through a people's referendum.

For various domestic and international reasons, the New Thinking vision could not be sustained and was soon replaced by the idea of Integration with the West. The new domestic coalition undermined Gorbachev's standing by insisting that Russia had been a country with a suppressed Western identity and that it now had to give up its socialist system in favor of a Western-style market democracy. Unlike New Thinkers, who sought to engage the West by developing the notions of global threats and common responsibility for their emergence, the new Russian leaders—Boris Yeltsin and his foreign minister Andrei Kozyrev—saw no major flaws in the West. They planned to rapidly gain membership in Western international organizations and to minimize relationships with the former Soviet states. These steps meant to soon bring Russia to the front-rank status of advanced European countries and the United States.

Opposition to the course of integration with the West was formidable, and the course began to unravel soon after attempts at its implementation. When a leading critic of this course, Yevgeni Primakov, was appointed the new foreign minister, the vision of national interest changed yet again. By selecting him, Yeltsin, to a degree, committed himself to a new perception of external threats and foreign policy objectives. Rather than proposing modernization and Westernization as Russia's key national interests, Primakov pointed to the dangers of a concentration of world power associated with the unipolar status of the United States. A realist rather than an economic liberal, Primakov proposed the vision of Great Power Balancing for the purpose of gradually turning the existing unipolar world into a multipolar one. In particular, the new minister sought to prevent, or at least slow down, the announced expansion of NATO toward Russia's western borders. The vision required integration of the former Soviet region under Russian leadership and seeking assistance from other powerful states, such as China and India, in order to balance the American hegemony.

Too many of Primakov's initiatives remained on paper only, and that contributed to the replacement of his vision with a new one. Vladimir Putin drew attention to the world's instabilities, such as terrorism, as well as some new economic opportunities. Unlike Primakov and similar to Gorbachev, Putin saw the need to engage the West in an ambitious joint project. However, unlike Gorbachev and Kozyrev, he visualized Russia as a great power and sought Western recognition of this. Putin redefined national interest as that of Pragmatic Cooperation of a great power. Rather than balancing the United States' power, the key objective was now pronounced as an economic modernization for the sake of preserving the great power status.

In attempting to reengage the West, Putin showed himself to be extremely active in developing relations with the United States, particularly after the September 11, 2001, terrorist attacks on that country. He offered a far-reaching intelligence cooperation and proposed new ways to develop Russian-U.S. energy ties. Putin was even more energetic when it came to activating economic and political ties with Europe. In some areas, such as visa relations with European countries, the president demonstrated his readiness to go much further than European leaders themselves. Yet Putin was no Gorbachev—his activism was pragmatic and driven by calculations of state power. On issues where Russian state autonomy was at stake, he was firm in limiting cooperation with foreign nations. Thus, despite his support of U.S. actions in Afghanistan, Putin sided with a number of European nations in condemning American intervention in Iraq without a United Nations mandate. And in his relations with Europe, he placed the emphasis on economic and energy cooperation, while restricting cooperation on security issues, such as Chechnya or peacemaking activities in the former Soviet region. In this, as in actively pursuing commercial sales of weapons abroad, Putin continued traditions of Primakov's diplomacy.

In the former Soviet Union, the vision of Pragmatic Cooperation implied an abandonment of Primakov's integration project in favor of less costly and mutually advantageous bilateral relations. In reestablishing bilateral ties consistent with his belief in economic modernization, Putin reasserted control over many of the ex-republics' strategic property and transportation, particularly electricity and energy pipeline facilities. He concluded a number of partnership and strategic partnership agreements in the Caucasus and central Asia, as well with Ukraine and Belarus. The Russian leader also took a different approach to security issues by emphasizing cooperation in counterterrorism and seeking to assemble on that basis his own coalition of the willing. He strengthened Russia's military presence in central Asia and the Caucasus by signing appropriate bilateral and multilateral agreements. Finally, Putin promoted new energy and transportation projects to further implement his vision of geoeconomically based and state-driven modernization.

Around 2005, Putin's vision changed in the direction of assertiveness. The Kremlin no longer believed in defensive cooperation with Western nations and insisted on greater acceptance of Russia's interests. Russia's leadership sharply criticized what it viewed as the United States' "unilateralism" in world politics and pursued more independent economic and security policies in the world. Following Putin's speech at the Munich Conference in January, the Kremlin was busy signaling its frustration with its inability to develop more equitable relations with the United States. Russia felt humiliated that it had to swallow the war in the Balkans, two rounds of NATO expansion, the U.S. withdrawal from the ABM treaty, military presence in central Asia, the invasion of Iraq, and plans to deploy elements of nuclear missile defense in Eastern Europe. In the wake of the Russia-Georgia conflict, Dmitri Medvedev stated, "[W]e will not tolerate any more humiliation, and we are not joking."[2]

However, after 2009 Russia's rhetoric began to change. In response to the global financial crisis, Medvedev declared that Russia needed to explore new opportunities for development and build new international alliances for modernization. In the post-Western world, this translated into Russia's efforts to improve ties with the West, while strengthening relations with BRICS countries. In the former Soviet region, the Kremlin's emphasis shifted toward initiating new projections of regional integration such as the Eurasian Union.

Finally, the return of Putin to the presidency was accompanied by the vision of state-civilization and new stress on assertiveness in relations with the United States and the European Union. Russia again was insisting on the West's recognition of its values and interests across the world. In Europe, Russia wanted a stronger role in defining security framework and a greater share in economic projects. In Eurasia, the Kremlin has initiated an ambitious idea of regional integration under the umbrella of the Eurasian Union by inviting several former Soviet states to join the union. In the Middle East, Russia fought against what it saw as a Western destabilization scheme behind the Arab Spring events. Instead of regime change, Moscow was committed to propping up existing governments such as the one led by Bashar al-Assad in Syria. In Asia, Russia sought to pool its resources with China in order to challenge the West-centered world. The Kremlin also contributed to the development of alternative international organizations such as SCO and BRICS—with the idea of taking advantage of new international opportunities outside the West. Finally, Russia reacted harshly to Western criticisms of its human rights record by insisting on Russia's own "civilizational" status and system of values.

Table 9.1 summarizes Russia's seven visions of the world and national interest.

Table 9.1. Russia's Seven Visions of the World and National Interest

	Perceived World	*National Interest*
GORBACHEV	Cold War crisis	New thinking and cross-cultural dialogue
YELTSIN/KOZYREV	Western institutional dominance	Integration with the West
PRIMAKOV	U.S. power hegemony	Balancing against the U.S.
PUTIN I	Terrorism & economic competition	Pragmatic cooperation with the West
PUTIN II	U.S. unilateralism	Assertiveness
MEDVEDEV	Opportunities for economic development	Alliances for modernization
PUTIN III	Competition between West and non-West	Promotion of Russia as a civilization

Understanding National-Interest Formation

Liberal and realist theories of international relations are too simplistic for understanding the described process and outcomes of national-interest formation. Each of them emphasizes either modernization or the need to maintain power as shaping foreign policy choices. Yet in reality both of these forces figure prominently in how nations determine their interests. In order to understand the formation of Russia's national interests, this book employed a complex framework that incorporates both types of influence. In the first chapter, I hypothesized that the vision of national interest is a product of the nation's interaction with the world, and Russia's strategic choices can be viewed as reactions to the behavior of the Western powers. At least since Peter the Great, the West has played a special role in Russian development, and much of the country's international behavior has meant efforts of the Russian Self to win recognition by its significant Other. Western actions are contested domestically, and local conditions are no less important in shaping a dominant vision of national identity and foreign policy. A closer analysis of Russia's foreign policy developments throughout the book has revealed three local factors that clarify the process of Russian interpretation of Western actions. These three—national tradition, current concerns, and state capacity—specify, rather than distort, the general causal mechanism of national-interest formation.

Gorbachev's New Thinking originated, in part, from the hostilities of the Cold War and unrealized opportunities presented by the brief period of détente. In contrast to the realists' emphasis on the West's economic and military strength, Gorbachev responded to social democratic ideas of détente's European supporters and the domestic tradition of reform social-ism, which was associated with the late Lenin, Bukharin, and Khrushchev. In putting forth his vision, the leader of New Thinking was hoping to garner and maintain a sufficient support among elites and within the broader society. It is no accident that his project contained elements of Westernism, Statism, and Civilizationism—the three main schools of for-eign policy thinking in the Soviet Union.

Yet the task of keeping the unstable coalition together proved to be untenable. Soon, conservative Civilizationists and Statists, on the one hand, and radical Westernizers, on the other, were attacking New Think-ing. The conservative and radical opponents wanted principally differ-ent—in fact, mutually exclusive—outcomes, and Gorbachev could have made progress only if he were to deliver on his promises to improve people's lives. Instead, busy persuading the West of the authenticity of his intentions and not getting as much as he expected in return, the leader of perestroika was rapidly losing the initiative and support at home. The perception was strengthening that the Russians were living through an unavoidable political disintegration and economic deterioration, and that was radicalizing the society and improving the political standing of Gor-bachev's opponents. After 1989, it was the vision of radical Westernizers, expressed by Boris Yeltsin, that was receiving growing social recognition.

The Westernist opposition skillfully exploited the newly emerged opportunities to challenge the ruling center. Unlike Gorbachev, Yeltsin was elected president of Russia by popular vote, and he continued to argue that economic deterioration could be stopped only by radical Western-style reforms. Yeltsin also entered a coalition with other republi-can nationalists and insisted that the efforts to preserve the union were doomed.

However, the new Westernist coalition was hardly a stable one. It con-sisted of pragmatic members of the former Communist *nomenklatura*, such as Yeltsin himself, and idealistic liberal reformers, such as Gaidar and Kozyrev. The new ruling coalition, therefore, tried to synthesize the influ-ences of Westernizers and former Soviet Statists, but the majority of the elites—military industrialists, the army, and the security services—remained excluded. The challenge that came from that majority was formidable, and the Westernist foreign policy course soon began to fade under powerful attacks from both Statists and conservative Civilizationists. The opposition took advantage of the attitude the Western nations had adopted toward the new Russia. Despite some considerable financial assistance given to the new Russian government, the West was clearly not eager to integrate Russia into its midst. NATO's decision to expand brushed aside Russia's hopes for transforming the alliance into a nonmilitary one or for being admitted as a full member of the organization. NATO's expansion also provided the anti-Western opposition with the required ammunition to construct an image of an external threat and question the objectives of the new government. Along with failure of the West-recommended liberal economic reforms, NATO expansion strengthened domestic Statists who advanced a different concept of national interests.

The new foreign minister, Yevgeni Primakov, articulated the new vision of Great Power Balancing and attempted to put it into practice. Working with the much less cooperative West, he sought to consolidate Russia's position as a great power and to resituate it into the center of the former Soviet region. The new minister—who subsequently became prime minister—also attempted to limit the power of the oligarchs in Russian economic and political life. The new course was not successful in delivering improved social and economic standards, and it unnecessarily alienated pro-Western forces, pushing them into opposition. The course was also quite expensive because it sought to restore the ties among the former Soviet republics primarily through subsidies by the Russian state. The vision therefore was not attractive to Russian business elites, and it also had little appeal to some isolationist-minded nationalists, who were formerly supportive members of Primakov's coalition.

As a result, when Yeltsin appointed Vladimir Putin prime minister and, subsequently, acting president, the new leader had a considerably different coalition of support behind him. In particular, he drew support from pro-Western commercial groups, formerly neglected by Primakov, and from state-oriented security services. Changed international conditions and Western attitudes assisted the new leadership in keeping the coalition together. Both the Russian economic recovery and the renewed threat of international terrorism made Russia important in the eyes of Western leaders. Russia's energy supplies were becoming critical in European economies, and Russian intelligence was now available to assist in American efforts to crush terrorism in Afghanistan and other areas of central Asia. At home, Putin's vision resonated with the need to stabilize the economy and defeat terrorism in the Caucasus. Although the war in Chechnya had its own unique characteristics, many Russians saw parallels between the Chechen rebels and Al Qaeda. So did the Western leaders, who softened their rhetoric regarding Russian violations of human rights in Chechnya and acknowledged the significance of Russia in fighting the threat of international terrorism. As a result, Putin was able to restore the state ability to govern, initiate a far-reaching military reform, and centralize governing institutions. Medvedev preserved Putin's institutional legacy while working to make political and economic institutions more inclusive of Russia's increasingly active society.

Putin and Medvedev's ratings remained high as they each adopted the more assertive and cooperative vision, respectively. The West, too, has had an important role to play. While George W. Bush's global regime change strategy worked to shape Putin's assertiveness, Barack Obama's effort to "reset" relations with Russia made it possible for Medvedev to formulate his notion of alliances for modernization. As Russia continues to be influenced by Western ideas and practices, Western policymakers and public-opinion leaders ought to be sensitive to the perception of these influences in Russia. A better appreciation of Russia's cultural distinctness and foreign policy concerns may encourage Putin and his successors to move further toward long-term cooperation with Europe and the United States. On the other hand, a more unilateral and isolationist approach is more likely to push the new regime in the direction of suppressing opposition at home.

Finally, both renewed Western pressures and Russia's domestic vulnerabilities help to understand Putin's transformation toward "civilizational" and West-assertive foreign policy. In his perception, the United States and the European Union failed to address Russia's concerns under Medvedev, but remained determined to preserve the West-centered world. As new, non-Western powers rose to prominence, Russia sought to position itself as an independent cultural and political center in a multipolar and multi-civilizational world. The new course was reminiscent of Primakov's Great Power Balancing, but was taking place in a changed international environment.

Such were some of the key foreign policy challenges confronted by the Russian leaders. Each of the leaders sought to creatively respond to various external developments, particularly those initiated in the West. Some, like Gorbachev, Kozyrev, and—to a lesser extent—Medvedev, wanted to engage the West in essentially liberal projects and to demonstrate their willingness to bring Russia into the family of Western nations. These leaders expressed Russia's eagerness to be recognized by the West as one of its own, and they saw the West as driven by essentially liberal motivations to spread justice and freedom in the world. Others, like Primakov and Putin, while avoiding direct confrontation with the West, sought to reassert Russia's power. Unlike their liberal predecessors, they were suspicious of the West's power motivations—both geopolitical and geoeconomic—and wanted to restore Russian national pride and independence. Russia faced multiple foreign challenges and opportunities—dangers of arms races, promises of post–Cold War economic and security cooperation, NATO expansion, and threats of global terrorism. Confronted with those challenges and opportunities, some leaders, in Albert Sorel's memorable formulation, arranged "their policy to suit the realities of the world," while others imagined "the world to suit their policy."[3] There will certainly be many other external challenges ahead of Russia, and they are likely to lead to other creative visions of national interest and foreign policy strategy. It is, as the same thinker put it some century ago, "the eternal dispute."

LESSONS FOR RUSSIA

What lessons can Russia learn from the past twenty years of its foreign policy? Are there particular steps it should take, or abstain from taking, that would preserve and enhance its status in the world?

Staying Engaged

First and foremost, it is important that in adjusting to new external challenges and solving its more specific domestic problems, Russia stay engaged with the world in general, and the West in particular. Lack of acceptance by the West should not prompt Russian leaders to take an isolationist path; rather, it should encourage them to double their efforts to explain their international policies as consistent with their vision of a global world. Isolationism cannot be practical in a world that has grown increasingly global in terms of both new opportunities and new threats. Russia should not deprive itself of new opportunities to participate in global flows of information, capital, and labor. Nor can it fully shield itself against new diseases or types of violence, or other crises of a transnational nature.

Isolationism, particularly an anti-Western one, remains strong in Russia. Hard-line Civilizationists, as well as some Statists, continue to argue that Russia is destined to oppose the West's civilizational and political influences across the globe. These forces insist on viewing the world in black and white terms and refuse to acknowledge that many of Russia's interests are best accomplished through participation in international organizations and joint activities. They continue to practice the old maxim "the enemy of my enemy is my friend" by recommending that Russia support anti-Western forces and work against those who are supportive of the West. In the post-Western world, these forces may become more

powerful especially if this world proves to be more unstable and dangerous than the world of the U.S. unipolarity. The former Soviet region has
emerged as an especially contested area in this respect, and the Russia-
Georgia conflict and Russia's annexation of Crimea confirmed failure of
international law to preserve peace in the Caucasus and Eastern Europe.

Despite all the flawed policies of New Thinking and Integration with
the West, the general effort of these philosophies to move away from
anti-Western isolationism must be recognized. One should remember that
before their failures, each of these courses had had a broad social appeal
and expressed some deep Russian aspirations. These aspirations must not
be neglected in the future, and they can be assessed based on the criteria
of security, welfare, and identity. Russians supported the vision of New
Thinking because it promised to prevent a threat of nuclear war and to
reform the heavily militarized economy. The society was eager to replace
the rigid economic and political system with one that would be more open
to the world. In addition, a considerable part of Soviet society identified
itself with the West culturally. Many in the post-Stalin generation saw the
need to move beyond the discourse of "irreconcilable contradictions"
between socialism and capitalism, and were open to ideas and cultural
products from Europe and the United States. Just as many Russians had
initially supported New Thinking, they did not initially oppose the strategy of Integration with the West. That strategy, too, was appealing for its
openness to the world. It was no accident that in being hard on Gorbachev
for his lack of domestic economic reforms, Yeltsin and Kozyrev took the
New Thinking as their point of departure in building relationships with
the West.

The post-Kozyrev Great Power Balancing did not mean to return to the
Soviet-like isolationism. Indeed, its principal architect, Yevgeni Primakov,
had been a New Thinking supporter and a member of Gorbachev's close
circle of trusted advisers. Yet, the strategy of balancing the United States
and building a multipolar world proved to contain elements of isolationism, some of which were unnecessary and did not serve Russia well.
Brought up in the tradition of Soviet class-based geopolitics, the father of
Great Power Balancing continued to be a geopolitical thinker and thought
more about defending his country's political independence and security
perimeter than about Russia's economic opportunities. Condemning
NATO's enlargement decision was one thing, but attempting to integrate
the former Soviet region at the expense of Russia's scarce resources in
response to the enlargement was an entirely different matter. The post-
Soviet integration was almost explicitly geopolitically driven and was
viewed by many as an isolationist-minded project rather than an
engagement-minded one. Along the same lines, developing closer economic and political cooperation with non-Western nations in Asia and the

Muslim world was fully justified and appropriate, but inviting them into an essentially anti-American balancing coalition was misleading and counterproductive. Putin's attempts to contain Western influences in the world can have only a limited effect if they are pursued from weak domestic foundations and without coordination with major non-Western powers. In addition, within the globalized world, staying engaged is not just an option, but a foreign policy imperative.

The vision of Russia as Eurasia, if pursued at the expense of Russia's ties with Europe, is also a flawed one. Insistence on Eurasia as anti-American and anti-European did a disservice to Primakov. Even if his own approach was more refined and pragmatic than that of the hard-liners, embracing Eurasia as a traditionally geopolitical notion added to Western perceptions of Russia's new foreign policy as essentially isolationist and could not resonate with the majority of the Russian public. "Western" and "Eurasian" coexist and overlap within the Russian psyche. Russia continues to be a multicultural, multiethnic, and multireligious community that has coexisted and interacted with the Asian and Middle Eastern region. That alone qualifies it to be a "Eurasian power." Putin's new initiative of building the Eurasian Union therefore has a certain public appeal and a chance to be sustained if it is pursued not at the expense of Russia's European-rich experience.

Following a National Path

It is no less important that in staying engaged with the world, Russian leaders do not lose sight of what has historically made Russia a special cultural community. Historically, Russia has played a vital role in European developments, while preserving special relations with Asia and the Muslim world. This special geopolitical and geocultural location has not harmed Russia's own identity development—the Russians have learned from their neighbors, while remaining a community with a distinct culture and history.

Globalization, too, is unlikely to erase Russia's distinctiveness, yet it does present the great challenge of finding an appropriate national niche in the new world. Russia must take advantage of the increased global flow of knowledge, goods, and capital. At the same time it must avoid some highly divisive social, economic, and political consequences of globalization, and that requires a considerable national creativity and imagination. The negative consequences of globalization are now visible everywhere. Instead of the earlier expected convergence of cultures and state policies in the world, scholars have observed new cleavages and divergences. Globalization has brought new poverty and socioeconomic divisions. It has created new areas of violence and lawlessness. It has reactivated arms races. And it has enacted new and intensified some old processes of cultural reformulations. Instead of relying on the protection and welfare of Western hegemony, nations often seek refuge in reformulating their interests to better protect their societies and readjust to their regional environments.[4] The struggle of the European Union to preserve its unity and cohesiveness after 2009 serves to validate this point. To Russia, this struggle for sustaining the European economy reminded it that the new regional and global arrangements may highlight and accentuate national differences, rather than reduce their significance. In the process of adjustment to new global challenges, institutional and cultural advantages are no less important than comparative and competitive economic advantages.

Russia's foreign policy, too, needs to reflect the realities of the increasingly global and yet persistently diverse world. Global adjustment can be successful if it is selective and does not come at the expense of vital national institutions and values. Properly applied, such institutions and values should assist Russia in successfully responding to some new security, economic, and cultural challenges during the era of globalization. In security matters, Russia is confronted with threats of terrorism, weapons proliferation, ethnic conflicts, and drug trafficking in the highly volatile Eurasian region. In economic matters, Russia is presented with the new challenges of transnationalization of capital, labor, and energy. And in cultural affairs, Russia has to preserve its identity as it faces a sharply intensified inflow of Western movies, literature, and other cultural products. In responding to these challenges, Russians are likely to empower their state with sufficient capabilities to formulate a strategy of global adjustment. While the state's areas of responsibility must be clearly defined, a strong state has been a part of national history and is likely to remain as such. It is through state leadership that a nation, like Russia, has a chance to successfully respond to the above-noted political, economic, and cultural challenges.

Russia's experience of the last twenty years suggests some errors, as well as accomplishments, in constructing a national path to a globalizing world. New Thinking and, especially, Integration with the West did not withstand the test of time partly because their proponents overestimated the liberal nature of globalization and underestimated the forces of divisiveness and conflict in the world. While advocating global engagement, they neglected the significance of national history and identity. As a result, their international engagement was not sufficiently supported at home, and it came at a very high price of domestic political, social, and economic disintegration. Both New Thinkers and Integrationists sought to solve their domestic problems by obtaining external material and institutional recognition. Both lost control over the economy—Gorbachev as a result of destroying the old centralized system of state orders without having a new one in place, and Yeltsin as a result of introducing price liberalization under the monopolistic structural environment. Both leaders had been stripped of some of their political power—Gorbachev ceded power to radical Westernizers, and Yeltsin made serious concessions to Statists and incorporated them into the ruling establishment. Most importantly, both had little faith in the ability of the state to lead the process of global adjustment. This, too, was a consequence of placing a much higher premium on transnational and global developments than on searching for a national formula of adaptation to these developments. Integrationism was especially guilty of holding an inflexible interpretation of some fundamental phenomena of the contemporary world, such as state power, regional economic differentiation, and cultural diversity. Rather than trying to rethink these phenomena and their role under contemporary conditions, Integrationists often denied their significance altogether under the pretext of the new era of the West-controlled global convergence.

Today, partly as the result of this earlier national amnesia, Westernist proponents of Russian foreign policy have considerably lost their domestic influence. In domestic foreign policy discourse, Westernizers continue to be active and visible, partly because they are in a position to draw public attention to impressive developments in the West, and partly because of the West's material support of their efforts. Western institutions, such as the Carnegie Endowment for International Peace, are particularly active in promoting the Westernizers' vision in Russia, and their experts in Moscow are influential participants in all major foreign policy discussions. The past failures have signaled, however, that the vision of Integration with the West is unlikely to succeed as long as it continues to view national tradition as a liability, rather than as an asset in global adjustment.

Great Power Balancing and Pragmatic Cooperation showed greater sensitivity to the national tradition in searching for a path to globalization. Primakov's major accomplishment had to do with restoring some important attributes of foreign policy autonomy. Working under the conditions of Russia's continuous economic decline and under a president committed to the previously articulated Westernist vision, the father of Great Power Balancing was able to take and sustain a considerably more independent line in Russia's relations with Yugoslavia, Iraq, and the former Soviet region. He also showed that Russia was in a position to improve its security environment in the former Soviet Union, once it had been willing to invest important diplomatic resources in it. Continuing to be engaged in the tough defense of what Primakov saw as Russia's national interest, while maintaining dialogue with the West, became an important example for Putin to follow. While softening Primakov's preoccupation with geopolitics and strengthening the emphasis on globalization and economic modernization, Putin followed the line of defending national interests as different from those of Western nations. Sensitive to the national tradition, the initiator of Pragmatic Cooperation differentiated himself and his strategy of globalization sharply from those associated with New Thinking and Integration with the West.

After being reelected to a third term as president, Putin has sought to revive Russia's national values and interests from which to engage the Western nations in joint economic and security projects. He indicated a desire to develop Russia's ties with the West, but not at the expense of Russia's own interests. This dilemma manifested itself in Ukraine when Moscow sacrificed its relations with the West to assert its interests in Crimea and the eastern part of Ukraine. The course resulted in political confrontation and mutual economic sanctions, yet Russia is likely to remain assertive in those areas it sees vital for preserving its values and interests. For example, Putin indicated his displeasure with the United States' stance on the Missile Defense System. He stood firm on Russia's distinct position on the Middle East by refusing to support the West-sponsored UNSC resolutions. And he continued bilateral pressures on Ukraine and other former Soviet states in attempting to strengthen Russia's influence in Eurasia. Russia's foreign policy under Putin is therefore likely to combine elements of cooperation and assertiveness.

Overall, Russia confirms the old wisdom that foreign policy is as much a science of revealing some patterns of behavior as it is an art of following them by creatively synthesizing national and global imperatives. Both vision and power are critical here—vision for a reality-grounded strategy formulation, and power for its implementation. Or, if we are to apply Carr's terms, both utopia and reality, free will and determinism, are essential in successful foreign policymaking.

LESSONS FOR THE WEST

Russia is sufficiently big and powerful, and that limits Western ability to influence its developments. Vast territory, enormous natural resources and military capabilities, and a significant political and diplomatic weight in the world have allowed and will continue to allow Russia considerable room for foreign policy maneuvering. It is hard to believe that the West will ever possess enough power to fully determine the shape and direction of Russia's developments. Yet, as this book has argued, one should not take lightly the role of Western ideas. When united, the West has been and will be influencing Russia in important ways. It is only when divided over issues, such as military intervention in Iraq, that the West would be unlikely to exercise this influence. The West remains Russia's significant

Other, and it should act with this in mind by avoiding serious disagreements and sending Russia a unified, rather than conflicted, message. One lesson we can learn from the past twenty years is that engagement, reciprocity, and patience should be the main principles guiding Western actions toward this nation. Carefully applied, these principles in time can bring more security and stability to the world.

Staying Engaged

The first principle that should guide Western actions toward Russia is engagement. A number of Western policymakers, particularly within the Clinton administration, well understood the significance of engaging Russia. Clinton felt "if Russia goes bad . . . we'll be back here talking about reversing our defense cuts and spending really big money to wage a new cold war."[5] In the late 1980s–early 1990s, many in Russia, too, believed in Western engagement and even predicated Russia's success on it. This attitude was far from a purely selfish expectation. A genuine Russia-West engagement is critical for making progress in arms control, counterterrorism, and the establishment of regional security arrangements in Eurasia. It is equally critical for developing cooperation in economic and energy matters.

Yet, the West's engagement with Russia has been modest. The majority of the political class in Western nations continued to mistrust Russia well after the Soviet disintegration and showed interest mainly in reducing nuclear threats coming from the region. Despite Gorbachev's and Yeltsin's expectations, the West never introduced anything remotely similar to the post–World War II Marshall Plan. Many in Russia and the West evaluated the absence of such a plan as a lack of engagement and a flaw of strategic significance on the West's part. In some ways, the West used Russia's ideological and psychological dependence on its approval and recognition, promising Moscow consistent engagement but limiting such engagement to the bare minimum. The Western leaders went only as far as to extend Russia some symbolic forms of recognition, such as membership in the G-7, while abstaining from more serious commitments to transforming the postcommunist economic and political institutions.

The efforts by President Barack Obama to "reset" relations with Russia promised a new way of engaging it, but proved to be limited and misguided. The fact that Obama's approach evolved from the "reset" to sanctions is of course a partial responsibility of the Kremlin. However, the U.S. side too bears responsibility for not trying a mutually beneficial engagement. A number of important issues that Russia views as of key significance remained unresolved. The Kremlin was critical of the U.S. proposal to develop the Missile Defense System jointly with the Europeans but separately from Russia. The Western nations were rhetorically supportive of the former Soviet states' bid for NATO membership, whereas Russia maintained its right to protect its interests in the former Soviet region. At the end of 2010, Moscow shelved its initiative to negotiate a new security treaty with European nations after not getting any support from NATO officials and the United States. The Kremlin also criticized the West's handling of the Middle Eastern crisis by going after the regime change in Libya and Syria. By the time the Western nations and Russia confronted the Ukrainian revolution, the Kremlin had little trust left in the other side's intentions.

Opponents of engagement with Russia in the West were equally strong and got even stronger since the Ukraine crisis. Some see problems with Russia's human rights record under Putin. Others charge that Russia presents a threat to the West's strategic interests and collaborates with dangerous regimes. Still others point to Russia's recent activism in the former Soviet region, seeing in it expressions of the Kremlin's new imperialism and attempts to muscle its way with the newly independent states at the expense of their sovereignty. In the wake of the Russia-Georgia war, U.S. secretary of state Condoleezza Rice compared Russia's role to the Soviet Union's invasion of Czechoslovakia in 1968, while Moscow's decision to incorporate Crimea prompted former secretary of state Hillary Clinton to compare it to those of Adolf Hitler before World War II.[6]

In both cases, the implication was that not only Russia had to be isolated, but also punished for its "aggression." Instead of engaging in a dialogue with the Kremlin, the West imposed sanctions against the Russian economy, offered military training for the Ukrainian army, and began to strengthen NATO forces on Russia's western border. Events were developing in a direction similar to what happened after World War II, when the two sides found themselves locked in a race to secure Europe on their own terms. It remains to be seen whether Putin's attempt to shift attention from Europe and engage the United States into a joint antiterrorist operation in Syria since late September 2015 will change the situation.

Punishing or isolating Russia is not likely to discipline it, however. Russia continues to be in a position not to yield to pressures from the West. Against expectations, such pressures are likely to strengthen anti-Western Russian nationalists and push Russia further away from the Western nations. Nationalists need an image of the West as a threat—they are dependent on it for their own survival. They will only be grateful to Western politicians for assisting them in constructing such an image. The examples of NATO's expansion, military interventions in Kosovo and the Middle East, as well as sanctions against the Russian economy, teach us that ignoring Russia or viewing it as a threat leads to a more defiant, not a more cooperative, Russia. Continuing along these lines risks getting

Russia off track by improving the position of nationalist forces and providing "proof" that the West is really interested in stripping Russia of its
international status, not in strengthening its economy and democratic
institutions.

Engaging on Mutually Acceptable Terms

Engagement will be especially effective when conducted on a reciprocal or
mutually acceptable basis. Anything short of reciprocity might result in
cheating by the sides involved. Hegemonic engagement on Western terms
will come at the price of Russia's own interests and perceptions. As
Thomas Graham wrote, "it is not Russia's strength that generates and
feeds the fear of it, it is weakness of the West and its lack of confidence."[7]
Rather than trying to dictate policies, the United States should acknowledge a strong and confident Russia that acts as a responsible protector of
its interests in the world. On the other hand, attempts to appease Russia
by jeopardizing the West's own interests are not likely to last either,
because of a lack of sufficient support within Western societies. Former
Cold War enemies will develop the required trust only when they openly
engage in direct negotiations of mutually acceptable forms of cooperation.

Unfortunately, the support in the West for hegemonic engagement
with Russia is stronger than for reciprocal engagement. Many in the West
are convinced that they are doing Russia a great favor by insisting on the
universal applicability of Western market democracy and pressing ahead
with making Russia in its own image. Russia's insistence on its own
interests and cultural specifics often gets dismissed as reflecting the views
of remnants of the Soviet "totalitarianism" and anti-Western nationalism.
Despite the West's decline relative to rise of non-Western economies,
many in the Western part of the world continue to believe that Western
civilization is in a position to teach the rest of the world about economic
and political institutions as well as moral standards. This attitude remains
a serious obstacle to the mutual understanding required for reciprocal
engagement.

As Western nations displayed the noted hegemonic attitude, Russia's
negative perception of the West grew strong. In particular, Russians have
resented the expansion of the U.S. and the EU economic, political, and
security institutions in Eurasia and elsewhere, while dismissing Russia's
opposition as pure paranoia. The conflict with Georgia and Ukraine, too,
became possible in part because the balance of power in the region had
long ago been violated by NATO's and the EU's decisions to expand its
infrastructure at the expense of Russia's interests. International law was
silent in the Caucasus and Ukraine just as it had been previously silent
when Yugoslavia and Iraq were attacked by Western powers without

approval of the United Nations of which Russia is a member. Similarly, the Western nations frequently engage in criticizing Russia's human rights record without considering how unpopular such criticisms are inside Russia.[8]

A genuinely successful engagement is therefore difficult to design and maintain. Given the history of hostilities between Russia and the West and divergent current interests, there will always be differences in the two nations' approaches to solving existing problems. Nevertheless, in light of the alternatives of an isolated and resentful Russia, engagement on mutually acceptable terms is worth a serious effort. When such engagement is in place, the two sides are able to deliver important results such as the new START in 2010 or the agreement on removing chemical weapons from Syria in 2013 or the nuclear deal on Iran in Vienna in July 2015.[9]

Tempering Expectations

In addition to engagement and reciprocity in relations with Russia, the West ought to be patient and not expect miracles. Unreasonable expectations about Russia have not been uncommon in the past and should not be a guide in the future. After the fall of the Berlin Wall, many hoped for Russia to quickly leave its past behind and to emerge as a market democracy with special relationships to Western nations. The reality proved different, and Russia's modernization so far has not really entailed Westernization. In the economic realm, Russia has built not a free-market model of capitalism, but rather an oligarchical capitalism, with the economy largely controlled by and divided among former high-ranking state and Communist Party officials. In the area of political and legal institutions, Russia developed a superpresidential system with few effective checks and balances. Utilizing this system, Putin tightened his grip over the legislature, party building, regions, and electronic media. As far as the relationship with the West is concerned, many polls indicate that many Russians see the West as a potential threat, rather than a friend or strategic partner.

The West bears a share of the responsibility for these unattractive outcomes. After all, Western officials pushed aggressively for shock therapy as a model for economic reform in Russia. They also deepened their relationships with Yeltsin beyond a reasonable level and supported him even when he relied on military force in relations with parliament and the rebellious republic of Chechnya. In the long run, the perception of Yeltsin as a "good guy" fighting "bad guys" or the "red-brown" opposition did a great disservice to Russia, and it worsened the image of the West. The choice to expand NATO by excluding Russia from it, despite available alternative ways to provide security in Europe, also did not and could not improve Western credibility in the Russians' eyes. Finally, the United States' strategy of global regime change served to exacerbate the Kremlin's perception of security vulnerability and regional instability.

To change the skeptical attitudes of Russians and the Kremlin, it is important to formulate some long-term objectives and to organize relationships with Russia with these objectives in mind. First, nations should select the bilateral relationships' most vital and pressing issues that would reflect broad social needs and the interests of whole societies. For example, the issue of domestic transformation should be put on the agenda only if it reflects the desires of both Russian and Western societies. Today, many in Russia do not see internal developments as a basis for a long-term relationship; instead, they emphasize the significance of security issues, such as counterterrorism and nuclear arms reduction. The second and related point is that Western policymakers must avoid developing exclusive relationships with either the ruling elite or the opposition. The personalization of relationships with Russian presidents may contribute to the emergence of a regime that will be only rhetorically pro-Western, but in reality will alienate the majority of Russians and serve the interests of very narrow political circles. On the other hand, attempts to build ties with opposition at the expense of the Kremlin will serve to strengthen the impression that the West engages in policies of regime change in Russia.

This way of determining a Western-Russian agenda is likely to take time, but over time it may produce more predictable relationships and help to weaken the current image of the West as overly pushy and opportunistic. As the world moves further into the twenty-first century, it will be increasingly important to recognize the economic, political, and geostrategic significance of Russia as a potential partner.

NOTES

1. Edward Hallett Carr, *The Twenty Years' Crisis, 1919–1939* (New York: Harper & Row, 1964), 11.

2. As quoted in Andrew Kuchins' notes from a meeting with Medvedev at the Valdai Discussion Club in September 2008 (Georgie Anne Geyer, "Russia First to Test New President," *Chicago Tribune,* November 14, 2008, www.chicagotribune .com/news/nationworld/chi-oped1114geyernov14,0,7013815.story).

3. Carr, *The Twenty Years' Crisis,* 11.

4. On national searches for strategies of adaptation to the global economy, see Erik Helleiner and Andreas Pickel, eds., *Economic Nationalism in a Globalizing World* (Ithaca, NY: Cornell University Press, 2005).

5. Strobe Talbott, *The Russia House* (New York: Random House, 2002), 58.

6. Philip Rucker, "Hillary Clinton says Putin's actions are like 'what Hitler did back in the '30s'," *Washington Post*, March 5, 2014, http://www.washingtonpost .com/news/post-politics/wp/2014/03/05/hillary-clinton-says-putins-action -are-like-what-hitler-did-back-in-the-30s/.

7. Thomas Graham, "Dialektika sily i slabosti," *Vedomosti*, June 29, 2007.

8. For some origins and consequences of such criticism, see Andrei P. Tsygankov and David Parker, "The Securitization of Democracy: The Freedom House Ratings of Russia," *European Security* 24, no. 1 (2015).

9. "Iran Nuclear Talks: 'Historic' Agreement Struck," *BBC News*, 14 July 2015, http://www.bbc.com/news/world-middle-east-33518524.

Further Reading

OFFICIAL VIEWS

Kozyrev, A. V. "Russia: A Chance for Survival." *Foreign Affairs* 71, no. 2 (1992).

Lavrov, S. "Russia and the World in the 21st Century." *Russia in Global Affairs* 3 (July–September, 2008).

Medvedev, D. Speech at meeting with Russian ambassadors and permanent representatives in international organizations. July 12, 2010, Kremlin.ru.

Primakov, Ye. *Russian Crossroads: Toward the New Millennium*. New Haven: Yale University Press, 2004.

Putin, V. "Rossiya na rubezhe tysyacheletiy." *Nezavisimaya gazeta*, December 30, 1999.

———. Speech at the Munich Conference on Security Policy. Munich, February 10, 2007. Kremlin.ru.

———. "Russia and the Changing World." *Moskovskiye novosti*, February 26, 2012.

———. Speech at meeting with Russian ambassadors and permanent representatives in international organizations. Moscow, July 9, 2012. Kremlin.ru.

———. Meeting of the Valdai International Discussion Club, September 19, 2013. http://president.kremlin.ru.

———. Address by President of the Russian Federation, Moscow, Kremlin, March 18, 2014. http://eng.kremlin.ru/news/6889.

———. Poslaniye Prezidenta Federal'nomu Sobraniyu Rossiyskoy Federatsii, December, 2014. http://president.kremlin.ru.

BOOKS

Allison, R. *Russia, the West, and Military Intervention*. Oxford: Oxford University Press, 2013.

Balmaceda, M. M. *The Politics of Energy Dependency: Ukraine, Belarus, and Lithuania Between Domestic Oligarchs and Russian Pressure*. Toronto: University of Toronto Press, 2013.

Black, J. L., and Michael Johns, eds. *The Return of the Cold War: Ukraine, the West and Russia*. London: Routledge, 2016.

Cadier, D., and M. Light, eds. *Russia's Foreign Policy: Ideas, Domestic Politics and External Relations*. London: Palgrave, 2015.

Cooley, A. *Great Games, Local Rules: US-Russia-China Competition in Central Asia*. New York: Oxford University Press, 2012.

Donaldson, R. H., and J. L. Nogee. *The Foreign Policy of Russia: Changing Systems, Enduring Interests*. Armonk, NY: M. E. Sharpe, 2009.

Freire, M. R., and R. E. Kanet, eds. *Russia and Its Near Neighbours: Identity, Interests and Foreign Policy*. Houndmills, UK: Palgrave Macmillan, 2012.

Hopf, T. *Social Construction of International Politics: Identities and Foreign Policies, Moscow, 1955 and 1999*. Ithaca, NY: Cornell University Press, 2002.

Legvold, R., ed. *Russian Foreign Policy in the 21st Century and the Shadow of the Past*. New York: Columbia University Press, 2007.

Libman, A., and E. Vinokurov. *Eurasian Integration: Challenges of Transcontinental Regionalism*. London: Palgrave, 2012.

Lo, B. *Axis of Convenience: Moscow, Beijing and the New Geopolitics*. Washington, DC: Brookings Institution, 2008.

Lukyanov, F., ed. *Rossiya v global'noi politike: Novye pravila ili igra bez pravil*. Moscow: Eksmo, 2015.

Mankoff, J. *Russian Foreign Policy: The Return of Great Power Politics*. 2nd ed. Lanham, MD: Rowman & Littlefield, 2011.

Marsh, C., and N. Gvosdev. *Russian Foreign Policy: Interests, Vectors, and Sectors*. London: CQ Press, 2013.

Molchanov, M. A. *Eurasian Regionalism and Russian Foreign Policy*. London: Ashgate, 2015.

Mouritzen, H., and A. Wivel. *Explaining Foreign Policy: International Diplomacy and the Russo-Georgian War*. Boulder, CO: Lynne Rienner, 2012.

Rangsimaporn, P. *Russia as an Aspiring Great Power in East Asia: Perceptions and Policies from Yeltsin to Putin*. Houndmills, UK: Palgrave Macmillan, 2009.

Rozman, G. *The Sino-Russian Challenge to the World Order*. Stanford: Stanford University Press, 2014.

Sakwa, R. *Frontline Ukraine*. London: I.B. Tauris, 2014.

Shakleyina, T. A., ed. *Vneshnyaya politika i bezopasnost' sovremennoi Rossiyi, 1991–2002*. 4 vol. Moskva: ROSSPEN, 2002.

Slobodchikoff, M. *Building Hegemonic Order Russia's Way: Order, Stability, and Predictability in the Post-Soviet Space*. Lanham, MD: Lexington Books, 2014.

Sotiriou, S. *Russian Energy Strategy in the European Union, the Former Soviet Union Region, and China*. Lanham, MD: Lexington Books, 2014.

Stent, A. *The Limits of Partnership: U.S.-Russian Relations in the Twenty-First Century*. Princeton: Princeton University Press, 2013.

Trenin, D. *Post-Imperium: A Eurasian Story*. Washington, DC: Carnegie Endowment for International Peace, 2011.

Tsygankov, A. P. *Russia and the West from Alexander to Putin: Honor in International Relations.* Cambridge: Cambridge University Press, 2012.

White, S., and V. Feklyunina. *Identities and Foreign Policies in Russia, Ukraine, and Belarus: The Other Europes.* London: Palgrave Macmillan, 2014.

Zimmerman, W. *The Russian People and Foreign Policy: Russian Elite and Mass Perspectives, 1993–2000.* Princeton: Princeton University Press, 2002.

ARTICLES, REPORTS

Casula, P. "Russia's and Europe's Borderlands." *Problems of Post-Communism* 61, no. 6 (2014). http://dx.doi.org/10.2753/PPC1075-8216610601

Forsberg, T., R. Heller, and R. Wolf, eds. "Status and Emotions in Russian Foreign Policy." A special issue of *Communist and Post-Communist Studies* 47, nos. 3–4 (2014).

Haukkala, H. "From Cooperative to Contested Europe? The Conflict in Ukraine as a Culmination of a Long-Term Crisis in EU–Russia Relations." *Journal of Contemporary European Studies* 23, no. 1 (2015).

Kaczmarski, M. "Domestic Sources of Russia's China Policy." *Problems of Post-Communism* 59, no. 2 (March/April 2012).

Kanet, R. E., and M. R. Freire, eds. "Russia in the New International Order: Theories, Arguments, Debates." A special issue of *International Politics* (July 2012).

Krickovic, A. "Imperial Nostalgia or Prudent Geopolitics? Russia's Efforts to Reintegrate the Post-Soviet Space in Geopolitical Perspective." *Post-Soviet Affairs*, vol. 30 (2014). http://dx.doi.org/10.1080/1060586X.2014.900975.

Kuhrt, N. "Russia and Asia-Pacific: From 'Competing' to 'Complementary' Regionalisms?" *Politics* 34, no.2 (2014). doi: 10.1111/1467-9256.12053.

Kuhrt, N., ed. "Russia and the World." A special issue of *Europe-Asia Studies* (July 2012).

Laruelle, M. *The "Russian World": Russia's Soft Power and Geopolitical Imagination.* Washington, DC: Center on Global Interests, 2015.

Lo, B. *Frontiers Old and New: Russia's Policy in Central Asia.* Paris: IFRI, Russia/NIS Center, 2015.

Lukin, A. "Eurasian Integration and the Clash of Values." *Survival: Global Politics and Strategy* 56, no. 3 (2014).

Malashenko, A. *The Fight for Influence: Russia in Central Asia.* Carnegie Endowment for International Peace, 2013.

Monaghan, A. *A 'New Cold War'? Abusing History, Misunderstanding Russia.* London: Chatham House, Russia and Eurasia Programme, 2015.

Nation, R. C. "Reset or Rerun? Sources of Discord in Russian–American Relations." *Communist and Post-Communist Studies* 45, nos. 3–4 (2012). http://dx.doi.org/10.1016/j.postcomstud.2012.07.011.

Petro, N. N. *Russia's Orthodox Soft Power.* New York: Carnegie Council, 2015. http://www.carnegiecouncil.org/publications/articles_papers_reports/727.

Sakwa, R. "The Death of Europe? Continental Fates after Ukraine." *International Affairs* 91, no. 3 (2015).

Simons, G. Russian public diplomacy in the 21st century: Structure, means and message. *Public Relations Review* 40, no. 3 (September 2014). http://dx.doi.org/10.1016/j.pubrev.2014.03.002.

Timofeyev, I. N. *Mirovoi poryadok ili mirovaya anarkhiya?* (World order or world anarchy). Moscow: Russian International Affairs Council, 2014.

Toward the Great Ocean—3: Creating Central Eurasia. The Valdai Club's Report, 2015.

Trenin, D. *From Greater Europe to Greater Asia? The Sino-Russian Entente.* Carnegie Moscow Center, 2015.

Tsygankov, A. P. "Vladimir Putin's Last Stand: The Sources of Russia's Ukraine Policy." *Post-Soviet Affairs* 31, no. 4 (2015).

Tudoroiu, T. "The reciprocal constitutive features of a Middle Eastern partnership: The Russian-Syrian bilateral relations." *Journal of Eurasian Studies* 6 (2015).

Welt, C., and S. Charap, eds. "Making Sense of Russian Foreign Policy." A special issue of *Problems of Post-Communism* 62, no. 2 (2015).

Wilson, J. L. "Cultural Statecraft and Civilizational and Cultural Themes as a Component of Russian and Chinese Domestic and Foreign Policy." *Politics* (2015).

Ziegler, C. E. "Contesting the Responsibility to Protect." *International Studies Perspectives* (2014). doi: 10.1111/insp.12085.

———. "Russian–American Relations: From Tsarism to Putin." *International Politics* 51, no. 6 (2014).

INTERNET SITES

Eurasia Daily Monitor, Jamestown Foundation. http://jamestown.org/edm.

Foreign Ministry of Russian Federation. http://www.mid.ru.

Johnson's Russia List, Center for Defense Information. http://www.cdi.org/russia/johnson/default.cfm.

Radio Free Europe/Radio Liberty. http://www.rferl.org

Russia in Global Affairs. http://eng.globalaffairs.ru.

Russia's President. www.kremlin.ru.

Russian and Eurasian Program, Carnegie Endowment for International Peace or Moscow Center. http://www.carnegieendowment.org/programs/russia/.

Topics for Discussion
or Simulation

Depending on their objectives, instructors can organize discussions around general or more specific topics related to Russia's foreign policy. For instance, one could assess a strategic international direction of Russia in terms of available courses of action as advocated by the Kremlin's critics at home.

Alternatively, a discussion can begin at the micro level of a specific foreign policy decision and its explanation by a variety of external, domestic, and psychological factors. Here, key questions should be (1) what forces/factors influenced the decision; and (2) what alternative course was available, if any.

Both options should assist in deepening student understanding of Russia-specific forces at play, as well as concepts commonly used in analysis of foreign policy and theory of international relations. What follows is a tentative list of possible themes and decisions broken down by relevant chapters. In each case, themes and questions may be specified further, particularly if the instructor assigns students specific actors and roles to play (simulation). Additional readings may be assigned as well.

CH. 1. UNDERSTANDING CHANGE AND CONTINUITY IN RUSSIA'S FOREIGN POLICY

Please discuss Russia's strategic choices from perspectives alternative to that of the Kremlin. Select one such perspective—pro-Western liberal, Civilizationist, or another—and then propose some historical intersections at which the Russian state could have acted differently. Examples might include state behavior before World War I and World War II or others. Consider what a different course of action could have meant for the country's overall direction and relations with specific foreign countries. Which policy course would have been best? Why or why not?

CH. 2. THE COLD WAR CRISIS AND SOVIET NEW THINKING

Strategic Alternatives: the Soviet conservative reforms at home and a limited dialogue with the West.

Individual Decision: Gorbachev's military withdrawal from Europe and acceptance of Germany's reunification, 1989.

CH. 3. THE POST–COLD WAR EUPHORIA AND RUSSIA'S LIBERAL WESTERNISM

Strategic Alternatives: limited market reforms at home, defense of great power and multipolar balance of power abroad.

Individual Decision: intervention in Moldova to prevent spread of violence and civil war, Spring–Summer 1992.

CH. 4. NEW SECURITY CHALLENGES AND GREAT POWER BALANCING

Strategic Alternatives: instead of trying to contain NATO expansion, focus on counterterrorist cooperation with the West.

Individual Decision: pressure on Serbia to accept Western conditions for peace after the NATO bombing campaign, June 1999.

CH. 5. THE WORLD AFTER SEPTEMBER 11 AND PRAGMATIC COOPERATION

Strategic Alternatives: continuation of Primakov's policy of multipolarity and reintegration of the former Soviet region.

Individual Decision: support for the United States following the 9/11 terrorist attacks, September 2001.

CH. 6. U.S. REGIME CHANGE STRATEGY AND GREAT POWER ASSERTIVENESS

Strategic Alternatives: continuation of Putin's earlier course of pragmatic cooperation with the West.

Individual Decision: official acceptance of the Orange Revolution in Ukraine, November 2004.

CH. 7. GLOBAL INSTABILITY AND RUSSIA'S VISION OF MODERNIZATION

Strategic Alternatives: return to Primakov's policy of building strategic ties with China and India.

Individual Decision: no veto on the UNSC resolution of the use of force against Libya, March 2011.

CH. 8. THE WEST, THE NON-WEST, AND RUSSIA'S "CIVILIZATIONAL" TURN

Strategic Alternatives: continuation of Medvedev's course of modernization and deepening ties with the West.

Individual Decision: military support and annexation of Crimea, February–March 2014.

CH. 9. CONCLUSIONS AND LESSONS

Strategic Alternatives for the West: patient, interest-based engagement with lowered pressures for democratization and protection of human rights.

Individual Decision: the U.S. president's decision to decline invitation to travel to Moscow to commemorate the 70th anniversary of Great Victory over Nazi Germany.

Index

Abkhazia, 165, 176n62, 201–02, 209, 216, 223, 225
Adamishin, Anatoli, 155
Afghanistan, 35, 157, 165, 178, 179, 196, 210, 218, 221, 227, 235, 255; anti-terrorism efforts, Russian assistance with, 201, 215, 244, 267; border patrol, 120, 224; Gorbachev, withdrawing troops from, 43, 45, 262; Kozyrev visit, 78; Putin, support of U.S. actions in, 145, 147, 149–50, 169, 263; stabilization efforts, 21, 215, 225, 244, 251; Taliban regime, 48, 115
Africa, 43, 98
Ahmadinejad, Mahmoud, 192
Akayev, Askar, 165
Akhromeyev, Sergei, 45
Albright, Madeleine, 112
Alexander I and II, 2–3, 5, 6, 9, 102
Alexander III, 3
alliance of oligarchs and chekists, 20, 138
Alliances for Modernization (AM), 21, 23, 29, 213, 214, 227, 264, 265, 268
Al Qaeda, 150, 268
Ambartsumov, Yevgeni, 69, 87, 89
Andropov, Yuri, 52
Angarsk-Daqing project, 154
Angola, 35
Annan, Kofi, 167

antiballistic missile (ABM) treaty, 145, 147–48, 164, 264
Arab Spring, 264
Arato, Andrew, 60
Arbatov, Aleksei, 76
Armenia, 50, 86, 87, 88, 117, 156, 251; CSTO, as part of, 156, 159, 224; elections, 157, 164; nonparticipation in union treaty, 48–49; as a Russian ally, 162, 189, 200
arms control agreements, 5, 25, 47, 52, 54, 76
arms sales, 77, 107, 114, 115, 116, 126, 152–53, 191, 192, 216, 220
Asia, 6, 40, 81, 92, 127, 160, 191, 197, 227, 236, 254; Asian identity of Russia, 20, 102, 191; Asian regions, Russian neglect of, 73, 77–79, 140; Europe and Asia, Russia as bridge between, 70, 197; Putin and, 152, 189, 198, 200; Russia, maintaining relations with, 25, 28, 106–07, 210, 249, 265, 270–71
Asian and Pacific Economic Council (APEC), 219–20, 221
Asia-Pacific region, 50, 114, 126, 197, 219–21, 235, 238
al-Assad, Bashar, 222, 242–43, 245, 249, 250, 265

assertiveness. *See* Great Power Assertiveness
Association of Southeast Asian Nations (ASEAN), 114
Atambayev, Almazbek, 224
Atsayev, Said, 222
Austria, 3, 5, 247
autarchy, 42, 104
autocracy, 2, 3, 6, 18, 171, 200
autonomy, 17, 22, *54*, 81, 90, 91–92, 125, *127, 203, 227, 255*; Gorbachev, troubles with, 26, 53, 263; Pragmatic Cooperation, role in, 28, 168, *169*, 171; Primakov and, 27, 112, 126, 273; Putin, calculations regarding, 24, 149, 169; Ukraine, demanding an increase in, 175n59, 252
Azerbaijan, *49, 75, 86, 88*, 115, *117*, 157, 164, 186, 192, 193, 202, 226; European energy agreements, 195, 219; GUAM/GUUAM, membership in, 130, 158; recognition of separatist territory, 183

Baikonur Cosmodrome, 158
Baker, James, 78
Balkans: Putin, policy towards, 147–48; Russian humiliation over war, 108, 264; security crises, 107; Supreme Soviet, criticism of Balkans policy, 79–80; Western agenda in, 27, 76, 92, 111–13
Baltics, 51, 160, 166, 167, 247; gas and oil pipelines, 157, 194, 217; NATO and, 112, 121; nonparticipation in union treaty, 48–49
Basayev, Shamil, 136, 162
Belarus, *6, 49, 88, 117*, 156, 159, 164; CIS affiliation, *44*, 50, 83; Custom Union, as part of, 123, 224, 226, 251; economic agreement with Russia, 155, 158; energy needs, Russian involvement in, 157, 200; Putin and, 200, 264; Russia-Belarus Union, 112, 121, 158; Russian alliance, 119, 162, 187, 189
Berezovski, Boris, 139, 154, 182
Berlin Wall, 40, 46, 262, 278
Berlusconi, Silvio, 167
Beslan hostage situation, 162–63
Biden, Joe, 245, 247
Big Treaty, 121, 123, 126

bin Laden, Osama, 137, 141
Black Sea, 121, 194, 221, 224, 226, 244
Blair, Tony, 142
Bogdanov, Andrei, 182
Bolsheviks, 3, 10, 18, 32n27, 34, 35, 61, 138
Bosnia, 76, 80, 111, 148
Boston Marathon bomber, 245
Brazil, 136, 171, 235, 249
Brazil, Russia, India, China, and South Africa (BRICS) alliance, 213, 219, 222, 235, 248, 250, 264, 265
Brezhnev, Leonid, 7, *9*, 38
Brezhnev doctrine, 44, 45, 262
Britain, 5, 111, 137, *151*, 247
British International Society school, 106
British Petroleum, 148, 168, 182
Brunei, 137
Bucharest summit, 194, 201
Bukharin, Nikolai, 37, 266
Bulgaria, 194, 217
Burbulis, Gennadi, 61
Bush, George H. W., 26, *44*, 60, 75, 95n26
Bush, George W., 142, 161, 164, 167, 268; on good *vs.* evil, 136, 141, 144; Iraq war and, 111, 150, 151; Putin and, 147, 153
Buzgalin, Aleksandr, 142

capitalism, 6, 7, 8, 38, 91, 187, 214, 239, 270; Civilizationist views on, 34–35, *65*; Gorbachev and, 37, 39, 53, 66; liberal capitalism, 33, 60, 142, 157; New Thinking and, 40, 46; *nomenklatura*, embrace of, 62; oligarchic capitalism, 93, 141, 278; Putin and state-dominated capitalism, 182; Westernizers, urging adoption of, 19, 60
Carnegie Moscow Center, 187, 214, 239
Caspian area, 115, 153, 157, 158; Trans-Caspian pipelines, 116, 159, 193, 200, 216, 226
the Caucasus, 157, 165, 201, 223, 225; CIS troop withdrawal, 78; ethnic conflicts, 98, 120; instability in region, 203, 212, 251; international law, failing to preserve peace in, 270, 277–78; Northern Caucasus, 161, 162–63, 196, 212, 222; Russian foreign policy in region, 211, 264;

Russian military presence, 120–21, 158, 170, 209, 226; terrorism in region, 28, 136, 138, 161, 162–63, 202, *203*, 217, *227*, 267; TRASEKA corridor, 160; U.S. military presence, 143; Westernist course in region, *91*

central Asia, 78, 83, 115, 116, 143, 145, 160, 161, 195, 198, 200, 201, 203, 219, 225, 226, 251, 253; destabilization in region, 98, 161, 200, 203; energy pipelines, 157, 193, 216; Medvedev visit, 197; Putin and, 28, 137; Russian foreign policy in region, 165–66, 211; Russian military presence, 87, 120, 157, 158, 170, 264; Russian relations, 123, 147, 162, 165–66, 202, 211; security concerns, 91, 120, 159, 192, 227, 244; terrorism in region, Russian and U.S. addressing, 196, 267

Chaadayev, Petr, 42

Chechnya, 19, 97, 113, 116, 124, 125, 157, 162–63, 179, 196, 202, 222; Chechen war, 111, 121, 129, 136, 137, 139, 267–68; OSCE mission, shutting down, 149; Putin and, 28, 140, 150, 152, 163, 169–70, 263; Russian military intervention, 72, 83, 97–98, 142, 170, 278; as a Russian security threat, 27, 28, 89, 91, 114

Cheney, Dick, 193

Chernenko, Konstantin, 35

Chernomyrdin, Viktor, 112–13, 122

Chicherin, Boris, 186

China, 21, 67, 99, 102, *106*, 120, 141, 142, 144, 153, 154, 160, 171, 180, 185, 186, 192, 214, 219, 225, 245, 253; as a consumer of Russian goods, 152, 198; Gorbachev, relations with, 77–78; growth of, 115, 198, 210, 211, 220, 224, 235; Medvedev visit, 197; Russia, prioritizing relations with, 227, 254; Russia-China alliance, 104, 114–15, 128, 158–59, 187, 188, 192, 200, 240, 248–49, 263, 265; Russian economy oriented towards, 236, 254; as a threat to Russia, 113, 115; tripartite alliance with Russia and India, 7, 19, 28, 105, 114, 116, 127; Yeltzin and Kozyrev, foreign policy towards, 81. *See also* BRICS alliance; Shanghai Cooperation Organization

Chubais, Anatoli, 30n6, 157

Churchill, Winston, xxvii, 10

citizenship law, 85, 127

civic identity policies, 85

Civic Union, 70–71, 72, 86, 122

Civilizationism and Civilizationists, 66, 85, 87, 92, 99, *105*, 110, 112, 115, 137, 143–44, 151, 166, 188–89, 247, 250, 254, *255*, 267; foreign policy assessment, *9*, *65*, *190*; Gorbachev and, 18, 38; integration of former Soviet states, in favor of, 118, 124; New Thinking, dislike of, 35, 40–41, 266; Putin and, 138, 172, 200, 237, 239, 240, 268; Russia as a distinct civilization, 8, 214, 237–41; Soviet Civilizationists, 8, 35, 104; state-civilization, 28, 238, 239, *241*, 255, 264; the West, attitudes towards, 22, 35, 66, 101, 103, 104–05, 269

Clinton, Bill, 13–14, 75, 275

Clinton, Hillary, 218, 244, 276

Cold War, 12, 33–35, 36, 46, 129, 168, 217, *265*, 266; liberal momentum of 80s-90s, Soviet defeat causing, 10–11; new Cold War possibility, 191, 194, 242, 275; Statist thesis of mutual responsibility for, 100; the West, victory of, 19, 26, 51, 60, 98

Collective Security Treaty, 83, 120, 143, 156, 158

Collective Security Treaty Organization (CSTO), 159, 225, 227

colored revolutions, 20, 171, 178–79, 183, 199, 210, 211, 224–25

Commissariat on Foreign Affairs, 35

Commonwealth of Independent States (CIS), *44*, 64, 78, 82, 83, 84, 103, 118, 121, 123, 125, *127*, 155, 156, 160, 199; Eurasian Union proposal, 223, 244, 251; Gorbachev resignation after creation of, 50; Primakov, CIS revival plans, 105; Putin, abandoning revival efforts, 158; Yeltsin as supporter of, 119, 120, 122

Communist Party and Communists, 3, 6, 35, 39, 61–62, 66, 182, 240, 278. *See also* National Communists; *nomenklatura*

Congress of Russian Communities, 87, 118

constructivism, 14–18

Contact Group, 111

Conventional Forces in Europe (CFE) treaty, 44, 77

Coordinating Committee for Multilateral Export Controls (COCOM), 76

correlation of forces doctrine, 7

Council for Foreign and Defense Policy, 70, 71, 100, 118, 155

counterterrorism. *See under* terrorism

Crimea, 6, 32n29, 102, 155, 164, 175n59, 186, 238, 243–44, 274, 276; Russian annexation of, 235, 246, 248, 249, 252, 254, 270

Croatia, 80

Cuba, 44

Customs Union, 122–23, 224, 226, 227, 240, 251

Czech Republic, 75, 112, 193, 194, 195

Dagestan, 125, 136, 179, 222

Darendorf, Ralf, 60

Dayton Accords, 111

Decree No. 472, 122

democracy and democratization, 3, 6, 75, 142, 161, 178, 200, 235–36, 277; democracy promotion as a peace-keeping method, 12; democratic peace theory, 13; democratic triumphalism of the West, 60; democratizing instincts of U.S., Russia threatened by, 211; European social democracy, 4, 5, 36; Gorbachev and democratization reform, 7; OSCE, pushing democracy in Eastern Europe, 195; Putin, favoring Statism over democracy, 137; in Russia, 5, 72, 77, 78, 93, 105, 129, 179, 183, 278; sovereign democracy, 184; the West, commitment to, 26, 33, 37, 61, 241. *See also* Social Democrats

Democratic Russia, 50, 81

Derzhava, 99

détente, 11, 34–35, 38, 40, 266

Donetsk, 175n59, 235, 252, 253

dual citizenship, 89, 124–25, 170

Duma, 108, 109, 110, 112, 145, 155, 167, 215, 226, 227, 234, 242

East Asia, 160, 197–98, 219, 220–21

Eastern Europe, 46, 80, 107, 195, 217, 218; Brezhnev doctrine of limited sovereignty in, 262; conservative approach of Russia, not supporting, 247; European Union, disagreement on Russian relations with, 243; freedom of choice principle, 45, 47; international law, failure to keep peace in, 270; Soviet decline, opening opportunities in, 60; victory over fascism celebration, 161, 166–67; withdrawal of troops from, 25, 40, 43, 44

economic diplomacy, 122

Economist, 147

Egypt, 211, 250

El Salvador, 44

end of history argument, 60, 98

Energy Charter, 195, 219

English, Robert, 11

The Establishment of the Strategic Course of the Russian Federation with Member States of the CIS (decree), 118

Estonia, 49, 75, 83, 86, 88, 117, 166

ethnic Russians, 70, 82, 84, 85, 87, 90, 117, 123, 124, 125, 164, 170, 212, 238, 241

ethnonationalism, 49, 118

Eurasia and Eurasianists, 8, 69, 70, 104, 118, 124, 153, 172, 183, 186, 190, 272, 275, 277; colored revolutions in, 225; Eurasianist dimension of Russian identity, 137; Eurasian Strategy for Russia, 160, 188, 189; Great Power Balancing as Eurasia-oriented, 28; hardline Eurasianists, 65, 66, 67; Izborsky club members as Eurasianists, 240; multicultural federalism, vision of, 125; Primakov as a Eurasianist, 19, 20, 128, 152, 271; Putin and, 144, 235, 248, 250; Russia and the West, disagreeing on policies in, 234; Russia as a Eurasian power, 105, 191; Russia-China-India partnership as Eurasian agenda, 114; Statists, importance to, 81, 99; Yeltsin, declaring Russia a Eurasian state, 71

Eurasian Union, 156, 220, 223, 235, 244, 249, 251, 253–54, 264, 271

Euro-Eastern civilization, 183–84

European Bank of Reconstruction and Development (EBRD), 74

European Economic Community, 30n2
European Union (EU), 187, 194, 217,
219, 220, 234, 242, 246, 247, 250,
272; Association Agreement offer
to Ukraine, 235, 244, 252; Common
Strategy of the EU on Russia
(document), 130; EU markets,
Russian access to, 75, 194, 217,
219; Eurasian Union as alternative
to, 253–54; EU-Russia Political
and Security Committee, 218, 226;
Medvedev and, 217, 268; Putin and,
148, 171, 234, 239; Russia, improving
relations with, 167, 195; Russian
exclusion, 149; Russian interest in
joining, 63; sanctions on Russian
economy, 243; shared values with
Russia, 213–14; U.S.-EU-Russia
alliance, 185

fascism, 7, 161, 166–67, 247
Federation Council, 153, 183, 212, 237,
238
Fedorov, Boris, 94n22, 155
500 days plan, 53, 74
Financial Times, 100
Foreign Affairs, 60
Foreign Affairs Committee of the
Supreme Soviet, 69
Foreign Intelligence Service, 68, 69–70,
80, 118, 120
foreign policy. *See* Russian foreign
policy
Founding Act on Mutual Relations,
Cooperation and Security between
Russia and NATO, 108, 112
Fourteenth Army, 87
France, 3, 5, 62, 104, 105, *106*, 110, 111,
143, 148, *151*, 218, 224, 226, 245, 247,
252
freedom of choice principle, 45, 47
French Revolution, 2, 3
Friedman, Thomas, 141
Fukuyama, Francis, 12, 60, 98
Furman, Dmitri, 176n15

Gabala radar station, 157
Gaddafi, Muammar, 218, 222
Gaidar, Yegor, 61, 74, 118, 155, 266
Garton Ash, Timothy, 60
gas and oil. *See* pipelines
Gazprom, 122, 182, 194, 199, 200, 217

Geneva Summit, 44
Georgia, *86*, 87, *88*, 91, *117*, 156, 170,
183, 186, 216, 218, 221, 270; Baku-
Ceyhan oil pipeline, passing
through, 158; blame for conflict on
NATO and EU, 277; CIS and, 121,
199; conflict compared to Soviet
invasion of Czechoslovakia, 276;
electoral changes, 157, 163; GUUAM,
membership in, 158; MAPs, Russia
blocking issuance of, 194; NATO,
desire to join, 178–79, 193, 201, 203,
211, 224; Rose Revolution, 161;
Russo-Georgian war, 209, 210, 211,
225, 233, 251, 264; sanctions placed
on, 202; South Ossetia, conflict with,
165, 178, 201, 217; union treaty,
rejecting, 48–49; U.S. arm sales to,
192
Germany, 3, 5, 62, 66, 104, 105, *106*, 136,
143, 144, 151, 218, 224, 247; Contact
group, as part of, 111; Minsk-II
agreement, as part of, 252–53;
Nazi-Germany, treaty with Soviets,
7; reunification of, *44*, 47, 53, 74;
Russian pipeline agreement, 160,
194, 217; Russian ties with, 148, 226
Gessen, Sergei, 186
global financial crisis, 20, 185, 203,
210–11, 212, 223, 236, 264
globalization, 21, 271–72, 273–74
Glukhovski, Igor, 156
Gorbachev, Mikhail: Afghanistan,
withdrawing troops from, 43, 45,
262; autonomy, troubles with,
26, 53, 263; capitalism and, 37,
39, 53, 66; China, relations with,
77–78; Civilizationists and, 18, 38;
conservatives and, 37, 40–42, 44–45,
46, 47, 49, 50; coup against, 50, 62,
77, 84; democratization reform,
7; election as general secretary
of Communist Party, 35; foreign
policy of, 5, 25–26, 33, 42–43, *44*,
51, 52–55, 66; globally integrated
national approach, advocating,
38–39; liberalism and, 11, 13, 18,
40, 41–42, 46, 49, 50, 52, 54; loss of
power, 18, 50, 51, 273; perestroika,
as leader of, 33, 36, 45, 49, 261–62;
Primakov, working for, 107, 270;
Russian national interest and, *265*;

Social Democrats, associated with, 65, 67; socialist nature of policies, 4, 5, 18, 21, 37, 41, 42, 60, 64, 73, 90, 168; UN and, 43, 47, 54, 262; the West, relationship to, 3, 4, 33, 34, 36–37, 43, 44–45, 46–47, 53, 54, 60, 73, 90, 145, 168, 266, 268; Westernizers and, 18, 62, 90, 91, 266, 273; Yeltsin as opponent of, 83. *See also* New Thinking
Gorchakov, Alexander, 6, 7, 9, 102, 103–04, 105, 129
Grachev, Pavel, 87
Graham, Thomas, 277
Great Power Assertiveness (GPA): contending views, *188;* as foreign policy, *23,* 177, 186, 189, 194, 202, 264; record assessment, *203;* Russian national interest, view of, *185;* Statist support for, *101*
Great Power Balancing (GPB): assessment of, 27–28; contending views, *105;* foreign policy record, *9, 127;* globalization, contending with, 273; lessons learned from foreign policy of, 128–30; Pragmatic Cooperation and, 167, 171; Primakov, as proponent of, xxvii, 9, 100, 139, 167, 187, 263, 267, 268, 270, 273; Statist support for, 126
Great Power Pragmatism, 177, 184, 203
great power status. *See under* Russia
Greece, 194, 217, 221, 246, 247
Gref, German, 180
Group of Seven (G-7), 63, 74, 75, 82, 275
Group of Eight (G-8), 71, 117, 236, 244
Group of 20 (G-20), 236, 249
GUAM/GUUAM economic security group, 130, 157, 158
Gusinski, Vladimir, 139, 182

Hamas, 196, 197
Hanssen, Robert, 146
Herzen, Alexander, 3
Hitler, Adolf, 7, *9,* 151, 167, 276
Houston energy summit, 147, 168
Hu, Jintao, 154
human rights, 4, 5, 19, *65,* 78, 95n26, 141, 241; in Helsinki Accords, 55n2; Magnitsky Act, sanctioning Russian human rights violators, 241–42; national unity language,

deflecting human rights pressures, 240; non-Western nations, not critical of human rights violations, 249; Putin and, 239, 244, 276; the West, committed to, 33, 61; Western criticism of Russian human rights record, 129, 234, 240, 242, 246, 265, 268, 276, 278
Hungary, 46, *75,* 112, 194, 247
Huntington, Samuel, 98
Hussein, Saddam, 98, 110–11, 150, 151

identity. *See* Russian national identity
India, 81, 99, 106, 142, 144, 153, 160, 186, 193, 203, 249; China and Russia tripartite alliance, 7, 19, 28, 105, 114, 116; growth of, 210, 211, 235; military ties with Russia, 77, 78; Primakov and, 19, 28, 102, 127, 128; Putin and, 137, 171; Russian arms purchases, 116, 152, 196, 198; Russian partnership, 106, 128, 185, 187, 248, 263. *See also* BRICS alliance
INF Treaty, *44*
Institute of Contemporary Development (INSOR), 213
Institute of Ethnology and Anthropology, 82
Institute of Oriental Studies, 107
Institute of World Economy and International Relations, 107
integration with the West. *See under* the West
intercontinental ballistic missiles (ICBMs), *52,* 76, 194
International Affairs, 79
International Monetary Fund (IMF), 14, 26, 63, 74, 79, 91, 109, 112
Iran, 66, 78, 120, 160, 193, 194, 197, 203; Eurasianists, advocating alliance with Russia, 188; nuclear program, 153, 178, 191, 192, 194, 195, 196, 215, 217, 218, 245, 249, 278; Primakov, promoting military cooperation, 105; Putin and, 140, 153, 221, 248, 250; Russian influence on, 221; Russian-Iranian relations, 115–16, 202, 250
Iraq, 27, 92, 98, 127, 128, 140, 142, 145, 149–51, 203, 250, 263, 264, 273, 277–78; Gabala radar station, Russian monitoring use, 157; intervention, Russian reaction

to, 113, 148, 162, 192; invasion of,
European opposition to, 143, 224;
military intervention, Russia and the
West divided over, 274; Primakov
and, 127; Putin, relations with,
140; Russian debt, 77, 110, 150; UN
sanctions against, 77, 110, 111; U.S.,
military activity, 77, 110, 114, 161,
178, 196, 235
Islamic State (IS), 245, 250
isolationism, 7, 81–87 104, 118, 120, 122,
124, 125, 129, 130, 155, 180, 268, 269,
270, 271; Soviet isolationism, 34, 52,
54, 62, 126
Israel, 196, 221, 227
Italy, 148, 221
Ivan IV (Ivan the Terrible), 8, *9*
Ivanov, Igor', 121
Ivanov, Sergei, 156, 186, 199
Izvestiya, 77

Jackson-Vanik amendment, 216, 242
Japan, 3, 6, 66, 68, 79, 102, 104, *106,* 114,
140, 153, 154, 199, 220, 249
Joint Declaration on a Multipolar
World and the Formation of a New
International Order, signing of, 114

Kaliningrad, 149
Kant, Immanuel, liberal internationalist
ideas of, 12, 13
Kapitsa, Pyotr, 4, 38
Karimov, Islam, 166
Katsav, Moshe, 167
Kazakhstan, *49, 75, 86, 88,* 95n40, *117,*
119, 156, 157, 158, 183; as an oil
and gas-rich state, 200, 226; China-
Kazakhstan-Russia transportation
route, 160, 253; CSTO, as a member
of, 159, 224; Customs Union, as
part of, 123, 224, 226, 251; Russian
pipelines in region, 193
Kerry, John, 242, 243, 245
Khasbulatov, Ruslan, 70
ibn-al Khattab, 136
Khodorkovski, Mikhail, 139, 171, 182
Khristenko, Viktor, 156
Khrushchev, Nikita, 3, 4, 7, *9,* 11, 30n2,
34, 37, 38, 266
Kim, Jong Il, 220
Kirill I, Patriarch of Moscow, 239
Klyuchevski, Vasili, 61

Kohl, Helmut, 75
Koizumi, Junichiro, 167
Komsomol, 62
Korea: Korean peninsula, Russian
security interests in, 78, 219, 220;
trans-Korean investments, Russia
facilitating, 221. *See also* North
Korea; South Korea
Kosachyev, Konstantin, 226
Kosolapov, Richard, 39
Kosovo, 108, 112, 113, 114, 116, 127, 146,
148, 185, 202, 217, 276
Kozyrev, Andrei: arms sales,
restrictions on, 107; Asia, negative
views towards, 77–79; Civilizationist
opposition to, 66; economic policies,
challenges to, 118; on ethnic
Russians, 85; Eurasianist attacks on,
104; foreign policy, *9,* 67, 69, 79–81,
83, 87, 92, 171; former Soviet region,
declaring as zone of interest, 87–89;
integration with the West, goal
of, 5, 26, 141, 161; isolation policy
towards former Soviet republics,
81–82, 87, 155, 160; as a liberal-
minded policymaker, 11, *65,* 266;
loss of power, 27, 68, 69, 70, 72, 97,
103; military forces, deploying to
Moldova, 84; on NATO, 76, 129;
Russian national interest, view of,
105; shock therapy of economic
reform, advocating, 62–63; U.S.,
supporting military actions of, 77;
Western international organizations,
policy of joining, 64, 108, 262; as a
Westernist, xxvii, 18–19, 20, 21, 27,
60, 61, 64, 70, 71, 72–73, 81, 89, 111,
146, 170, 262, 268, 270
Kuchma, Leonid, 158
Kudrin, Aleksei, 180
Kuril Islands, 79, 221
Kurman-Bakiev, president, 225
Kyrgyzstan, *49, 86, 88, 117,* 120, 123,
178, 211, 225; CSTO, as a member of,
159, 224; Dustan torpedo plant, 226;
Eurasian Union, membership in, 156,
251; revolution, 165, 178; Russian
air force base, establishment of, 158;
Russian partnership, 166, 227

Latin America, 43, 192, 210
Latvia, *49,* 50, *86, 88, 117,* 167, 217

Lavrov, Sergey, 165, 245
Lebed, Alexander, 87
Leites, Nathan, 10
Lenin, Vladimir, 7, 8, 10, 38, 53, 266
Lenin-Trotsky doctrine, 8, 9
Liberal Democratic Party, 66, 182
liberalism and liberals, 4, 7, 12, 17,
    21, 55, 65, 66–67, 68, 82, 84, 98,
    155, 180, 241, 247; failure of liberal
    experiment, 14, 267; foreign policy,
    4, 12, 14, 16, 18; foreign policy
    liberalizations of Khrushchev, 37;
    Gaidar and Kozyrev as liberal
    reformers, 266; Gorbachev and,
    11, 13, 18, 40, 41–42, 46, 49, 50, 52,
    54; liberal internationalist ideas
    of Kant and Wilson, 13; liberal
    momentum of 80s-90s, 10–11; liberal
    Westernizers, 5, 21, 41, 49, 62, 64, 71,
    141, 143, 145, 161, 164, 166, 187, 191;
    Medvedev, arguing for liberalization
    of system, 5–6; new *vs.* old liberals,
    186; pragmatic liberalism of new
    Westernizers, 105; Putin and, 7, 163;
    Yeltsin and, 46, 100, 273
Libya, 77, 211, 216, 218, 222, 227, 249,
    276
Ligachev, Yegor, 45, 47
Lithuania, 49, 50, 86, 88, 117, 149, 166
Litvinov, Maksim, 7, 9
Luhansk, 175n59, 235, 252, 253
Lukashenko, Aleksandr, 158, 200
Lukin, Vladimir, 69, 81
Lukoil, 110, 122
Lukyanov, Fyodor, 253

Madrid Summit, 112
Magnitsky, Sergei, 216, 234, 241–42,
    243, 246
Major, John, 75
Malaysian civilian airplane downing,
    244
Margelov, Mikhail, 153
Marshall Plan, 33, 74, 275
Maskhadov, Aslan, 136
McCain, John, 193, 244
Medinsky, Vladimir, 240
Medvedev, Dmitri: diversification
    policy, 240; European Union and,
    217, 268; foreign policy, 21, 209–210,
    213–15; liberalization of economic
    and political system, arguing for,

5–6; modernization policy, 21, 28,
    197, 212–13, 233, 239, 264, 265,
    268; NATO and, 217–18; Obama,
    establishing ties with, 194, 210, 234;
    Putin and, 180–82, 214–15, 223, 234,
    235, 239, 251, 268; Russian influence,
    preserving, 226; trans-Korean
    pipeline, favoring, 220; Ukraine and,
    207n64; the West, relations with, 185,
    212–13, 213–15, 233, 234, 264, 268
Membership Action Plans (MAPs), 194
Middle East, 21, 73, 102, 137, 147,
    178, 196, 213, 218, 249, 255, 276;
    democratization efforts in Middle
    East, 161; EU nations, seeking
    common solutions to solving
    Middle East conflicts, 195, 217;
    fears of destabilization spilling into
    Russia, 214; Kerry, admitting U.S.
    errors in handling, 243; Primakov,
    relations with, 106–07, 114; Putin,
    Russian position on, 242, 245, 249,
    274; regime changes, 211–12, 264,
    276; Russia, relations with, 77, 202,
    221–22, 271; Russia, strengthening
    ties in region, 227, 254; U.S., failure
    to stabilize, 235, 242; Western and
    Russian disagreement on Middle
    East policies, 234–35
Migranyan, Andranik, 69, 155
military industrialists, 19, 80, 86, 119, 267
Milošević, Slobodan, 112, 148
Milyukov, Pavel, 5, 9, 11, 61, 186
Ministry of Defense, 79, 83, 87, 110, 119,
    131n13
Minsk II agreement, 253
missile defense system (MDS), 148,
    194, 218, 227, 243, 274; antimissile
    defense system of Russia, 195;
    Russian exclusion from U.S.
    development proposal, 275–76; U.S.
    plans to develop, 110, 114, 145, 152,
    193, 203, 210, 216, 246, 276; Western
    plans for MDS in Europe, 21, 218,
    234, 255, 264
modernization. *See under* Medvedev,
    Dmitri
Moldova, 86, 88, 91, 117, 149, 170, 186,
    187, 199; ethnic conflicts in, 98, 120;
    GUAM/GUUAM, membership,
    130, 158; Kozyrev, addressing civil
    strife, 27; Primakov, diplomacy

efforts towards, 119, 126; Russian military presence, maintaining, 87; Transdniestr negotiations, 84, 202; union treaty, rejecting, 48–49; U.S. demand for Russian troop withdrawals, 216; weakness of elected bodies of power, 225, 251

Molodaya gvardiya, 67

monarchies, 2–3, 5, 6

Mongolia, 125, 137

Mongols, 2, 6, 8

Monroe Doctrine, inspiration for former Soviet territory, 69, 155

Moscow Institute of International Relations, 104

Moscow Institute of World Economy and World Politics, 39

multilateralism, 39, 83, 101–02, 122, 123, 127, 130, 133n49, 156, 158–59, 169, 185, 195, 197–98, 199, 202, 217, 225, 264

multipolarity, 103, 104, 106, 114, 128, 139, 140, 143, 155, 167, 184, 223, 238, 263, 268, 270

Munich Conference on Security Policy, 177

Muslims: alliance of Russian and Muslim countries, proposal, 144, 197; Bosnia, fighting with Serbs over, 76; cultural unity of Slavs and Muslims, Eurasianists advocating, 118; Denmark cartoon controversy, 196; Kosovo Muslims, Iranian support for, 116; Muslim republics, support for Eurasian federalism, 125; Muslim state activities, as a threat to Russia, 120; Primakov, advocating stronger ties with, 107, 270–71; Russia, maintaining ties to, 25, 28; Russian Muslim leaders, reaction to U.S. military campaigns, 145; Russian neglect of, 77–78; terrorism, associated with, 141, 179; Uighur minority of Xinjiang, 114, 159

Naftogas, 226

Nagorno-Karabakh, 78, 83

National Communists, 65, 66, 67, 68, 69, 144

National Security Concept of 1997, 102

NATO. *See* North Atlantic Treaty Organization

Nemtsov, Boris, 166

New Thinking: assessment of, 25–26; autonomy, record on, 54; Civilizationists, dislike of, 35, 40–41, 266; failure of, 25–26, 47, 51, 54, 92, 272; Gorbachev, associated with, 9, 25–26, 36–40, 43, 46, 48, 53, 92, 99, 261–62, 266; initial support for, 270; liberals and, 14, 41–42; origins of, 11; Soviet Union, contributing to breakup of, 50–51; Statists and, 38, 40–41, 100, 266; Westernism, paving way for, 64, 262

Nicaragua, 44

Nicholas II, 3

Niyazov, Sapurmurat, 157

nomenklatura, 38, 41, 61–62, 72, 93, 266

North Atlantic Treaty Organization (NATO), 44, 47, 78, 83, 89, 127, 157, 194, 215, 235; eastward expansion, 20, 23, 27, 48, 68, 70, 76, 80, 92, 98, 105, 107–08, 113, 114, 116, 119, 120, 121, 129, 145, 146, 201, 263, 267, 269, 270, 276, 277; former Soviet states, U.S. support of bids to join, 216, 276; Georgia, desire to join, 178–79, 193, 201, 203, 211, 224; Khrushchev, proposing disbandment of, 38; Medvedev on, 217–18; missile defense plans, Russia threatened by, 35, 216, 218, 227; Primakov, negotiating with, 28, 126; Putin and, 178, 211, 246; Russian exclusion, 20, 278; Russian interest in joining, 63, 71, 76, 107, 147; Russian refusal to cooperate with, 80; Ukraine, desire to join, 121, 178–79, 201, 203, 211, 224; Yugoslavia, military intervention in, 28, 110, 111–13, 128

North Korea, 78, 79, 137, 191, 197, 198, 199, 220, 249

Novgorodtsev, Pavel, 186

Nuclear Non-Proliferation Treaty, 78

Nunn-Lugar Cooperative Threat Reduction Program, 246

Obama, Barack: envoy created for Eurasian energy, 193; at G-20 summit, 249; Magnitsky Act, signing, 242; Medvedev, strengthening relations with, 194, 210, 234; reset diplomacy with Russia, 211, 215–16, 234, 268, 275; START treaty, proposed amendments, 243; Syria, desire for Assad's departure, 222; Ukrainian conflict, reaction to, 244

oil and gas. *See* pipelines

Okruashvili, Irakli, 201

oligarchy and oligarchs, 20, 32n27, 93, 138–39, 141, 154, 171, 180, 182, 236, 247, 267, 278

Olympic games of Sochi, 242, 246

Orange Revolution, 28, 161, 166, 199, 201

Organization for Security and Co-operation in Europe (OSCE), 47, 64, 71, 76, 84, 89, 107, 149, 182, 194, 195, 217, 218

Organization of the Islamic Conference, 197

Orthodox Church and religion, 2, 8, 41, 124, 239–40, 251

Ossetia: North Ossetia, 124, 162, 163, 179, 216, 222; South Ossetia, 165, 176n62, 178, 201–02, 209, 217, 223, 225

Owen, David, 76

Pakistan, 120, 159, 248

Palestine, 196, 197, 221

Pankisi Gorge, 157

Paris Club, 75

Paris Peace Treaty, 102

Partnership for Peace, 80

Pavolvski, Gleb, 183, 205n24

Payment Union, 123

Pereslegin, Sergei, 189

perestroika, 4, 29, 33, 36, 37, 38, 45, 47, 49, 50, 261–62, 266

Permanent Joint Council, 108

Perry, William, 107

Peter the Great, 2, 5, 6, *9*, 265

Pikayev, Alexander, 83

pipelines: Baku-Ceyhan pipeline, 116, 158, 159, 193; Baku-Novorossiysk pipeline, 121; Blue Stream pipeline, 194; Caspian pipelines, non-Russian nations favoring, 200, 226; dependence of former Soviet states on Russian pipelines, 123; Energy Charter and third party access to Russian pipelines, 195, 219; Gazprom pipeline to Germany,

160, 217; Putin and, 264; Russia as an energy pipeline hub, 198, 199, 225; Russian pipelines in former Soviet regions, 157, 193; Siberian oil reserves and, 153–54; trans-Caspian pipelines, 115, 116, 159, 216; trans-Korean pipeline, 220; Turkey, Russian pipelines going through, 221, 226, 250

Poland, 46, *75*, 112, *151*, 160, 193, 195, 217

Portugal, 140

Pragmatic Cooperation (PC): autonomy, record on, *169*; Bolsheviks, as foreign policy of, 3; challenges for, 161–67; contending views, *144*; in ex-Soviet states, 154–56; future dilemmas, 170–72; globalization and, 273; Great Power Balancing as forerunner, 135, 167; limitations of, 28; national interest, view of, *140*; Primakov and, 101, 111; Putin and, *9*, 20, 28, 146, 150, 169, 263, *265*, 274; record of, 168, *169*, 170; security threats, policy influenced by, *23*, 28; state-civilization and cooperation with the West, *239*, 247; Statists and, 20, 28, 143–44, 161, 170

Presidential Administration and Security Council, 70

Presidential Decree No. 909, 125

Primakov, Yevgeni: autonomy, actions regarding, 27, 112, 126, 273; eastward expansion of NATO, reactions to, 80, 107–08; economic independence, aiming to restore, 109; economic integration policy, 122–23; as a Eurasianist, 19, 20, 128, 152, 271; foreign policy, 7, 14, 19, 20, 100–01, 104, 106, 113–14, 114–16, 126–28, 128–29, 143, 154, 170, 177, 187, 263, 273; Georgia, failing to stabilize, 120–21, 126; Great Power Balancing, as proponent of, xxvii, 9, 100, 139, 167, 187, 263, 267, 268, 270, 273; India and, 19, 28, 102, 127, 128; integration of former Soviet states, 116–19, 127–28; integration with West, as critic of, 262; Iran, promoting military cooperation with, 105; Kozyrev, replacing as foreign minister,

27, 70, 100; Muslims, advocating stronger ties with, 107, 270–71; NATO, confronting, 28, 111–12, 126; as a Statist, 19, 65, 68–69, 99, 100, 108, 122, 137; Tajikistan, diplomacy efforts towards, 115, 120, 126; Yugoslavia, guiding Russian relations with, 110, 111–12, 126, 273
privatization, 53, 75, 84, 139, 157
Program of Economic Cooperation, 123
Prokhanov, Aleksandr, 138
Pussy Riot, 241
Putin, Vladimir: Afghanistan, support of U.S. actions in, 145, 147, 149–50, 169, 263; Asia and, 152, 189, 198, 200; Asia-Pacific region, focus on, 219–20; Assad, supporting, 222, 243, 249; autonomy, calculations regarding, 24, 149, 169; Chechnya and, 28, 140, 150, 152, 163, 169–70, 263; CIS and, 158, 244; Civilizationists and, 138, 172, 200, 237, 239, 240, 268; economic focus, 152–54, 168, 169, 213; Eurasia and, 144, 235, 248, 250; Eurasian Union, proposing, 223, 235, 251, 271; European Union and, 148, 171, 234, 239; foreign policy, 7–8, 14, 140, 148–49, 154, 168–70, 170–72, 185–86, 198, 233, 234, 237–39, 240, 263, 274; globalization, contending with, 273–74; Iran, relations with, 140, 153, 221, 248, 250; liberalism and, 7, 163; Medvedev and, 180–82, 214–15, 223, 234, 235, 239, 251, 268; Middle East, position on, 242, 245, 249, 274; NATO and, 178, 211, 246; normal great power vision, 161, 182, 241; policy autonomy, restored, 24; Pragmatic Cooperation and, 9, 20, 28, 146, 150, 169, 263, 265, 274; public support for, 136, 189; Pussy Riot, praying for ouster of, 241; as a realist policymaker, 11; Russia at the Turn of the Millennium (speech), 137, 182–83; START II and, 110; state-civilization, supporting idea of, 28, 238, 264; as a Statist, 21, 138, 240; terrorism, responses to, 8, 10, 20, 27, 28, 136–37, 138, 142–43, 150, 163, 168, 169–70, 263, 267, 268; third term as president, 180, 188, 237, 274; transportation initiatives, 159–61;

Turkish energy agreement, 157, 193, 250; Ukraine and, 164–65, 247, 248, 252;, 264, 274; United Nations and, 142, 148, 150; U.S. and, 8, 20, 138, 140, 141, 142–43, 145, 146–48, 148–49, 149–51, 168, 234, 239, 243, 246–47, 263, 274; Westernizer criticism, 187; Yeltsin, appointing as prime minister, 267. *See also* Pragmatic Cooperation

Rakhmanin, Oleg, 45
Rasmussen, Anders Fogh, 218
Reagan, Ronald, 35, 44, 47
Realism and Realists; foreign policy, 10–11, 14, 16, 21, 103; international anarchy, notion of, 11, 12, 13; limitations of realism as an international relations theory, 127; New Thinking, as critical of, 37, 64; strength, emphasis on, 17; the West as focus of, 14, 266; Western realists, goal of Soviet-West power balance, 34
Reykjavik Summit, 44, 45
Rice, Condoleezza, 147, 276
Rodionov, Igor, 151
Rogov, Sergei, 160
Romania, 84, 194
Rose Revolution, 161
Rosneft, 182, 188, 216
Rossiyskaya gazeta, 145–46
Royal Dutch Shell, 182
ruble, 25, 84, 123, 236
Rumsfeld, Donald, 141, 147
Rumyantsev, Oleg, 68
Russia: backwardness of, 5, 6, 42, 61; conflict and cooperation with the West, 241–44, 244–47; economic issues, 14, 26, 27, 86, 135–36, 140, 152–54, 179–80, 181, 213, 225–26, 236; ex-republic dependencies, comparison to, 88; external aid and investment, 75; great power status, xxvii–xxviii, 7, 19, 20, 21, 27, 66, 68, 70, 89, 97, 102, 105, 119, 126, 140, 143, 167, 185–86, 187, 189, 263; gross domestic product (GDP), 59, 115, 136, 140, 180, 211, 236; imperialism charges, 69, 99, 123, 129, 183, 187, 188, 193, 210, 244, 276; little Russia concept, 63; middle class, 180, 189,

204, 215, 239, 240; military budget, *139*; power capabilities and resources, *106*, *117*; Russia-victim argument, 82; security concerns, 4, 6, 8, 80, 91, 113, 120, 137–38, 162, 180, 210; U.S. cooperation and rivalry, 191–94

Russian foreign policy, 10, 13–14, 35, 107, 125, *145*, 149–51, 199–200; Asia and, 81, 92, *127*, 210; assertive foreign policy, 185–87, 209–210; autonomy as a factor, 22, 24, 26, 27, 28, 53, 90, 91–92, 126, 149, 168, 169, 171, 263, 273; change and continuity in, 9–10, 254–55; criteria for evaluation, 22–24, 26, 28, 53, 90, 127, 168, 212, 214, 270; expansionism policy, 3, 8, 10; Foreign Policy Concept of 2000, 103; Foreign Policy Concept of the Russian Federation, 87; future corrections and challenges, 203–04; globalization, adjusting to, 272; lessons to preserve and enhance status, 269–71, 271–74; liberal foreign policy, 4, 12, 14, *16*, 18; local conditions, taking into account, 16, 17, *23*; minimax policy towards U.S. and Iran, 116; multilateral policy orientation, 101–02; near abroad policy, 70, 94n20, 127; post-Soviet foreign policy views, *23*, 65–66; of pre-Soviet era, 2–3; pro-Western foreign policy, departure from, 90; public satisfaction and support for, 24, 25, 189–91; rational interests as a foreign policy motivation, 73; Review of the Russian Federation's Foreign Policy (report), 184; social construction of, 18–22; transnational ties, importance of, 12–13. *See also* Civilizationism; Statism; Westernism; individual prime ministers and presidents

Russian national identity: Alexander II, redefining, 2; alliances for modernization, *213*; citizenship law and civic identity, 85; civic nation identity, 82, 87, 89, 125; as distinct from the West, 113; Eurasianist dimension, 137; as a Euro-Eastern civilization, 183–84; identity coalitions, 16, 17, 19, 20, 122, 137–39, 180–82; as independent from the West, 238; liberal identity in post-Soviet Russia, 4, 19; New Thinking, failure as an identity project, 47, 51, 53; post-Soviet identity, 19, 25, 93, 170, 236; pro-Western vision of, 59, 73, 138; Russian empire identity, 8; Russian socialist identity, 33; significant Other, role in defining, 15, *16*, 17, 18, 22, 24; Soviet collapse, as opportunity for establishing new identity, 64–65; Westernist dimension of Russia's identity, 61–62, 100, *255*. *See also* social constructivism

Russian national interest: constructivists on social contexts of, 15; defining, 10; domestic debate on, 185–91; Gorbachev, bringing new understanding to, 33, 42; Great Power Assertiveness view, *185*; under Kozyrev and Yeltsin, 26, 70, 105; liberal scholars, undermining concept, 12; national identity, importance to, 17, 22; national interest formation, 265–69; New Thinking on, 39–40, 48; post-Soviet concepts, *23*; Pragmatic Cooperation response, *140*; Primakov's view of, 108, 128; private sector, helping to advance, 130; Putin, influence on, 20, 140, 141, 147, 150; Realist views, 11; state-civilization understanding, *239*; Statist concept of, 19, 100–01, *105*; summary of main views, *265*; Westernist concept of, xxvii, 62–65, 68, *69*, 90. *See also* Alliances for Modernization; Civilizationism; Great Power Assertiveness; Great Power Balancing; Integration with the West (under the West); New Thinking; Pragmatic Cooperation

Russian Security Council, 70

Rutskoi, Aleksandr, 70, 87

Saakashvili, Mikhail, 157, 166, 201, 217, 224

Sakharov, Andrei, 4, 38

Saudi Arabia, 159, 168, 171, 250

Schroeder, Gerhard, 163, 167

Sechin, Igor, 188, 214

September 11 terrorist attacks. *See under* terrorism

Serbia, 76, 111, 112, 113, 247
Shanghai Cooperation Organization
 (SCO), 158–59, 192–93, 198, 213, 219,
 235, 248, 250, 265
Shanghai Five. *See* Shanghai
 Cooperation Organization
Shevardnadze, Eduard, 39–40, 46, 49,
 157
Shevtsova, Liliya, 187
shock therapy of economic reform, 26,
 63, 66, 79, 84, 91, 92, 278
Siberia, 153–54, 182, 219, 220–21, 248
Sidanko, 122
Silk Road initiative, 253–54
siloviks, 138, 180, 182
Skokov, Yuri, 70
Slavic unity, 8, 200
Slavophiles, 41, 240
Snowden, Edward, 235, 243, 246, 249
Sochi Olympics, 242, 246
social constructivism, 14–18
Social Democrats, 5, 34, 38, *65*, 67, *69*,
 103, 104, 142–43, *145*, 189, *190*
socialism and socialists: competition
 with capitalism, 34–35; Gorbachev,
 socialist nature of policies, 4, 5, 18,
 21, 37, 41, 42, 60, 64, 73, 90, 168;
 New Thinking as a development
 of socialism, 38, 46, 51; perestroika,
 reviving socialist values, 261–62;
 reform socialism, 266; socialist
 Civilizationists, 11; socialist identity
 of Russia, 33; socialist Statists, 9
Sorel, Albert, 269
South Korea, 78, 199, 220
Soviet Union, 5, 11, 26, *37*, 43, 45,
 46, 47, 66, 116, 167, 262, 277;
 Afghanistan, withdrawal from,
 48; behavior, three rules guiding,
 10; CIS, replacing, 82; Cold War,
 33–35, 60; Czechoslovakian invasion,
 276; debt, Russian liability for,
 75; disintegration of, 4, 18, 19, 27,
 60, 81, 119, 124, 275; economy,
 undermined by energy price
 decline, 195; ethnonationalsim, rise
 of, 48, *49*; foreign policy, 33–35;
 identification with the West, 34,
 270; isolationism, 34, 52, *54*, 62, 126;
 middle class, 34, 38, 41, 54; national
 interest, rethinking, 38–40; as a
 natural geopolitical form, 104; New

Thinking, opposition to, 40–41, 42,
 45, 51; Russia as an internal colony
 of, 63, 81; Soviet Civilizationists, 8,
 35, 104; Soviet liberals, 42; Soviet
 Statists, 18, 34, 35, 102, 266
Spain, 125
Stalin, Joseph, 6, 7, *9*, 10, 35, 36, 39, 66,
 79, 167
de-Stalinization, 3, 4
Stankevich, Sergei, 19, 70, 78, 81
State-Civilization (SC), 28, 238, 239, *241*,
 255, 264
State Duma. *See* Duma
Statism and Statists, 85, 87, 89, *105*,
 118, 143, 151, 155, 164, 166, *188*,
 240, 240; foreign policy, 6, 7, *9*, 81,
 99, 104, 113–14, *145*, 214, 240; great
 power status, focus on, *65*, 66, 68, 99;
 identity coalition, 103, 126, 130, 137;
 institutional advantages, 69–71; new
 Statists, 19, 66, 69; New Thinking
 and, 38, 40–41, 100, 266; Pragmatic
 Cooperation and, 20, 28, 143–44, 161,
 170; Primakov as a Statist, 68–69,
 122; Putin as a Statist, 21, 138, 240;
 revival of Statist thinking, 67, 68–69,
 89, 97, 98; Soviet statists, 18, 34, 35,
 102, 266; the West, stance towards,
 6, 7, 38, 68, 70, 89, 99, 100, 101, 161,
 240; Westernism, opposition to, *65*,
 66, 70, 71, 79, 89, 267; Westernist-
 Statist consensus, 154–56; Yeltsin,
 concessions made to, 273
Strategic Arms Limitations Talks (SALT
 II), 35
Strategic Arms Reduction Treaty
 (START), *44*, *52*, 243
Strategic Arms Reduction Treaty II
 (START II), 21, *52*, 76, 110, 113, 215,
 278
Strategic Defense Initiative (SDI; Star
 Wars), 35
Strategic Democratic Initiative (SDI),
 74
Struve, Pyetr, 186
Suez Canal, 153, 220
Supreme Soviet, 69, 70, 78, 79–80
Syria, 192, 196, 211, 216, 221, 222, 227,
 235, 242, 245, 250, 276, 278; Assad
 regime, Russian support for, 264–65;
 UNSC resolutions, Russia not
 supporting, 218, 222, 246, 249, 274

Taiwan, 197
Tajikistan, 49, 86, 88, 91, 117, 119, 123, 156; CSTO, as part of, 159, 224; dual citizenship, rejecting idea of, 125; Kozyrev, addressing civil strife in, 27; Primakov, diplomacy efforts towards, 115, 120, 126; Russian intervention in, 84; Russian military base in, 158, 230n56
Talbott, Strobe, 13
Taliban, 48, 107, 115, 147, 149, 165, 169, 178, 221
Tashkent Collective Security Treaty, 158
terrorism, 25, 120, 156, 157, 159, 178, 224, 248, 252, 269, 272; Beslan school hostage crisis, 162–63; in the Caucasus, 28, 136, 138, 161, 162–63, 202, 203, 217, 227, 267; in Chechnya, 162–63, 222; counterterrorism efforts, 146, 148, 154, 157, 158, 163, 169, 179, 191, 201, 210, 244–45, 254, 264, 267, 275, 276, 279; Islamic terrorism in Russia, 212, 222; Putin, combating, 8, 10, 20, 27, 28, 136–37, 138, 142–43, 150, 163, 168, 169–70, 263, 267, 268; September 11 terrorist attacks, 20, 136–37, 138, 140, 141–43, 144, 145–46, 147, 149, 151, 217, 263; war on terror, 150, 161, 179, 196, 211
Thatcher, Margaret, 44, 47
Tiananmen massacre, 77
Tishkov, Valeri, 82, 85, 89
Totski, Konstantin, 145
Transdniestr area, 84, 202
Trans-Pacific Partnership, 220–21
Trans-Siberian Railroad, 160, 220
TRASEKA, 160
Trenin, Dmitri, 214
Tsarnaev, Tamerlan, 245
Tuleyev, Aman, 119
Tunisia, 211
Turkey, 78, 115, 151; energy pipelines, 158, 159, 194; Eurasian development, proposed part of, 253; European energy agreements, 195, 219; Russia, expanding ties with, 221, 227, 254; Russian energy pipeline project, 221, 226, 250;
Turkmenistan, 49, 75, 86, 88, 117, 125, 160; as an oil and gas-rich state, 200, 226; ethnic Russians in, 123; Putin

energy agreement, 157, 193; Russia, guarding borders of, 120

Ukraine, 21, 86, 88, 117, 119, 157, 175n59, 183, 186, 210, 225, 227, 234, 250, 277; 2004 presidential election, 162, 163–64, 172; Big Treaty with Russia, 121, 123, 126; CIS membership, 44, 50, 83; Customs Union, invitation to join, 224, 226, 251; as energy-dependent, 155, 187; ethnonationalism, rise of, 49; Eurasian Union, membership in, 156; GUAM/GUUAM, membership in, 130, 158; MAPs, Russia blocking issuance of, 194; military training, Western offer to Ukrainian army, 276; NATO, desire to join, 178–79, 193, 201, 203, 211, 224; Orange Revolution, 28, 161, 199, 201; Primakov, strengthening relations with, 121; Putin and, 164–65, 248, 264, 274; Russian subsidies to the economy, 199, 200; Statists' views toward, 164; Ukrainian revolution, 178, 252–54, 276; Western reactions to Russian intervention, 164, 235, 242, 243–44, 247, 248, 249, 252, 254, 276
Union of Industrialists and Entrepreneurs, 86, 213
Union of Right-Wing Forces, 141
unipolarity, 11, 66–67, 100, 101, 103, 110, 115, 128, 144, 186, 189, 213, 235, 236, 263, 270
United Nations (UN), 48, 61, 78, 111, 151, 263; Gorbachev and, 43, 47, 54, 262; Iran resolution, Russian support for, 215; peacekeeping forces, 76, 83, 89, 120; Primakov, upholding power of, 106; Putin and, 142, 148, 150; Russian membership in, 278; Statists, favorable view towards, 100; Yugoslavia and, 76, 80, 112, 277–78
United Nations Security Council (UNSC), 61, 106, 111, 113, 117, 163, 192, 216, 218, 222, 245, 246, 249, 274
United Russia (UR) party, 215
United States, 13, 37, 47, 52, 60, 68, 74, 75, 78, 162, 179, 222, 225, 277, 279; Afghanistan and, 215, 235, 244; anti-American sentiment, 67, 151; Baku-

Ceyhan oil pipeline, supporting, 158; counterterrorism cooperation with Russia, 8, *140*, 142, 147–48, 210, 244–45, 276; hegemony of, 28, 106, 127, 143, 144, 249, 263; Iraq and, 110–11, 149–51, 161, 178, 196, 235; Kozyrev, supporting military actions, 77; Medvedev and, 182, 212, 217; missile defense system, plans to build, 110, 114, 145, 152, 193, 203, 210, 216, 246; Putin and, 8, 20, 138, 140, 141, 142–43, 145, 146–48, 148–49, 149–51, 168, 234, 239, 243, 246–47, 263, 274; resentment towards U.S., 26, 91; reset of relations with Russia, 211, 215–16, 226–27; Russian cooperation and rivalry, 191–94; sanctions against Russia, 244, 247; Snowden surveillance scandal, 235, 243, 246, 249; Syria and, 242–43; Trans-Pacific Partnership proposal, 220–21; Ukraine crisis, reactions to, 234, 242, 244, 247, 254; unilateralism, Russian offensive against, 184, 192, 224, 264; unipolarity of, 11, 66–67, 100, 103, 115, 128, 186, 236, 263, 270; U.S.-EU-Russia alliance, 185; Yeltsin, relations with, 63, 71, 76–77. *See also* September 11 terrorist attacks

USSR. *See* Soviet Union

Uzbekistan, *49, 86, 88, 117*, 158, 159, 170, 193; CSTO membership, 224, 225, 227; Russian pipelines in region, 193; violence in region, Russian response to, 165–66

Vance, Cyrus, 76
Varga, Yevgeni, 39
velvet revolutions, 163–65
Venezuela, 192
Vernadski, Vladimir, 4, 38
Vietnam, 35, 249
Vike-Freiberga, Vaira, 167
Vladivostok summit, 50, 220, 221
Vlasov, Yuri, 68

Wall Street Journal, 147
Warsaw Pact, 38, *44*, 47, 48, 159
the West, 42, 98, 112, 128, 163, 216, 245, 262; Civilizationists, attitude towards, 22, 35, 66, 101, 103, 104–05, 269; Cold War, as victors of, 19,

26, 51, 60, 98; colored revolutions, supporting, 178, 183; conflict and cooperation with Russia, 241–44, 244–47; engagement with Russia, maintaining, 274–79; Gorbachev, relationship with, 3, 4, 33, 34, 36–37, 43, 44–45, 46–47, 53, 54, 60, 73, 90, 145, 168, 266, 268; hegemonic actions of, 66, 112, 272, 277; human rights record of Russia, as critical of, 129, 234, 240, 242, 246, 265, 268, 276, 278; Integration with the West, *9*, 19, 23, 26, 62, 63, 64, 68, 72–81, 89, 90, 92, 140, 161, 177, 187, 193, 234, 237, 239, 262, *265*, 270, 272, 273, 274; lessons for, 274–77, 277–79; Medvedev, relations with, 185, 212–13, 213–15, 233, 234, 264, 268; power shift away from, 210, 236, 237–38, 241; pragmatic cooperation with West, 141–42, 143–44, *239, 265*; Primakov, strategy for dealing with, 106; Putin, relations with and attitudes toward, 21, 146, 150, 169, 171, 185, 233–34, 237, 239, 245–46, 263, *265*, 267, 268, 271, 274; recognition of Russia, xxviii, 37, 47, 63, 71, 73, 89, 90, 92, 126, 146, 264, 268; rejection/ exclusion of Russia, 18, 20, 267, 269, 278–79; Russian conservatives, negative attitude towards, 40–41; sanctions placed on Russia, 236, 242, 244, 246, 248, 249, 254–55, 276; as significant Other of Russia, 18, 20, 33, 79, *265*, 274–75; Statists, stance towards, 6, 7, 38, 68, 70, 89, 99, 100, 101, 161, 240; Ukraine crisis, reaction to, 164, 235, 242, 243–44, 247, 248, 249, 252, 254, 276; Yeltsin, Western support for, 13, 75, 109, 278. *See also* North Atlantic Treaty Organization

Westernism and Westernizers, *69*, 77, 80, 103, 105, 107, 115, 151, 152, 278; early Westernizers, 4–5; foreign policy course, *9*, 62, 64, 68, 71, 79, 90–92, 190, 194, 267, 273; Gorbachev and, 18, 62, 90, 91, 266, 273; Kozyrev as a Westernist, xxvii, 18–19, 20, 21, 27, 60, 61, 64, 70, 71, 72–73, 81, 89, 111, 146, 170, 262, 268, 270; liberal Westernizers, 5, 41, 49, 64, *65*, 71, 141–43, *145*, 161, 164, 166, 187; loss

of influence, 35, 69, 71–72, 267, 273;
Medvedev, Westernizers support
of, 213; national identity, influence
on, 61–62, 90, 100, 128; national
interest, concept of, 62–65; New
Thinking and, 37–38, 266; post-
Soviet Westernizers, 82; pragmatic
Westernism, 139–40; Primakov
and, 262, 273; Putin and, 137, 138,
245; record of Westernist course,
91; Soviet Westernizers, 34; State-
Civilization and, *241, 255*; Statists,
opposed to, 19–20, 66, 79, 89, 92,
99, 101, 267; Westernist-Statist
consensus, 154–56; Yeltsin as a
Westernist, 5, 18–19, 26, 41, 60, 62,
64, 72–73, 89, 97, 262, 266. *See also*
liberalism and liberals
Wight, Martin, 29
Wilson, Woodrow, 12, 13
Witte, Sergei, 3
World Bank (WB), 26, 74, *75*, 91, 246
World Trade Organization (WTO), 21,
28, 150, 168, 182, 193, 200, 216
World War I, 3, 5, 197
World War II, 7, 79, 166, 167, 248, 276

Xi, Jinping, 248, 253

Yabloko Party, 141
Yakovlev, Aleksandr, 46
Yakunin, Vladimir, 239
Yanukovich, Viktor, 164, 174n59, 244,
252
Yavlinski, Grigori, 141, 142, 155
Yazov, Dmitri, 50
Yeltsin, Boris: CIS states and, 70, 78,
82–83, 118, 119, 120, 122; Contact
Group, initiating, 111; Decree
No. 472, 122–23; Democratic
Russia as umbrella organization,
50, 81; election as president, 55;

Energy Charter, signing, 195, 219;
expectations of Western aid, 63, 74,
275; Foreign Intelligence Service,
access to, 69; foreign policy, 76–77,
78, 85, 92, 97–98, 103, 112, 114,
116, 125; Fourteenth Army and,
87; on hegemonic role of Russia,
132n34; liberal support for, 46;
loss of support, 68; national idea,
initiating, 128; New Thinking, as
point of departure, 270; oligarchs,
role in reelection of, 138; partnership
with West, failure of, 145; Putin,
appointing as prime minister, 267;
shock therapy of economic reform,
advocating, 62–63, 84; Statists,
making concessions to, 71, 100, 273;
transnational community, reviving
identity of, 124; U.S., relations with,
63, 71, 76–77; vision of the world
and national interest, xxvii, 72, *265*;
as a Westernizer, 5, 18–19, 26, 41,
60, 62, 64, 72–73, 89, 97, 262, 266;
Western support for, 13, 75, 109, 278;
Yeltsin-Kozyrev course, failure of,
79–81, 92–93
Yugoslavia, 28, 76, 77, 80, 128, 192;
Primakov, guiding Russian
relations with, 110, 111–12, 126, 273;
Western military strikes, 109, 113,
114, 277–78
Yukos, 122, 139, 154
Yurgens, Igor', 213
Yushchenko, Viktor, 164, 166, 175n58,
207n64

Zatulin, Konstantin, 155
Zavtra, 138
zero-sum situations, 11, 14, 42, 77
Zhirinovski, Vladimir, 13, *65*, 66, 80, 182
Zyuganov, Gennadi, *65*, 66, 104, 108,
182, 240

About the Author

Andrei P. Tsygankov is professor of international relations and political science at San Francisco State University. He is the author of many books, including *Russia and the West from Alexander to Putin* (2012). He has also published dozens of book chapters, journal articles, and academic papers on Russia, foreign policy, and international relations.